THE ANCIENT MONUMENTS OF ROME

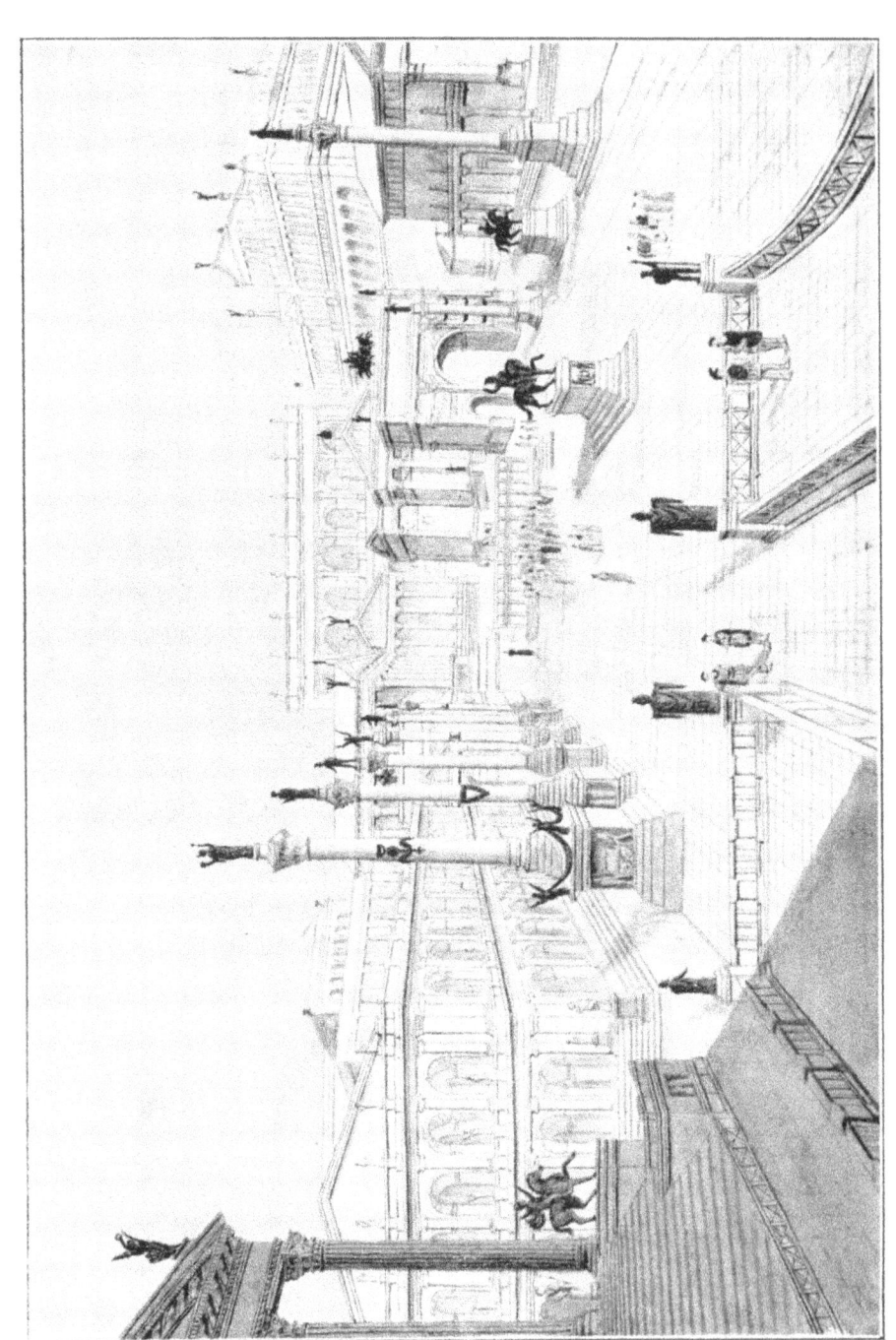

ROMAN FORUM. (Reconstructed).

Frontispiece

THE ANCIENT MONUMENTS OF ROME

BY
THEODORE PIGNATORRE

Author of
"Ancient and Mediæval Architecture"

With Sixty-one Illustrations Drawn by the Author

LONDON:
TREFOIL PUBLISHING COMPANY
"BANGOR HOUSE"
66 & 67, SHOE LANE, E.C.4

Made and printed in England by Purnell and Sons, Paulton (Somerset) and London

CONTENTS

CHAPTER		PAGE
	Prologue	ix
I.	Introductory	13
II.	Habitations	20
III.	Habitations (*continued*)	30
IV.	Habitations (*continued*)	40
V.	Habitations (*concluded*)	51
VI.	Forums	56
VII.	Temples, Chapels, Shrines	72
VIII.	Temples, Chapels, Shrines (*continued*)	84
IX.	Temples, Chapels, Shrines (*concluded*)	97
X.	Walls and Gates	113
XI.	Aqueducts and Drains	123
XII.	Circuses and Stadiums	129
XIII.	Amphitheatres	136
XIV.	Theatres	144
XV.	Bridges	149
XVI.	Arches	158
XVII.	Columns	167
XVIII.	Obelisks	173
XIX.	Porticos and Fountains	180
XX.	Basilicas	187
XXI.	Baths	194
XXII.	Mausoleums and Tombs	202
XXIII.	Mausoleums and Tombs (*continued*)	210
XXIV.	Mausoleums and Tombs (*continued*)	218
XXV.	Mausoleums and Tombs (*concluded*)	233

LIST OF ILLUSTRATIONS

Roman Forum . . . . . (Reconstructed) *Frontispiece*

PLATE		FACING PAGE
1.	Roma Quadrata	19
2.	Library of Augustus	23
3.	Palace of Caligula	25
4.	Portico of Pedagogium	27
5.	House of the Vestals	30
6.	Chapel of Vesta and Temple of Castor and Pollux	32
7.	Sanctuary of Juturna	38
8.	Villa of the Quintilii	47
9.	Kryptoporticus, Villa of Hadrian	53
10.	Platea Aurea, Villa of Hadrian	54
11.	Temples of Dea Matuta and Dea Fortuna	57
12.	Temple of Saturn	60
13.	Screen of Trajan	64
14.	Mamertine Prison	67
15.	Temple of Jupiter	83
16.	Temple of Roma Aeterna	88
17.	Temple of Mars Ultor	91
18.	Temple of Minerva	95
19.	Temple of Neptune	96
20.	Temple of Hercules	98
21.	Temple of Vesta	102
22.	Pantheon	108
23.	Temple of Antoninus and Faustina	111
24.	Temple of Vespasian	112
25.	Aurelian Walls	117
26.	Porta Tiburtina	120

LIST OF ILLUSTRATIONS

PLATE		FACING PAGE
27. Arch of Martian Aqueduct	. . . . . .	123
28. Arches of Claudian Aqueduct	. . . . .	124
29. Aqueduct of Claudius	. . . . . .	126
30. Mouth of Cloaca Maxima	. . . . . .	128
31. Stadium of Domitian	. . . . . .	133
32. Amphitheatre Castrense	. . . . . .	136
33. Flavian Amphitheatre	. . . . . .	138
34. Theatre of Marcellus	. . . . . .	146
35. Aemilius Bridge	. . . .	151
36. Fabricius Bridge	. . . .	152
37. Arch of Titus	. . . .	158
38. Arch of Janus	. . . .	160
39. Arch of Septimius	. . . .	162
40. Arch of Septimius	. . . .	164
41. Arch of Gallienus	. . . . . .	166
42. Arch of Constantine	. . . . . .	167
43. Column and Forum of Trajan	. . . . .	169
44. Column of Aurelius	. . . . . .	171
45. Obelisk of Thothmes	. . . . . .	178
46. Portico of Octavia	. . . . . .	181
47. Basilica Aemilia	. . . .	187
48. Basilica Julia	. . . .	189
49. Basilica Flavia	. . . .	190
50. Basilica Maxentia	. . . . . .	192
51. Antonine Baths	. . . .	197
52. Tomb or Cenotaph of Eurysaces	. . . .	203
53. Mausoleum of Caius Publicius Cestius	. . .	204
54. Mausoleum of Hadrian	. . . . . .	210
55. Mausoleum of Caecilia Metella Crassia	. . .	221
56. Tomb of Seneca	. . . .	223
57. Tomb of Hilarius Fuscus	. . . . .	226
58. Mausoleum of Messala M. Velerius	. . .	230
59. Tomb of P. V. Marianus and of R. Maxima	. .	234
60. Mausoleum of the Plautii	. . . . .	236

PROLOGUE

THOUGH it is obviously my purpose to give a description of the Ancient Monuments of Rome and not to write her history, as any account of them must include a reference to the two main standpoints of all similar national works, the historic and the artistic, to omit all mention of the former, at least cursorily in so far as history is connected with these Monuments, would be to deprive them of what is generally considered their prime interest and value.

Rome has occupied and occupies an absolutely unique position in the world, her sphere of influence and fame, although successively assuming different forms, has something of the perpetual and universal, to a degree that no other city has ever possessed or possesses. The distinctive attributes of her famous antetemporaries and contemporaries, such as Athens, Jerusalem, Carthage, were limited to one nationality, one creed, one direction or one epoch, and the same may be said of Rome's post-temporaries, mediaeval and modern, such as Constantinople, Paris, London, and similarly of the noted cities of still more recent birth.

Taking Babylon as an instance of the extreme earlier period, and New York as typical of the latest, it will be admitted that if the first possesses a past—great indeed but obscure and almost unrealizable to us—she has no existence as a living city at present nor apparently any prospect of a resurrection in the future, and if, on the other hand, the second has a conspicuous position in the present—and in so far as can be foreseen with regard to the problematical " to come " every chance of a prosperous future—she holds a place of minor importance from the historic and artistic view-points.

Rome, in her palmy days, was the recognised capital not of a nation or creed but of the then known universe, and what is far more, this hegemony did not derive solely or chiefly from the right of conquest. Alexander of Macedon and others conquered mighty states and vast territories, but they, or their people, did not attain any lasting world pre-eminence, or leave deep traces of their domination and influence after them. Rome alone gained and maintained that durable all-round ascendancy which could only be produced by the fittest of all. Briefly, to employ an astronomical simile, Rome Æterna relatively to other famous cities holds the place of a planet to meteors.

This unparalleled pre-eminence was indeed amply justified, for what a prodigious race were these Romans, these world's Aristoi, whose patricians were taken for gods by the Gauls, whose Senate was designated by other nations " an Assembly of Kings ", and whose burgesses were the recognised equals of the nobles of other peoples. These unrivalled legislators whose Code of Laws, because it could not be improved upon, was and is adopted as the basis of all legislation by the most civilized States, whose Constitution has never been equalled, whose language is one of the two parent tongues of those of the superior races of mankind, without some knowledge of which no one can have much claim to a higher education, whose works in literature and art hold their secular sway as standard models, and from whose polytheistic form of religion so many of the rites and symbols of our Christianity are borrowed.

These wonderful builders, whose palaces, villas, baths were cities of marble, whose forums were hypæthral museums with their units unmutilated and perfect, whose temples and basilicas were the classical archetypes of the edifices of this category, whose amphitheatres and circuses were capable of containing an audience equal in number to the population of a middle-sized town, whose magnificent tombs had the dimensions and strength of fortresses, into which they were converted by succeeding generations, and whose insuperable roads, aqueducts and drains in Italy and elsewhere lasted for over twenty centuries, accomplishing their several functions perfectly, and would have lasted much longer if ordinary care had been taken of them instead of wanton neglect and destruction.

And wherever these great colonizers and conquerors of antiquity planted their all-triumphant Eagles, they subdued nature as well as nations, not for their needs only but even for their pleasures. To cite one instance out of scores, we have the example of the Theatre of Orange, the façade of which was erected before a mountain whose huge flanks were opened merely to cut the " gradus," or rows of seats, for 8,000 spectators; and all these splendid and mighty works were, it must be remembered, produced by man-power alone, unaided by such artificial factors as steam and electricity.

The definite and official surrender of Rome's political throne with the ending of her Empire, heralded her inheritance of another, the religious one—a fair exchange, and the Seven-hilled City, by what seemed a natural evolution, instead of being the Capital of Romanism became the Metropolis of Christianism, as extensive and influential a domain as any; for, as we know, the Roman Sovereign-Pontiff, besides his purely religious supremacy and his own secular sovereignty, was then politically always the " De Jure " and often the " De Facto " overlord and disposer of both rulers and peoples. And even after the religious secessions of the two Reformations, Orthodox and Protestant, and after the loss of the pontifical temporal power, Rome still continued to be the head and centre of Roman Catholicism—that is, of the most ancient Christian Church, and which counts the most numerous, united and disciplined adherents.

Since A.D. 1870 the Eternal City has possessed a twofold though separate sovereignty, the sole modern city so distinguished, by comprising in herself the Spiritual Crown of the Church, in an absolute and comprehensive sense such as no other Head of any other form of Christianity has ever enjoyed, with the Temporal Crown of the Kingdom of united Italy, now recognised as one of the Great Powers of the World.

With regard to the purely material point of view also Rome can compare favourably, in matters of development and progress, with any other, and there is no reason to prognosticate for her a future less brilliant and prosperous than that of any existing city.

It would be impossible in these conditions that innumerable authors and artists of all grades and varieties should not have devoted their learning, talents and energies to the work of commemorating and depicting Rome in almost every respect and aspect, and the difficulty of presenting anything regarding her in a new light is, therefore, proportionally great. But every medal has its obverse as well as reverse side, and thus it is precisely this all-embracing interest attaching to the Eternal City that provides a place for all, because the subject matter, being practically inexhaustible, is greater even than the legions of successive writers and workers whose abilities and activities it has served to engross and display.

The elimination of all heterogeneous matter—that is, all reference to other than the ancient classic Roman monuments, except when a cursory mention of mediæval or modern ones is called for in connection with the former—and the classification of these monuments by dealing with each category of building in a separate chapter or chapters, arranged in each chapter chronologically or topographically, are, it is assumed, calculated to concentrate the attention successively on each monument and class of monuments, and rivet the memory on a subject certainly vast and important enough of itself to require undivided study.

The illustrations comprise a practically almost complete series of the surviving monuments in the city and some of the environs.

In brief, to adopt a homely metaphor borrowed from culinary language, an appetising, substantial, well-known, almost cosmopolitan dish is offered, but served in a different sauce and dressing. Fortunately every person who has thought or learnt anything on any subject, if he or she be at all possessed of any individuality, must naturally introduce something of this quality in their productions—in other words their own point of view, their reflections and deductions, differing necessarily from those of others; and it is from this diversity of feeling and vision that arises the never-failing novelty and charm even in traversing a well-trodden path, infinitely the more so if this path be full of the most powerful and varied interest.

Some of the personal reflections and conclusions of the author, suggested by the works of this great and all-pervading ancient civilization, might possibly at first sight appear to be somewhat irrelevant to the subject matter, but the main object of studying these wonderful remains being to learn the lessons they are pre-eminently calculated to teach us, the expression of the thoughts they excite cannot rightly be considered unsuitable or irrelevant, but, on the contrary, as a natural and useful result.

The indulgence of the readers for all errors of omission and commission is claimed chiefly on two grounds. The one, peculiar to this subject, is its inherent difficulties (besides its diffusion) which while precluding freedom of imagination and action, permitted in works of fiction or semi-fiction, does not, in compensation, provide the accurate and entirely reliable sources on which treatises on art, science or business are founded, and therefore while purporting to be a work of information, depends in a measure on conjecture and assumption. The other, a general one, is applicable more or less to all works, and this is that man is admittedly a fallible machine, a watch, let us say, warranted, in spite of guarantees, not to go right usually but nearly as often perhaps to go wrong.

Nevertheless, it is permissible to hope that any contribution dealing with a subject of such comprehensive magnitude and historic value, whatever its imperfections, will be welcomed for the sake of its purpose. If, therefore, this attempt be not formally convicted of exceeding the average percentage of defects, and considered as productive of any profit in any direction, it will have obtained all the success expected and all the satisfaction desired by the author.

THE ANCIENT MONUMENTS OF ROME

CHAPTER I

INTRODUCTORY

ITALY, the long and narrow European peninsula in the shape of a top boot between the other two Southern peninsulas, Spain and Greece, extending from the Alps to the Straits of Messina, traversed longitudinally by the Apennines and their branches, bounded by the Alps on the north, the Adriatic Sea on the east, the Tyrrhenian Sea on the west and the Ionian Sea on the south, surrounded by a galaxy of islands, large and small, of which the largest, Sicily, is one of the finest in Europe, well watered by numerous rivers and lakes, with its advantageous situation, its singularly fertile and varied soil, its admirable climate, is as especially favoured by nature, as it has been rendered surpassingly renowned in history, literature, science and art by the genius and talents of its inhabitants.

Like its gods of old, this country has several names—viz., " Esperia," from " Esperas," signifying, in Greek, evening, otherwise the land to the west of Greece, the Occidental or Evening land; " Saturnia," from Saturnus, the God of Agriculture who migrated to this country, settled here and was the first who taught its people this branch of knowledge, whence it was designated the Saturn or Agriculture-land; " Camenese," from " Camenae," the demi-deities whose particular function it was to sing the praises of kings and heroes, and, as in this country of melodious voices and improvisator-poetical capacities persons gifted with these qualifications were naturally more numerous than elsewhere, it was called the Camenese or Singers-land; " Oinotria," from " Oinos," wine, owing to the abundance and excellence of its vineyards, otherwise the Wine country; " Italia," from " Italus," a mythical and prehistoric hero or king, possibly both in one, or, according to another version supported by Varro, from " Vituli," calves, owing to the multitude of an excellent breed of cattle reared here, it was denominated the Hero-King or Cattle-land. The other names were Ausonia, Opica and Argissa, apparently derived from particular districts.

Speaking in a general sense it seems that the bulk of the primordial inhabitants of both Greece and Italy came of the same stock originally. The population of the latter was later, it appears, divided into five principal races, each subdivided into several branches—namely, the Umbrians in the north, the Etruscans, the Sabines and the Latins in the centre, and the Iapigians, gradually absorbed by the Greek settlers, in the south, wherefore this part came to be known as Magna Græcia or Great Greece. All accounts, however, of the earliest peoples of Italy, being necessarily based mainly on hypothesis and myth, are inevitably of a very uncertain and conflicting character.

In the prevailing obscurity of this primæval age a few epoch-making figures stand out as landmarks to link the prehistoric to the historic period of Rome.

The first recorded king or ruler of Italy was Janus, or Dianus, mythologically son of Apollo and the nymph Creusa, or of Caelus and Hecate, who gave his name to the hill Janiculus, where he resided, and who was the host and benefactor of the agricultural deity Saturn. Janus, or Dianus, was, after his decease, deified as the offspring of Apollo, the Sun, or, of Caelus, the Heavens, and as his own name, a derivation of Dies denotes, was originally identified with that beneficent luminary and the day, but later the powers and functions attributed to him, as will be seen further on, were of a totally different nature.

The next who emerges is Evander of Arcadia (Greece) who migrated here, settled on the Aventine Hill, became Ruler and was much venerated as the first who introduced the rudimentary arts of life and the religious rites in these parts. Hercules shortly followed, and was much favoured by Evander, who gave him his daughter in marriage, and the issue of this union was named Pallas, in memory of Pallantium, an Arcadian town, after which, as some opine, the Palatine Hill took its designation. Aeneas, the third prominent figure, who brought the famous Palladium or mysterious effigy of Pallas or Minerva from Troy (from which some assert that the name of the Palatine Hill originated) and who was the son of Anchises and Venus, landed here at the head of a colony of Trojans and was hospitably received by Latinus, who granted him territory to settle on, and his daughter, Lavinia, as his wife. Aeneas founded Albalonga (precise date uncertain, approximate one a few years after the fall of Troy) the parent city of Rome, destroyed by Tullius Hostilius, 670-639 B.C. This town was called "Alba," white, from the incident that a white sow was observed near at the time of the foundation, a tradition perpetuated in the City Arms, and "Longa," because it was long and narrow. Albalonga rose to be the metropolis of the Latin Confederation, that is, of the peoples then occupying the lands now comprising the townlets of Marino, Ariccia, Castelgandolfo, Albano, Genzano, Rocca di Papa, Rocca Priora, Frascati and their environs.

King Latinus, having been killed in a battle with King Turnus and the Rutuli, Aeneas succeeded him and ruled over both the Trojans and the Latins, who had to a great extent amalgamated. To curb the growing power of Albalonga, a league was formed between the Rutuli and the Etruscans, under Maretius, and in the ensuing campaign the Latins were victorious, but their king was slain, though his body was not discovered on the battle-field, which disappearance was explained as a miraculous Ascension, and he was henceforth worshipped as Jupiter Indiges, or Latialis.

Aeneas was succeeded by his son, Ascanius, or Julius, to whom the foundation of Albalonga is by some ascribed, and from whom the celebrated Gens Julii trace their origin, and through whom Julius Cesar claimed to descend from Venus. The successors of Ascanius left no mark of their passage, but whether this was due to their mediocrity or to the lack of annals or to both, is not certain. Livius and Dionysius have drawn up a list of their names only, for the accuracy of which, however, these historians do not vouch, and which was probably compiled with the intention of filling a large part of the years that elapsed between the foundation of Albalonga and that of Rome. To furnish a copy of this list would serve no useful purpose in the present case.

We now come to one of the latest Sylvii Kings (the Alban Sovereigns, after Latinus Sylvius, all took this surname, which was thus applied to the reigning dynasty) named Procas, who had two sons, Numentanus, or Numitor, and Amulius. On his death the throne devolved by right of primogeniture and the father's choice, on Numentanus, but Amulius, by right of might, usurped his senior's crown, to whom in compensation he left the possession of part of the paternal private estates. Numentanus had two children, Egestus and Rhea, and both had to be disposed of before their uncle could feel that crown and life were effectually secured to himself and issue; he therefore had Egestus killed and Rhea compelled to become a Vestal. Only the policy of cutting off his brother's progeny was not carried out thoroughly and consistently by Amulius, and in consequence did not succeed eventually.

It is true that if wrong-doers were thorough and consistent, right-doers would have little chance, and it is equally true that the punishment of misdeeds, or their failure to succeed, does not arise generally from the evil qualities or acts of the perpetrators, but, on the contrary, from their good ones. This, which at first sight may appear paradoxical and strange, is, for those who possess any knowledge of logic and psychology, a very natural result.

Amulius, by his cold-blooded murder of his nephew, secured his own future position and immunity, so far, while by his consideration for his brother, who though dethroned he left alive, free and wealthy, he constituted a permanent menace to himself, and by his compassion for his niece, which prevented him from killing her and induced him to honour her by making her a Vestal, he prepared the fatal blow of retribution which was to destroy him, so incontrovertible it is that thoroughness and consistency in right or in wrong have the greater part, barring luck, in success.

Rhea, in the service of Vesta, was in the Nemus, or Sacred Grove, the customary woody accessory of the religious edifices in antiquity, when the sudden presence of a wolf so terrified her that she took refuge in an adjacent cave, where Mars appeared and either overpowered or seduced Rhea, promising an illustrious progeny to this semi-divine, semi-human union. However, either during her absence in the cave or later at the birth of her twin boys, Rhea had necessarily neglected the Sacred Fire of Vesta, which thereupon became extinguished and, according to the then law (afterwards it seems abolished and commuted to scourging) she was in consequence condemned and executed, and her children put in a water-tight basket and thrown into the Anio, a tributary of the Tiber.

It is significant that, though by some tentatively suggested, it is not stated that Rhea was sentenced for violation of the law regarding chastity, which was usually the crime for which a death penalty was inflicted on the Vestals, and the reason is obvious. For though capital punishment was perfectly legal when applied in these cases to two mortal trangressors, it does not at all follow that it was equally so when one of the two was a Deity. To condemn the woman Rhea would be tantamount to condemning the God Mars, in other words to declare that humanity could sit in judgment on Divinity, which it is quite evident no theology can ever admit.

But legend also takes another turn, and, rejecting the version altogether that she was executed for whatever cause as a condemned culprit, relates that Rhea, by favour of the gods, after having herself consigned her twins in a boat-cradle to the river, miraculously exchanged her ephemeral existence for an eternal one, which proved that Mars' influence outweighed that of the outraged Vesta.

The site where these events occurred was on and around Mons Sacer, which afterwards became prominent in history on account of the secessions here of the Roman plebeians on strike.

The babies floated down the river until their boat-cradle stranded at the foot of the northern slope of the Palatine, near the Fig-tree, which was styled, in consequence, the "Sacrus Ficus Rumanalis" figuring so frequently in Roman history, at the spot where the sarcophagus, conjectured to be that of Faustulus and Aca Laurentia, the foster parents of the twins, is now shown in a cavern.

In these circumstances it is not surprising that the infants did not feel exactly comfortable. Who would in similar conditions? Nor that they proceeded, after the manner of their kind, to give expression to their feelings by whimperings and yellings. Anyhow the noise they made attracted a prowling she-wolf, who approached, and being either a stupid wolf who mistook them for her cubs, or an abnormally good natured wolf, or acting under supernatural inspiration, instead of devouring the toothsome mites, as any true-born, self-respecting wolf would have done, she, on the contrary, helped them to live by suckling them. But however willing, her assistance went no further, though, as some opine, a certain amount of licking was also occasionally added by her.

In any case, her ministrations were insufficient, for a wood-pecker, a bird sacred to Mars, and sent by him, supplemented and varied the infants' nourishment by other articles of food, procured soft substances for them to lie upon and, moreover, called together other birds as a bodyguard to protect the offspring of the War-god both from the attacks of reptiles and insects with their beaks and talons, and from the inclemencies of the weather by forming with their bodies and wings a sort of impenetrable cupola over them whenever the case called for it. Faustulus, a shepherd of King Amulius, who witnessed this remarkable scene, then took the children and confided them to the care of his wife.

The twins, who were given the names of Romus, of which Romulus is the diminutive, and Remus, grew up to be the ablest and boldest of the herdsmen around, the best protectors of the flocks against the assaults of robbers and wild beasts, and having thus acquired a superiority over their comrades, each had his following, those of Romus being called Quintilii and those of Remus, Fabii, and from these Gens two of the noblest families of the Roman Patriciate derived their origin.

The neighbouring Aventine Hill was the pasture land of the livestock of Numentanus, between whose herdsmen and those of Amulius on the Palatine, conflicts frequently occurred, in which the twins distinguished themselves at the expense of their adversaries. The Aventine men thereupon resolved to revenge themselves, and selecting the "Lupercalia," a pastoral fête of the Sylvan-god Lupercus or Pan, made a surprise attack that proved successful. Romus fled for assistance to Faustulus and Remus was captured and brought before Numentanus, who somehow recognised in the prisoner one of his grandsons, whose fate had been hitherto enveloped in mystery, and, it is superfluous to add, released him at once and treated him as a near kinsman. In the meantime Faustulus revealed to Romus the true parentage of the twins, so that when Remus returned the brothers decided to assemble a force with the object of overthrowing their great-uncle and of replacing their grandfather on the throne. In this enterprise they succeeded; Amulius was slain and Numentanus restored.

The twins, after this, stayed for a while at Albalonga, but though the favourites of the king, their former free life rendered them impatient of the restraints of a city, as their knowledge of their exalted semi-divine extraction, too ambitious for a subordinate position, with the result that they formed the resolution to found a town of their own on the site where they had spent their earliest years, and which had been the scene of their first exploits. The volcanic eruptions, too, prevalent at that period in the highlands of the Latium, were doubtless also an incitement to emigration.

The twins gathered together a large following, composed in part of their own comrades from the Palatine, called "Rumni" or people of the "Rumen" (fertilizing river), subsequently renamed "Tiberis," Tiber, but principally of Albans, Latins and Trojans, among whom were many of their nobles. This project was no sooner matured than the question naturally arose as to which of the two brothers was to assume the leadership. On the advice of Numentanus the candidates left the decision to the gods, to be manifested by the flight of vultures.

This colony, mainly consisting of a vigorous, pastoral, mountain race emigrating from the Alban highlands, to settle first on the Palatine and Aventine Hills and valleys about them, was, therefore, destined to be the nucleus of the mighty Roman State.

The Palatine is a rocky elevation of about one mile and a quarter in circuit and 160 and 170 feet in height, divided into two sections, the "Cermalus" and the "Palatinus," and the opposite Aventine, probably an extinct volcano, partitioned likewise by soil depression into the "Aventinus" and "Pseudo-Aventinus," is about 140 and 150 feet high. The origin of the name of the first has already been given, that of the second has three versions, some authorities deriving it from King Aventinus Sylvius of Albalonga, one of the numerous sons of Hercules, others from Avens, a Sabine river, and others again from Avis or bird, this hill being much frequented by the feathery tribes.

Romus selected the Palatine and Remus the Aventine as their respective headquarters, and on the day appointed for the prophetic vultures to manifest the divine will, which was to decree to whom the sovereignty was to be allotted, each candidate seated himself on his hill to watch. Remus had the first augury, beholding six vultures flying over him; Romus shortly after however perceived twelve, and each interpreted the omen in his own favour, Remus on the score of precedence in time, Romus on that of number. The majority of the colonists seem to have sided with the second, either because they were convinced that the gods had pronounced in his favour, or, what was more likely, because they had more confidence in him as a leader.

In any case, the result was a tragedy. While Remus remained inactive on the Aventine, apparently undecided whether to yield or to oppose, Romus set to work to trace the boundaries of his new city on the Palatine. On seeing this Remus left his hill and ascended that of his brother, and either in derision or aggression, leapt over Romus' boundaries with some disparaging remark as to their efficiency, and was instantly killed by Celer,* or a Celer, a follower of Romus, or by the latter himself.

There is no more proof that the one was the author of Remus' death than the other, but as the majority of mankind delight in the sensational, this act has been almost universally set down to Romus' account, because, for the morbid appetite, what is such an ordinary occurrence as that of an assailant being killed by an unknown stranger in comparison with a thrilling fratricide by the hand, too, of a twin, who, moreover, is a famous historical figure? Indeed, if anyone was to prefer the first much less interesting version most of the few who care or know anything about history would feel aggrieved and shocked at the authenticity of one of their cherished, pet, emotional theories being even questioned.

The net outcome was that Romus was thus freed from a rivalry or partnership (by an act however blamable in itself) which would in all probability have proved very detrimental to the infant State, then in the throes of its birth, whose development would have been inevitably retarded by internal dissensions or by divided power. Rome was destined to play a great role in the history of the Universe, and in furtherance of all such world missions it is the hard but unavoidable necessity that individuals should be sacrificed. Concentration of authority, as experience uniformly teaches, generally advantageous in all stages of a State's existence, is indispensable, particularly in two cases, at its birth, and, after, at its critical moments. Compatibly, therefore, with the welfare of Rome there was no room for both the twins, so one had to go, and probably he who remained was the abler of the two, as from the first Romus seemed to take precedence. It was a case of the survival of the fittest.

The corpse of Remus was carried back to the Aventine and interred under the rock where he had sat a short time previously watching the fateful vultures, and henceforth this rock was denominated " Rupes Sacrae." It appears that Romus suffered great remorse owing to the death of Remus, for not only did he erect a Temple to him called " Remuria " over his grave, and, in obedience to an apparition of Remus to Faustulus, he instituted the " Lemuria," or Feast for the Dead, to appease his brother's spirit; but, moreover, had a throne, a crown and a sceptre, exactly similar to his own, placed always side by side with his. It may be noted here that the six Vultures of Remus were held to have prophetically symbolized the six centuries of the duration of the Republican régime, which, by the way, is a very approximate calculation, as the Republic did not last 600 years, but considerably less, and the Twelve Vultures of Romus the twelve centuries of the entire existence of the Roman State, 753 B.C.—A.D. 476, which is somewhat more accurate.

The exact date of the foundation of Rome is still a disputed question. Any of the years between 753 B.C. and even earlier and 727 B.C., have been assigned as possible, but the one which is based on firmer grounds of authenticity is 753 B.C. The Palatine was chosen for the residence of the highest order of settlers and the Aventine for the lower, and Romulus, after the religious ceremonies by which all public undertakings were then inaugurated, proceeded to trace the quadrangular space on his hill, now known as the

---

* Some historians use the word " Celer ", swift, on this occasion as a personal name or surname, but as Romulus called his bodyguards " Celeres " it probably means in this case one of these guards.

ROMA QUADRATA. PALATINE,
HUT OF ROMULUS, B.C. 753. TEMPLE OF CYBELE, B.C. 191
QUARTERS OF THE PRETORIANS (PALACE OF TIBERIUS), A.D. 15–30.

Plate i.

"Roma Quadrata." In the centre he caused a rectangular pit to be dug with a square Altar inside, to which was afterwards added a wall of tufo covered at the top, designated "Mundus," a Latin word of several significations, century, world, its inhabitants, heavens and clean. The Mundus, which is still to be seen, after each settler had thrown in a handful of his country's soil, was used as a receptacle for the first products of the land, placed therein in small quantities three times a year, accompanied by the ritual performances, as offerings to the "Dei Mani," or Spirits of the Dead. The "Scalae Caci," or Stairs of Cacus, the robber-monster of an earlier period, descend here by the south-west declivity.

Subsequently Romus built the "Domuncula Romuli," or Hut of Romulus, the present remains of which are a few scarred tufo blocks set together without cement on this spot. Tufo is a porous stone, an amalgamation of sand and calcareous sediment, somewhat friable in certain regions and hard in others, of a whitish, yellowish or greyish colour. The Sacrus Ficus Rumanalis aforementioned, was transplanted here from its place at the foot of the hill, and later the Temple of Jovis Victor was also built near.

Romulus drew a furrow encircling the Palatine, this furrow made to incline inwards was cut by a bronze ploughshare drawn by a bull on the outer side and by a cow on the inner, symbolic of strength and courage without and of fertility and docility within the city, and over all the spots where the gates were to be placed the plough was raised and carried, and hence, from the verb "Portare," to carry, is derived "Porta," gate. The Plebs, or commons, were not permitted to dwell within the sacred area except in the capacity of servants or temporarily in cases of imminent danger as refugees within the walls, and, although the Aventine was also eventually encircled by the Servian Wall it was never included in the aristocratic region. Even much later, in the latter days of the Republic, long after the removal of the material barriers and the relaxation of class distinctions, the Palatine continued to be what would now be termed the residential quarter of the Upper Ten, only marked and regulated by a greater degree of exclusiveness.

On the walls of one of the halls of the Capitoline Museum there are some fresco paintings, valuable rather as illustrative of historical events than as specimens of art, and one of these represents Romus directing the "Sulcus," or furrow.

This new town on the Tiber became, in a short time, powerful enough to wage frequent wars with Albalonga, and finally, in consequence of the historic triple duel of the Horatii and Curiatii in the reign of Tullius Hostilius, third King of Rome, to overcome the parent-city and to transport her inhabitants to people the Caelian Hill which the Romans had added to their others.

There is more than one version of the origin of Rome, but after due research and comparison of competent sources, the most reasonable and authentic, allowing, of course, for the interweaving of legend and fable with history, seems to be the one of which the above is the outline.

CHAPTER II
HABITATIONS

AMONG the various qualities that concurred to render the ancient Romans a master race was their constructive ability, and in no direction was this more conspicuously exemplified than in their private habitations, every category of which, from the hut to the palace, were described collectively by the Latin word "Domus."

It would doubtless be far easier for us to portray to our mental vision the primitiveness of the earlier and humbler Roman dwellings than the magnificence of the later and grander ones, as imagination, in common with other faculties, has a much more facile task when dealing with the primitive and simple than with the developed and complicated. Moreover, despite the differences arising from the diversity of race, climate and epoch, the lower class of buildings of those times and these, have, necessarily, some general points of resemblance, both being low, unadorned and provided, at best, with the more elementary requirements only, whereas the edifices of a higher order, offering as a matter of course a much wider field for the display of art, taste and variety, the dissimilarity between the two periods and peoples is inevitably much greater.

Relatively to the details respecting the dwellings of the commonality in ancient times there is no sufficient or reliable information, because the two principal sources from which it can be gathered, documentary evidence and material vestiges, are, for obvious reasons, particularly in this case, almost entirely lacking.

In two respects, however, the ancient "Domunculae" (little houses) seem to have been better than their modern town counterparts. Their material and build were more solid, and they stood on, and not partly below, the level of the soil. The reprehensible custom so prevalent in modern cities whereby a great number of the inhabitants live underground, even in good class houses, thus sacrificing the health of the public in order to economise space, in other words for the few to obtain a larger pecuniary profit, is certainly no proof of our wisdom or of our vaunted civilization. And unaccountably enough our enlightened legislators and philanthropists, after the lapse of so many centuries, have never attempted to remove this particular evil, or even to denounce it.

As regards the Roman patricians, however, it is indisputable that they, as a class, were luxuriously and splendidly housed. Their superiority in respect to the materials used was incontestable and striking. Where we employ bricks or stone for our best modern mansions, the Romans adopted marble, either in slabs as a casing for a core of concrete, brickwork or stone, or exclusively in huge, monolith blocks. In place of the slate or earthenware tiles of our roofing, they used massive bronze ones often chiselled.

Instead of our wood, mortar or stone floors, they had pavements of variegated marbles, frequently inlaid or carved in relief, or, of artistic mosaics. Our panes of glass were substituted either by fine "Laminae," or plates of "Lapis Specularis," a species of talc as transparent as glass and less fragile, or, by a glass very similar to ours, an invention of the Phoenicians, the window frames being ornate, costly and massive.

The entire habitation, with its grace and dignity of classic architecture and sculptural accessories, standing like a jewel in a befitting setting, surrounded by tastefully laid out gardens, with their fountains, grottoes, etc., which meant that the Domus had another notable advantage, that of being independent and separate, and not, as our houses, joined and crowded together.

Regarding, therefore, the external and internal aspect of the classic Domi from the aesthetic point of view, it would be idle to attempt to compare these ancient to our modern structures. For though we have some modern private habitations with a beautiful interior, the exterior does not correspond usually, and besides this there are very few, comparatively, to the Roman edifices of this class. Ours are the exceptions, theirs the rule.

To counterbalance the acknowledged supremacy of former generations in the above respect, moderns claim a certain superiority relatively to the plan and comfort of their private residences. Is this so? The more regular and harmonious divisions of the "Domus Patricia," the greater height of the apartments, the larger size of the doors and windows (in addition to which there was often the "Clypus"; an aperture in the centre of the ceiling with a movable bronze disk that opened and shut at option), the massiveness of the entire construction, were all better calculated to ensure a light, dry and wholesome atmosphere.

Besides this, the ancient Romans understood and practised the art of making nature minister to their wants better than we do, by their systematic application of the logical principles of hygiene relatively to a favourable position, and hence their houses were situated so as to run between east and west, and thus possessed two main sections respectively cool and warm in the forenoon and afternoon. The fresh and hot water and internal heating appliances were scientific, simple and solid. Large lead pipes, often with mouths of massive, chiselled silver, ran round the building, severally fed by a spring or cistern, and by the "Hypocaustus," subfurnace, placed in the strong and ample substructions.

The Romans of the classic age objected, and with reason, to many-storied houses which are less convenient, less healthy and less independent, not being so short-sighted as to barter these positive and inestimable advantages for lucre or any other objects of minor importance, but in those cases, when their buildings were comparatively high, elevators, moved by hydraulic or man-power, spared the occupants all excessive fatigue, otherwise much diminished in Roman houses by the low and broad steps of their stairs; and to this day one of the hall-marks by which the class of building is recognised in Rome more than anywhere else, is the depth and width of the steps; the flatter and broader they are, the better the class.

So far as has been gathered, the internal divisions of the Domus were broadly as follows. The first section reached, the entrance, was called the "Vestibulum," vestibule; next came the "Atrium," reception-hall, which led to the "Cavaedium," or court, within the body of the house that opened on the "Triclinium," dining-room, "Tablinium," drawing-room, flanked by the "Alae" wings, or side-chambers, and from thence to the "Cubiculae," bed-rooms, upstairs, with their "Piscinae," bath-rooms, and behind these came the "Pinacotheca," picture-gallery, the "Bibliotheca," library, the "Proeceton," servants' apartments, the "Coquina," kitchen, and "Promptuarius," pantry. In some houses, besides these apartments, there was the "Peristylium," at the extremities of which were the "Ceci," or halls, intended, according to some authorities, for repasts, and, according to others, for receptions.

In the higher class Domi there were several suites facing north, south, east and west, inhabited according to the seasons and according to their special purposes as, for instance, those intended for study, painting or hand-work faced north to ensure an equality of light, for the bed-chambers the east was preferred on account of the morning sun, for the dining-room the west to profit by the declining sun, and for the reception saloons, the south aspect.

The edifices whose scant vestiges cover the Palatine naturally first claim our attention. In the following account, unavoidably brief and incomplete, not the chronological but the topographical sequence has been preferred, starting from the south-eastern declivity by which we enter.

The road laid bare leading from the "Summa Sacrae Via," crowned by the Arch of Titus, to the Palatine, has been identified as the original "Clivus Palatinus." By this incline we first reach the hollow between the Cermalus and the Palatinus, upon which once stood the "Regia," or Royal Abode of Ancus Martius, fourth King of Rome, and the ancient "Porta Mugonia," though what sort of structure this "Regia" was no one seems to have the remotest idea. On this depression of the hill, about seven centuries later, the Emperor Vespasian, A.D. 69-79, after levelling the existing buildings to the ground and using the lower compartments by filling them up with concrete as the foundations of his constructions, began to erect, A.D. 70, a group of edifices collectively denominated, "Domus Flaviorum," which was finally completed by Domitian, A.D. 86.

The entrance of this Flavian Palace was a grand arcaded Propylaion (Pro—fore, Pile—gate), the bronze, gilded doors of which gave access to a State-hall surrounded by Corinthian columns of Phrygian marble, sustaining a richly-decorated vault, the walls adorned with niches containing statues of equally valuable marbles. At the furthest end stood the apse, in the centre of which was the imperial throne on a dais. There were two openings to this hall, the one to the right led to the Basilica Flavia, the other to the left, to the Aedes Flavia or Imperial Chapel. This last was renamed "Lararium," or receptacle for the Lares, after the Emperor Heliogabalus had the Seven Sacred Emblems of Rome placed therein.

Next in line with the throne-hall came the Peristylium, that is a court or saloon, with an encircling colonnade, where the Sovereigns, the Imperial Princes and their courtiers retired, "To amuse themselves, not only with flowers and birds, as the ancient chronicler hastens naïvely to add, but also with diversions of a more exciting nature." This hall was unroofed, and formed of arcaded walls lined with two species of marble, Marmor Numidicum and Porta Santa, so highly polished that Domitian believed himself safer here from assassination than anywhere else, because he could perceive by the lucid reflec-

LIBRARY OF AUGUSTUS. PALATINE.

Plate ii.

tion cast on all sides those who approached. In spite, however, of this and other precautions, this monarch was eventually assassinated in this palace, and with him this short-lived dynasty of three Sovereigns, who reigned collectively twenty-seven years, terminated. From this hall a narrow staircase descends to constructions of a period prior to the Augustan, in one of the chambers of which were exposed some exquisite arabesques on golden ground unearthed in 1720.

Next to the peristylium came the Triclinium, of which the only detail gathered seems to be that it had a pavement of "Opus Sextilis," that is, of sawn pieces of marble arranged in a pattern. It was from this hall that that conscientious reformer, the Emperor Elvius, Publius Pertinax, went forth to his death at the hands of the Praetorians A.D. 193, after a reign of eighty-seven days. The dining-room of every well-planned Roman house opened on the "Nymphaeum," Chamber of the Nymphs, which in this palace had niches, statues and pavement all of alabaster. The limits of this assemblage of palatial edifices, so enthusiastically extolled by Statius, were bordered on the south by a row of Corinthian columns of "Marmor Carystium", or, as the above writer terms it "Undosa Carystos."

This marble extracted from the quarries of Carystia, in the island of Euboia, is one of the varieties of the much valued and used marble denominated anciently "Lapis Phrygius," and also called "Marmor Caepelium," or Cipollino from "Caepa" or Cipolla, onion, on account of its peculiar veins green, blue or grey which resemble those of this vegetable. This marble, which has been styled "The Marble of the Antonines," owing to its extensive use by the monarchs of this dynasty, is likewise to be found in some parts of France, Corsica and Italy.

Passing onwards over a space conjectured to have been occupied by the vanished bibliotheca annexed to the Domus Flaviorum, a ruin is reached supposed to have been a small theatre, overlooking the Vallis Murtia, Myrtle Valley, lying between the Palatine and the Aventine, famous as the site of the Circus Maximus.

A little further on once stood the disappeared Domus Hortensia belonging to L. P. C. Hortensius, 114-50 B.C., of which no particulars have been attained, though it is in general recorded that the mansions and villas of this celebrated man were of a high standard. Hortensius was first the rival and after the colleague of Cicero, and they were so nearly equal in reputation at the time, that it was only when the former tacitly but publicly recognised the superiority of the latter by conceding to him the concluding speech in a great case in which both were engaged on the same side, that the question was finally decided in favour of Cicero.

Turning to the left we meet the scattered remains of another group of buildings once forming the Domus Augustiana, constructed by Octavius after the battle of Actium had rendered him sole and absolute master. They consisted of four principal edifices, viz.: The "Aeditus" or entrance, the "Templum Apollonis," Temple of Apollo, the two joined "Bibliothecae," libraries, and the "Domus Imperialis," Imperial Palace. The Aeditus was an arch surmounted by a quadriga guided by Apollo and Diana, a masterpiece of Lysias, erected in the Via Apollinaris.

It is recorded that it was the eccentric custom of Octavius, after fortune had so conspicuously favoured him, to sit for a whole day every year at this entrance-arch in the character of a beggar soliciting alms from the passers-by, and that this was done in obedience to a vision whereby he was informed that he could thus appease Nemesis, Goddess of Vengeance or Retribution, and so escape a reverse. As it would be difficult to admit that the person of the monarch, even in this humble disguise, or the day fixed for the propitiatory performance could be unknown to the public, it may be safely assumed that Octavius amassed in his one begging day considerably more in coin and kind than any bona fide mendicant, whether a professional or an amateur, an unfortunate or a rogue, could manage to do in one year. It was an annual spectacle, and spectacles are generally paid for; only this particular one had the inestimable advantage of being accessible to all alike at any price they chose to offer. And who would not be ready to give a piece of bread or a coin of infinitesimal value to see and touch a live Emperor—a " de facto " one too, so renowned and great as to be almost a god—in the guise and attitude of a supplicant and a beggar, which was exceedingly interesting; to patronise him, which was delightful; and possibly to attract his particular attention and even future favour, which might be extremely advantageous. This performance, presenting the unusual feature of not being a penance for a past misdeed but a precaution to avert a future catastrophe, reveals the highly provident and prudent character of Octavius.

With regard to the second building mentioned, the Temple of Apollo, see Chapter VIII A colonnaded portico led to the third, the libraries, the central aula or hall of which was extolled by the writers of the period, especially for the decorations, statues and other art treasures furnished from almost all parts of the then known world. Among these may be cited the bronze statue of Octavius, and the colossal statue of the patron deity of strength, Hercules, and Bacchus, discovered here in A.D. 1724, and now preserved in the Museum of Parma. The fourth, the Imperial Palace, was quadrangular, its peristyle being approached by a double colonnaded portico, and at its south-west side an exedra was annexed from which the sovereigns could conveniently view the games of the Circus Maximus beneath. A staircase at the north conducted to the ground floor apartments which were marble-lined and adorned with statuary. In the eighteenth century a firm of antiquity merchants, who had hired these apartments for this laudable purpose, carefully stripped them of all this valuable material and work with business-like thoroughness.

We next come to the " stadium," and close to it the Domus Septimii. This edifice, the most extensive, highest and last of the great palaces of the Palatine, was constructed A.D. 198-211, partly on the ruins of that of Hadrian (of which, strangely enough considering Hadrian's reputation as a builder, no information has been obtained) to the south-west of the hill facing the Church of San Gregorio and the Jewish cemetery.

So far as can be gathered from meagre records and dilapidated remains this Domus Septimii was undoubtedly of a grand scale and design, it is alleged, for the political purpose of impressing the African compatriots of this Emperor, whose sight on approaching the Eternal City was thus first struck by these imposing edifices. It was called " Septizonium," sevenzoned, on account of its seven zones or stories, each adorned with a range of columns of seven Orders of Classic Architecture, viz: the Etruscan, the Greek Doric, the Roman Doric, the Greek Ionic, the Roman Ionic, the Corinthian and the Composite in their usual gradations.

PALACE OF CALIGULA, A.D. 38–40. PALATINE.

Plate iii.

There is a divergence of opinion with regard to these constructions, some affirming that they were only a Palace, others that they were divided into two distinct though connected buildings, the one a Domus, the other a Mausoleum. It is known that Septimius was an exceedingly capable man, and an emulator of his renowned predecessors Octavius and Hadrian. There is therefore, nothing surprising in his vying with them in architectural erections, as in fact we see by his works in the stadium, the Antonine baths, his arch in the Roman forum and in these ruins, that served as a model for celebrated artists. But it does not follow that emulation should banish common sense, as would be the case if Septimius had built a family Mausoleum which he did not intend to be used as such, seeing that both he and his son, Caracallus, were interred in the then established Imperial Mausoleum for all Sovereigns, that of Hadrian. Wherefore, simply by attributing ordinary common sense to one who was admittedly a particularly sensible man, we may conclude that the famous Septizonium was exclusively an Imperial Palace with its accessories, but not a mausoleum.

Taking the opposite direction, that is to the right of the Flavian Palace, we come to the Roma Quadrata, on this space close to the Mundus are the remains of the Temple of Cybele. A series of cells near this temple have been identified as the guard-rooms of the Praetorians on service at the Palace of Tiberius, of which these cells formed a part, and which comprise all, except the shattered north wall, of the vast Domus Tiberii, its former area, as well as the extension palace of his successor, Caligula, built A.D. 38-40, having been covered by the Orti Farnesiani. Of the Domus Caligulae the only remains are the Cryptoporticus, a small portion of riven walls and substructure, and a broken marble transenna over a gate with a half-effaced panelled soffit to be seen from the Clivus Victoriae, below, so called, it is stated, from the Ara Victoriae, Altar to Victory, erected by Evander, long before the foundation of Rome, on the summit of this incline, and conjectured to be the earliest altar raised in these parts with the exception of the Ara Saturni, on the Capitoline Hill.

Retracing our steps by the aforesaid Praetorian quarters we reach the paved portion of a street called Vicus Germanicus, that skirts the Domus Germanicus or Liviae, discovered in 1867. It seems almost a pity that a relatively good state of preservation should have been reserved for this structurally modest and historically unimportant habitation, rather than for the principal stupendous Palatine edifices, renowned as the theatres of historical events and as creations of art. But as all classic remains have their value, the one in question may claim it on the ground that it serves as a specimen of the small secondary Roman houses or rather a sort of modest private retreat of the period. It must be borne in mind that Germanicus and Livia were members of the Imperial family, and that this, therefore, was not their regular official residence, which was of course the Imperial Palace, compared to which this Domuncula was as what might now be termed a gentleman's rural cottage to a Royal Palace.

This little rectangular house, built mainly of tufo and concrete, was entered by a covered corridor with a mosaic pavement of simple pattern leading to the Atrium which opened into four principal rooms. Beginning from the right is the Triclinium, appropriately painted red, with frescoes of animals, birds and flowers. Next, at the angle of this chamber and the following one, comes the entrance to the cellars, still containing some Amphorae, and a narrow staircase conducting to the upper storey, divided into the Cubiculae. After this we find one of the Alae, that is one of the two rooms flanking the central chamber and hence called its Alae or wings. The walls of this Ala are decorated with frescoes of columns with intersecting garlands, flowers, fruit and masks. The Tablinium, or sitting-room follows next. Though all the frescoes are good, those of this chamber are the best and most interesting, representing the following mythological subject. The nymph, Io, of whom Juno, doubtless with good reason, was jealous, had been consigned to the custody of the Hundred-Eyed Argus (otherwise to be guarded and watched by many eyes) which one would have thought might have been sufficient to guarantee Juno's tranquillity, provided, of course, the said Argus was faithful, and that no Deity interfered. But unluckily the latter happened, and the painter has chosen the moment of this untoward occurrence as the scene of his work, when the nymph, Io, is about to be released by Mercury, always a meddlesome God, who is very gallantly advancing to her rescue. In this room are also kept fragments of leaden pipes belonging to the heating apparatus of the house.

Lastly comes the fourth chamber, that is, the second Ala, possibly used as a minor reception room, which has been too much, if not too well, restored, to retain an equal degree of interest with the others. A true restoration is not limited to mending or strengthening a building, but also aims at a facsimile resurrection of it. What little survives at present of the original fabric is enough for us to judge that this Domus Liviae can compare favourably with the modest modern habitations of its class in all respects except one, artistically, wherein it decidedly excels them. On the outside, adjoining this house, is an ancient cistern, very well built, and said to be coeval with the foundation of Rome.

Previously, that is to say, during the Republican period, the mansions of several celebrated Romans were built on the Palatine. Among these may be mentioned the Domus Catulus, with its Porticus Catuli; this man was the constructor of the Tabularium, poet, historian and colleague of Marius against the Cimbri; the Domus Gracchus, that of Cicero, of Aemilius Scaurus, of the wealthy patrician, Clodius, who purchased the two mansions of Catulus and Scaurus, the latter alone costing about £30,000, and incorporated both in his more sumptuous Domus, the mansions of M. Lucius Crassus and Marcus Antonius, the Triumvir, and others.

Of these superb edifices there are literally no traces existing, and the records are too vague and scant to enable anyone, however dowered with intelligence, imagination and zeal to describe or represent them by pen, pencil, brush or chisel in anything like they once were. We are told, for instance, that the aforesaid Domus Crassii was styled the "Venus of the Palatine," adorned with columns of Hymettian marble, a rare species from the quarries of Mount Hymettus, in Greece, and had its walls inlaid with massive, chiselled bronze decorations. Also, we hear that the Domus Scaurii was adorned with perfectly modelled columns thirty-six feet in height, and a wonderfully worked pavement of costly materials, but these and similar fragmentary notices do not yield any satisfactory information relatively to dimensions, style and plan.

In reference to the aforementioned Hymettian marble, it may be noted here that Mount Hymettus is equally famed for its fine marble and for its exquisite honey, and

PORTICO OF PEDAGOGIUM. FOOT OF THE PALATINE. WEST SIDE.

Plate iv.

therefore the name appeals to the connoisseurs and amateurs in sculpture and architecture as well as in gastronomy; to the artist and to the gourmet.

The famous Domus Aurea Neronis, Golden House of Nero, A.D. 54-68, the name of which we hear so often, and of which we know so little, extended from the south-eastern declivity of the Palatine over part of the Caelian, and included the north angle of the Esquiline, with the valleys between them. This palace was chiefly remarkable for two features, its vast dimensions as above, and its lavish splendour. We hear vaguely of its gold-plated walls, its ceiling panellings of lapis lazuli and agate and its other decorations of more precious stones, its silver and gold domes, tubes, balustrades and cornices, its exadrae, gardens, porticos, lakes, statues, but we have no positive detailed accounts from the structural, architectural and engineering standpoints; and there are barely any traces of this enormous edifice.

Claudius, Cesar, Nero (Nero in the Sabine language signifies Strong) fifth Emperor of Rome, was an absolute monarch of the greatest known Empire, but no connoisseur. It follows, therefore, that he had many courtiers and flatterers, and that he could at will assemble heaps of treasures and multitudes of workmen, but the first could not give him what he lacked—taste and knowledge, and the second could only produce something gorgeous and immense but not equally artistic. Moreover, this construction, a caprice of his megalomania, had a very few years' existence, though, in spite of this, a world-wide notoriety, which may be accounted for partly by its size and lavish costliness, but mainly by the infamous notoriety of its builder.

One of the few vestiges, except part of the shattered walls and ground vaults, of Nero's palace still extant *in situ*, is an accessory, the wrecked pedestal of his statue facing the Flavian Amphitheatre, said to have been of gilded bronze, 118 feet high and with a halo on the head representing Apollo with whom Nero identified himself.

The nimbus, halo or aureole, with or without rays, was the emblematic head ornament of the statues and effigies of the Roman Emperors in their divine character, its brilliancy symbolizing the sun and its spherical shape, eternity. Till the fourth Christian century the heads of Holy personages of the Church were distinguished by a triangular or quadrangular accessory, and it was only after that period that the nimbus as above was borrowed from the Pagans and introduced by the Christians as a sign of Holiness and even of Divinity.

At the foot of the west slope of the Palatine, among a host of unknown, nameless, mutilated statues, fragments of capitals, entablatures, shafts, pedestals strewn about, there are three constructions in a way surviving. Beginning from west to north we first meet the " Domus Gelotiana," House of Gelotius, later converted into a Pedagogium, college, the elementary school being, it seems, the " Paedagogium ad Caput Africa " on the Caelian hill, of which no traces remain.

The Porticus of the one in question now consists of a series of square-topped apertures flanked by brick piers sustaining a marble entablature, with two Corinthian pilasters in the centre and the capitals and bases of two pilasters at the extremity. It is said that originally a range of granite columns was erected here. On the walls there are so-called " Graffiti " (from " grafo " to write) that is, inscriptions cut with the stylus, in this case, evidently by the pupils. Of these the following are still decipherable: " Corinthius exit de Paedagogio," "Marianus Afer exit de Paedagogio," "Labora Asello quamodo ego laboravi et proterit tibi" (Work little Ass as I have done and it will profit thee), with the figure of a small donkey turning a mill, now almost effaced. The most noteworthy incision is the one found originally in the fourth chamber, and now preserved in the Kircherian Museum of Rome. It represents a caricature of the Crucifixion, a human body with an Ass' head on a Cross with a worshipper beneath and the inscription "Alexamenos adores his God," in Greek letters, which is generally believed to be of the time of Alexander Severus, A.D. 222-235, and the earliest attempt to portray the manner of Christ's death by incision.

The second erection in sequence as above is an altar of travertine, the "Ara Calvinus," and the third at the foot of the northern declivity, a rough sarcophagus in a cave, is conjectured to be that of Faustulus and Aca Laurentia aforementioned.

Some restorations of the historic edifices of this aristocratic hill were accomplished much later by the Emperor Theodoric on which it is said he spent £8,000. The Emperor of the East Constans was crowned in the Domus Flavia, and Pope John VIII, A.D. 872-882, made the Domus Caligulae his official residence, so that the Pontifical Bulls were issued, after over eight centuries, from the Palace from which the Pagan Emperor had promulgated his Decrees. During the Middle Ages the Palatine structures were transformed into fortresses by the Roman Barons, notably the Frangipani and the Annibaldi, and in the fifteenth century a great portion of this hill became the property of the Farnese family, and reverted, subsequently, by right of inheritance, to the Bourbons of Naples. After the fall of this Dynasty, in 1860, these so-called Orti Farnesiani were purchased by the Emperor Napoleon III for the sum, it is stated, of £10,000, and when he, in his turn, lost his crown and went into exile in England, 1871, he sold this property, the sole relic of his estates and Empire, to the city of Rome.

For the information which enables posterity to identify some of the edifices of the Palatine, partly or entirely destroyed, we are indebted to surviving inscriptions, to the Imperial and Mediaeval descriptions and annals and especially to the works of Plutarch, Tacitus and Ovidius.

It must, however, be duly borne in mind, that owing to the secular lapse of time, and far more to the almost uninterrupted and deliberate destruction, passively by neglect and ignorance and actively by internecine disturbances and foreign invasions, inflicted on these, and, of course similarly, on other monumental remains of Roma Vetus, it would require more than the scholar, the archaeologist and the scientist to accomplish even an imperfect resuscitation in facsimile of them. A wizard alone might succeed in doing this, if these beings were not some of them fabulous and all shams. The literary magician of the historical Romance type, the only one that is not a myth or a fraud, is the sole exception to a certain extent. Of these Sir Walter Scott, so aptly styled "The Wizard of the North," Alexander Dumas and in a lesser degree, E. Mezzabotta and others, are instances.

Their works, the products of an always fecund and patriotic imagination, bring back the past very vividly and delightfully to us, but they do not and cannot claim to be an accurate, absolute resurrection of it.

The real and important service these gifted authors render to mankind is of a different nature, and consists in arousing and reviving an interest in history in many who, after the information gained through their tasks at school, usually neglect and forget all about it in after life, for which alone they are ever taught anything. This service is naturally more useful to the more earnest and studious, in whom these splendid Historio-Romantic works excite a desire to go further in utilizing them, that is, by consulting history, if possible contemporaneously, to discover how far the magic authors altered, travestied and embellished events, persons, places, structures, etc., to suit their plots. This analytical examination and comparison, results, by a pleasant path, in redeeming History from dryness by the glamour of Romance, and thus in making History not only more attractive and in consequence more studied, but also in fixing it more thoroughly and firmly in the memory.

CHAPTER III

HABITATIONS—(*continued*)

LEAVING the Palatine from the eastern declivity and descending by the Via Victoriae to the Roman Forum, we reach the Domus or rather the Coenobium Vestalium, usually known as the House of the Vestals.

Fire being an indispensable element it was worshipped by primitive but practical peoples of antiquity as a Deity. Vulcan and Vesta were its chief representatives in Roman Polytheism, with the difference that whereas the first was the patron also, and primarily, of ironsmiths and armourers, that is, of fire when adopted for the manufacture of implements, utensils and arms, the second was exclusively the patroness of fire alone and unsubjected by man.

Though this is not perhaps generally known, mythology recognises two divinities bearing the appellation of Vesta, viz: Vesta Prisca, or Ancient Vesta, and Vesta Virgo, or Virgin Vesta. The first was the spouse of Uranus and the mother of Saturn, and is often identified with "Terra," earth, the progenitrix of the worlds and of weather, wherefore she is represented with a drum in hand to indicate that as the drum contains air the earth holds the winds and fire enclosed. The second, on whom eternal virginity was conferred, was the daughter of Saturn and grand-daughter of the first. She is usually represented with a lighted torch or lamp. Their temples were circular in shape, symbolic of the globe, which even then was believed to be round, with internal fire in the centre.

In those times, when the process of procuring and igniting fire was more difficult, it was customary to keep the "Focus Publicus," or public fire uninterruptedly alight in the residence of the Chief or King of every community; later, however, every dwelling had its own fire, and it is surmised that the term "Vestibulum," derived from Vesta, arose from this habit.

Numa Pompilius, second King of Rome, erected two shrines in proximity in the Roman Forum, the one to Vesta, or Fire, and the other to Juturna, or Water, and appointed four Vestals, or Fire-attendants, to the service of the former, though we do not hear of his having shown a similar attention to the latter, which neglect may be attributed to the fact that Juturna did not hold brevet rank in the celestial hierarchy, being a nymph and not a goddess. These priestesses were subsequently increased to six, according to Dionysius and Polibius, by Tarquinius Priscus, fifth King of Rome, and, according to Plutarch, by Servius Tullius, sixth King of Rome. This institution lasted over eleven centuries, till the reign of the Emperor Flavius Theodosius Magnus, A.D. 378-395, who formally abolished the Sisterhood. King Numa and his consort regarded the Vestals as their spiritual daughters, and the Flamens, or Priests of Quirinus, Jupiter and Mars, as their spiritual sons, thus constituting a sacerdotal family the members of

HOUSE OF THE VESTALS. ROMAN FORUM.

Plate v.

which were entrusted, under the sovereigns' presidency, with the functions of the State religion. It may be mentioned in connection that the marriage ceremony among the ancient Romans was ritually typified on the woman's part by her symbolic acceptance of "Fire and Water," to signify that she undertook the care and responsibility of the man's hearth and home.

The structures, mainly composed of bricks cased in some parts with marble, in others of marble, forming collectively the Coenobium Vestalium, may, so far as has been gathered, be divided into four principal sections, namely: the Atrium or court, the Penus Vestae or reliquary, the Virginea Domus, as Martial terms it, or habitation, and the Templum Vestae or Temple of Vesta. The Atrium was surrounded by a two-storied arcade, with columns of Breccia Coralina for the lower storey, and of Marmor Carystium for the upper. The "Breccia" presents a speckled aspect of pink, yellow or green on white ground, and consists of various amalgamated fragmentary elements, and, according as the finer or coarser predominate, is more or less susceptible to polish and carving. There are three principal varieties, viz: the "Breccia Gialla or Tenera," yellow or tender; the "Coralina," coraline or pink; and the "Verdognola or Dura," greenish or hard, and of a more homogeneous nature.

This colonnaded Atrium was decorated further with statues of the Abbesses and distinguished Sisters to the number of one hundred, of which a few still exist. The two best specimens were transferred to the National Museum of Rome, the former Balneae Diocletiani, the more dilapidated were replaced in this court. The inscriptions give the following names and dates: "Occia," 38 B.C.; "Junia Torquata," A.D. 19; "Vibidia," the intercessor in favour of Messalina; "Cornelia Maxima," executed by order of Domitian; "Praextata Mumisia Maximilla," A.D. 200; "Terentia Flavola," A.D. 215; "Campia Severina," A.D. 240; "Flavia Mamila," A.D. 242; "Flavia Publicia," A.D. 247; "Cloelia Claudiana," A.D. 286; "Terentia Ruffila," A.D. 300; "Cloelia Concordia," the last but one of the Abbesses; and another whose name has been erased, it is surmised, because she became a Christian. In the centre of the Atrium there are two marble-lined tanks to collect and retain rainwater, none other being permitted by the rules for the personal use of the Vestals, while for religious rites in the Temples and elsewhere the sacred water of Juturna's spring was adopted.

At the south-west angle of the Atrium there was a chamber of apsidal form conjectured to be the "Penus Vestae," or "Lararium," the receptacle of the sacred emblems of Rome. Behind this Penus once grew the "Nemus Vestae," or Vestal Grove; a sacred clump of trees skirting the foot of the Palatine.

The Roman Pagan Creed recognised three categories of spirits in connection with the deceased, called respectively "Penates," "Lares," and "Manes." According to Cicero the word Penates, derived either from "Penus," aliment, or from "Penitus,"—internal, was used to designate the patron deities of the household, represented by small statues placed on the hearth. The word Lares has likewise two disputed derivations, arising either from the Etruscan term "lar," king, lord or hero, or from "Lara" a nymph, whose issue by Mercury were called after her "Lares," and was the name given to the good spirits of the deceased of the family headed by its founder who watched over and protected their survivors and descendants. This custom, like the analogous institution called "Jus Imaginum," was, in fact, the tangible expression of a sentiment innate in humanity, especially high-class humanity, the ancestral cult, though in ancient times stronger than at present. The Lares were divided into two categories, the public and the private, the first again subdivided into three, viz: the "Lares Praestates," patrons of cities, the "Lares Rurales," of the country, and the "Lares Viales," of streets and roads. The "Manes" were also spirits of the dead, but connected in particular with their place of burial, and the sepulchral epigraphs were accordingly headed with the initials, D.M.S., "Dis Manibus Sacrum," or Sacred to the Gods or Spirits of the Dead.

The third section of the Coenobium was the Virginea Domus, the habitation, consisting of two stories, the first, or ground-floor, on an elevation reached by steps, was composed of a central hall surrounded by three smaller chambers, into which it opened directly by three doors. This hall is conjectured to have been the Triclinium, or, in monastic language, the refectory, and the three smaller rooms the official Cellae of the Vestals on duty. On the west side of these were the domestic compartments, namely the kitchen and storerooms, and on the east a larger chamber containing bins and a "Mola Versatilis," or mill. The upper storey was partitioned into the Cubiculae, bedrooms and adjoining bathrooms, with the indispensable Hypocaustus underneath. To the south stood the Domus Publicae Sacrum, the official residence of the Pontifex Maximus.

In the year following the death of Lepidus, 12 B.C., Octavius granted this Pontifical abode to the Vestal Sisterhood, and it was henceforth included as an integral part of the Coenobium. The dignity of Pontifex Maximus had been accorded to Lepidus in compensation for his loss of power on the dissolution of the second Triumvirate, of which he was a member, owing to the death of Marcus Antonius and the elevation of Octavius to autocracy.

The fourth section of the Coenobium was the Templum Vestae, a small structure somewhat resembling that of the Dea Matuta, in the Forum Boarium, coated with marble and erected on a platform of a height sufficient to exclude the possible inconvenience or danger from occasional inundations, which might otherwise extinguish the Sacred Fire, then considered a fatal occurrence equivalent to a national disaster. This "Ignis Perpetuus," perpetual fire, blazed for over eleven centuries on the altar of the Cella, which was surrounded by two circles of twenty Corinthian columns each, in all forty, sustaining a cupola of gilt-bronze tiles. The temple doors were either of cedar or cyprus wood, a still disputed question, and there were the usual regulation apertures for the emission of the fragrant smoke of the fire, fed solely by sweet smelling wood, and the pit in the centre of the Cella served as the receptacle of the ashes of the sacred logs.

This temple, besides suffering other damage, was destroyed by fire alone four times, namely: during the Gallic invasion 390 B.C., in 241 B.C., when the then Pontifex Maximus lost his sight in endeavouring to save the Lares, under Nero, A.D 64, and under Commodus, A.D. 191. It was rebuilt, on a grander scale, by the Emperors of the Flavian Dynasty, and for the last time by Domna Julia, the wife of Septimius Severus, A.D. 193-211, after which it continued in fairly good preservation up to A.D. 1489, and was finally demolished in A.D. 1549, the ruined stylobate and the ashpit being the sole surviving vestiges.

Eastward of the above Temple, and near the main entrance of the Coenobium, are the remains of the Aedicula Vestae, chapel of Vesta, where in simpler times the goddess

CHAPEL OF VESTA AND TEMPLE OF CASTOR AND POLLUX. ROMAN FORUM.

Plate vi.

was represented by her element, but in later and more fastidious and artistic ages by a statue. One of the original Ionic marble columns, with a riven incomplete entablature, is still standing, the other has been replaced by a rude brick pilaster by the inadequate restoration of 1898. The inscription on the frieze runs thus: "Senatus Populusque Romanus pecunia publica faciendum curavit."

As has been said, the Sacred Fire was kept burning uninterruptedly day and night, except once, at the close of every year, when the Pontifex Maximus extinguished and rekindled it instantly in the presence of the Vestals. The penalty inflicted on the Vestal on duty who allowed the fire to expire was flogging by rods and in the dark at the hands of the Primate or Pontifex Maximus, and it would be curious to speculate how each of the two parties, active and passive, felt during these operations. The revelation of any secret confided to their keeping was rigorously punished, but always according to its importance as affecting the interests of the State, and to the Vestal proved guilty, before a College of Flamens erected into a Judicial Bench, of the offence of having violated her vow of chastity by an amorous connection, the sentence was extremely severe and cruel.

On the same principle that the knights of old, before undergoing a heavy punitive sentence had their spurs hacked off and were deprived of the emblems of knighthood, as, later, military men in similar cases were primarily shorn of the distinctive marks of their profession, so the condemned Vestal was first degraded by being stripped of her sacerdotal vestments and insignia, in token that she was unworthy to wear them any longer. She was then scourged, and after placed in a closed litter and carried from the Coenobium, through the Roman Forum, followed by her relatives and friends as in a funeral cortège, to the Campus Sceleratus, wicked field, near the ancient Porta Collina, on the site now occupied by the Ministry of Finance. In this field a vault underground was already prepared containing a lamp, a couch and a table with food. On reaching this spot the Pontifex Maximus, after uplifting his hands and inwardly uttering a short prayer, proceeded to open the litter and lead out the captive to the summit of the ladder conducting down to the subterranean cell and there consigned her to the common executioner and his acolytes, who, in their turn, took her down to the said vault, left her there, reascended, drew up the ladder and filled the pit to the level of the soil. The partner paramour was likewise, after being deprived of the insignia of any rank he might possess, punished in an atrocious manner, being scourged to death in the Roman Forum.

The ostensible theocratical theory was that as the erring Vestal had, while alive, deliberately offended the Deities of Light above earth, she had to be delivered, also alive, to the Gods of Darkness below, and that it was equally necessary to shed in pain the blood of him who had co-operated wilfully in the rebellion and pollution, as a propitiatory offering to placate the outraged Divinities and avert their wrath. But the real crime, and the real reason for the awful penalties meted out to the transgressors, did not lie in the private amorous intrigue in itself, towards which the State authorities were merciful so long as these transgressions did not entail injury or danger to the Commonwealth, but to the fact that in this particular case of consecrated servants of religion all lapses were universally regarded as the causes as well as the omens of evil to the State, the gravest of all crimes in the eyes of all true Romans, for the prevention of which no measure could be too strong and no penalty too severe. So great, indeed, were all crimes against the State held to be, whether of the above nature or entirely dissimilar made no difference, that whenever they occurred the expiation was not limited to the culprits alone, but in a less degree to all the inhabitants, irrespective of grade, age or sex.

Among the members of the Sisterhood who were buried alive in consequence of this State crime, the names of the following have been transmitted to posterity: Panuria, Oppia, Popilia, Minuria, Scotia, Popimia, Caporonia, Cornelia, Murica, Aemilia, Mucia and Veromila, and as all records have not been preserved, there may have been and probably were others. But if we consider that the number of Vestals did not exceed six contemporaneously (though some assert that on one or two occasions their number was temporarily increased to twelve) even supposing that the above list comprised all the delinquents it yields a fair percentage of criminal Vestals, counting the convicted ones only, of the small total number of Sisters: which proves that these ladies of antiquity, like moderns, found, with the perversity inherent in human nature as a rule, in all races and epochs, that the more strictly anything is prohibited, provided it be more or less agreeable (or even disagreeable in certain cases *per se*) the more attractive it becomes, and the greater number of devotees it counts, owing mainly to this very prohibition. The first human couple proved the truth of this very clearly.

The Vestals resembled in some respects and differed in others from their Christian successors, the nuns; or rather they were a combination of priestesses and nuns, under the direction of a Superior or Abbess styled " Virgo Vestalis Maxima." The qualifications for admission to this select religious body were: first, the age limit, not under six and not over ten years; second, to be free of personal defects or blemishes; third, to possess both parents living; and fourth, until the reign of Octavius, to be of patrician descent. The Pontifex Maximus chose the fittest among the applicants, and when the voluntary eligible candidates began to fail, the " Lex Popea " was passed in virtue of which he selected twenty children belonging to the most conspicuous families, from whom the name was drawn by lot to fill the vacancy. The child on whom the lot fell was then and there, in full public assembly of magnates, invested with the sacred bands, stole and mantle. It was obligatory for the novice, on first entering, to have her hair cropped close and appended to the " Lotus Capillata," or hair lotus-tree, but the tonsure was not repeated, and the hair was allowed to grow to its full length. This was the votive offering to Vesta from the child, who had nothing else of her own to give. The dress of the Sisterhood consisted chiefly of white woollen cloth, white being then, as now, the usual emblematic hue of purity, and was composed of the " Vittae " twined in ropelike folds about the head, a long sleeveless gown bound at the waist by the " Zona," or girdle, the " Stola," stole, with sleeves, and the " Pallium," or full, many-plaited garment. When attired in full canonicals the Vestals wore the " Siffibulum," or oblong wimple, with a purple border fastened to the breast by a " Fibula," buckle, to which some added a metal necklet.

The period of service was thirty years, ten of novitiate, ten of official functions and ten of training the novices, at the expiration of which they had the option of either remaining Vestals or of retiring, and, if matrimonially inclined and the opportunity offered, of marrying. This re-entry into secular life, however, rarely occurred, and

Tacitus mentions an instance, probably not a unique one, of a Vestal of fifty-seven years of unbroken service.

Although the wives and female relatives and friends of high officials, tribunes, censors, senators, praetors, consuls and emperors, naturally possessed and exercised, then as now, that indirect and unavowed influence in social and public affairs, which has been and always will be the main participation of the female sex in similar concerns, the Vestals were the only women constituted in a regular corporation, who both individually and collectively were legally invested with definite rights and privileges regarding matters of the State. Among these stands foremost the prerogative of officially interceding with all the Courts and Judges, before and after a sentence, and to this was annexed another rather curious one, that if a condemned individual happened to meet a Vestal on his or her way to execution, provided the encounter was fortuitous, he or she were at once set at liberty unconditionally. Of this last we have a replica in much more recent times. Previous to the unification of Italy, in some of the States, if a condemned person accidentally came across the cortège of the Viaticum, that is, the priest and his acolytes on his way to administer Extreme Unction, the condemned man or woman were instantly released.

The Vestals were also instrumental in obtaining, not only by private recommendation but by official action, various important posts for their protégés in the public services. They were, as aforesaid, the guardians of the Sacred Emblems of Rome till A.D. 218, and of course the precincts of the Coenobium were an inviolable asylum for fugitives of every description. During the Republic the patricians and later also the emperors confided to their keeping State documents as well as private ones, including testaments and secret deeds of all kinds, and they continued to be the custodians of private archives after the public ones had been transferred to the Tabularium (from " Tabulae," tablets, on which the Laws were inscribed). The Tabularium, the peperino foundations of which still exist on the southern slope of the Capitoline Hill, was built by C. Catulus, it is uncertain whether in 79 B.C. or 85 B.C.

In the way of honorary distinctions the place assigned to them in national ceremonies and public spectacles was amongst the highest Orders and personages; they had precedence over all civil and military ranks with the exception of the Senators and Consuls, and, similarly with the highest dignitaries, they were accompanied by lictors. The right of burial within the city boundaries was conceded to the Sisterhood; a privilege only shared exceptionally by the most illustrious and deserving of the Romans.

The Vestals had their own horses, vehicles, stables, cattle and estates, all appertaining, of course, to the Order, and in the course of time the ever-accumulating property and wealth of the corporation became great enough to excite the cupidity and rapacity of the later emperors, particularly those of the fourth century, and this opulence resulted in affecting seriously the material interests of the Sisterhood, and sometimes also the personal safety of its members, but this, of course, occurred in decadent times, when tyranny and corruption prevailed, and not during the classic age, when it would have been impossible.

The case of the wealthy military-monastic Order of the Templars offers, in some respects, a parallel. King Philip IV, " Le Bel " of France, in co-operation with his creature, Pope Clement V (Bertrand de Goth), suppressed the Templars in order to seize their possessions in A.D. 1314. Tradition relates that on this occasion, when the Grand Master, Jacques Molay was on the stake, where he was burnt alive as a sorcerer and criminal, he summoned the two "Accursed," as he termed the king and the pontiff, to appear before the Tribunal of the Almighty, the first within a year the second within forty days, to answer for their crime towards his Order and himself condemned by them unjustly to extinction, torture and death on false accusations, that served as a pretext for the confiscation of their possessions coveted and appropriated by their persecutors. This prophesy was, so far as regards the dates of the respective deaths of the two potentates, fulfilled to the letter, and what happened to them subsequently before the Judgment Seat of the Omnipotent it is certainly not within our province to enquire or within our power to learn.

Julius Caesar owed his life during the political persecutions of Sylla to the interposition of the then Vestalis Maxima, supported by Aurelius Valerius, to whom the Dictator had promised to grant the first favour he asked of him. Sylla had refused to accede to all other appeals in favour of Cæsar and in reluctantly consenting on this occasion, he warned the two applicants and the others who supported them, that in asking him to withhold his hand in the case in question they were committing a fatal error as regarded the independence of Rome and the integrity of her great institutions, an error Rome would have to pay for very dearly later, because in the single person of Cæsar, the then effeminate, dissolute and voluptuous spendthrift, he foresaw many and more dangerous Mariuses incorporated. And as regards the real greatness of Rome, her moral supremacy, his prediction was not at fault, which is not remarkable, as Sylla, besides being an exceedingly clever man, was of aristocratic lineage, belonging to that class, the patrician, which is generally characterized by perspicacity and foresight in a greater degree than the plebeian.

The intercession of another Vestalis Maxima later with the Emperor Claudius on behalf of Messalina was not successful, but it might have had a different result if the Abbess' conference with the Sovereign had not been temporarily postponed by the conspirators who took care to hasten the execution at once before there was time for another attempt by the Vestalis Maxima. These two instances are, of course, well known on account of the personages concerned, but many others could be cited and many more are unrecorded.

It may be noted here that the Emperor Darius Bassianus, A.D. 218-222, better known by the name he assumed of Heliogabalus, created a female Senate to deliberate and regulate fashions, diversions and etiquette; one of the rare sensible acts to his credit, for otherwise he was notorious for all sorts of eccentric and abominable excesses, among which were two sacrilegious ones connected with the Vestal Corporation. The one was marrying as a third wife the Vestal Aquilea Sabina, reckoned, by the way, the best looking of the Fire-priestesses of the time, in the belief that the offspring of this union would be divine or nearly so on both sides, and the other, still greater in patriotic eyes, of removing the Palladium from the Penus Vestae to his Palatine Palace. His justification for these acts was, that as he had been ordained, previous to his assumption of the Throne, High-Priest of Baal, he was doubly endowed with impeccability and infallibility.

If it were not otherwise abundantly refuted, the above fact would suffice to dispose of the curious idea some people have conceived, that the Dogma of Infallibility of 1870 was a papal invention, whereas the modern dogma was in reality only a pale, limited, belated reassertion of an ancient principle.

Among the signs of progress which modernity claims as peculiarly its own is the so-called emancipation of women. Facts, however, do not confirm this claim. Besides the Vestal Corporation, endowed with special and high privileges, of which no woman or body of women possess even a tithe now, they were then admitted equally with men to be consecrated members of the religious hierarchy; in other words, they were held to be worthy of fulfilling functions from which they are now debarred as unworthy. In the military profession, in many nations of antiquity, women formed regular corps, composed of officers and soldiers of the female sex; that is, they were accepted in a service that they are now considered incapable of performing. Women could then be Sovereigns in their own right as well as in some countries now, and we have examples in ancient times of female deliberative assemblies, which, however rare then, have no counterparts in our times. Added to all this, the position and dignity in general not only of the Roman matron but also of women of some other peoples, the Scandinavian for instance, was higher than that of the modern lady. Thus the status and importance of the female sex, in a public sense as well as in a private and social one, could, to say the least, compare favourably with the present. If, therefore, this movement, rather hysterically manifested, whatever its merits or demerits, is put forward as an indication and proof of progress, and as something quite novel we are also in these respects in a state of retrogression as compared with the ancients, and only feeble imitators of principles and systems of days long past.

Adjacent to the Coenobium Vestalium was, as aforesaid, the Regia Numae, one of the most ancient buildings of the Roman Forum, and, it is said, more extensive than its present scant remains would seem to denote. Ovidius, however, refers to it in these words: " Hic fuit parvae antiqua Regia Numae," but probably he alludes to the original structure, and, if so, his description was accurate, because it was erected in primitive times by the unostentatious King Numa, who occupied this little fabric in his double capacity of king and pontiff, and it afterwards became the Chapter-house of the College of Flamens.

This building, after various destructions, alterations and renovations, was entirely reconstructed by the Pontifex Gn. Calvinus 36 B.C. in solid marble; and ornamented with statuary from Greece. The new Regia is reported to have contained separate shrines for all the Pagan Deities, but as they were nearly, though not quite, as numerous as the Christian Saints, and as the building could scarcely have been vast enough, however extended, to contain the shrines of all the members of Polytheism, it may be assumed that this comprehensive phrase was intended to mean the Chapels of the principal gods and goddesses.

The wife of the Pontifex Maximus, styled " Regina Sacrorum," presided here in virtue of her office at the sacrifice of the Black Sow to Juno Lucina, and on the 25th of August the Vestals performed in this building the annual rites in worship of Ops, otherwise Cybele. Here, again, we have another example that women occupied a higher status in ancient than in modern times. The wife of a Protestant Bishop does not participate officially in any religious functions; that is, she is a nobody as regards the Church in which her husband holds a high rank; she does not share his functions, honours or authority, and, as if to mark the difference between the two more clearly, she does not bear an equivalent title by courtesy at least, he is " My Lord Bishop," " His Lordship," she is Mrs. Somebody. On this head no comparison can now be made with regard to the Roman Catholic hierarchy, because celibacy has been imposed on all members of the clergy.

The Regia, before the façade of which were planted two laurels, the trees sacred to Mars, also served as an astronomical and seismological Observatory. In the shrine of the War-god were suspended two Hastae, or Spears, as the chronicler phrases it: " Hastae Martis in Regia sua sponta motae ", and there was a priest constantly on guard to watch and report to the Senate every oscillation of the spears caused by telluric vibrations. On these occasions the Salii, dancing-priests of Mars, were ordered to the Regia to sing the Carmen Salia, which was intended as a specific to avert evil consequences. This structure was also the depository of the sacred implements employed in sacrifices, so that it held an important place in the religious life of Rome.

The present remains consist of the foundations containing, among broken scattered fragments, a hollow circular Sacrarium, or altar, to Mars, and a Tholos, or vault, to Ops. Some archaeologues, official and free-lances, contest, however, both these versions, and assert that the first is a mediæval cistern and the second a coeval cellar. In the Capitoline Museum there is a fresco illustrating a sacrificial scene of Numa assisted by the Vestals.

Although the neighbouring Juturna structures cannot by any stretch of licence be classed as habitations, yet as they are connected locally, and chronologically with the Coenobium, a brief reference to them here may not be deemed inadvisable, as it might facilitate the assimilation of the subject matter.

This district of Juturna, in the Roman Forum, is small in extent but comprises the remains of three distinct buildings, namely, the " Puteal," wellhead or fountain, the " Lacus," or pond, and the " Sacellum," or shrine of Juturna, all originally erected by Numa, and consisting of brickwork, in some parts coated with marble or of marble. The Puteal, a solid construction, is surrounded by marble fragments, among which are two Stelae. The Lacus, marble-lined, served, as legend narrates, to assuage the thirst of the steeds of the Dioscuri, who, apparently not sharing the divine nature of their riders, felt the very common material want of thirst. The Sacellum contains a headless, fractured statue of Juturna with a child in the main recess, and in a smaller cavity to the left a bust on a bracket of some unidentified individual, which some suppose to be that of Numa and others of Aesculapius, and on the right wall the lower half of a female statue.

These constructions were subsequently surrounded and built upon by the Status Aquarius, Water-Board, and, later again, in the eighth and ninth centuries one of the halls of this Board was converted into an oratory dedicated to the Forty Martyrs. Another shrine was consecrated to this nymph or demi-goddess later by L. Catulus, 241 B.C., near the Virgo Aqueduct and also another, probably near the Arch of Janus by her spring, but it is evident that Juturna never attained much importance, because we do not hear of any temple being dedicated to her.

SANCTUARY OF JUTURNA. ROMAN FORUM.

Plate vii.

The following building likewise cannot be, strictly speaking, included in the category with which we are dealing now, still, as it is a habitation though not a private one, and seems to stand alone and unconnected with any other, a brief description at the end of this chapter would not be more out of place here than anywhere else.

In the year 1866 G. Gagliardi discovered, eastward of the old Church of San Chrysogono, about twenty feet below the street level, the remains of a fabric identified as that of the ancient Exhubitorium, or Quarters of the VIII cohort of the Vigiles, fire-brigade. The modern staircase leads down to a courtyard with a pavement of Opus Signinum and a fountain in the centre, a chapel on the right and some rooms with square windows furnished with a heating apparatus. The dilapidated wall frescoes and the pavement must have been fairly good, but the most noticeable feature is the great doorway, a fine specimen of a peculiar style of architecture in brickwork, with its two flanking pilasters, the shafts of red bricks and the capitals of yellow, supporting the arched cornice of terra cotta, dentellated and otherwise ornamented. On some of the bricks was found the date of A.D. 123, and various Graffiti by the Stylus or writing-stiletto of the reign of Alexander Severus A.D. 222-235. These graphical incisions generally commenced with the consular date, followed by the number and rank of the writer, and concluded with his reflections or exclamations. The frequent repetition of the word " Sebaceria," from " Sebum," suet, is accounted for by the use of this substance for the lighting of the Exhubitorium, as " Ceroleria," from " Cera," wax, was adopted to signify illumination by wax candles. The institution of the Vigiles, or Watchers, or rather their organization and formation into units called " Cohortes Urbanae " nine in number, is attributed to Octavius after he had developed into Augustus.

The name of Heliogabalus had been inscribed also here, as some faint traces still discernible reveal, but it is evident that it was subsequently erased by the Senatorial decree whereby the names of the defunct Sovereign were cancelled from all public buildings. On the medals bearing the effigy of this extraordinary monarch, he is designated by the other names he took, that is, Marcus Aurelius Antoninus, the identical ones of Caracallus, whom he succeeded, and whose illegitimate son he is said to have been; and hence the two are sometimes confounded, a confusion of identity at which neither could have reasonably objected, seeing that were on the whole equally unworthy.

CHAPTER IV

HABITATIONS—*continued*

THE class of construction to which the term "villa" applies was a private residence comprising habitations, gardens, orchards, and in many cases also temples, circuses, baths and other similar establishments. The habitation proper was divided into three distinct sections, viz: the "Urbana," or residence of the proprietor, his family and immediate attendants, the "Rustica," destined for the shelter of horses and cattle and the depository of implements of husbandry, &c., and the "Fructuaria," for the storage of crops.

Villas were and are a national institution peculiar to the ancient Romans and modern Italians, with the difference that those of the former were, as a rule, like most things, on a grander and more artistic scale. Within the "Urbs Romae" the word villa was likewise used to describe public edifices, such as the two Villae Publicae, the one in the Roman Forum and the other in the Campus Martius, both vanished. On the other hand, in modern Italy the term is employed to designate public gardens and parks as well as private residences. Other nationalities in due course adopted this class of habitations, borrowing even the name in proof of their origin, though few of the dwellings in other countries, grandiloquently styled villas, resemble or equal the typical modern Italian, and far less the ancient Roman, villas.

The villas of the Eternal City and environs were naturally superior in number and importance to those of other parts of Italy, in fact the extent of some of them was so great as to resemble rather that of townlets than of private residences, but they have all perished or nearly so. The exercise of a little knowledge and reflection will suffice to explain the causes of the greater degree of destruction suffered by the private edifices in comparison with the public ones. The authorities and people were naturally more interested in the preservation of the latter buildings, which belong to all, on the score both of public utility and historical association; and for those of a religious character, there was an additional protection in spiritual prestige. The conservation of some of these public edifices of great solidity, was, remarkably enough, prolonged by the feudalism of the Middle Ages, owing to the prevalent system of transforming the amphitheatres, baths and mausoleums into fortresses and the temples into churches.

One category of private constructions alone has in a measure escaped this extensive obliteration, the "Houses of the Dead," the sepulchral structures, but this may be partly accounted for by the profound and universal veneration, so peculiarly Roman, in which the deceased and everything connected with them was held, and which manifested itself

HABITATIONS

materially by elevating these sepulchres, often of magnitude and magnificence, to the rank of national monuments.

The Caelian Hill, Mons Caelius, situated between the Palatine and the Esquiline Hills, was first called Mons Querquetelanus, or Mount of Oaks, because it was covered by a forest of these trees. It was subsequently renamed Mons Caelius from Caelius Vibena, an Etruscan chief who was the ally of Tarquinius Priscus, and who eventually settled on this elevation. If the period occupied by the reign of Tullius Hostilius, about thirty-one years, be excepted, during which he built his Regia on this hill and transported the population of Albalonga to inhabit this elevation, the Caelian, with the Viminal, have figured less in history and tradition than any of the other hills. But if the Caelian possesses fewer national monuments and records it seems to have been one of the preferred sites for villas.

The Villas Vectliana and Annea, covering the space after occupied by the Military Hospital on this hill, have been rescued from oblivion so far as their names go, chiefly owing to the fact that the philanthropist and philosopher, Emperor Marcus Aurelius, A.D. 161-181, was born in the first in A.D. 121, which was the dwelling of his grandfather, and reared in the second. The Villas Patricia, Casali and Tetricia; likewise on the Caelius, the last named served as the gilded prison of Tetricius T. Pesanius, one of the thirty tyrants of Gaul mentioned by Tribellius Pollonius, and also probably of his son proclaimed Caesar, both protégés of the Emperor Aurelianus A.D. 270-275. Of these structures and others there are no known traces left.

There was another noted house on this hill, which although not of the classic times, can scarcely with propriety be omitted, as it was the home of Pope Gregory A.D. 590-604, distinguished by the three titles of "First," "Saint" and "Great." This dwelling of his wealthy parents, Saints Gordianus and Silvia, in which the future Pontiff was born A.D. 450, stood opposite the present Church of Saints John and Paul. The family name of this celebrated Pope, as well as the status and profession of his father, are still subjects of dispute, some authorities contending that Gordianus was a scion of the Anicii, an ancient Roman Patrician stock, others that he was a member of the Conti, a powerful feudal family, some maintaining that he was a Senator, others that he was a Saint, though there is no apparent or cogent reason that the two should be incompatible in one person, as in fact happened with his son Gregory, who though a Saint held the office of Prefect.

It appears that the Pincian, Janiculan and Esquiline Hills were, like the Caelian, studded with villas now vanished. On the first, the present well known public park, anciently denominated "Collis Hortorum," Hill of Gardens, and now Pincio, formerly stood the Villa Acilia on the site of the present Villa Medici, later French Academy.

The Patrician Gens Acilii rose to eminence by the Consul Acilius Glabrius Marius 191 B.C., who, with his colleague, the renowned M. Portius Cato, defeated Antiochus and the Aetolian league. His homonymous grandson was appointed 70 B.C. Praetor Urbanus in place of the fraudulent Verrus, and later commander of the Roman forces, contending with Mithridates, one of the most powerful and inveterate foes of Rome, whom Acilius vanquished. Under Domitian another Acilius was in command of the Roman army operating in Pannonia (a vast tract comprising parts of modern Hungary, Carinzia, Croatia and Sclavonia) together with M. Ulpius Trajanus, who became subsequently the celebrated Emperor. Indeed, during the Republican and Imperial eras the names of various members of this family occur no less than eleven times in the Fasti Consulares. The Acilii were among the earliest converts to Christianity of the Roman aristocracy, as is attested by the tombs of Verrus and Priscilla, in the catacombs of Sta. Priscilla, who were son and daughter of Acilius Glabrius Consul in A.D. 151. The Pincii, an influential family of the later imperial times, succeeded the Acilii in the possession of this estate, and from them the hill took its present appellation of Pincio.

The greater part, however, of the ancient Collis Hortorum was occupied by the Villa Luculli, reckoned as one of the most magnificent in Rome as were all things connected with comfort and luxury of that refined voluptuary Lucius Lucinius Lucullus. The life of this distinguished man, born 115 B.C., presents two distinct and opposite phases; the first, that of an able and successful statesmen and warrior, the second, that of a sensual and luxurious but cultured votary of pleasure. But history teaches us that the Romans of the upper class, besides being more versatile than we are, knew how to grace even their sensuality by the cultivation of literature and the Fine Arts. There was the usual proportion of good and evil in them of course, but in virtue or vice there was nothing sordid, low, unintellectual or superficial about these high-souled patricians.

There are probably few acquainted with Roman history who will fail to recall to mind the celebrated banquets, whose fame has survived to our day, that Lucullus gave in his various Triclinae, named severally after the gods, as for instance the supper to Pompey and Cicero, perhaps the best known, not because it was more sumptuous than usual (though it is said to have cost 50,000 lire, £2,000 at par) but on account of the two historic guests. In evidence of the system and style with which he regulated his household it was his custom to name the dining-room in which he intended to take his repast to his majordomo, but neither the number of guests, if any, or other particulars and this alone sufficed, as also is the answer, so often quoted, he gave to an unexpected guest and surprised new attendant, who manifested their unbounded astonishment at such an elaborate and exquisite meal with its splendid accessories, when no one had been invited, "That Lucullus was going to sup with Lucullus." But that he was no mere empty pleasure seeker must be admitted not only in view of his previous life and services but also by the admiration and lifelong friendship of such men as Pompey, Horatius, Cesar and Cicero.

The above villa susequently passed into the possession of Valerius Asiaticus and became the theatre of the two following tragical episodes in sequence. The famous or rather infamous Empress Messalina Valeria coveted this beautiful seat, and with her there was but one step from this to the suppression of the proprietor. She accordingly induced her lover, Silius, to accuse Asiaticus of corrupting the army, a State crime, and also, strangely enough as coming from her of all people, of the private sin of leading a dissolute life. Asiaticus was a typical Roman of the old school. He first, as a duty to himself, defended himself and so eloquently as to draw tears even from Messalina, genuine crocodile tears, of course, and then without waiting for the sentence, the chances of a reprieve or acquittal, or making any attempt to escape, arrange or bribe, all of which his position and wealth rendered quite possible, he resolved to have done with the whole matter at once in the lofty Roman way. He proceeded to bathe and perfume himself and sup luxuriously, had his funeral pyre prepared which he inspected and ordered to be removed so as to prevent any injury to the trees by the flames, and then calmly severed his veins and died.

Silius, in the meanwhile, throwing off all disguise, went so far as to celebrate the religious ceremony of his marriage with Messalina, while her consort Claudius was at Ostia, which this monarch so greatly contributed to enlarge and embellish. Some of the numerous enemies of the newly-wedded couple conspired, and taking advantage of this fresh feat, hastened to inform the Emperor, and at last even the easy-going Claudius was aroused to punish the accumulated enormities of the Empress. While she was still engrossed in her orgies at this iniquitously acquired villa, the Emperor suddenly returned to Rome, and finding Silius and some of her other paramours opportunely in the city, had them promptly arrested and executed. It was remarked that he contented himself with this effectual disposal of her chief lovers, but that if he had thus drastically suppressed all those who had valid claims to be her left-handed spouses, it would have been tantamount to ordering a veritable hecatomb.

Messalina made an attempt to meet the Emperor in Rome accompanied by their children Brittanicus and Octavia (ladies frequently make use of and rely a good deal on these diminutive and not verbally eloquent advocates to cover their shortcomings or crimes) and also by the Vestalis Maxima, whom she persuaded to plead for her, and who, as aforesaid, had the right in virtue of her office, to interpose and suspend an accusation or a sentence. But the Empress, with her escort, were prevented from approaching her outraged consort by those who had resolved to have done with her, the Abbess being put off by some plausible reason and promise of a hearing later.

This attempt having, for the time failed, Messalina at once addressed a supplication to Claudius, the wording of which revealed the internal strife between her habitual insolence and her abject fears. The Emperor still procrastinated, divided between his desire for vengeance and his compassion for the " poor creature " as he called her, but Narcissus, once her accomplice now her inveterate foe, turned the balance of the still swaying scales against her, by interpreting the first words the Emperor had uttered in his wrath on hearing the startling news, " It is too much, she must die," as an official order, and thereupon commanded a Tribune with some Centurions to put the Imperial sentence instantly into execution, well knowing that he had to choose without delay between her immediate death and that of himself and his accomplices.

During the days, all too many, of Messalina's prosperous fortune, her mother and she had been at bitter variance, but maternal love, one of the strongest feelings of humanity and of all living creatures, asserted its power and would not permit the mother to desert her child however culpable in the latter's dire distress and peril. Vibidia, in the true Roman fashion, which had begun to fall into disuse, then urged her daughter to make amends for a bad life by a decent death. " After all," she is reported to have said, " existence in this world must have an exit, yours is on the threshold, prefer therefore a voluntary dignified dissolution rather than the end of a condemned criminal at the hand of others." But Messalina, who had arrogance and audacity only when above danger and in prosperity, but no becoming pride or courage, and who, moreover, was utterly demoralized by her debaucheries, could not obey her mother's injunctions. So when the military arrived accompanied by Evodius, a freedman sent with them as a sort of Civil Commissioner to supervise and see the deed duly accomplished, they found Messalina in the gardens lying beside her mother in a state of despair. This man proceeded to load her with brutal reproaches, well deserved if any ever were, but cowardly towards a being so fallen in every respect, and she made a feeble attempt to destroy herself, but was immediately despatched by a Centurion's sword.

When her death was announced to Claudius he received the report with philosophic indifference, neither elated by the accomplishment of his vengeance nor depressed by the sudden, unedifying and violent death of his spouse, nor even much surprised that she had been dealt with so summarily without his express and formal order: and the Senate, being then reduced to an Assembly of Courtiers obsequious only and always to those in power, decreed that the names and titles of the defunct Empress should be forthwith erased from the Imperial Palaces and all public buildings and her statues, effigies, portraits and busts, broken and destroyed.

This villa, reckoned by Plutarch as superior to a royal residence, was finally ravaged and demolished by Theodoric, King of the Ostrogoths A.D. 455-526, who transferred its rare decorative works to Ravenna. The sole remaining vestige of it now is a portion of a mosaic pavement beneath N. 57 of the Via Sistina and of N. 46 of the Via Gregoriana.

The Villa Aurelia, on the Janiculus, was especially noted for its fine situation and luxuriant vegetation, and these assets seem to have furnished for a long period equally attractive prey to goats and to municipal authorities, who vied with each other in the work of devastating the beautiful and varied garment with which nature clothes herself; with the difference in favour of the former that the quadrupeds limited themselves to eating the vegetation suitable for their sustenance, whereas the bipeds could not claim this practical excuse for their destructive propensities, nor that their ravages were only confined to grass and shoots.

The numerous, chiefly Imperial, villas, of the Esquiline have all vanished, the scant remains, still surviving a few years back, having been demolished to make way for the invading modern buildings. This hill was also, it seems, the chosen residential quarter of the Roman Equites and it is recorded that the Domi or Villae of Cicero and Pompey, once stood here. Relatively to the House of Cicero we have no information except that it is stated that the world-famed orator was born in it, and in respect to Pompey's, that it was built near the Templum Telluris, and that it was decorated externally with Rostrae in commemoration of his naval triumphs, and internally with frescoes representing sylvan scenes. Antonius the Triumvir appropriated this building, enlarged and embellished it, and later it became the favourite residence of the Emperor Antoninus Pius.

It is recorded that one of the two villas of Maecenatus was constructed on the slope of this hill near the Servian Agger, and Propertius, who was frequently the guest of the proprietor, describes this villa in glowing terms. The site it occupied, called "Malanno dei Morti" from being a desecrated cemetery, was transformed into the beautiful villa, or "Horti Maecenati," with a tower, the identical one, it is affirmed, wherefrom Nero afterwards viewed the conflagration of Rome, of which the Christians were denounced as the incendiary authors, thus furnishing a pretext for further persecutions.

The other Villa Maecenati, a quadrangular construction measuring as computed 640-450 feet, was at Tivoli, and its ruins of which a few vestiges remain, formed formerly one of the most conspicuous features of that enchanting region. On the side facing Rome this villa was bounded by arcades comprising a theatre in the centre flanked by two halls. The Porticus was arched and adorned with pilasters of the Doric order, while the entire building appears to have been surrounded by pillars of the Ionic Order enclosing a " Herculeum " or Temple of Hercules. The decorations, stuccoes, arabesques, frescoes, mosaics and especially the interior of the heliocaminus are stated to have been remarkably fine.

Claudius Clivius Maecenatus was a member of the Clivii, one of the few families of Etruscan extraction incorporated in the Patriciate, flourishing up to the early Imperial times. Although this eminent man was appointed by Octavius, of whom he was the close friend and trusted counsellor, Vice-Regent of Rome and all Italy, a high post he filled with credit and success, this was not his principal claim to renown. Almost all conspicuous Romans distinguished themselves in various, and, apparently to us, incompatible directions and careers, priest, soldier, orator, legislator, sailor, governor, statesman, builder, writer, &c., were often all combined in one individual and sometimes all in an eminent degree. But the fame of Maecenatus was, in its line, unique and supreme, he emerges above all others as the great, munificent and enlightened patron of literature, science and art, and in this capacity he overshadows so completely all other qualities in himself as well as eclipses all other known patrons, that to this day in Italy, and in a lesser degree in other countries, a powerful and competent protector is a " Maecenatus," so that ceasing to be the appellation of a man it became conventionally a qualificative epithet denoting a patron of culture. His protégés were innumerable, but among the most celebrated may be mentioned Virgilius and Propertius. Maecenatus was also a writer of merit, and above all a first rate reviewer and critic of the works of others. He was born in 73 B.C. or 63 and died in his Esquiline villa 8 B.C.

In our times we lack men like Maecenatus, and therefore art and literature, or rather the apostles thereof, do not have equal chances with those of these earlier times, and of the rebirth of these times, otherwise what is styled usually the " Renaissance " period. The patrons in our age have a very different and inferior conception of patronage of this nature. None of them make it their life's chief study and purpose, for them this patronage is rather a pastime than an important business, fit to be taken up in a dilettante fashion at idle moments and preferably when retired from life's active arena, and when, therefore, the faculties are generally decaying, and in these cases what does it usually consist of? Acquisition of real or mock antiquities, of decoration good or bad for their own private domiciles, and, rarely, of giving and sometimes, of bequeathing, certain sums to societies, not to individuals, and always without possessing the will or the ability of directing how these sums are to be employed.

All this forms a striking contrast to the procedure of the ancients in this direction, who besides giving money with greater liberality and discrimination during their lifetime, which constitutes a real difference; devoted their life's knowledge and energy to this sublime work, whereby obscure but gifted persons were enabled to do justice to their talents to the great advantage of the entire community and eventually to humanity in general. If the precious plants of talent and genius be discouragingly rare in our times, the vivifying and fostering sun of professional, enlightened and disinterested patronage is altogether absent; therefore if we flatter ourselves that there may possibly be among us Apollodoruses, Buonarottis, &c., their productive ability is blighted and barren to a great extent, because there are certainly no Maecenatuses, Hadrians or Medici and Valois now.

The villa or gardens of Sallust, the " Horti pretiosissimi ", as they were styled by his contemporaries, covered the area now known as the Ludovisi quarter of Rome, including the present Palazzo Margherita up to the former Porta Collina. This villa comprised several considerable structures, the principal of which were the Domus Sallustii, the Baths, the Porticus Milliarensis, so-called because it measured 1,000 feet in length, the octagonal Temple of Mars Prestans and Venus Eryxina and the obelisk, and above all the Circus, which was so extensive that it was used in substitution of the Circus Maximus when the latter became temporarily unavailable. Up to a few years back the temple's remains and numerous marble fragments still existed *in situ*, and a section of the wall left standing, the last vestige of which was blown up by gunpowder as late as 1884. After the death of its founder's grandson this villa became successively the favourite residence of the Emperors Vespasian, Nerva and Aurelius and was destroyed by Alaric who entered by the adjacent Porta Salaria.

The constructor and proprietor Caius Crispus Sallustius 86 B.C.-A.D. 34 was an erudite, elegant and concise writer and his works are among the earliest in Rome that merit the title of historical, two of them deal with the conspiracy of Cataline and the Jugurthan war. He was a great scholar and affected the Greek style of literature, and is by some considered the peer by others the superior of the celebrated Thucidides Livius, as well as Seneca, mention him with praise, though the criticisms of the first are not so favourable as those of others, which is by some attributed to envy.

Sallustius was accused of adultery and deprived of his rank of Senator in consequence, which proves that the standard of private morality in connection with political life stood high then. His expulsion from the Senate was not, however, followed by any penal sentence, and the explanation offered by some for this act, was that it may have been a party move, seeing that Sallustius was a partisan of Cesar and the majority of Senators adherents of Pompey, their political perspicacity, as usual right, having made them decide that of the two rivals the latter was the least dangerous to their valued institutions.

The rehabilitation and readmission of Sallustius to the Senate was due to Cesar, as also his appointment as Praetor and second in command in the Jugurthan war and to the Governorship of Numidia. It was on his return from thence that the latter, and as some opine, the better part of existence began, when he retired to private life, built his villas and devoted his powers to historical research and composition. He had also a villa at Tusculum and another at Pompeii, of which recent excavations have brought to light the fine work and material.

Two other Sallusts are recorded. The one a neo-platonic philosopher and Prefect under the Emperor Julian, A.D. 360-363, and the other a cynical philosopher in Alexandria of the fifth century, strongly anti-platonic, who signalized himself for his school in that city and the uncompromising vehemence and fearless persistence with which he

VILLA OF THE QUINTILLII. CAMPAGNA.

Plate viii.

assailed the immorality of his contemporaries in all its various forms. In principle he seems to have been a sort of later day Cato, only possibly not his equal in purity of life and perhaps his superior in tireless and violent aggressiveness.

Cicero also possessed a villa on the slopes of the Janiculus, which was thickly studded with these residences, and another at Tivoli. Various fragments of the former were found *in situ* corresponding with a description he gave of this villa in a letter, among which may be mentioned a Hermathene, or joint statue of Mercury and Minerva, both Deities representative of mental qualities and, as such, peculiarly suitable to the abode of the highly intellectual proprietor, a table supported by effigies of the gods, a headless bust of Cicero himself, with his name, and two relics, one of a young philosopher and the other of a military man with huge legs. Little is known of these villas, but they are Cicero's villas, and that is enough to render them famous, whatever they may have been architecturally.

The great family of the Quintilii possessed two superb villas, a summer and a winter one, the first at Tusculum, the second at a locality called Torre Mezzavia about seven miles distant. This villa, where leaden tubes for internal heating were discovered bearing the names of the brothers Candianus and Maximus, covered an area of about half a square mile, its ruins now being one of the features of the Campagna. It was subsequently confiscated by the Emperor Commodus, A.D. 181-193, where he was besieged by the Roman populace who issued in revolt from Rome, like the French, sixteen centuries later, from Paris to Versailles, and so terrified the tyrant that to save his own head, he threw down to appease the mob, the severed one of his detested Minister Cleander, perhaps not quite so bad as his master to equal whom it would have been no easy matter.

The following anecdote in connection may not be found devoid of interest. In one of the attempts against the life of Commodus two brothers Quintilii were protagonists. It was arranged that they should assassinate the Emperor in his passage through the Cryptoporticus leading from his Palace to the Flavian Amphitheatre; they both attacked him suddenly and simultaneously, but this unworthy son of Aurelius was a giant in strength, and he succeeded in strangling one of his assailants, and the other, named Quadratus, escaped. They had each taken with them as a last resource a bladder full of hare's blood, so like the human, and the fugitive on the approach of the pursuing Imperial Guards, filled his mouth with the fluid, let it flow over him, suddenly dropped from his horse and lay motionless on the ground. It was dark and the Praetorians, on coming up, mistook him for dead, left him and reported accordingly, and he thereupon got up and made good his escape. This family was very wealthy, in fact for centuries afterwards explorations and excavations were repeatedly made about this villa in the hope of discovering the hidden gold and other treasures. As for Commodus, who appropriated their estates, it may be added that he was at length poisoned by his chief mistress Marcia, and, to make sure, contemporaneously strangled by his favourite athlete Narcissus.

Now for the sequel. Septimius Severus ascended the throne, and Rome breathed again freely in the interval between Commodus and Caracallus, when rumour suddenly diffused the news that Quintilius had reappeared and returned to Rome. In his quality of patrician he had easy access to the Sovereign, and accordingly presented himself to

Septimius to reclaim his forfeited inheritance. This monarch was severe as his name denotes, but just, determined, and above all clear sighted. He apparently beheld the Quintilius Quadratus he had known in bygone days, but still he doubted, and, as he had conversed with him formerly in Greek, then the scholarly tongue, he addressed the petitioner in that language as a test. The latter hesitated, and then said, that owing to his long sojourn among barbarians he had almost forgotten the tongue of Homer and Demosthenes. "No matter," responded the Emperor in Latin, "that does not hinder my giving my hand to an old friend." The claimant dare not refuse the honour. "Oh, what is this," exclaimed Septimius when they had clasped hands. "This is not the hand of a Patrician, it is that of a slave, or, at best, of a plebeian, to whom Scipio Nascica once said, 'Friends, is it your custom to walk on your hands?' but avow all, and if you have not committed any heinous crime I will pardon." The man at this fell on his knees and confessed he was no patrician or Quintilius, of whose existence he was ignorant until a Senator at Etruria met him and hailed him as Quintilius Quadratus and as a friend, then a second, a third and others followed. He denied this personality, but they all refused to believe him, telling him that he was wrong in concealing his identity, for Septimius was now reigning, and strongly advised him to return to Rome and reclaim his rights, which he would now assuredly get.

At length he was persuaded to make the attempt, seeing that the estates had not been claimed. On his arrival in Rome all those who had known the slain, proscribed or disappeared patrician, recognized him as Quadratus, and, as he pointed out, even the perspicacious emperor himself had at first subscribed to the general verdict. The chronicle adds that Septimius, touched by the sincerity of the confession, considering the temptation too for a man of his condition, and also that he was not trying to dispossess the legitimate owners, as the Quintilian estates were still unreclaimed, forgave him and even allowed him a small annuity in compensation for his sincerity and disappointment.

A twofold moral may be drawn from this incident. Firstly that whenever anyone undertakes to personify someone else, he must not only be sure as to physical resemblance between himself and his proposed double, but also if the social and cultural conditions between the two are different, to render them equal and similar, before making the attempt. In this case, though the personal likeness was perfect, the impostor's ignorance of Greek, that is, of difference or inferiority in culture, was a disastrous blow to his hopes, entirely destroyed by the finishing stroke administered by the shape and cuticle of his hands, that is, the difference or inferiority in lineage and social status. Secondly, that frauds are not so frequently successful as many people believe them to be, with whom it is an article of faith, a dismal and unfounded one, however, that wrong almost invariably triumphs and right nearly always succumbs, in this world at least.

Some rugged, utterly shattered walls, with apertures now remain to attest the site rather than anything else of this once imposing and historic villa. The Quintilii and the Fabii, it may be noted, were the "Luperci" or priests of Lupercus by hereditary right, wherefore these Pontefices were divided into two orders named after the above families, who were among the earliest Roman "Gens Gentilia."

Some ruinous vestiges skirting the Via Appia about seven miles from Rome and not far from the Villa Quintilii, are the remains of the Villa Servilii, of which nothing has been authentically ascertained. The Gens Servilii, originally patricians, were subsequently divided into two branches, the second being plebeian. The first and last of the family, curiously enough, were the two most celebrated, P. Servilius Priscus Struttus 490 B.C. and Servilius Silanus A.D. 198.

In the Via Ardeatina, near the catacombs of Saints Nereus and Archilleus martyrized at Terracina, eunuchs in the service of Flavius Clemens and Flavia Domitilla, are the ruins of a villa belonging to this Christianized lady discovered in 1817, but it does not seem to have been a vast or sumptuous abode, and if built after the conversion of Domitilla, who was a Princess of the Imperial Flavian family, most probably not so, because Christianism was at that time the declared enemy of art and luxury.

The Via Flaminia traverses at about eight miles from Rome a defile called " Prima Porta," on a hillock on the right of which are the remains of the " Villa ad Gallinas Albas ", villa of the White Fowls, unearthed in 1867. The frescoes and arabesques of flowers, birds and insects were finely executed, and when first exposed in good preservation, but a German artist covered them with a waxy composition for their conservation and this experiment had the contrary effect. The statue of Octavius, now in the Vatican Museum, was found here.

It appears that this Emperor was very much attached to his consort, Livia, whom he married after she had been divorced, and it is related that his last words were " Preserve the memory of a husband who has loved you very tenderly." The other deathbed utterance of Octavius, just previous to this one when he bade farewell to his ministers and courtiers " Have I acted well in the comedy of life? If so, applaud me," is much more generally known and quoted, but it depicts his many-sided character quite as well as his last words to Livia, though from another and less amiable aspect.

History has not generally portrayed this lady very favourably, but it is evident that she possessed the great quality, or rather combination of qualities, that go to make a good wife. Dion Cassius narrates that the Empress on being asked how she managed to acquire and retain her ascendency in the affections and esteem of so cold, sceptical and calculating a man replied, " My secret is a very simple one. I have made it the study of my life to please him in all things, and, while showing in all that concerns him an unfailing interest, have never exhibited any curiosity relatively to his public or private affairs." And there are many who think that her example in this respect might be followed more generally, as calculated to promote conjugal harmony, an invaluable boon all round. There is a legend connected with this villa which has been transmitted as follows.

One day, when Livia Drusilla, before she married Octavius and became Augusta but when she was engaged to him, was seated at her villa of Veies an eagle high above dropped a white chicken on her lap with a laurel branch in its beak, which, to her astonishment was not hurt or even frightened. This unusual occurrence she accounted, as was customary then, as a portent, and consulted the Auruspices for its interpretation and for guidance. They announced that she must nourish the fowl and plant the branch to ensure the prosperity and power of her family, that depended on the existence and multiplication of these two. She immediately put these instructions into execution, selecting a villa of the Cesars on the Flaminian Way for the purpose, which henceforth took the name of " Ad Gallinas Albas." The result was miraculously successful, for a vast number of chickens were quickly born and reared of the white fowl and the branch speedily produced shoots that became trees numerous enough to form the nucleus of a forest, and the might of Livia's family was extended and sustained. But just before the death of Nero, the last and worst of the Claudian dynasty, when he was preparing to sing in the theatre, it was reported to him that both birds and trees, so flourishing heretofore, had suddenly, unaccountably, ominously and simultaneously all perished, and with this Emperor the Julian and Claudian dynasties became extinct.

At Albano, anciently and modernly a favourite site for villas, on and around the grounds now occupied by the Villa Barberini, were formerly the Villas of Clodius and Pompey, later incorporated into one by Domitian. Among the few remains of these edifices, as yet discovered, are a part of a Cryptoporticus, a shattered wall and water conduits. Trajan also had a villa here, but of this one and of others nothing positive has been recorded except some doubtful names, and there were others which have not been identified.

CHAPTER V

HABITATIONS—*(concluded)*

TIBUR, now Italianized into Tivoli, owing to its fine situation, hilly and varied surface, luxurious vegetation, abundance of excellent water, salubrious climate and health giving "Aquæ Albulæ," was always a much frequented resort and therefore adorned with numerous villas, the traces of which exist in the shape of wrecked substructions and mutilated marble fragments. Among the vanished edifices may be mentioned, besides the aforesaid ones of Cicero and Maecenatus, the villas of Cesar, Octavius, Propertius, Piso, the Quintagliolo of Quintilius Verrus, the Truglio of Catullus, and the villa of Hortensius, which stood on the spot now occupied by the Church of Sant Antonio.

Although the Villa Hadriani, at Tivoli, may justly claim the title of "Queen of Villas," not only as being probably the most splendid and certainly the most extensive of all the magnificent erections of that Emperor, but also as so unique and excelling all other works of this nature, yet the descriptions concerning it depend, despite the efforts of generations of learned men, largely on conjecture, and leave much to be desired. Nevertheless the customary topography and terminology will be employed on this occasion in default of better, which may be the result of renewed attempts.

Hadrian's vast conception, so admirably realized in his design and execution, was to create a city from which everything mean or even ordinary should be rigorously excluded, a thing of beauty but none the less of use and comfort, composed of palaces, temples, theatres, baths, etc., amid gardens, groves, lakes and fountains. In other words a collective reproduction in marble, bronze, ivory, silver and gold by the best artists from models of all the works this much travelled monarch had admired, studied and selected with his well known taste and judgment. To this assemblage were added as decorations art treasures of all the subject nations which he chose to take, the whole concentrated in an area, as computed, of 160 acres of a fertile and beautiful land, peopled by the concourse of the most distinguished personalities in every branch which the colossal Empire could produce, protected by 10,000 picked men of the Imperial Guard and served by a host of trained attendants and slaves.

During his twenty years' reign, A.D. 118–138, Hadrian continued to design, lay out, build, embellish and collect for this harmonious assemblage of artistic structures. He was of Spanish extraction, but his predilections favoured the pure Greek school of art, and in consequence he preferred as models, for the most part, the Greek works he had studied during his sojourn in Greece, and frequently gave his reproductions the

Hellenic names of their prototypes, such as "Lyceum" from "Lykion," "Hippodrome" from "Ippothromos," "Odeum" from "Othion," "Naumachia" from "Navmahia." At the same time it must be understood that this villa was not all Greek in style, for Hadrian modified the Greek type occasionally, and also introduced Roman and Egyptian art in some parts, as was to be expected from a man of his individuality and broad views.

Proceeding from the Pons Lucanus, to the right a pathway is reached leading to the entrance of the Villa opening into an avenue of cypresses, known as the Viale dei Cipressi, and conducting to the first ruin, consisting of the vestiges of the foundations and of a row of seats with a wrecked, solitary fluted Greek Doric column, conjectured to be those of the Greek Theatre. Continuing we come to the remains of the Palestra and close to it those of the Roman Theatre, after which comes the Poicile, a rectangular space surrounded once by a colonnade with a pond in the centre and an Aedicula annexed at the angle. The wall which bound the Poicile on the north, 660 feet in length and still partly standing, had a series of arcades, now disappeared, on either side running between west and east, otherwise a sunny and a shady side, and therefore assumed to be a Heliocaminus Ambulatory. Next comes the now so-called Sala dei Filosofi, Philosophers' Hall, with seven niches for the like number of absent statues, and followed by a circular construction variously denominated "Teatro Marittimo," Maritime Theatre, or "Natatorium," swimming-bath, that contained a small artificial lake with an islet encircled by columns, five of which are still standing, and close by, it is said, was once the dual Temple of Venus and Diana.

In reference to the Philosophers' Hall built in honour of the Seven Wise Men of Greece, it may be observed that this appellation applied to them, like those of "Sybilline Books," "Draconian Laws," "Elysian Mysteries" and other similar ones, are for most people rather a phrase representing something that existed in antiquity which is repeated vaguely without much or anything being known about it. At the same time it must be admitted in extenuation that even for bona fide seekers, trustworthy and positive information of many of these subjects is difficult to obtain.

The traditional origin of this sect is the following. Certain fishermen had acquired by purchase piscatorial rights from the Milesians, and it happened that one of their nets brought up a tripod, and in consequence a contestation arose between the lessors and the lessees with regard to the proprietorship of this object. The dispute being apparently incapable of amicable or inimical settlement, it was decided by common consent to appeal to the arbitration and sentence of the Oracle of Delphos, who responded that the disputed tripod was to be given to the wisest. It was accordingly offered to Teletus, who passed it on to another whom he considered his superior in sagacity, and this other in his turn to another, for the same reason, and so on till it came to the hands of Solon, who returned the tripod to the Umpire or Oracle of Delphos, saying that the wisest of all was God.

The number of these Wise Men has been variously estimated at Seven, Eleven and Sixteen and their names, or at least, the best known of them, handed down to us, are: Pittacus of Mytilene, Solon of Athens, Cleobulus of Lindo, Periandros of Corinth, Chilon of Sparta, Teletus of Mileto and Biantus of Priene. As to date it seems that these

KPYPTOPORTICUS, VILLA OF HADRIAN. TIVOLI.

Plate ix.

men lived in the sixth pre-Christian century, and it is evident that they were not only philosophers but also statesmen. Greece was at that epoch traversing the initial stage, when life is necessarily less complicated and artificial, and therefore the code of morality was single and simple instead of the several codes now, public, private, real, conventional, etc. The Wise Men being nature's Aristoi (because despite the idle dreams of Utopists and the insincere and selfish cant of demagogues equality between man and man never has and never can exist) they naturally assumed the leadership of the young, strong, undeveloped peoples, constituted them into communities regulated by means of maxims and precepts, in place of bills, bulls, edicts, etc., comprising and defining in terse and energetic terms the fundamental principles of moral wisdom, otherwise of individual and general equity and interest. These maxims, which were derived from logic and experience, had the force of laws, in place of the intricate, contradictory copious maze of legislation born of the multitude of artificial wants and conflicting interests of a complicated society, which subsequently, an indigestible legislative plethora in its declining stages, degenerates into corruption and practically into a confusion of right and wrong, thus defeating its real aim and raison d'être.

To resume. Parallel with the Poicile runs a vast substructure called the Centumcellae, now Italianized into Cento Camarelle, consisting of three stories of vaulted halls destined for the accommodation of the attendants of the Imperial Household. Leaving the Centumcellae, the road passes on the right some ruins termed the vestibule, and on the left the remains of two bathing establishments, designated respectively the Bagni Piccoli and Bagni Grandi, small and great baths, the first of which is in a slightly less ruinous condition than the second.

This road proceeding reaches the artificial valley, which it skirts, denominated the "Canopus." There are two versions regarding this name. Strabo derives it from a town 120 stadii from Alexandria, which took this name of the pilot of Menelaus of Troy fame, who died there, but the more probable one is, that this epithet arose from Canopus, the Egyptian Divinity corresponding to the Roman Neptune and Greek Poseidon. This hypothesis is corroborated by the fact that Hadrian had set apart this section of his villa as the Egyptian district, where the Egyptian festivals were celebrated and a Temple to Serapis, another deity of this nationality, was erected with a lofty cella with niches, alcoves and typical hieroglyphics and reliefs, now scarcely traceable, and a statue to Serapis and other Egyptian works found here now in the Vatican Museum.

In this Egyptianized region there was, however, one note of Hellenism, the name of Peneus, given to the artificial rivulet after the renowned Greek river, and which supplied in part the hydraulic power required for the services of the lifts and other mechanical appliances of the various establishments of the villa. The quarters of the Imperial Guard ran parallel with the Canopus and next came the Academia, followed by the Odeum, Music Hall, with its traces of a stage and rows of seats.

The origin of the term Academia, Academy, is perhaps not generally known. Some philologues maintain that it springs from Academus, an Athenian who made a donation of part of his property to his fellow townsmen, for the purpose of its being converted into a public park in Athens, others that it arose from Bacchus Academus to whom a temple on that site was *ab antico* consecrated. Aristocles, best known as

Plato (an epithet given to him by his grand father on account of the breadth of his forehead or of his shoulders), selected this spot in which to assemble his disciples for lectures, and hence this sect as well as others later, were styled Academicians, and the seat of learning, Academy. Near this edifice of the Villa Hadriani is a simulacrum of the Styx, now of course, waterless, which leads to a vast subterranean hall measuring 330 by 110 yards, intended to represent the pagan Hades, the prototype of the Christian Hell.

Returning in an inverse direction, we first meet a mausoleum of which nothing seems to be known, and then the "Platea Aureae," Piazza d'Oro, Golden Square, distinguished by this name owing to the gold plating of the walls and massive ornaments, it was originally encircled by a colonnade of 88 columns, alternately of oriental granite and cipoline marble, of which little more than broken fragments survive. The purpose for which this structure was used has not been ascertained, but it is surmised by some that it was a Reception-Saloon. Two paths bifurcate from the Platea Aurea, the one to the left conducts first to a lofty building, supposed to be the Exhubitorium, Firemen's Quarters, then to the Piscina, reservoir, the Cryptoporticus and finally to the Stadium. The other path to the right, to the Imperial Domus with its fifty-eight marble columns, of which a few broken shafts remain, with its Nymphaeum and its Exedra on each side and its annexed gardens. There is a quadrangular space here the purpose of which is unknown.

From the Imperial Domus we pass to the Ospedale, Hospital, with its regular partitions and some traces of frescoes and mosaic pavement. Between the Ospedale and the Sala dei Filosofi lies the Atrium Bibliothecae, court of the Libraries, Latin and Greek, situated contiguously, this court was a Doric Peristyle by which the first named library was approached, and near is the Heliocaminus aforementioned and two theatres with which we began.

The artificial lakes of the Villa were severally supplied with sea and spring water, for the purpose of breeding and preserving the two species of fish, each in its own element, so that they could be had at a moment's notice quite fresh.

At a sign from the Emperor at any time of day or night, the theatres, circuses, groves, lakes, etc., became instantly animated with histrionic and musical performances and sports of all kinds, with the wild denizens of the animal kingdom and with mimic warfare by land and sea. Hadrian habitually kept by his side his favourite scribe or private secretary, Phlegon, to whom he dictated his memoirs that mainly referred to his travels and wanderings. This monarch also built other villas at Praeneste (Palestrina) and Antium (Anzio) and the works he produced in the Eternal City alone during his reign of twenty years, if their number, magnificence and artistic excellence be duly considered, albeit the creations of an absolute Ruler, can hardly be said to have been surpassed, if indeed equalled, by any other in similar conditions at any period.

The Villa Hadriani, after its creator's death at Baia, was inhabited by his immediate successor Antoninus, and after the latter's decease it gradually, but more rapidly than usual, fell into decay and ruin. This is not surprising if we realize that to keep in good preservation a similar assemblage of artistic and costly edifices at some distance from the capital would have required the dedication of a great part of the lives of a succession of men in power not far inferior to the founder in disposition and talents, otherwise a

Plate x.

PLATEA AUREA, VILLA OF HADRIAN, A.D. 118-138. TIVOLI.

sequel of Hadrians, which could hardly be expected, though even a moderate amount of care would have sufficed to prolong its existence. But this vast and splendid villa was, in any case, even discounting the damages inflicted by neglect, ignorance, plunder and disorders, destined to be short lived, being afflicted by " congenital debility " to borrow a medical term, because it was a beautiful anomaly, a fancy city, that is, above and out of all proportion to the ordinary course of mundane conditions.

Constantine, A.D. 312–337, the arch pillager, who constantly despoiled the productions of others and moreover attempted to pass them off as his own, carried away most of the art treasures of this villa to Byzantium. Under the pontificate of Alexander VI (Rodrigo Lancol Borgia) A.D. 1492–1503, some explorations were initiated in search of antiquities missed or left by previous depredators, and in one of the shattered halls the statues of the Muses, now in the Vatican, were discovered. The painstaking Pirro Ligorio, painter, designer, architect and above all archaeologist of merit, made a plan of the Palatium Hadriani, as it came to be denominated, and this design has been of material help in locating the various structures.

All those who visit for the first time the wrecks of this world-famed villa, must be prepared, in order to avoid disappointment, to find on its site little more than vestiges, traces, and broken masonry, a dismembered, crumbling skeleton, all else having disappeared owing to the above noted causes. It may be as well to emphasize this, because a great name often carries with it great disillusions, and all tourists may not realize adequately the peculiar conditions that rendered the production of this abnormal work possible and its conservation impossible, and that about eighteen centuries have elapsed, full of vicissitudes, since its creation.

CHAPTER VI
FORUMS

WITH the ancient Roman the term Forum had two significations and therefore these city centres may be divided into two classes. The one, the "Fora Venalia," chiefly for the supply and sale of edibles and the other commodities of life, has its counterpart in our markets. The Fora Boarium and Holitorium belong to this category, to which may perhaps be added the Forum Esquilinum. The other, the "Fora Civilia," were mainly or entirely destined for the transaction of public affairs, and as other countries, with the exception of Greece, whose "Agora" was a Forum, had no exactly similar centres in their cities, there is no corresponding word in other languages to designate them.

Besides the Forum Romanum or Magnum, which though chiefly of the latter class comprised both varieties, and as appears from recent excavations also the Forum Trajani, though we include it in the second class, there were, so far as we know, seven Fora Civilia, viz.: The "Julium" and the successive Imperial Fora of Augustus, Vespasian, Nerva, Trajan, Antoninus and Aurelius. Every Forum, whatever its particular plan and character, was provided with at least one temple for the performance of religious rites, one basilica for judicial functions and one porticus for business purposes, and most Fora had more than one of these edifices.

The "Forum Boarium," or cattle-market, is the most ancient of the Eternal City, its antiquity reaching back to mythological times, as is attested by the legend of Cacus, which may briefly be narrated as follows. It appears that a certain king named Geryon reigned in those days in Baetica, the modern Andalusia, and that this monarch was the possessor of numerous herds of cattle and physically a triple giant, a species of bodily trinity, that is, three bodies comprised in one individuality, and moreover was guarded by a dog with two heads and a dragon with seven. Hercules was commissioned, it is alleged, by Euristheus, to suppress this monster and his extraordinary bodyguard, and at the same time, not neglecting business, to undertake the transfer of the live-stock to the proprietorship of a more normal and respectable master, that is, to Euristheus himself. The demi-god accomplished the double task successfully, he slew the remarkable sovereign and his attendants and brought away his herds as spoils, which last feat, if we consider the number of cattle he conveyed single-handed by such a long, perilous and arduous journey as that, is not the least noteworthy of this hero's exploits, though history and mythology do not seem much impressed by it, possibly because it is not miraculous and sensational enough.

Plate xi.

TEMPLES OF DEA MATUTA AND OF DEA FORTUNA. FORUM BOARIUM.

On his return home, Hercules selected the site on which this Forum was built, now occupied in part by the Piazza Bocca della Verita, for his cattle, and from this incident and choice the name of Boarium originated. But as there was a disturbing factor in the neighbourhood matters were not destined to go quite smoothly yet. Cacus (from kakós, bad) mythologically son of Vulcan and therefore cousin of Hercules, described as a monster emitting flames, was, in sober language, really a remote predecessor and prototype of the Fra Diavolos, Mamones, etc., of recent times, and this professional robber made a raid and carried off the cattle in the absence of the demi-god, regardless of the claims of relationship, to his haunts in the woods and caverns of the Palatine and Aventine Hills, taking the precaution of dragging them up by their tails so that the traces of their hoofs might be misleading. The stone steps descending from Roma Quadrata are pointed out as the "Scalae Caci." Hercules did not take long between the discovery of the theft, of the perpetrator of it and of the latter's condign punishment, though, to be sure, the identification of the robber in those circumstances, was not a detective feat requiring a Sherlock Holmes. It is related that he settled the matter promptly by dragging Cacus out of his grotto, and, oblivious of their kindred, killing him by a blow of his club, retaking, of course, the cattle and leading them back to their abode.

In after times a brazen bull, the work of the celebrated statuary Myron, was brought here, as Pliny states, from Egina, and appropriately placed in the centre of this Forum as a befitting emblematic figure. It may be mentioned in connection that in Florence opposite the Palazzo Vecchio, a colossal group by B. Bandinelli, representing Cacus subdued by Hercules, commemorates this episode.

The ancient Forum Boarium extended from the present Church of San Giorgio, in Velabro, to the Tiber banks, and of all the structures it contained, among which was a temple to Hercules, the only four remaining, though in tolerable preservation, are the two temples,* one to the Dea or Mater Matuta, and the other to Fortuna, and two arches, one to Janus Quadrifrons, which is conjectured to have the Aeditus, or entrance, to the Boarium by the Vicus Jugurthus, and the other, the Arcus Argentariorum.

It was in this Forum that the first gladiatorial combats witnessed in Rome were introduced by the brothers M. and D. Brutus, 264 B.C., on the occasion of their father's obsequies. The Boarium was twice the scene of a most barbarous act, caused by a passage of the Sibyline Books to the effect that the Gauls and Greeks would possess Rome. The first time this tragedy was perpetrated was during the Gallic invasion, the second after the three successive victories with which Hannibal opened his campaign in Italy: and it must be admitted that on both these occasions Rome stood within an ace of complete annihilation at the hands of a triumphant and apparently irresistible foe. Two Gauls and two Greeks, one man and one woman of each nationality, were buried alive in each case, in the belief that by giving them, in this way, the soil of Rome, the two races would not possess it in any other sense, and in consequence the Sibyline prophecy would be fulfilled, in the letter, without her subjugation by these two nations.

The reason for the sacrifice of the two Gauls is comprehensible as representatives of the savage invaders, but the choice of two Greeks is less obvious. The only explanation is, that probably the Greeks, being among the few peoples known, or well

---

* For these two Temples see Chapt. IX., and for the two Arches see Chapt. XVI.

known, by the Romans of that period, they were held to represent in general the foreign element; in this case in an inimical point of view, especially if there were no Phoenicians available for sacrifice at hand. The reason that the victims were buried alive and not dead is evident; the living can possess or acquire, the dead cannot.

In any case, this sinister prediction, despite the horrible immolation, was verified in after years by both Gauls and Greeks and other peoples besides, because if Rome conquered almost every known nation in turn, during her period of greatness, she, or at least Italy, became in her decadence the prize of many other countries.

The ancients were more earnest and thorough than we are, and dreadful as were sometimes the excesses to which they were urged by animosity, the sacrifices they made for love or a noble cause were equally great, and in either case inspired usually by high motives, such as for example in the above instance, when the atrocity exercised had its root in an impersonal and honourable desire to save their country, then in extreme danger. Moreover, if their patriotism had not been misguided by superstition and fanaticism (which, by the way, are the excuses generally advanced in extenuation of Christian bigots), it would undoubtedly have manifested itself in a manner worthy of its origin and aim, of which history records so many glorious examples among this great people. And we must always bear in mind that it is as unjust as it is illogical and futile, to judge, by our own particular standard and code of morality of the moment, others in totally different conditions and circumstances.

But, besides this, in a general sense, it must be remembered also that there was a vast and vital difference between the Romans of the Royal and Republican Rome, on the one hand, and of the Romans of Imperial Rome, on the other. The Romans of the pre-Imperial epoch were a superior race, and as such did not descend, as a rule, to cruelty and injustice, which are the distinctive features, in particular, of unregenerated or degenerated peoples; thus in the Imperial times tyranny, license and corruption bore their customary fruit and gradually transformed them into degenerates.

Unfortunately cruelty and injustice are not the exclusive characteristics of any epoch or people; they are innate in human nature, but to religion, morality and law, if well understood and practised, has been confided the sublime mission of subduing, eradicating or at least moderating these two fiendish and other evil natural propensities.

In the Mediaeval times, nevertheless, so many centuries later and despite the teachings of Christianity, we find cruelty and injustice forming the basis of a system sanctioned and legalized by religion and law in the legal torture inflicted by ecclesiastical and lay tribunals, not for high purposes only such as the above cited of the Boarium, but in the ordinary course of procedure even for trifling faults or misdemeanours, or simply to force the victims to confess or declare what the prosecutors desired; and this system was not abolished in its entirety till the nineteenth century.

Nor are moderns, if we look below the surface, much better in substance in this respect, though the external manifestations and forms have altered, owing partly to the softer lives and more sensitive physical constitutions of the people of these times.

The "Forum Holitorium," or vegetable market, was situated on and beyond the space now occupied in part by the present Piazza Montanara. It was surrounded by porticos called, according to the different purposes they served for, "Minucia" and

"Frumentaria," and contained, besides other unrecorded buildings, the "Columna Lactaria," and four temples erected in proximity to each other and dedicated respectively to "Juno Sospita," to "Spes," to "Apollo Medicus" and to "Janus," the last named near the Theatre of Marcellus and subsequently rebuilt by Tiberius, all of which have now vanished.

On the walls of the Church of San Niccoló in Carcere there are three columns of stone, one of the Ionic and two of the Doric Order, which, it is conjectured, belonged to one of the above temples, or more probably to another, consecrated to "Filial Piety," on the ruins of which this church was raised. Judging by the traces and references it may be safely assumed that this ancient Forum Holitorium was not only incomparably better built and more ornamental, that goes without saying, but also much more extensive than its supplanter, the modern quaint but sordid Piazza Montanara, with its mean, poor houses around.

The prisons of the Decemvirs originally stood here, which gave the sobriquet of "in Carcere" to the above-mentioned church, and were the scene of an example of filial affection which it would be wronging human nature, so full of faults, to pass over in silence. A prisoner, whether a man or a woman is still a disputed question, condemned to die by starvation herein, was kept alive by the daughter nourishing her parent with her own milk till the fall of the brief tyranny of the Decemvirs. Many people are touched by the mere act of her giving her milk, but the real merit in this daughter did not lie in so trifling a gift, but in the danger to herself, if discovered, which she so bravely faced. The Roman Senate, in accordance with its noble traditions, ordered these prisons to be demolished to obliterate even this tangible evidence of the tyranny they had overthrown, and at the same time the above temple to be raised in their place, in honour of the daughter—who had done her duty, regardless of danger to herself—to perpetuate the memory of this act of filial piety.

The third in point of antiquity of the Fora Venalia seems to have been the "Forum Esquilinum," but almost everything concerning it is enveloped in obscurity, except that it was extensive and mainly, if not entirely, a market.

The "Forum Romanum." The extent and boundaries, as well as the structure, of this famous focus of the political, social, religious and commercial life of the Eternal City cannot be established with desirable accuracy; not so much for lack of records, as history abounds in references to it, but because the extent changed and the buildings were successively in a great measure supplanted by others in the course of time. The marshy valley on which the "Magnum" stood was about twenty-two feet above the river level and about thirty-six above the sea; in fact a backwater of the Tiber, drained by the Tarquin kings. On this space once raged the conflicts between the Romans, under Romulus, from the Palatine and Aventine, and the Sabines, under Tatius, from the Quirinal and Esquiline, before they both became, after the rape of the Sabine women by the Roman men, joint sovereigns of the amalgamated State.

The nucleus of this Forum consisted at first of two main sections viz.: the "Comitium" (derived from "Co-ire," to go together) and the "Forum" (from "foris," out of doors), the first serving as a centre for citizens' assemblies, the second lined with "Tabernae," or shops, as the market place. Time and development wrought their

E

inevitable changes. The Comitium became the seat of more select and organized public assemblies, and the popular meetings were transferred to the Forum quarter; and hence men congregated there for other purposes besides buying and selling; the butchers and fishmongers were removed further north, and confined for their business to enclosures called " Macellum," slaughter or flesh market and " Piscatorium," fish market, and their former shops reoccupied by jewellers, money-changers and the like. This section was also the locality where the funerals of the patricians and other public ceremonies took place, and, after 264 B.C., occasional gladiatorial combats.

The earliest edifices of note of the Forum seem to have been the Aediculae or Sacelli Vestae and Juturnae, by Numa; the Curia Hostilia, senate-house, built by Tullius Hostilius; the " Carcer Tullianus " or " Mamertinus," prison, by Servius Tullius; the Temples of Saturn, of Castor and Pollux; and later that of Concord. After the close of the first Punic war, 241 B.C., the Forum Romanum was further embellished by three Basilicas, the " Porcia," the " Aemilia," and the " Sempronia," followed later by the " Basilica Julia," and still later by the " Maxentia "; but this happened when the Porcia and the Sempronia had disappeared. The emperors successively added many monuments to this Forum, which continued to retain its qualificative epithet of " Magnum" even after the creation of that of Trajan, which was more extensive.

Besides the usual inherent difficulties of all excavatory undertakings of this nature, there are special factors in the case of Roman antiquities that militate against any thorough operations. Ancient Rome, like other cities of remote times, has been demolished above ground and buried under ground, only more so, because the others have not been similarly built upon. The surface level, too, is considerably higher now than formerly, in the case of this Forum from twelve to thirty feet. To execute a complete exploration it would have to be preliminarily drained here and in some other parts by a Cloaca like the Maxima, and the existing structures everywhere levelled and their materials removed. Roma Vetus, therefore, is a mysterious, half-buried city.

The Via Sacra, a continuation of the Via Triumphalis, the latter now renamed Via San Gregorio, began at the Arch of Constantine and, curving to the left, ascended between the Palatine and the Velia, and, through the Arch of Titus, traversed the Forum from south to north longitudinally, to terminate by two branches up to the Capitol. From the Arch of Titus issued two streets, the Clivus Palatinus, ascending to the Palatine, and the Clivus Sacer or Via Sacra aforesaid, descending to the Forum. Between the two above arches the street was bordered in classic times by various vanished edifices, of which all that now exists, are, to the right, the remains of the Temple of Venus and Rome on the summit of the Velia, and to the left those of the Temple of Jovis Statoris and Nero's Palace.

From the Arch of Titus the ruins of the principal constructions flanking the Sacred street may be taken in the following sequence. On the right, the first is the Basilica Maxentia and a triangular space opening into the Forum Vespasiani, or Pacis behind. To the fore, follow in continuation the Aedicula Romuli, chapel of Romulus, the Carceres, prisons; the Sepulcretum, cemetery; the Fornix Fabianus, the Temple of Antoninus and Faustina; the Basilica Aemilia, the so-called Lapis Niger, Black Stone; the Curia with the Comitium in front; and the Arcus Septimii, under which the street

TEMPLE OF SATURN, B.C. 497. ROMAN FORUM.

Plate xii.

passes to incline upwards by the Clivus Capitolinus, between the Temples of Vespasian and Concord, to the Capitol.

On the left, recommencing by the Arch of Titus, first comes a space now covered with the ruins of the fourth century superstructed fortifications, the traces of the prisons of Augustus, the Domus Publicae, the Regia Numae, the Aedicula and façade of the Coenobium Vestae, the Juturna structures, the Rostra Julia, the Forum Square, containing the Equus Domitiani (horse or equestrian statue of Domitian), the Lacus Curtius, the Columna Phoca, the Plutei Trajani, screens of Trajan, and outside the said square, the Rostra Flavia and Ara Vulcanis, altar of Vulcan, reaching the Clivus to the Capitol.

At the aforesaid Rostra Julia, the Sacra Via bifurcates, one branch being the one already traced, the other turning to the left, runs between the said square and the Temple of Castor and Pollux. On reaching the angle of the square it turns again to the right and therefore runs parallel to the original main Via Sacra, thus having the square between the two branches of the street. This second or west branch is bordered, on one side by the Columnae Honorariae, honorary columns, the Miliareum Aureum, golden milestone, the Ombelicus Romae, navel of Rome, and on the other by the Basilica Julia and the Temple of Saturn, and passing under the vanished Arch of Tiberius, winds up again to the Capitol.

From this second branch of the Via Sacra, three tributary streets cross over in parallel lines to the Palatine and Forum Boarium, the first beginning from the south called Vicus Vestae, spanned by the Arch of Augustus, connected the Rostra Julia with the Library and Temple of Augustus at the foot of the Palatine. The second, named Vicus Etruscus, because the Etruscans inhabited this quarter of the Forum, led up from the Forum Square to the Horrea Germanicus on the Palatine and to the Circus Maximus. The third, denominated Vicus Jugurthus, leaving the Forum Romanum by the Arcus Tiberii, conducted to the Forum Boarium.

Of the remains of the structures of the Romanum, exclusive of the monuments dealt with in their respective chapters, the following is a summary account.

At the northern angle of the Basilica Maxentia, is a row of five low brick arches which are all that survives of the Horreum, or grain stores, built during the fourth century, and which are said to have extended from here to the Arcus Titi; and nearly opposite, on the other side of the Via Sacra, are some ruins alleged to be those of a guard station. Between the Chapel of Romulus and the Temple of Antoninus and Faustina are a series of cells to which the name of Carceres, or prisons, has been given on account, it is said, of their plan and situation. The Sepulcretum, another relatively recent discovery, appears to have been a cemetery of the primitive inhabitants of these regions, the earliest interments having been dated as far back as 1100 B.C. and the latest at 450 B.C. Thirty tombs of four different categories, with their special potteries and skeletons laid in hollowed trunks of trees, have been found here, together with the ritual food such as grapes, pulse-cakes and fishbones.

Standing in front of the Basilica Aemilia is a circular stone mound identified as the "Ara Veneris Cloacina," altar of the Drain-Venus. This distinctive, but not very honorary, title was bestowed on this Deity in her general capacity of patroness of drains, swamps and sewers, and in this case to invoke her protection, in particular, for the Cloaca

Maxima which opens here. The original shrine, decorated with two female statues and a transenna, containing this altar, is reproduced in coins of M. Longinus, 43 B.C.

Backed by the present Church of Sant' Adriano are the remains, a few scattered marble fragments, of the Curia or Senate-House, the seat of the most efficient, patriotic and greatest Assembly recorded in history, by whose deliberations and decisions the fate of the peoples of the world was shaped. The earliest Curia of the " Patres Conscripti " was a hall of stone built, as already mentioned, by Tullius Hostilius, and approached by a flight of steps down which the body of this king was flung by the Tarquins. This building was destroyed by fire and reconstructed by Faustus, son of the celebrated Sylla, and again by Octavius, who renamed it Curia Julia, in honour of the Julii. After the fire of A.D. 282 it was rebuilt by the Emperor Diocletian. The Secretarium Senatus, a section of the Curia reserved for the secret meetings of the Senators, formerly occupied the site of the present church of SS. Luca and Martina. A marble balustrade, adorned with statues, separated the Curia from the Clivus Argiletum, Clay Street, behind, that led to the Suburra, one of the worst quarters of Rome.

The Curia was connected with the Comitium by a flight of steps, the core of which is still visible, with its superb bronze doors transferred to the Lateran by Pope Alexander VII (Fabio Chigi) A.D. 1655–1667, but the jambs are still discernible in their original places in the Curia. Regarding the plan and decorations of this edifice little is known, but it may be assumed that they corresponded with the high and important functions for which it was destined. The reconstructed Curia was calculated to afford sitting accommodation for six hundred members, and although the number fluctuated like the British House of Peers or the Hungarian House of Magnates, they were rarely fewer after the fall of the Royal régime. In the earlier times, however, the Senate was composed of one hundred members, increased under Tarquinius Priscus to three hundred, during the Republic to about six hundred, under the Triumvirates to one thousand, and in the Imperial times the membership depended on the will of the monarch, but then the Senate had lost its prestige and importance.

The seats of the senators were denominated "Sellae Curulae" (derived from the Sabine city of "Cura") from which people, the Sabines, many of the customs and laws, especially the aristocratic ones, of the Kingdom or Commonwealth were taken. These seats were usually of marble, with inlaid and carved ivory, and somewhat resembling in shape the chairs now distinguished by the name of Savonarola. The Sellae Curulae were only used in Rome, for in the provinces the seats of the highest magistrates were called "Bisellium." The sceptre of the Sovereigns was termed "Verga Curulae," and there was a "Juno Curulae" venerated at Tivoli. Some archaeologists opine that the word "Curula" is derived from "Curus" or car, but this hypothesis does not seem well founded.

The adjoining Comitium, the site of which is likewise marked by a few mere fragments, served for two purposes, one as a centre for the meetings of the citizens, to express their political views and to elect subordinate magistrates and priests by votation, the other, as the place where the sentences of those considered guilty were pronounced and sometimes carried out; a place of judgment and execution in one. Under the

Imperial régime the Comitium figured almost exclusively in the second capacity, because political and electoral meetings of subjects, even of a tranquil, academical nature had become practically aimless and obsolete, and those of an independent and tumultuous one, of course impossible.

The reconstruction of the Comitium was commenced by Cesar and completed by Octavius, who added a porticus of fifteen columns. The building itself had eight columns in front and eight behind; of these eight pedestals were discovered between the Curia and the Comitium, at the foot of the aforesaid connecting marble steps. These pedestals stood on the third layer of tufo and travertine which alternately composed the four successively superposed pavements of the Comitium. The marble staircase was separated from the rest of the building by a marble transenna, and around a gutter was grooved to carry off the rain water and a fountain placed in the centre. The Comitium, originally uncovered, was roofed about A.D. 222–226. During the Middle Ages the high rear wall of the Curia was turned into a Columbarium and the Comitium into a Sepulcretum.

Owing to the removal of some paving stones in 1898, possibly those placed for the triumphal march of the Emperor Charles V in A.D. 1527, there was discovered close to the Comitium, about three and a half feet below the Forum surface, a slab of black celtic marble with white veins measuring twelve by thirteen and a half feet in area and ten inches in thickness, two pedestals of the Etruscan style, a cone of yellow tufo, a broken stela, an altar and various votive offerings—such as dice, beads, armlets, rings—twelve diminutive bronze statues and some equally small amphorae. The imperfect archaic epigraph concludes with the laconic ritual phrase of "Jovis Estod," that is, "Let the violator be devoted to Jupiter"; otherwise slain. The shape of the remains and the votive offerings alike justify the assumption that this was a sacrificial shrine and a depository for sacred relics. To this collection the appellation of "Lapis Niger" has been applied. A paragraph of Festus, surmised to refer to this identical slab, reads as follows: "The Black Stone of the Comitium betokens an unlucky site intended, as some say, for the Tomb of Romulus, but not used for that purpose, and, as others assert, for the grave of Hostus Hostilius, the father of King Tullius." It may be that the above passage of the said Festus, a Latin grammarian of the third century, gave birth to the name of Lapis Niger, but however appropriate this name may be relatively to the marble slab alone, it is not equally so when applied to designate collectively all the above objects unearthed, which, moreover, may be unconnected with the "Stone."

In critical times of danger the Sacred Relics of Rome were concealed underground to save them from abstraction, contamination and destruction. Livius records a senatorial decree relatively to the repurification and reconsecration of monuments and relics after sacrilegious touch and presence. Those, however, which were considered beyond redemption were permanently covered over and committed to the custody of the Deities of the lower regions, and as black was the colour, then as now, assigned to infernals, it may reasonably be concluded that these relics, endangered and polluted possibly during the Gallic invasion, were consigned here in this spot, denominated by the ancients "Locus Religiosus et Funestus" under their black lid, to the guardianship of the infernal Pluto and his crew. Taking, therefore, into consideration the name and reputation of this site, and the obvious character of these relics, perhaps a more appropriate epithet would be "Sacrarum Reliquiarum Theca" (Receptacle of Sacred Relics).

The Forum Square measured, it is affirmed, 400 feet in length by 165 in width, though authorities differ as to its dimensions and shape, and contained several monuments of which the following, in a way, survive. The rugged pedestal styled "Equus Domitiani" has been conjectured to have supported either the Equestrian Statue of this Emperor, or, as some opine, that of his horse only. The discovery of this fragmentary pedestal led, in 1894, to a more important one, of a pit close by, thirty by twenty feet, paved and lined with travertine, and identified as the "Famosisque Lacus," as Statius terms it, otherwise, the Lake of Curtius. Cesar, in his construction of the galleries for the Forum Games, abstained from encroaching on this historic pool and had an altar erected, and a fig tree, declared sacred by the Flamens, an olive tree and a vine, all planted here.

There are three traditions connected with the Lacus Curtius. The earliest recorded is that a warrior named Curtius when returning from his pursuit of the enemy, instead of waiting for a boat to ferry him over the swampy backwater, plunged in at this spot to rejoin his friends on the Capitol. The second version is that this locality was considered "Fulgiretum," or subject to thunderbolts, and that the Consul Curtius 446 B.C., had it completely covered up with soil as a prophylactic measure. The third refers to an occurrence when Rome was visited by inundation, earthquakes and plague, 362 B.C., which, according to the Oracles, could only be stopped by the sacrifice of the most precious object possessed by the Romans. This object was by unanimous opinion held to be the Eques Curtius Marcus, and in consequence he voluntarily flung himself, armed, armoured and mounted, into the lake, which immediately closed over rider and steed. But whichever of the three versions be accepted, the Lacus Curtius was associated with acts of service to the country, and Valerius Maximus wrote in reference to this historic tank, evidently in allusion chiefly to the self-immolated Curtius, as follows: "Many and noble deeds have given glory to the Roman Forum, but not one of them radiates to our day such splendid light as did this deed of Curtius."

The Emperor Servius Sulpicius Galba was killed here A.D. 68, and his adopted son, Piso Lucinianus, despite the refuge he had taken within the precincts of Vesta's Temple, was dragged forth and likewise slain. Caius Tranquillus Suetonius, Latin historian, annalist and grammarian, A.D. 75–160, informs us that it was the custom of the Roman people to throw a coin into this lake as an offering for the preservation of the Emperor. It seems scarcely reasonable to conclude from this that the inhabitants of Rome were equally anxious for the health and life of "all" the Emperors indiscriminately, but Suetonius was the contemporary of Trajan, Hadrian and Antoninus, which may account for the custom in his times; probably then a spontaneous act and possibly continued subsequently from servility, expedience or fear.

Trajan's two marble screens, with their interesting and fine reliefs, were probably used originally as decorations of his Forum. From the artistic standpoint they are incomparably the best of the surviving relics now in the Forum Square. They are commonly known as the "Anaglypha Trajani," but might be more correctly termed, "Plutei or Diathyra Trajani," that is, partitions or screens of Trajan, seeing that

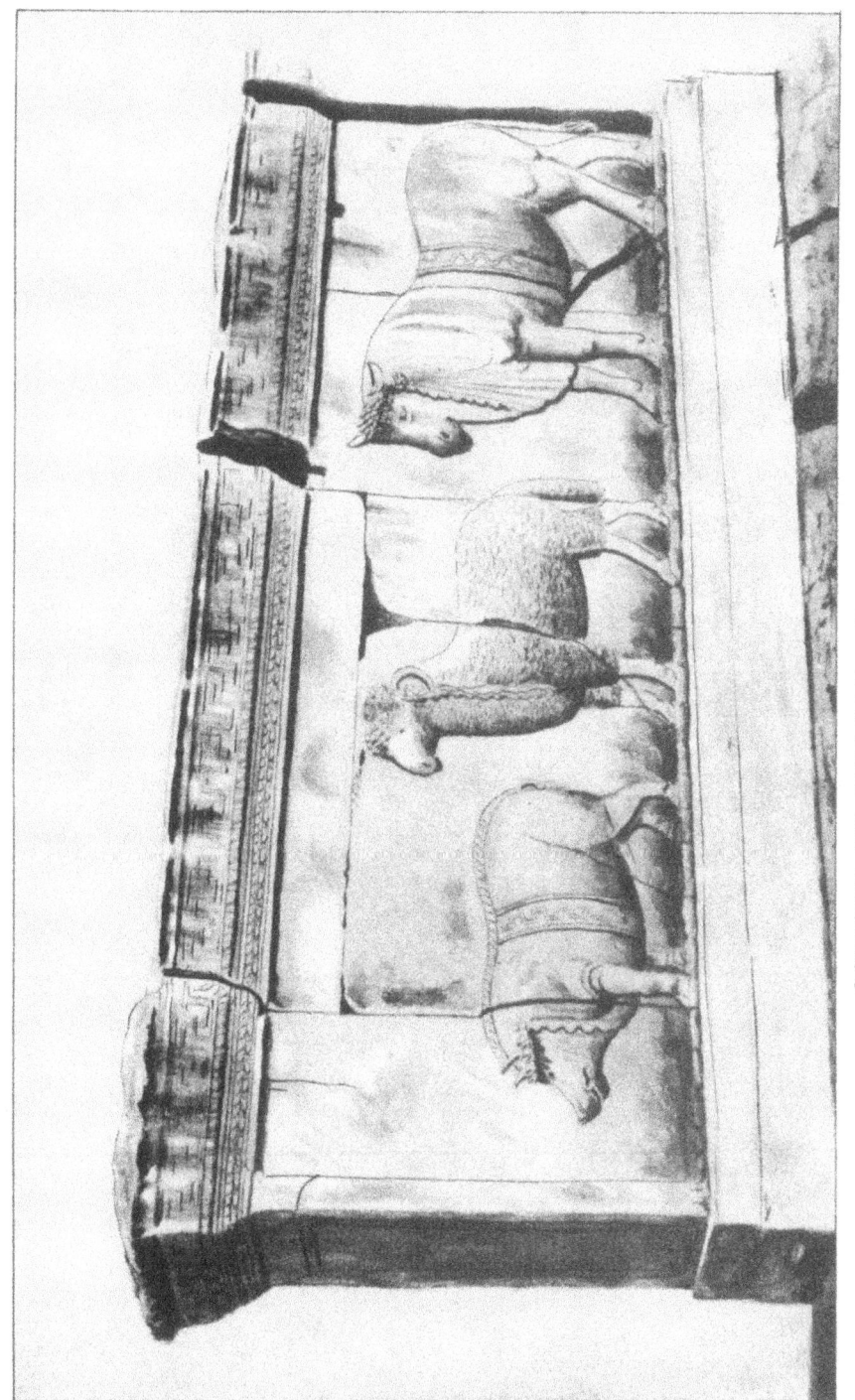

SCREEN OF TRAJAN. ROMAN FORUM.

Plate xiii.

"Anaglypha" is Pliny's term for "Extypa," as "Toreuma" is Cicero's, signifying reliefs in general, and not screens as these two are.

The sculptured work on one of them refers to Trajan's institution for poor children, called "Alimenta," and illustrates on the right the figures of the Emperor and of a woman, representing Italy, with two children, one in her arms and the other led, on the left, the Monarch, accompanied by lictors proclaiming his Edict from the Rostra with the acclaiming people, and in the background an unidentified Arch, the Curia Julia, an unknown street, the Sacred fig tree and the effigy of Marsyas. The reliefs of the other screen represent the remission of taxes, the documentary records of which are in the process of being burnt in Trajan's presence, and behind, a reproduction of the Temple of Concord, the Basilica Julia, the fig tree and Marsyas. On the obverse sides there is a boar, a ram and a bull, the three animals sacrificed in the ceremony called "Lustrationes," the preliminary rite being the "Suavetaurilia," which consisted in leading these animals, bedecked, to be sacrificed, around the building to be repurified.

The Rostra, the Latin for beak, otherwise the Oratorical Tribune, was an elevated platform which took this name from the metal beak-like prows of ships affixed to its sides. The first time these marine ornaments were employed in this manner was in 330 B.C., after Antium had been made a port colony and her ships destroyed. The earliest Rostra was placed in the Comitium, as aforesaid, but as population and demand for public speeches increased, the space became insufficient and orators had frequently to address their audience from the Temple of Saturn or from that of Castor and Pollux. Cesar remedied this insufficiency by commencing to construct another Rostra of greater dimensions, 45 B.C., completed by M. Antonius and Octavius, opposite the Temple of Antoninus and Faustina, where the remains, an utterly shattered wreck, are still to be seen.

Judging from a reproduction of this Julian Rostra on the Denarii of the Lolia family, it appears to have been of the earlier Republican style of architecture, with its portico of arches measuring, it is said, five by five and a half feet, the arcade being sixty-three feet long by seven feet high. The Subsellium or Tribunician Throne was encircled by an ornamental parapet with a pavement of black tesserae. From this Rostra Marcus Antonius delivered his famous funeral oration of Cesar, which was in fact an astute though impassioned political speech, that, striking while the iron was hot, went far to discredit the Republican party by associating it with its artfully denounced leaders, Cassius and Brutus, the authors of Cesar's assassination; and thus paved the way to the total overthrow of institutions, admirable in themselves and to which Rome owed her power, prosperity and glory, but already undermined and tottering in consequence of the invading corruption.

In other words, in order to be effective, institutions and peoples must be reciprocally fitted for each other, and this the Romans were fast ceasing to be. A good Government depends for success even more on the worth of the individuals who have the practical handling of the institutions than on the institutions themselves, however excellent they may be.

It is related that on the occasion of Cesar's obsequies the excited populace seized the furniture of the neighbouring Basilica Julia and used it as fuel for his funeral pyre.

The ashes of the cremated Dictator were taken to the Mausoleum Julium, in the Campus Martius, of which remarkably enough, nothing certain has been known, even so far as regards its exact site. About two years after the battle of Actium, 31 B.C., when Octavius erected the " Aedes ad Divi Julii " in proximity, he also further decorated the above Rostra with the prows of the vessels captured in that naval action. In A.D. 14, that is, fifty-eight years after Cesar's funeral, the body of Octavius was likewise placed on this Rostra, and on this occasion Tiberius pronounced an Epikithion (from " epi," on, and " kithia," funeral) or funeral oration, of course excessively eulogistic, over the corpse, after which it was removed, cremated, and the ashes deposited in the Augustan Mausoleum.

Close to the Arch of Septimius another fragment has been identified as the third or Flavian Rostra. In shape it appears to have been a rectangular platform sixty-eight feet long by eleven feet high, coated with white marble, now almost disappeared, but the orifices made by the insertion of the ship prows and some metal pins, are still visible on what is still standing of the barrier-wall. It is superfluous to add that it was not from either of the latter Rostrae that the heads of the victims of Marius and Sylla were exposed, or that the oratorical contests of the Patricians and Plebeians did not rage around the last, but it was from this Flavian Rostra that the Emperor Septimius delivered his eloquent and touching oration over his murdered predecessor's corpse, the excellent Publius, Elvius Pertinax, A.D. 193, at the latter's funeral. Dion Cassius, an ocular and auricular spectator and participator in his quality of senator at the time, gives a graphic account of these obsequies, which were among the most magnificent ever known.

The remains of a shrine to Vulcan, or Vulcanal, were recently also discovered near the above Arcus Septimii. It was on this site that Tatius and Romulus used to meet as on neutral ground to transact public affairs when these required the joint co-operation of the colleague kings, and it was here also that, according to Plutarch, Romulus was killed by the enraged senators in consequence, it is stated, of his attempt to usurp absolute power, as happened over six centuries later to Cesar in the Curia Pompeia.

Primitive Rome consisted very largely of timbered houses and huts; it is not, therefore, surprising that the inhabitants at this initial stage should hold the Fire-god Vulcan, on whose good will so much depended, in especial awe and worship, and equally natural, subsequently, this cult should decay when the materials employed were less vulnerable to fire and the means of extinguishing it greater. His festivals, called " Vulcanalia," took place annually on the 23rd of August, and Terentius Varro relates, commenting on the inconsistency, " that fishes, creatures of water, the extinguisher of fire, were anomalously selected as the animals to be sacrificed to him," though animosity might explain the seeming incongruity. King Tarquinius Priscus, who built porticos and shops around the earlier Forum, offered up to Vulcan here the spoils taken from the Sabines, if so, presumably of the Separatist Sabines, and Octavius restored the Altar and erected a statue to Vulcan on this spot.

Not far from the Vulcanal are the remains, mere scarred cones, of two small but interesting monuments of classical times. The one denominated " Ombelicus Romae," Navel of Rome, marked at that period the theoretical central point of the City, and the other, called " Miliarium Aureum," Golden Milestone, was originally a bronze

MAMERTINE PRISON. FOOT OF CAPITOLINE HILL.

Plate xiv.

gilded pillar surmounted by a ball with a spike, erected by Octavius, 28 B.C., on which were engraved the principal roads and postal stations diverging from the City gates.

The "Carcer Mamertinus, or Tullianus," now under the Church of San Giuseppe dei Falegnami, at the foot of the Capitoline Hill, in the Via Marforio, derives its first name, like the street, from the now disappeared statue of Mamer or Mars, and its second from Tullius, or from tullianum, a well. It was built, according to some authorities, by King Ancus Martius, and according to others by King Servius Tullius. The probability is that the first erected a small prison, which the second, as the population increased, naturally enlarged, especially as we hear that Tullius built a series of cells, all of which have vanished, with the exception of the one in question. And, indeed, considering the number of those we hear of as contemporaneously incarcerated, it could scarcely have been otherwise.

This prison cell is composed of blocks of travertine, with a conical roof, and was divided into two sections, the upper being called "Robur" and the lower "Latomia." Robur is a Latin word of divers significations, viz.: strength, hardness, oak, the rod used for beating prisoners, their prison and their place of execution. Latomia is the Latin term for quarry, pit, or cave, and in this case applied to the subterranean dungeon. Sallustius, after the lapse of about five centuries, describes it almost as we see it now, in the following words translated verbatim. "There is a dungeon chamber named Tullianum about twelve feet below the level of the soil, surrounded by stone walls and covered by a vaulted stone roof, but its aspect is repulsive and terrible on account of the neglect, darkness and odours."

Though possibly smaller than the Augustan prisons in the Roman Forum and others, the Carcer Mamertinus is the sole one of which any remains survive in good preservation, and also the most interesting historically, owing to the notable persons who were immured and perished there. Among the Romans may be mentioned, Manlius, the adherents of Caius Gracchus, who were strangled therein, the accomplices of Catiline, who likewise underwent the same fate, so laconically announced to the public by Cicero in his one word "Vixerunt," they lived, Sabinus and Sejanus, Ministers of Tiberius, the first beheaded the second hurled from the Tarpeian Rock, the partisans of Vitellius who were led from this prison to be precipitated from the "Scalae Gemoniae" (Stairs of Groans). Among foreigners, may be noted Sifac and Jugurtha, Kings of Numidia, Perseus, King of Macedon, Batuitus, King of the Averni, Vecingetorix of Gaul, Simon Bar Jonas of Jerusalem and forty-two Anatolian Princes.

Christian legendary lore has not failed to contribute its quota to the annals of the Tullianum. Saint Peter was incarcerated here in the reign of Nero, where he converted his jailers, who were in consequence canonized as the martyred Saints Processus and Martinianus. In order to baptize them, however, it seems that the indispensable element was wanting, and the legendary miracle consists in St. Peter's causing, like a second Moses, water to issue from the stone walls. Pope Sylvester I, a Saint both by his own right and by inheritance, being the son of Santa Giusta, A.D. 314-335, consecrated this State prison to Saints Peter and Paul, and, in the fourteenth century the present Church of St. Joseph of the Carpenters was built over it.

The "Forum Julium" was situated on the space lying between the Roman and Augustan Forums, now traversed crosswise by the Viae Marmorella and Cremona. Suetonius states that the price paid for the area alone, quite irrespective of all other expenses, amounted to 100,000,000 sesterces. The very scant vestiges are now reduced to a few arches of peperino with springers and keystones, of concrete and divided by pilasters, half embedded in the soil and all thoroughly defaced. The recorded vanished monuments of this Forum founded by Cesar, 47-45 B.C., comprise a temple to Venus Genetrix (the reputed ancestress of the Julii on the paternal side, and on the maternal King Ancus Martius), containing a statue of the Goddess by Archesilaos, a group of Ajax and Medea by Temomacus and a statue of Cleopatra. Facing the temple was an equestrian statue of the Dictator, the bronze horse of which, supposed to be a reproduction of the famous "Bucephalus" (Bull-headed steed) had the physical peculiarity of Cesar's own charger, that of divided hoofs.

The Imperial Fora that followed the "Julium" connected the Romanum, the centre of old Rome, with the newly-risen quarter of the Campus Martius and other city extensions. Being built on a plan they eclipsed the Forum Romanum in regularity and harmony, and might have done so in other respects if the historical associations attached to the latter had not diverted so considerable a portion of art productions to its adornment even after their foundation.

The "Forum Augusti" occupied the site between the Forum Nerva and Forum Trajani, beginning at the Julium and ending about the present Salita del Grillo, near the family house of the Marquises del Grillo, whose representative of the eighteenth century made himself so notorious, and is still so popularly known and remembered in Rome, for his wit, eccentricities and practical jokes, mostly done for a useful purpose and as a lesson, and who has been the theme of novels and popular plays.

The first intention of Octavius appears to have been to erect a Temple to Mars Ultor, here, in grateful recognition of the protection this God had vouchsafed him in the battle of Philippi. To this Temple he subsequently added his Forum on the site known by the name of "Pantano," swamp, from its former marshy soil, and hence the old "Arco dei Pantani" which opens on the Via Bonella, the street that now bisects the space once covered by this ancient Forum. Among the various works of art therein were the statue of Octavius triumphant amidst subdued provinces, four statues of Apollo, and the Genius of War seated on piles of arms, with hands bound behind to signify that war was bound to keep the peace. The porticos were decorated by statues of all the Latin and Roman Kings and Dictators from Aeneas to himself, and bronze statues of victorious Consuls who had been honoured by public triumphs, with "Elogiae" or Eulogistic Epigraphs inscribed by order of the Emperor, occupied the Exedrae. Below the present street, at about twenty feet, the vestiges or rather the place of one of the Exedrae is still to be seen, thus marking the original level of this Forum, which was of irregular oblong shape owing to the exigencies of the proprietors around. Details concerning the plan and style of the Augusti, restored and almost entirely rebuilt by Hadrian, are somewhat vague and, what is worse, contradictory.

The "Forum Vespasiani," or Pacis, situated behind the Temple of Antoninus and Faustina, covered, it is said, a square area of about 500 by 500 feet, now traversed by the Vie Cavour, Miranda and Alessandrina. The centre of this Forum was occupied by the Templum Pacis, which served as a Museum, wherein were kept the famous Seven Branched Candlestick and other Jewish spoils, as well as several art treasures from the dismantled palace of Nero. The present remains consist of a travertine gate walled up, a portion of a wall, a small part of a fine pavement, cumbered with a mass of masonry, with twelve steps, which, detached from the adjoining Basilica Maxentia, has fallen down here, and the "Forma Urbis," or Marble Map of Rome, originally affixed to the northern wall. The fragments of this map or plan, joined together, were taken to the Capitoline Museum. Pliny also mentions another work belonging to this Forum, a reclining statue of the Nile surrounded by playing children; possibly the identical group now in the Vatican Museum. At the angle of the Vespasian Forum, behind the former Romulus chapel (now graced by the curious epithet of "Heroun Romuli"), otherwise behind the present church of SS. Cosimo and Damiano, once stood the Templum Sacrae Urbis, Temple of the Sacred City, built by Vespasian A.D. 78. The conflagration of A.D. 191, which entirely destroyed the aforesaid Forum Pacis likewise consumed this Temple of the Sacred City, but the latter was restored by Septimius and Caracallus.

The "Forum Nervae, or Transitorium," very narrow relatively to its length, about 550 by 165 feet, was wedged between the Forums of Augustus and of Vespasian, its former site being now traversed from opposite directions by the Vie Alessandrina and Croce Bianca. It was designed and commenced by Domitian, and terminated by Nerva M. Coccejus, who reigned A.D. 96–98, from whom it took one of its names. The other of "Transitorium," arising from its position and purpose as a transition or passage Forum, wherefore it was provided with a main intersecting street as an artery of communication. Of its structures two have been recorded, the one a Temple dedicated to Janus, of which no information has been gathered, and the other to Minerva (See Chapter VIII).

In connection with this Forum it is related that the Emperor Nerva, having discovered that Vetronius Terenius made an unscrupulous, false and venal traffic of his interest at Court, condemned him to be suffocated by smoke, and the execution of his sentence took place here, while a Herald proclaimed, "Fumo punitur qui venditit Fumum" (Smoke punishes him who sold smoke). This species of punishment was not much more painful than that of hanging, by the neck, now in vogue, and if such strong penalties can in any case be admitted as indispensable for the prevention of greater evils, they are certainly justifiable when applied by a strong race that required strong measures like the Romans of ancient times. In ours, if indeed any kind of penalty is meted out to a criminal of this description, it is generally limited to a mild, expostulatory paragraph in some newspaper, or at most, a dismissal from office, or a quite disproportionate fine. Naturally, in these conditions the ill-doer can hug himself and his illicit profits in the consciousness that it is not he, the defrauder, who will pay the penalty of his misdeeds, but rather his victims, a result which he endures, as a rule, with exemplary philosophic equanimity.

One of the symptomatic and significant features of our times is that what really shocks us generally is rather the name than the deed; what scandalizes and horrifies us is calling a spade a spade. So long, therefore, as we substitute the words "Sharp practice" and "Kleptomania" (and a classic term goes a great way towards white-washing villainous actions) for fraud and robbery, the misdeed, even if discovered and published, is socially condoned and excused and legally practically unpenalized.

The "Forum Trajani or Ulpianum," adjoining the Forum Augusti, took its name from its founder the Emperor Trajanus Ulpianus Crinitus, and was according to the general consensus of opinion the best planned, the most extensive and the first as regards the harmonious execution and arrangement of its monuments, of all the Fora of the Eternal City. In order to construct this Forum the neck of land that connected the Capitoline and Quirinal Hills was hewn down about 128 feet and the space thus lowered, with other land around, covered by the Ulpianum, which has been calculated by some authorities as measuring 670 feet in width, and although its length has not been equally specified by them, it was estimated as much greater. But this calculation, besides being incomplete, errs, according to many authors, on the side of reducing the dimensions of the Ulpianum, which the latter compute at about 2,000 feet in length by 1,000 in breadth.

This Forum, designed A.D. 111 by the renowned Apollodorus under the Emperor's direction, was completed in A.D. 114. It was divided into seven sections, viz.: First, the Propylaion or Entrance; second, the Platea or Square, with the Equestrian statue of Trajan in the centre; third, the Basilica Ulpia; fourth, the Latin and Greek Bibliothecae; fifth, the two Exedrae; sixth, the Column; and seventh, the Templum Trajani. The Forum commencing from the Propylaion, dignified by a triumphal Arch erected near the present via del Priorato, terminated at the above Temple, the exact site of which is doubtful. The two hemispherical Exedrae, extended on either side of the square, and the entire Forum was a perfectly arranged assemblage of superb edifices and monuments, constituting one great collective masterpiece of art at its prime. The decorations were rich and artistic, but not too many. The cornices of the buildings were sculptured and moulded representations of most illustrious actions of the Emperor, as also the statuary in marble or bronze, isolated or in groups.

Ammianus Marcellinus, a Greek historian born in Antioch A.D. 333, died in Rome A.D. 390 (whose history of the Roman Emperors beginning from where Tacitus ends, that is, from the reign of Nerva to that of Valentinian, A.D. 98 to A.D. 375, is justly considered to be of great value) in referring to this Forum uses the expression "Singolarum sub omni Coeli structura," "Unique structure under the Heavens." A miniature reproduction of the Upianum on a rare gold coin, now preserved in some unknown corner of a private or perhaps public museum, is reckoned to be a faithful representation of it, so far as its minuteness can admit. Up to the present, it seems that only less than one third of this Forum has been excavated.

The "Forum Antonini," founded by the Emperor Antoninus Pius A.D. 139–160, and situated on the ground now occupied by the Piazze di Pietra and Colonna, must have been, if so, relatively extensive. Two important monuments have survived, viz.: the Temple of Neptune, in the first-named square; and the Column of Aurelius, in the second, though neither were erected by its founder, the temple long before and the column soon after the Forum constructor's death. It is a pity that this Forum is an almost unknown quantity.

The adjacent "Forum Aurelii," equally an unsolved mystery, occupied, it is affirmed, the present Montecitorio quarter where some rugged huge blocks incorporated in the base of the walls of the present Chamber of Deputies are pointed out as indicating its former site. The usual canonical buildings must have been raised here, but no traces of them exist. The well known equestrian statue of the Emperor M. Aurelius was found here, and is now on the Capitol platform.

These Fora were a series of open air museums as well as city centres, very dissimilar from their modern substitutes, markets and squares. The former combined utility, beauty and instruction; a combination more common in the classic ages than in ours.

CHAPTER VII

TEMPLES, CHAPELS, SHRINES

THE sense of the frailty of his nature and the brevity and precariousness of his existence which are continually forced on man, give birth to a craving for support different from and superior to that emanating from himself and his fellow creatures. In infancy this need is, it is true, supplied by the parents or the adults who replace them, relatives, tutors, guardians, but in after life they no longer suffice, because we are compelled to recognise that these seemingly superlative beings of our earliest years are by no means omnipotent, or even much dissimilar to ourselves, and we are then driven to look elsewhere to satisfy what is, from the ultra religious bigot to the extreme atheist with all their intermediate grades, a want and a law of humanity.

Though ostensibly diametrically opposed, the difference between the religious devotee and the self-styled materialist is more apparent than real, because both believe in a supernatural world and agencies, the miracle working saint, the mysteries, etc., of the former being substituted by the divining clairvoyant, the seances, etc., of the latter. This being so, the religious, having faith in a post mortem eternal and superior existence, have a manifest advantage over the non-religious whose ideals and beliefs are painfully ill-defined and unsatisfactory.

It is true we generally treat the superstitious beliefs of ancient and mediaeval times with a condescending superior indulgence for which there is no call, because we have as many and as fantastical ones as they had, though differing in form, as every age has its own special superstitions, it being evident that mankind cannot exist without them, not excepting the greatest of men and women. Our lucky mascots and days, our salt-spilling, Fridays and number thirteen, etc., etc., are quite as unfounded, wild and unreasonable as any that ever obtained at any time.

It would be difficult to imagine a being more impressionable and even gullible than the average man or woman, by means of show and sound. No form of Theology, therefore, however perfect, has ever succeeded in supplying the abovesaid spiritual want, unless its teachings are supplemented by external and material manifestations, such as images, symbols representative of supreme, superhuman beings, and altars, temples or churches for the performance of the rites established for their worship and the invocation of their protection. Among the many beautiful lessons of original, unperverted Christianity is the one that informs us " Wherever any number of men are assembled in the name of the Almighty there would He be also with them." There is no mention here of cathedrals, effigies, rich sacerdotal vestments, etc. But man is pre-eminently a creature of the senses, and, unless some miraculous change be wrought, will always be such. In consequence, the error does not lie in the use of symbols or forms, which, though in themselves nothing, are in our conditions indispensable, but in our giving them an equal or superior value to the spiritual essence of Religion, which is everything. This fundamentally false conception, though unavowed or denied, too often obtains not only with the "masses" but with the "classes," who ought to know better.

There is no doubt that Christianity has greatly improved and elevated mankind, but it is to its spirit alone that this is owing, not at all to its symbols and forms, which are mostly replica copies of the Pagan rites and emblems. For example, the "Aqua Lustralis" of the Pagans is the Holy Water of the Christians, the "Indegetes" and "Lemones" of Paganism are the prototypes of the Angels and Saints of Christianism; the worship of statues is continued in the worship of Images, the "Artolaganus Consecratus" by the Consecrated Bread or Wafer, the sanctuary of the Temple by that of the Church, the "Galerus" of the Flamen by the Mitre of the Bishop, the "Acera" by the Incense-box, etc., and one might go on furnishing an endless list of examples in proof that we do not exactly shine in the inventive faculty as regards the external forms of Religion, any more than we do in other directions.

Religious sentiment first manifested itself in the primitive form of Feticism, still prevalent among the lowest and most savage peoples, and is based on the belief in the supernatural attributes of material objects, mostly trifling ones, such as beads, hairs, pieces of glass, wood or stone and also insects and reptiles. To this form succeeded Polytheism from Asia, passing to Egypt, Greece, Rome and the Scandinavian, Celtic and Teutonic peoples. Among the Egyptians, Polytheism was a belief in animals such as cattle, birds and amphibians, in two capacities, in their own right, as principals, and as representatives of their gods and goddesses. But this Egyptian national creed never reached the development attained by that of the Graeco-Romans, in which the lower creatures were discarded as principals and only admitted as accessories or as emblems of their Deities, and in which philosophy, poetry and art concurred to embellish, elevate and perpetuate the Faith. Among the other peoples of Europe, Polytheism, corresponding to their conditions, was of a ruder and simpler type.

Roman Polytheism was not, correctly speaking, a Mythology or Myth-lore; it was rather a Polytheology, because it was based on the elements of nature and the attributes of man, and these are realities and not myths, though they were symbolically incarnated in supernaturalized human forms exalted by miracles and legends. For example, the Sea, a mighty element, was symbolized by the God Neptune, and its natural but prodigious activities, its currents, its whirlpools, its tempests, etc., which may be explained scientifically by man, but cannot be altered or controlled by him, were declared by Polytheology to be the miracles of Neptune, who might be modified and rendered favourable by prayers, sacrifices and votive offerings. All living creatures are hunters; man in the wilds seeks his game, birds and beasts; in cities, his competitors. This instinctive quality was represented by the Goddess Diana, and it is undeniable that the vicissitudes and dangers of the chase are all facts and not myths, although interpreted in an embellished guise as her miracles.

This system, which, after all, Christianism repeats in a way, in the legends of saints and other miracles, was calculated, being poetical, easy and attractive, to impress more favourably the masses than dissertations on Divine attributes, deductions regarding the phenomena of nature or psychic research, all of which are for the few, and which, therefore, the greater portion of mankind cannot be expected to understand or to be interested in.

The infinity of human wants and the fecundity of human imagination was never better demonstrated than by the multitude of Deities and Semi-Deities invented by Polytheism, numbering among the Romans about 30,000, divided into three Orders, which were respectively sub-divided into classes, as follows. The highest Order of Divinities were styled "Dei Majorem Gentium," sub-divided into first, the "Dei Consentium or Duodecim Deorum," namely: Jupiter, Juno, Neptune, Minerva, Mars, Venus, Vulcan, Vesta, Apollo, Diana, Mercury and Ceres; and second, the "Dei Selecti," namely: Jupiter, Cybele, Saturn, Bacchus, Pluto, Janus, Quirinus, Rhea, Sun, Moon and Genius. The second Order, termed "Dei Minorem Gentium," was again sub-divided into two categories, viz. the "Indegetes," or Demi-Gods and Goddesses, and the "Lemones," or Demi-humans. Among the former are numbered Hercules, Castor and Pollux, Proserpine, Psyche, etc., among the latter, Perseus, Theseus, Achilles and other heroes of primaeval ages. The third Order was composed of genuine but secondary Deities, who were not, however, the issue of the Highest Gods, such as Terminus, the Landmark God; Lupercus, the Wood God; Vertumnus, the Vegetable God; Vaticanus, the Divining God; Flora, the Flower Goddess, and so forth.

It is noteworthy that the direct issue of the highest Deities, even if semi-human, took precedence of the secondary Deities, who were not their direct issue, even though the latter were of an entirely divine nature.

But besides these specified Supreme Beings of Paganism, their forests were peopled, as is well known, with fawns, nymphs and satyrs; their rivers, lakes and seas by tritons, mermaids, etc., because to the exuberant and poetical imagination and sentiment of the ancients, especially the Greeks and Romans, a lifeless, senseless nature was a thing at once inconceivable and repulsive, and even now, with our fairies, phantoms, etc., though feeble and limited repetitions of the classic conceptions, we recognize the existence of this innate feeling.

It must be emphasized that the Polytheology of the Romans was pre-eminently a political and state Religion, consistently with their main principle that the State was supreme in all things. Numa regulated and systematized the beliefs of the three races, Sabines, Romans and Etruscans. The Roman hierarchy therefore did not constitute a distinct caste, or possess the overwhelming power of the Egyptian or Chaldean priesthoods. The Roman lay authorities and military leaders were often invested with ecclesiastical offices, and it was not incompatible, for instance, for a Consul or Censor to be also contemporaneously or subsequently an Augur or a Pontifex.

There was, besides, another remarkable feature in the earlier Roman Paganism, the fact that for about 170 years after the foundation of the City the gods were worshipped without the aid of any images, and it was Tarquinius Priscus, who, initiated in the Samothracian Mysteries, introduced this custom; and the first statues probably erected to any Deity by the Romans were those of Jupiter, Juno and Minerva, for the Temple he built on the Capitoline Hill.

The religious edifices of Rome, at first naturally very primitive, gradually augmented in elegance, dimensions and splendour as time and refinement progressed. A list alone of these ancient structures in the Eternal City and its environs would cover some pages, and any attempt at a thorough description, almost impossible from lack of data, would, if accomplished, require several volumes.

Of the Seven Hills of Rome, three, namely: the Quirinal, Viminal and Esquiline were, it seems, originally Sabine; three, the Palatine, Aventine and Caelian were occupied by the Romni, the Alban and Trojan settlers afterwards called Romans; and the one, the Capitoline, changed hands until the two races were incorporated into one State. Four of these hills, viz.: the Quirinal, Viminal, Esquiline and Caelian, have been likened by fertile imagination to four fingers, of which the Campagna is the palm, of the mighty hand that seized and held the world. The classic ancients, as aforesaid, possessed the faculty denied to us, of incarnating, as it were, and vivifying nature, and the above Seven Hills were accordingly looked upon as the living features of their homeland by the Romans, and hence held in a species of veneration and affection inconceivable to our prosaic selves. Ovid records that a Festival, called the "Septimontale Sacrum" was annually observed in December with all due ceremonies and sacrifices. From these elevations, formerly higher than they are now, Rome took by periphrase the designation of "Urbs Septimontalis," Città delle Sette Colli, or Sevenhilled City.

Besides the above seven there were three other hills, the Janiculan, Pincian and Vatican, which, if included officially, would have entitled the City to be styled "Ten-Hilled." The Janiculus and the Pincius have already been mentioned, and as regards the Vaticanus its name is said to have been derived from the Divination-deity Vaticanus, who had his headquarters on this hill, which was held in horror by the ancient Romans, partly on account of its unhealthy emanations till Heliogabalus rendered it more habitable by removing the tombs there. Tacitus, in referring to this hill, calls it "Infamia Vaticani Loci." Now, as is known, the Pontifical Palace and Cathedral of St. Peter occupy the ancient Mons Vaticanus.

The principal structures destined for religious functions were termed "Templum" or "Aedes," the difference being that the first were consecrated by the Augurs and the second not. The smaller erections were called "Aedicula," chapel, "Sacrarium" or "Sacellum," shrine, and "Ara," or "Altare," altar. The earliest constructions, so far as is known, of this class were dedicated to Evander and Faustulus on the Palatine, to Saturn on the Mons Saturnus or Capitoline Hill, to Quirinus or Mamertinus on the Quirinal and to Janus on the Janiculan, probably altars protected by a shrine. Next in date came, it is conjectured, the Vestal and Juturna structures.

There is naturally much uncertainty as regards the first regular temple erected, but broadly speaking the priority of date must be conceded to the Sabine buildings, because the Sabines were already established in these parts as a constituted State before the advent of the Romans.

The Sabine word "Quiris," signifying lance, gave a name to one of their hills, the Quirinal, to one of their gods, Quirinus, and to themselves, as they were denominated, Quirites. On the amalgamation of the two peoples later, the term was adopted also to designate one of the Orders of the State, the Quirites or Equites (Lance-men or

Horsemen), and hence the initials composing the National Motto, " S.P.Q.R.," the first being that of " Senatus " from " Senex," elder, the second " Populusque," or people, the third " Quirites," or knights, and the fourth " Romanus," which last word included the indigenous Sabines, the Roman settlers and the Etruscans as one, in other words " The Roman Senators, Knights and People."*

Regarding the style, size and plan of the original Sabine Temple of Quirinus on the Quirinal and its restoration by Numa, who rededicated it to Romulus, identifying him with Quirinus, the Sabine War-god, there are no certain records as yet attained. The third reconstruction of this Temple was the work of L. Papirius Cursor, 293 B.C., to commemorate his victory over the Samnites, and he also added a " Solaria Horologium," sundial, which not being in a correct latitude, was replaced by C. Marcus Philippus. The fourth renovation was due to Octavius who encircled the Temple with pillars, as Dion Cassius relates, corresponding in number to the years of his life at the time. This edifice was situated near and over the space now occupied by the Church of Sant' Andrea a Montecavallo, where its ruins were discovered, and, it is added, destroyed in A.D. 1628.

In connection with the Templum Quirini, we are indebted mainly to Pliny for a tradition sufficiently remarkable and unique to warrant mentioning. Two myrtle-trees grew in front of this temple, corresponding to the twin laurel-trees of the Regia aforenoted, and were as celebrated in a political sense as the latter were in a military. One of these myrtles was named " Patricia " and the other " Plebeia," and they were each credited with reflecting and sharing the changing fortunes of their respective Orders with marvellous fidelity and precision. For about seven centuries fortune fluctuated between the two, but on the whole the scales inclined in favour of the patrician cause, wherefore Patricia, with occasional intervals, flourished vigorously at the identical time and rate in which Plebeia declined, and of course vice versa, but during this secular series there were likewise periods when both prospered equally, and those were the golden days of Rome. Under the Imperial régime the twin myrtles deteriorated, being ravaged by a raven (the Empire), hovering over them, but Patricia, despite slight rallies, was the greater sufferer of the two. This was a natural result, because the one man rule has proved itself even more disastrous to the classes than to the masses; both are degraded, but the first loses most, having most to lose, and, besides, this, autocrats very often rely on the mob's help to destroy the aristocracy, who, being more independent and stable and less gullible, constitute a greater obstacle to monocratic despotism.

In the course of time the scene changed again. Autocracy was substituted by Oligarchy that is, by the Feudal Barons, the unworthy successors of the Roman Patricians, who had regained or rather usurped more than the beneficent power of the latter, and if the twin barometer-trees had not disappeared previously, they would have been expected to duly register this evolution, that is, the " Raven " would have become a powerless, inoffensive shadow, " Patricia " exuberantly if not beneficially flourishing, and " Plebeia " a withered plant. But long before Feudalism had arisen, to radicate itself so strongly that it survives even now to some extent, the miraculous emblematic

* There is also another interpretation of this Motto as follows :—S. Senators, P. People, Q. Quirites or Sabines, and R. Romans, that is, " The Sabine and Roman Senators and People."

twin myrtles, linked indissolubly with the great Roman State alone, had terminated their mission apparently, and hence pined and withered synchronously and mysteriously with the extinction of the Roman Empire of the West under Romulus Augustulus, A.D. 476, who, significantly enough, bore the diminutives of the two names respectively of the first Roman King " Romus " and of the first Roman Emperor " Augustus."

On the Mons Quirinalis besides the above Temple of Quirinus there were several others, of minor note, among which may be mentioned the adjacent one to " Publica Fortuna," another to " Salus," or health, from which Porta Salutaris of the Servian wall took its name, and another to Flora. Of the illustrious Sabine families who resided on this elevation are recorded the Cornelii, after whom a street was called Via Corneliorum, the Aemilii and the Flavii. The Emperor Vespasian, of the last-named family, had a brother called Sabinus, taking the name of the race, and a son called Titus in memory of King Titus Tatius, the colleague of Romulus.

Between Rome and Albano there are the ruins of a well-proportioned rectangular building with Corinthian pilasters which claims the distinction of being probably the sole surviving remains of the various temples raised by the Romans to Salus, a practical people who duly appreciated the greatest of earthly physical blessings, health. In consequence of one of those errors that cannot always be explained, this temple has been supposed by some to be an unknown tomb, although there are none of the typical features of a sepulchral structure about it, not even a half effaced D.M.S. to justify the assumption.

The diminutive bronze temple to Janus Quirinus, probably movable, and corresponding to the Ark of the Covenant of the Jews, is referred to as standing between the Basilica Aemilia and the Comitium. Janus, besides being the first recorded King of Italy, was a Deity of no slight importance. He presided over the four seasons, wherefore he is often represented with four visages facing the four cardinal points, and is styled Janus Quadrifrons, four-fronted Janus; he was the symbolic barometer of peace and war, whence his title of Janus Quirinus, in the first case his doors being closed, in the second opened. He was the patron of arches of the two vaulted type, named after him Jani, of ingresses, egresses, gates, viaducts, roads and bridges. But his highest attribute was that of being the custodian-porter or janitor (another derivation of Janus) of the Heavens, the Pagan archetype of Saint Peter, wherefore he is represented with a key in one hand and a stick in the other. In the latter functions two faces are assigned to him, turned in opposite directions.

It is worthy of note as proving the status of this God, that during the anti-Christian persecutions, when judgment was delivered in the Roman Forum, the test applied to those accused of Christianity was for them to burn incense on the Altar of Janus Quirinus, and in case of acquiescence they were sometimes acquitted, while in case of refusal, condemned. Wherefore this Templet played a conspicuous part in Roman history, and is frequently mentioned by writers such as Propertius, Livius, Horatius, Ovidius.

Among the various temples erected to Jupiter, the King of Gods and Highest Deity of men in Paganism, the incarnation of supreme authority, naturally very numerous and imposing, the following are almost all those that have escaped oblivion. The "Templum Jovis Statoris," the site of which is still marked by a few scarred blocks at the foot of the Palatine to the left of the Via Sacra before reaching the Arch of Titus was built in accomplishment of a vow by Romulus during an encounter with the Sabines. On this occasion it appears that at first the Roman forces were routed, but after their King's invocation, he succeeded in checking the flight of his men and in redeeming the day, wherefore this especial Jove received the distinctive title of "Stator" or the Rallier, though this word also signifies usher, court-attendant and servitor. Romulus, having obtained the boon he asked for, proceeded, like an honest man, to pay the price he had offered in return, only as he did not hurry himself he died before he had accomplished more than laying the foundations and commencing the construction of this temple, which was completed long after by Attillius Regulus, 290 B.C., and rebuilt again in the early Imperial times. Except that its columns were of the Roman Corinthian Order in this last reconstruction, nothing much has been gathered, so far as we know, concerning the size, style and other details of this building.

From another point of view the chief interest attaching to the Templum Jovis Statoris lies in a probable conjecture and a political event, viz.: that it was the first Temple erected by the Romans to any Deity, and that the famous meeting of Marcus Tullius Cicero and Lucius Sergius Catiline took place here. This remarkable encounter was a turning point in history not brought about by military action, but by the prowess of brain and dialectic skill and eloquence. Cicero, by one of the feats of his extraordinary powers, compelled Catiline, a bold, astute and worldly man, to avow himself, against his own interests and will, hostile to the existing institutions, and to reveal his plans in part, all of which he had hitherto contrived to conceal, and thus Cicero by unmasking him, rendered him less dangerous, and prepared the way for the conspirators' fall which secured the safety of the Republic. It was on this occasion, when Cicero, without arms, defeated an armed conspiracy, that he composed his poem beginning with the famous phrase "Cedant arma togae" (Let arms cede to the robe) otherwise, Let the military yield to the civil power.

The "Templum Jovis Capitolinus Optimus Maximus," probably the second of the authentic Jupiter temples in point of date, once stood on the site of the present church of Ara Caeli on the Capitoline Hill, its entrance facing south. It was begun by King Tarquinius Priscus in observance of a vow, terminated by King Tarquinius Superbus, seventh and last king of ancient Rome, and consecrated by Horatius Pulvilius, in this first year of the Republic. This temple was the finest, as well as the last, of the great edifices of Royalty, and measured, it is said, 800 feet in circumference and belonged to the pure Etruscan school of architecture, with a triple colonnade before the façade and sides. It contained three Cellae, the central and largest for Jupiter, flanked on one side by that of his spouse, Juno, and on the other by that of Minerva, the offspring of his brain alone without the co-operation of the other sex. This edifice lasted over 400 years, and would have had a far greater longevity if it had not been burnt down during the internecine war of Sylla and Marius, 82 B.C. In the following year the former, then Dictator, commenced the reconstruction of this temple and adorned it with columns of Pentelic, a very fine Greek marble, which he had brought away from the Temple of Jupiter Olympus, in Athens, but he did not survive for the completion of his work, which was terminated about twenty years later, 62 B.C., by L. Lutatius Catulus.

In the struggle between Vespasian and Vitellius, A.D. 69, with the Imperial throne as the prize of the victor, it again fell a prey to flames ignited by the soldiers of the latter, who threw their lighted torches on the pavement together with the body of Vespasian's brother, Sabinus, whom they had killed. On this occasion Domitian, Vespasian's son, escaped the fate of his uncle disguised as a priest, and he subsequently erected a chapel, Aedicula Jovis Conservatoris, containing an altar whereon was engraved an inscription recording his above adventure. The victorious competitor, Vespasian, had the temple rebuilt on the lines of the original fabric. A few years after the Templum Jovis Capitolinus succumbed to fire and was rebuilt by Domitian, A.D. 82. The restored edifice, said to measure 200 by 185 feet, reproduced the three original Cellae in the same order of the aforesaid Trinity. It was erected on a lofty terrace adorned with columns of which Plutarch extols the exquisite workmanship,—having seen them himself modelled in a renowned laboratory in Athens—with numerous statues of ivory and marble, with the dome and doors plated with gold and a mosaic pavement of a very delicate and symmetrical pattern. It is affirmed that twenty-two of these columns are those of the church of Ara Caeli here.

The first image of the titular Deity, the product, as stated, of the Tarquins, was of terra-cotta and represented Jupiter attired in the "Tunica Palmata," or Tunic of Triumph, and the "Toga Pictor," the painted and embroidered mantle of the Supreme Chief, with the emblematic thunderbolts in the right hand and a spear in the left. Later this statue was substituted by one of gold, and subsequently, in Martial's time, the statues of the three divinities were of gilded bronze. The present well known sitting statue of Saint Peter, of which there are so many copies—the original being that of Saint Peter's Cathedral in Rome—is credited or discredited with being this identical statue of Jupiter, one of the three above-mentioned of Domitian's reconstructed temple discovered here, and, bereft of its thunderbolts and spear, which were replaced by the emblematic keys in the left hand and by the uplifted right in the canonical shape for benediction, was thus transformed, so far as material alterations went, from the Pagan God to the Christian Saint.

It is related that when all the effigies of the other Deities, except the said trio, were removed from this temple, the God Terminus, consistently with his character, refused to budge, and therefore quite exceptionally was honoured with a shrine therein, his presence being permitted, independently of his powers of passive resistance, on the score doubtless of his holding the position of adjutant or secretary to Jupiter, the land and property God *par excellence*.

The Jovis Capitolinus remained for several centuries the chief Temple of Rome, in modern language, the Cathedral, the ancient Roman Westminster Abbey or Notre Dame, but with a political as well as religious character. Here the Sibylline Books were kept, the oath of fealty to the State taken by the newly-appointed officers, civil, clerical, military, and the most important national ceremonies performed. The deliberate demolition of this building began actively in A.D. 404 under the Emperor Honorius, when his general, Stilichus, stripped off the gold platings of the doors to pay the arrears of the soldiers, and the second blow was administered by Genseric, A.D. 445, who carried away the statues and bronze tiles to decorate his African palace. Still out of the fragmentary marble remnants of this grand edifice various artists contrived, centuries later, to produce decorative works, among which may be mentioned Flaminio Vacca who carved the lion now in the Villa Medici in Rome, and Vincenzo de Rossi, the author of the statues of the Prophets in the present church of Sta. Maria della Pace.

Near this temple was an altar dedicated to Jupiter Pistor (the baker) in commemoration of an episode of the siege of Rome by the Gauls, the beleaguered Romans having thrown down loaves of bread on the besiegers in evidence that their food supply was plentiful. A gigantic statue of Jupiter, moulded from the armour captured from the vanquished Samnites, was also erected here, of which Pliny states, in proof of its colossal size, that it could be plainly discerned at a distance of several miles. The Temple of Jovis Feretrius (from Feretrim, bier) was also begun, it is alleged, by Romulus, but this is doubtful, and in any case it was never completed by him. It was situated contiguously to his ayslum for fugitives, slaves and outlaws, whom he thus attracted with a view of increasing the population in quantity if not in quality, as he could not afford to be fastidious, and it was in this unfinished temple that he offered up the spoils taken from Areas who waged a war of reprisal against him in consequence of the rape of Vallis Murcia.

King Titus Tatius besieged and partly captured Mons Saturnius or Capitolinus, aided by the treacherous or thoughtless connivance of Tarpeia, daughter of the Governor Spurius Tarpeius. There are two versions of the causes and results of Tarpeia's act on this occasion. The one, that she was dazzled and seduced by the gold armlets and other ornaments of the Sabine warriors, much more sumptuous than the Romans of the times in their attire, and engaged to admit them if they made over to her these costly articles, and the Sabines entering, fulfilling the letter but not the spirit of the agreement, flung on her all their heavy ornaments so that she was crushed to death. The other, absolving her from venal complicity, attributes the motive of her treason to her intense love for Tatius, and he, combining love with policy, thus gained her and the Capitol at one stroke, married her, but we do not know if they lived happy ever afterwards, as, in our childhood's tales at least, invariably happens. By both versions she betrayed her father, kin and country, only in the first it was for the low motive of dress greed and in the second for love, the most beautiful of human feelings.

In consequence of this event this hill was called "Rupes Tarpeia" or Tarpeian Rock, a name it still retains for the ridge overhanging a sheer precipice from which condemned persons were thrown to be dashed to pieces below, and it is significant that the same crime, treason to the State, which gave it its name, was also the same one for which the accused were in after times hurled down. The present altitude of this part of the hill is about sixty feet, but it was much higher, because its summit has gradually crumbled away and the falling material has raised the surface at the foot.

According to legendary tradition this lady still sits covered with ornaments, but enchanted and motionless, in the centre of the Tarpeian Rock, her secular confinement differing somewhat from that of the giant Enceladus imprisoned under a very much vaster elevation, Mount Etna. The Giant, says mythology, was imprisoned by order of Jupiter, but not enchanted or motionless like Tarpeia. The flames and smoke of the eruptions of Etna were imagined to be his breath, and the telluric shocks to which the Sicilian volcano and island were subject, to be caused by the movements of Enceladus, who, when he bestirred himself, occasioned slight vibrations, and when he periodically attempted to burst his mountain prison, great earthquakes.

Among the functions of the Vestals was a yearly procession here to the Tomb of Tarpeia. Some authorities assert that she was a Vestal herself, and attribute this annual ceremony to her membership, but if she had been a Vestal she could not have been living with her father; and would still less have been entitled to this homage if she violated the statutes of the Order by marrying. The most probable hypothesis is that Tarpeia having favoured the Sabines to some purpose, as we have seen, King Numa Pompilius, who organized the Sisterhood, being himself a Sabine, thus wished to honour the friend of his race by this yearly tribute.

It was here, after the entrance of the Sabines, when the conflict between them and the Romans was about to begin, that it was arrested by the interposition of the thirty Sabine women. By the treaty of peace and amalgamation that followed, the two kings reigned jointly with equal powers over the peoples of the two races, and of a third, the Etruscan, constituted into one State, divided into three Tribes, named respectively "Tatiensi," from Tatius, "Romensi," from Romus, and "Lucumonensi," from Lucumonus. These three Tribes were sub-divided into ten "Curiae" each, in all thirty Curiae under a chief called "Curion," and named severally after the thirty Sabine women, whose supplications, addressed to their fathers and kindred on one side, and to their husbands on the other, had the felicitous result of transforming a field of battle into a field of peace and union, and was the initial and sentimental prelude to the definite treaty that fused the two adverse races into one. The thirty Curiae were again subdivided into ten "Decuride," totalling three hundred Decuriae, with a "Decurion" each as chief.

As regards classes, the most cultured, well-born, intelligent and bravest composed the Patrician Body, the rest, the multitude, the Plebeian. To these two Orders a third was added later, an intermediate one, the Equites, or knights, distinguished by the peculiar insignia of their Order, a massive gold ring. The Patricians were the King's hereditary counsellors; to them was entrusted the cult of the State religion, the administration of justice and of the public funds and civil and military leadership. To the Plebeians were assigned the minor State offices, agriculture, the care of the live stock, mechanical arts, commerce and military service. Both were subordinated to the Sovereign, who, though not an absolute ruler, directed, controlled and, in ultimate appeal, decided.

This primitive regal constitution with the natural evolutionary modifications, continued substantially in force for about two and a half centuries, that is, till it was overthrown and replaced by a new form of government called "Res Publica" (Public Thing) or Republica, Republic, in this case signifying an Aristo-democratic constitution, but without a life President or one elected by the suffrage of the population. By this system the power of both the Orders was augmented as both appropriated part of the Royal authority which had been abolished. The Patrician, by the appointment of two of its members annually as Consuls, Magistrates whose prerogatives differed but slightly from those of the former kings, and the Plebeian, by the election of Tribunes from their Order to moderate and balance the power of the Consuls. Later the Plebeians secured the right of electing a Plebeian Consul as colleague of the Patrician. For the offices of Pontifex Maximus, Censor, Aedile, Augur, Praetor, Questor, the Plebeians as well as the Patricians were eligible, though in earlier times these posts and dignities were held exclusively by the first Order, and in the later, mainly by them.

At the close of five years of joint reign of the two first kings, Tatius was assassinated by the relatives of the Ambassadors of Laurentia, whom he had caused to be executed. Subsequently Romulus reigned alone and his ultimate fate is uncertain. Some authorities affirm that he was slain, as aforesaid, because he attempted to usurp autocratic powers, others favour the tradition that he disappeared unaccountably in a military review. The latter lame version is supplemented by some writers with a miraculous legend as follows. When the review was terminated a terrific tempest occurred, during which the King vanished, to reappear shortly afterwards to the Senator Proculus Julius. This Patrician reported that Romulus appeared to him as a resplendent, supernatural figure, and charged him to say to the Romans, that their King, having completed his terrestrial mission, had now rejoined his Father-God (Mars his reputed Sire) in the heavens; that he prophesied that his people would attain and maintain the highest pinnacle of human greatness, power and prosperity so long as they were virtuous, wise, valiant and steadfast; that he, spiritualized as the God Quirinus, would continue to protect them, and that he granted them twelve centuries of existence as a State, and in fact from his own reign to that of Romulus Augustulus, about 1,200 years elapsed, though we do not know if this prophecy like other numberless wonderful predictions, was not invented after the event.

The devout and sagacious King Numa erected two other temples on the Mons Capitolinus, one to "Fidus Publicae," Public Faith, wherein the officiating priests performed the service with fillets on their hands in token that verbal faith was as binding as material links; a very wise, honourable and progressive principle, not so generally practised in our times as to warrant our assumption of superior morality and civilisation. The other temple was dedicated to Terminus, a Deity who enjoyed a far greater degree of importance in earlier times than he did subsequently.

The "Temple of Jovis Victor" was built on the Palatine by Fabius Maximus 295 B.C., in fulfilment of a vow made by him at the battle of Sentinum. No information regarding its construction has been gathered, and its remains are reduced to a rugged platform, the podium of the former temple, approached by modern steps, and the vaults beneath, originally quarries, were afterwards used as cisterns for water storage. On the above steps was once a cippus with the inscription "Cn. Domitius Calvinus Pontifex," in commemoration of his triumphs in Spain 36 B.C. It seems that this man, like most Romans of some eminence, had held ecclesiastical, civil and military offices, as he was twice consul, 54 B.C and 46 B.C., and served also as one of the commanders under Cesar at the battle of Pharsala 48 B.C. There is a travertine altar restored by another Calvinus, likewise an ecclesiastic, originally placed in the Via Nova in obedience to a mysterious warning of the approaching Gallic invasion, but removed after to the spot it now occupies at the foot of the Palatine because it obstructed the building of the Domus Caligula. The epigraph on this altar, "Sec. Deo. Sec. Deovae. Sac. C. Lentius Calvinus, 90 B.C.," evidently refers to the restorer, but its erector not having been identified, it has been called "Ara Calvinus."

TEMPLE OF JUPITER. PORTICO OF OCTAVIA. ROME.

Plate xv.

The "Temple of Jovis Libertas" was built by Tiberius Sempronius Gracchus, grandfather of the celebrated liberal reformers, the brothers Tiberius and Caius, on the flank of the Aventine adjoining the Censor's Hall, where these officials met to transact business and where the archives of this service were preserved. This temple was rebuilt by Asinius Pollius who added to it a public library, the first of this description in Rome. The Asinii were a plebeian family of mark and this Pollius was a distinguished orator, poet, historian and patron of literature, and he had once held the dignity of Consul. Hortensius and Virgilius mention him with praise no less than Cicero whose friend he was.

It is said that a Temple was also erected on this hill by Hercules to Jupiter Inventor, in gratitude for the aid the Sire of the Gods had vouchsafed him in the discovery and recovery of the cattle robbed by Cacus. Besides this doubtful pre-Roman temple, there were others on the Aventine dedicated to Remus, Juno, Diana, Hercules, Victory, Vertumnus and the Hecates. This hill, as aforesaid, had once been an active volcano, and the fact that it became the favourite haunt of Cacus accounts for the superstitious belief that the flames which issued from its crater were those emitted from the mouth and nostrils of the monster. This and the death and burial of Remus thereon rendered the Aventine an ill-omened place, and its official inclusion in the city circuit and privileges was postponed till the reign of the unprejudiced Claudius, A.D. 41–54.

Regarding the "Temple of Jupiter Lyaconius," on the Tiberine Isle, and for the twin Temples of Jupiter and Juno within the Porticus Metelli, see Chapters XV. and XIX. The Temple of Jupiter Tonans (the Thunderer) of which no traces survive, was built by Octavius so close to the aforesaid one of Jovis Capitolinus that it came to be considered as an annex of the latter. This Emperor's well known nervousness with regard to thunderstorms induced him to erect this temple in observance of a vow made by him when a thunderbolt struck the litter in which he was travelling during an expedition against the Cantabrii, the modern Biscayans, which killed the slave beside him while he escaped unscathed.

The Corporation of priests appointed for the special service of Jupiter were called "Flamines Diales," from Diovis, Jovis, and naturally held the most elevated rank in the hierarchy, and had to maintain the highest standard of dignity and unstained reputation.

CHAPTER VIII

TEMPLES, CHAPELS, SHRINES (*continued*)

THOUGH of the Seven Hills of Rome the Capitoline is reckoned politically as the most notable, its extent and altitude have not been computed with precision. Approximately its area is said to measure about three-quarters of a mile in circumference and its height between 190 to 200 feet, owing to which superiority in elevation poets have termed it " Celsus," " Sublimus " and " Altus." Janus gave this hill, opposite his own, the Janiculus, to his guest Saturnus (a derivation of Saettare, to sow) from whom it took its first recorded name of Mons Saturnus. As is known, Saturn, probably a capable foreigner who taught the aborigines agriculture, became the supreme male agricultural Deity, the female being Ceres, the Greek Demeter. The second appellation given to this hill was Tarpeius, from Tarpeia, and the third, Capitolinus, or Capitolium, was owing to the severed head " Caput," discovered when the foundation of the aforesaid temple to Jupiter by Tarquin was being laid. As almost every incident, especially if out of the ordinary, was accounted an omen to be explained by the official interpreters, this head was solemnly declared to indicate that Rome would become the head of the world. The " Arx Capitolii " otherwise the fortified area, the Citadel, contained, it is affirmed, sixty temples, chapels and shrines, no small number considering its extent. The present designation of Campidoglio or Field of Dolour, was first adopted in the Middle Ages on account of this hill being the theatre of many scenes of cruelty.

The earliest temple to Saturn was erected, it is asserted, on the site occupied by the Ara Saturni which marked the confines of the asylum already mentioned for the fugitive outlaws within the precincts of which they were theoretically safe. The Porticus of this temple was reached by a flight of steps, the road leading to them, part of which has been laid bare, reveals its ancient and superior construction by its pavement of polygonal slabs well finished and fixed together in contrast to the Mediaeval thoroughfares, with their rough, smaller, ill-joined stones. The succeeding Temple of Saturn at the base of the hill is likewise of unrecorded date of foundation and name of founder, but its reconstruction took place 497 B.C., a very respectable antiquity, by the Consuls Sempronius and Minutius. It was restored by Munatius Plancus, 42 B.C., and after suffering considerable damage by fire, was twice renovated, by the Emperor Carinus and by the Emperor Gratianus. The present ruins in the Roman Forum, consisting of eight Ionic columns dissimilar in diameter and quality, and a riven entablature, proclaim it to be the remains of one of the later and indifferent reconstructions. The inscription on the entablature, much effaced, runs as follows: Senatus, Populusque, Romanus incendio consumptum restituit.

We are informed that this temple and that of Castor and Pollux were the only two in Rome wherein it was made compulsory for the priests and worshippers to uncover their heads. The great annual fêtes in honour of this god, the Saturnalia, the precursors of the Christian carnival, took place on the 17th of December, when, as Cicero puts it, "All Rome went mad," and during their celebration, masters and slaves, patricians and plebeians, creditors and debtors, all mixed familiarly in perfect equality. Dion Cassius relates that the slaves on this occasion were permitted to wear citizens' attire. The general popular feeling with regard to these fêtes was embodied in the proverb, "Non semper sunt Saturnalia," meaning that it is not always a Saturnalia, otherwise, every day a holiday.

There are two versions relatively to the origin of these agricultural festivals. Aurelius Ambrogius Macrobius offers the hypothesis that they were a Pelasgic importation, and due to King Tullius Hostilius' initiative, while Livius and Dionysius of Halicarnassus support the theory that they were an institution of the aforesaid consecrators of the temple, the Consuls A. Sempronius and M. Minutius, and contemporary with its consecration. Their duration was first fixed at one day, under Octavius increased to three and later to five.

It was from this temple that Cicero delivered his famous oration in favour of the expiring Republic, in which on one occasion he made a personal appeal to Pompey, then in the plenitude of his power, who was among the audience surrounded by his adherents, clients, and officers. This edifice served as the depository of the archives of the Questors and as the "Aerarium Publicum," or public treasury. Pompey, in his flight from Rome, took the keys of this Temple-Treasury, but left the money, and Cesar, less scrupulous and more thorough, on arriving forced the doors with his satellites, in spite of the Tribune Manlius' strenuous defence, and seized the cash to finance his campaign against his rival. This temple appears to have been a handsome and symmetrical structure with its portico of graceful Ionic columns, its podium decorated with emblematic reliefs of bunches of grapes and ears of corn and its bronze statues, two equestrian, respectively of Janus and Saturn on each side of the landing of the steps, two pedestrian in a group at the summit of the pediment of Saturn and Ceres, and two other symbolic figures at its angles. This edifice was considered to be one of the finest specimens of the Roman Ionic Order of the Eternal City.

The Temple of the Dioscuri, Castor and Pollux, was begun 496 B.C. in grateful recognition of the personal and visible aid of these twins extended to the Romans in the memorable and decisive battle of Lake Regillius, 499 B.C., where they defeated the Latins led by the Royalist Pretender Mamillus Octavianus, son-in-law of the last King Tarquinius Superbus. By this victory the Romans secured the stability of their peculiar form of republican constitution and their supremacy in the Latium. The lake Regillus, like so many others in Italy, is the crater of an extinct volcano, and is now known by the name of Lago di Castiglione or Lago di Sta. Prassede.

The term "Dioscuri," a composite Greek word of "Theos," Dios, genitive of "Zefs," Zeus, Jupiter, and of "Kuros," child, that is, the Children of Jupiter, was in particular applied to these twins of all his numerous progeny. It is related that Castor and Pollux did not content themselves with their miraculous active participation on this occasion, but proceeded to announce, *in propria persona*, the victory, and stopped to water their steeds on their arrival at the pool of Juturna in the Roman Forum, wherefore this spot was chosen for the erection of their temple, which was by all accounts a superb octastyle edifice, finally completed and consecrated 484 B.C., by the Dictator Postumus Albinus.

The present remains, however, are not those of the original building, but of a reconstruction of Tiberius and Drusus, A.D. 7, contemporaneous with the re-edification of the Temple of Concord by the former, and consist of a broken but handsome entablature supported by three beautiful marble columns, forty-seven feet high by five in diameter, and which, though wrecked, are still one of the finest specimens extant of the Corinthian Order. The Emperor Tiberius utilized for some of the decorations of both these Temples the spoils taken in the wars of the period. If, however, the above date be correct and not rather the more probable one of A.D. 17, then Tiberius accomplished these stupendous works when he was still a doubtful heir apparent or presumptive only, having succeeded his step-father, Octavius, in A.D. 14, and it is not likely that the latter monarch, who did not favour him, would have granted him the power and means to re-erect these two temples on such a grand scale, especially as Octavius considered architectural building his own particular province; as we know by his not altogether unjustified boast, " That he found Rome of brick and left her of marble."

Suetonius relates that the Emperor Caligula subsequently annexed the Templum Castoris and Polluxis as the vestibule of his palace on the Palatine, and had his statue placed between those of the deified twins in order to secure, to his effigy at least, some share of the worship lavished on the divine horsemen.

The anniversary of the battle of Regillus was solemnized annually by a State procession of the Roman Knights, of whom Castor and Pollux were the special patrons, issuing from the Temple of Mars, near the Porta Capena, to reach this Temple, clad in their richest attire, crowned with olive leaves and bearing trophies. This edifice was constructed on so costly and splendid a style that Verrus, the Praetor Urbanus, demanded for the reproduction of its columns alone, although it was not a Peripteral, the sum of 500,000 sesterces. During the excavations various fragments of the equestrian statues of the Dioscuri were found, but we have not heard of any attempt at a recomposition by reuniting and supplementing the pieces, possibly because this would have proved impracticable. The standard weights and measures of the city were affixed to the walls of this temple.

The Templum Concordiae, Temple of Concord, of which a few scattered marble fragments now mark its former site at the foot of the Capitoline Hill, opposite the Arcus Septimii, was constructed 366 B.C. by M. Furius Camillus, in commemoration of the great national event of the reconciliation of the Patricians and Plebeians, rebuilt by the Consul Opimius 121 B.C., and as aforesaid, finally by Tiberius. This temple, in its last reconstruction entirely composed of Luna marble, except its pavement of variegated, was on the plan of the class of structures distinguished by the term " Augustea," that is, rectangular and oblong, with the canonical Cella 130 by 82 feet, and its spacious Pronaos measuring eighty-eight by forty-six feet, approached by a broad flight of steps to its elevation twenty feet above the street level.

TEMPLES, CHAPELS, SHRINES

The architecture, all harmoniously Corinthian, was of great richness and purity of design, as is also materially attested by some of the fragments still existing. The Cella contained eleven niches adorned with the statues of Zeus, Athena, Ares, Demeter, Hermes, Apollo, Diana, Latona with the infant Apollo, Aesculapius and Hygeia, with three paintings portraying Bacchus, Cassandra and Marsyas, and four elephants of "Lapis Obsidianus," all masterpieces of the renowned Greek artists Ephranor, Piston, and others.

The Lapis Obsidianus or Obsidian, is a dark stone with black, greenish or brown hues, of a felspathic nature and undoubtedly of volcanic origin, and so hard that it is capable of making an impression on glass by scraping. There is a variety of Obsidian called "Veturinata" containing grains of other lighter substances. The carving of the four above elephants was, therefore, a wonderful example of skill, patience and labour, as well as a proof of the degree of excellence which their implements had at that time attained.

The earlier edifice served sometimes, in an emergency, for the meetings of the Senate, and it was on one of these occasions that Cicero delivered his fourth denunciatory speech against Catiline and his accomplices. The later, rebuilt as above by Tiberius, was used as a national Museum also.

One of the finest, if not the finest, temples dedicated to Juno was constructed 425 B.C. on the Aventine near and on the site of the present church of Sta. Sabina. No positive particulars relating to this building have been gathered, and the only relics surviving are the twenty-four columns of Parian marble, discoloured by years and neglect which now adorn the said church.

The Templum Junonis Moneta, near and opposite to the much greater aforementioned one of Jovis Capitolinus, Optimus Maximus on the Capitoline Hill, was erected by M. Furius Camillus 409 B.C. in observance of a vow, and here it was that the Sacred Geese of the Goddess were reared and kept, the famous geese that gave the timely alarm, which enabled Marcus Manlius, surnamed Capitolinus in recognition of his services on this occasion, and the Roman garrison, to repulse the surprise assault of the Gauls. The title of "Moneta" bestowed on this Juno is derived from the Latin verb "Monere," to admonish, but owing to the fact that this temple was used as the depository of the current coin of the State, the term Moneta took a very different conventional meaning, that of money, which it still retains in the Italian language, the sole, modern, genuine, direct offspring of the classic parent tongue.

Near a pool on the Esquiline Hill which emitted poisonous exhalations was erected the temple to Juno Mephtis or Mephitical Juno, and close to this another to Juno Lucina, Luminous Juno, mentioned by Ovid as follows:

> "Monte sub Esquilio multis incaeduus annis
> Junonis Magnae nominae locus est."

According to Verrus Flaccus, the epithet of Esquiline applied to this hill is derived from "Ex-cultus," literally "Out-cultivated," an assumption not based on etymological grounds but on the fact that trees were planted here, outside the then Urbs Romae, by

King Servius Tullius, viz. the Fagutalis, beech-grove and the Nemus Argiletum on the space now traversed by the Via Sta. Maria del Monte. Another and more probable hypothesis is that the name originated from " Ex-quil-ae," external or suburban habitations, as the Esquiline was a suburb of Rome till the Emperors practically incorporated it in the City by covering it with villas, temples and other buildings. The corresponding word " In-quil-inus," internal inhabitant or tenant, is invoked in corroboration seeing that both have the same root " Quil," qualified by the particles " In" and " Ex," signifying respectively, " in " and " out."

The Esquiline has three elevations, namely: the " Cispius " anciently occupied by the palace of Servius Tullius and the temple of Juno Lucina, now supplanted by the Basilica of Sta. Maria Maggiore, the "Oppius," the former site of the palace of Tarquinius Superbus and Trajan's baths, now occupied partly by the Church of San Pietro in Vincoli, and thirdly the hillock, Fagutalis, crowning the slopes towards the Caelian. The height of the Esquiline varies and has been calculated at about 165, 175 and 180 feet severally, and it has been found difficult to estimate its area, as its limits are very ill-defined, though we know that it is the most extensive of the Seven.

It is recorded that there were five altars raised on this hill, one to Juno, by the survivor of the historic triplets Horatii, one to Nulla Fortuna, one to Minerva and two to Janus. Bordering the ancient Via Carina, a street connecting the Esquiline with the Palatine, once stood the Aedes Tellus, or earth, erected 290 B.C., of which we learn that it was large enough to accommodate the Senate when they were summoned here by Marcus Antonius. The Templum Junonis Sospita in the Forum Holitorium, and that of Juno Gabina, identified by some vestiges among the ruins of the ancient Gabii, the modern Castiglione, close the best known list of the Juno Temples, though there were others.

The same may be said of the Venus Temples, namely: the Venus Victrix of Pompey's Theatre, the Venus Genetrix of Cesar's Forum, the double one of Mars Prestans and Venus Erixyna on the Capitol, and the Templum Venus Libitina on the Esquiline.

The term " Libitina " was comprehensive, and denoted all that appertained to post mortem functions, such as registrations, funerals, burials. Some assert that Venus, others that Proserpine, was worshipped especially in this capacity. Though Plutarch favours the first theory, the second seems the more logical of the two, because it would be singularly inappropriate to select as patroness of similar offices to the departed, with whom all carnal senses and desires are extinct, of all others precisely the goddess of beauty and sensuality, in preference to the dark, sombre deity of the under world. But whether both were the joint titular divinities of the above temple or one of them, the fact remains that it was much frequented and, practically useful, as it was the ritual custom of the Romans to throw a coin therein for every individual that died, and these coins served as the statistical tallies of the number of deceased during the year.

The only Temple of Venus, but not exclusively dedicated to her, of which some remains exist, is the double one consecrated to " Venus Felix " and " Roma Aeterna," on the Velia, on the right of the Via Sacra, before reaching the Arch of Titus, the Pronaos of which alone covered the space now occupied by the Church of Sta. Francesca Romana,

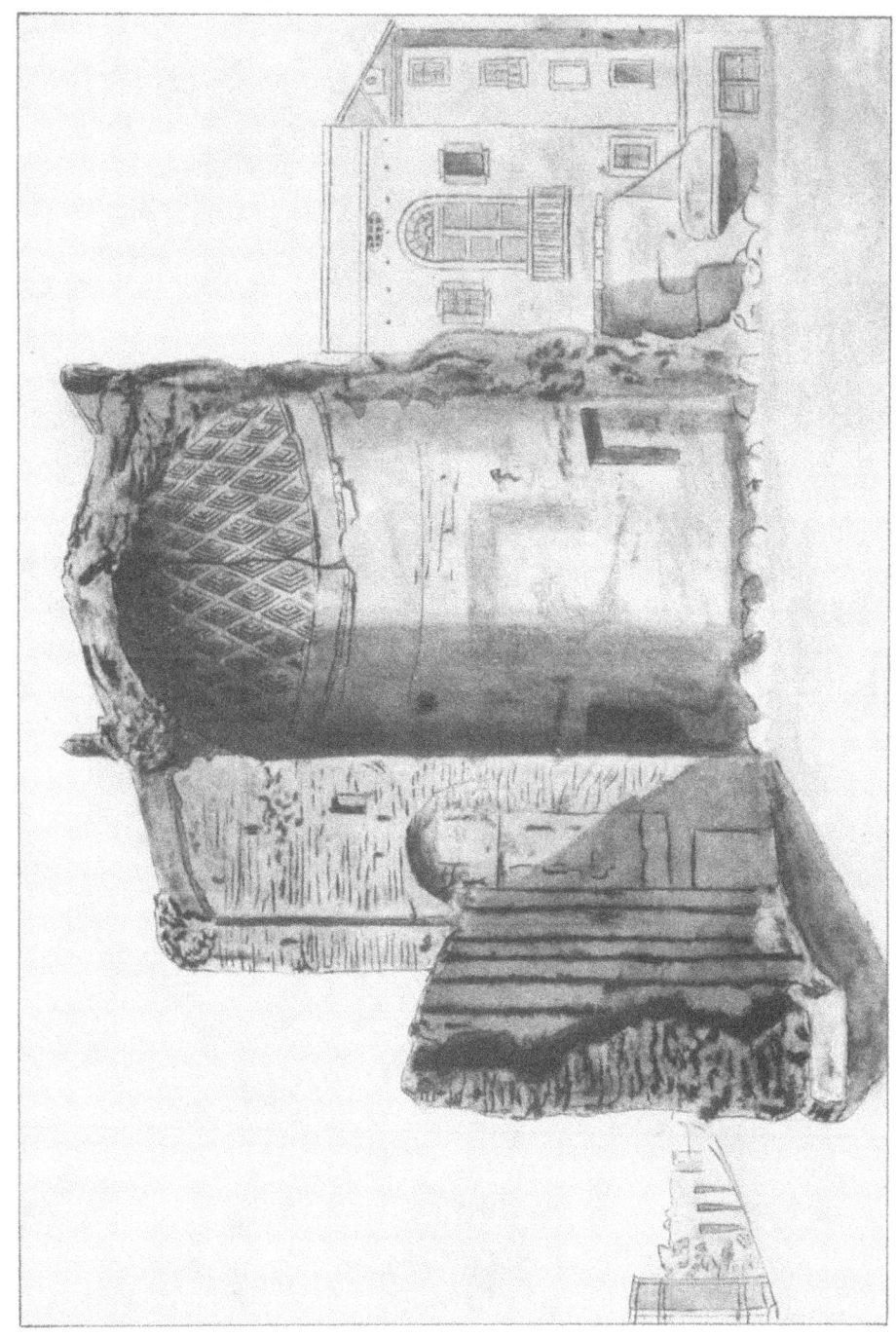

APSE.—TEMPLE OF ROMA AETERNA, A.D. 135. VELIA, ROME.

Plate xvi.

TEMPLES, CHAPELS, SHRINES

was designed by Hadrian, A.D. 135, and the execution under his supervision was entrusted to the celebrated Apollodorus, but the Emperor, of whom it was one of the most magnificent creations, died before its completion, accomplished under Antonius Pius, and after its partial destruction by fire it was restored by the Emperor Maxentius in A.D. 307. The length of this double peripteral temple is stated to have been 180 yards and its width 110, probably rather exaggerated estimations. It was composed of two Cellae covered by one dome of chiselled bronze, lined entirely with the rarest marbles, each Cella containing respectively the colossal statues of Venus and Roma, and each provided with a separate opposite entrance, the one facing the Capitol and the other the Flavian Amphitheatre. The entire edifice was bounded by sixty Corinthian columns of Parian marble disposed as follows, ten at the façade, ten at the back and twenty at each side. There was besides another encircling colonnade of 150 columns with shafts of oriental granite and capitals and bases of Parian marble.

The present remains, *in situ*, are reduced to a wrecked apse, to a cella in the adjacent convent, to a fragment of an exquisitely sculptured cornice and to some broken pieces of the external colonnade strewn about. Such are the meagre vestiges and records of what was once the largest, and, possibly excepting the Jupiter Temple of the Capitol, the most splendid Temple of Roma Vetus. This dual temple was closed by the Emperor Theodosius, but remained substantially intact till A.D. 630, when Pope Honorius I stripped it of the bronze tiles of the dome.

The ruins of this temple became from the twelfth to the fourteenth centuries the preferred abode of sorcerers, and the light issuing from the apertures was imagined to illuminate their performances and orgies, or, as it is also related that this ruined pagan edifice was used by poisoners for the brewing of their death dealing drugs, and that they took advantage of its evil repute as the laboratory of black magic, to protect themselves from indiscreet curiosity, which might otherwise have seriously inconvenienced them.

The renowned poisons of the Borgias, which, as is known, were of so subtle and perfected a nature as to defy detection even by a post mortem analytical examination, and, moreover, so contrived as to simulate the various hereditary diseases in the families or those peculiar to the individuals whom the Borgias desired to remove permanently from this sublunary existence, were not manufactured here, because the above and other high-class poisoners had no need to leave their palaces and castles for this purpose. Their humbler imitators in the science, however, of an inferior status in life, had to resort to similar uncanny spots to operate in secrecy and safety. In all probability, as poisoning and sorcery were in those times frequently allied professions, these artists combined both, and thus administered to two classes of customers.

Among the few religious structures on the Caelian Hill was the Temple of the Camenae, with its Nemus, or Sacred Grove. It was set on fire by the notorius Clodius and partly consumed, with the object of thus destroying the documentary proofs of his debts preserved therein. This Templum or Aedes Camenae covered the space now occupied by the Church of San Stefano Rotondo, with its ghastly, indifferently executed frescoes of martyrs, or, to be more precise, the Pagan Temple was converted into the Christian Church, a very common transformation at the time. The Templum ad Divo Claudio erected by his niece, and widow, Agrippina, formerly stood where the Church of SS.

John and Paul, with the monastery of the Passionist Fathers now is, but little is known of this temple.

The above Saints were officers of the household of the Princess and Saint Constantia, daughter of the Emperor Constantine I, and these two men having been converted to Christianity, refused to recant, otherwise to re-abjure and return to the Pagan religion, during the reactionary reign of the Emperor Julian, A.D. 361–363, who is known, owing to his reversion to, or perhaps steadfast adherence to, his ancestral Faith, as the "Apostate," and who in consequence of the obstinate and rebellious heresy of John and Paul, in his opinion, peculiarly aggravated in officers of the Imperial Household, had them both beheaded.

Mars, who is best known as the God of War, was originally among the primitive Romans, the patron Deity of vegetation and live-stock, and this is the reason that the priests appointed to his service were termed "Salii," or leapers, because they leapt as high as possible from the ground, the altitude they attained in their acrobatic performances being held to prognosticate a corresponding height in the corn of the coming harvest. But in the course of time Mars succeeded or superseded Quirinus as the Supreme War-god, and he surrendered his attributes as the agricultural and pastoral Deity entirely to Saturn. The importance of both the military and agricultural interests having developed correspondingly with the progress of the State, their respective duties were separated, the military art and service were undertaken by the Roman citizens, while the culture of land and the care of cattle became gradually relegated to freedmen, prisoners and slaves.

The evolution was reflected in the Campus Martius, which from a crop-growing and pasture district became the exercise and parade field of the armies that, directed by the sagacity, foresight and patriotism of the Senate, the arm with the head, conquered all and subjugated most of the nations of the then known Universe. But besides being the War-god of a people pre-eminently and scientifically warlike, Mars was also the titular sire of the Roman race, and nevertheless no temple of commensurate importance, so far as has been recorded, had been erected to his exclusive worship before that of Mars Ultor, by Octavius, and this, too, is the only one of which some vestiges exist.

In the earlier times the principal Temple of Mars stood on the left of the Porta Capena, built by T. Quintus, who was Duumvir Sacris Faciendis, in accomplishment of a vow made during the Gallic wars of 390 B.C. There are naturally references to this edifice in Roman history but no detailed description so far as has been gathered, though it may be assumed in view of the stage of art at that period in Rome, this early Templum Martis was not a very imposing or highly artistic fabric. It is related that this Temple had a portico which fell down at the prayer of St. Stephen, who if he was a saint need not necessarily have been a monumentoclast, the deliberate destroyer of interesting historical works.

It may be noted that a temple to Hercules Custos was also erected near the famous Porta Capena, so that the principal entrance to the Eternal City was appropriately flanked by the two supreme divine representatives of Strength and Valour.

The twin temple to Mars and Venus on the Capitol was vowed, after the battle of Trasimene, so disastrous to the Roman arms, to placate the wrath the gods manifested

TEMPLE OF MARS' ULTOR, B.C. 2. ARCO DEI PANTI.

Plate xvii.

TEMPLES, CHAPELS, SHRINES

so unequivocally on that occasion, and was consecrated, 215 B.C., by the Consuls R. Fabius Maximus and T. Otacilius, though some writers affirm that the Consuls of the year were Q. Fabius Maximus and Tib. Sempronius Gracchus.

The fate of the decisive battle of Philippi fought, 42 B.C., between the republicans led by Brutus and Cassius and the absolutists under Antonius and Octavius, hung for some time in the balance, because the success achieved by the wing of the army commanded by Antonius was neutralized by the defeat sustained by that under Octavius, and the latter, morally dauntless but not a hero physically, vowed, in his sore straits, a Temple to Mars to be built conditionally, that is, after that god had granted a complete victory to the votary.

To this temple, Octavius subsequently added his Forum. The religious edifice was consecrated 2 B.C. to Mars Ultor, or the Avenger of Cesar, on his foes and assassins, the above-mentioned chiefs of the Republican forces who were defeated, as the Triumvir doubtless believed, in consequence of his timely vow. The Templum Martis Ultoris was recognized as one of the architectural and sculptural masterpieces of ancient Rome, ranking as the equal of the Basilica Aemilia in the Roman Forum and the Temple of Apollo on the Palatine. But independently of its artistic value this temple possessed two other attributes, a moral and a material one, the first, that it was used as the edifice wherein were preserved the trophies taken from the vanquished enemies of Rome, and among these were also the standards, captured by the Parthians from the Triumvir Crassus and restored by them to Octavius, 20 B.C.; and the second, that it served as the Aerarium Militare, Military Treasury, of the Empire, the money being stored in the cellars of the substructure.

The remains of this temple, which contained many art treasures, are now reduced to the massive, neat-hewn peperino blocks that mask the convent of the Annunciata in the Via Tor di Conte, and which were a section of the outer encircling wall of the temple and Forum, still in good preservation despite their over nineteen centuries' existence, and three superb Corinthian columns, a pilaster and a broken entablature, all of Luna marble which formed part of the right colonnade.

The earliest recorded temple to Apollo was the one erected 430 B.C. by the Consul C. Julius on the Campus Martius, of this one, as of the other of Apollo in the Forum Holitorium, it may equally be said that beyond names and dates, nothing positive and precise is known. The chief Apollonian Temple, so far as has been gathered, seems like the Martian, also to have owed its existence to Octavius, and was one of the group of Augustan edifices on the Palatine, and the handsomest of the group. It was rectangular and composed entirely of solid marble, like, for instance, the diminutive mediaeval Church of Sta. Maria della Spina of Pisa, an architectural jewel, but superior to the latter in dimensions and differing in architectonic style. The Cella was adorned with statues of the Nine Muses, the attendant bodyguard of Apollo, and three others, namely: the statue of Apollo by Scopas, of Diana by Timotheos and of Latona by Cephisodotos, which were almost priceless on account of the renown of the artists who created them. On the dome stood a colossal group representing Apollo in a quadriga. The Porticus was decorated by one hundred statues, fifty equestrian of the fifty sons of Aegyptus and fifty pedestrian of the fifty daughters of Danaus, their wives, and in front was erected an altar flanked by four bronze gilded oxen, the work of the celebrated Myron. There was also a dependent Templet to Vesta attached to the main building.

The Temples of Diana have vanished almost completely. There was the celebrated one dedicated to her mentioned by Propertius and Martialus on the Aventine, on the site now occupied by the smaller and very inferior Church of Sta. Prisca. Our knowledge of this temple is limited to a comparison, a detail and a legislative act, as follows: That this edifice was constructed in imitation of the world famed Temple of Diana of Ephesus, which is in itself no slight argument in its favour, that the horns of a cow, the divine Huntress' favourite sacrificial victim, were suspended emblematically on the façade, and that the law of Icilius was engraved on a pillar placed in the Cella.

Spurius of the prominent plebeian family of the Icillii, framed and succeeded in getting the above law passed, 492 B.C., in favour of the political Tribunes. In cooperation with his colleague, the celebrated Junius Lucius Brutus, Spurius obtained an order to execute Coriolanus by having him thrown from the Tarpeian Rock, but the attempt to carry out this order was frustrated by the Patricians, a fate, which the less fortunate M. Manlius Capitolinus, first the saviour of Rome from the Gauls, after the aggressive foe of her institutions, underwent later.

Lucius Icilius, as political Tribune, 456 B.C., persuaded the Senate to cede the Aventine entirely to the people and subsequently took part in overthrowing the Decemvirs. His colleague, Virginius, slew his daughter Virginia, the betrothed of Icilius, to save her from the iniquitous sentence of the Decemvir Appius Claudius. The Tribune lover's impassioned appeal over her corpse served to excite the Romans of all classes, already exasperated against the Decemvirs for so many cogent reasons, and thus, the time being ripe, their downfall was accomplished by Icilius and Virginius under the leadership of the Senatorial Delegates Valerius and Horatius.

The aspirations of the Romans to possess a more regular Code of written Laws induced them to send a deputation of three Senators to Athens, 454 B.C., who were empowered to collect material for the above purpose, as the Athens of Pericles was considered then the most enlightened centre. This mission eventually resulted in the abolition of all other magistratures in favour of the creation of an annually elected body of ten members styled " Decemviri Legibus Scribendi," who were entrusted with the compilation of a Code and invested with dictatorial powers in 451 B.C. The laws were first inscribed on ten and later on twelve " Tabulae " or Tablets, and hence called the Laws of the Twelve Tables, which constituted the nucleus and foundation of the legislation in which the Romans have been the world's teachers.

The failure of the institution of the Decemvirs as the sole governing instrument offers one more proof of the value of the oft-taught lesson that to endow any individual or corporation of individuals, from whatever source originating, with absolute irresponsible authority, is the hugest of political errors, except in two cases, in the infancy stage of a State and during its critical periods, and even then, only a temporary dictatorship of proved devoted servants of the State. This was the principle and practice of the Romans, our masters in statecraft, so long as they were true to themselves, who, more intelligent and whole hearted lovers of their country than moderns are, made short work of any species of tyranny by whatever spacious name it might be called, whether in reality autocracy, oligarchy, militarocracy, plutocracy or mobocracy. But moderns are, mostly, hopeless word-mongers, and are therefore habitually duped and ruled by euphemistic phrases and words in place of being guided by principles, acts and facts.

There were three Orders of Decemvirs, viz.: First, the above-mentioned " Decemviri Legibus Scribendi " (Decemvirs Law Writers); second, the " Decemviri Litibus Judicandi " (Decemvirs Lawsuit Judges); and third, the " Decemviri Sacrum Faciendi " (Decemvirs Sacred Performers) also called " Decemviri Sacrorum," these being the guardians and exponents of the Sybilline Books. These three Orders are mentioned and defined here, because as a rule, whenever the term Decemvirs is used, people only know and think of the first, that is to say, of the legislative, administrative, political Decemvirs.

In connection with these legal " Tabulae," it may be as well to make some reference to another sort of publication also inscribed on Tablets, adopted by the ancient Romans and corresponding to our modern Press. To some persons it may come as a surprise to hear that in the classic ages this people had anything resembling and substituting our Press, which is supposed generally to be an exclusively modern product.

The formal introduction of journalism or its counterpart in antiquity among the Romans, may be broadly fixed at the period when the Scipios were predominant, about 240–210 B.C. The learned Victor Leclerc informs us that the term " Diarium," diary, journal, was first used by Asillius S. Sempronius military Tribune under Scipio Africanus, as the title to his written narrative of the events he had witnessed, and in which he had participated. This word adopted in the plural " Diaria " was the generic term to denote Press, while to describe in particular that branch of it which we now style newspapers the word " Acta " was used with the qualificative indicating the several purposes, viz.: " Acta Diurna," " Acta Urbis," " Acta Senatus." The publication of these journals was, as we see, established long before Cesar's times, who objected to the journalistic system altogether, and more particularly to the Acta Senatus, which his successor Octavius suppressed, nor is this at all surprising, because autocrats are not usually in favour of any kind of Press, and above all of an independent Press.

There is a marked difference between the Roman Acta and our newspapers with regard to purpose, contents and diffusion. The purpose of our journalism is chiefly to ensure a pecuniary profit to the owners, on one hand, and to sway and divert the public on the other, in consequence the news is expressed so as to suit these two aims. The Acta were not connected with any sort of pecuniary or other interests, and therefore an entirely disinterested summary of necessary information to the public of internal or external events, proclamations and edicts. This information was diffused by affixing these Acta to the Album Praetorium of the Praetors' Hall, at the Curia and the Domus Publica, where they could be freely perused and also copied by all, and the public officials and patricians usually sent their scribes for this purpose daily, and these copies the latter distributed among their clients.

As it is probable that only vague notions prevail in general in respect to the relations that existed between Patrons and Clients, it may not be amiss to say something briefly also on this fundamental feature of the social life of the ancient Romans. Dionysius defines the respective reciprocal duties and ties of the " Patronus " (from Pater) and of the " Cliens " (from Clino, to incline) broadly as follows. The former undertook to expound the law to the latter, to represent him in the Courts of Justice, and to further and protect his interests material and otherwise in all things, the Client in return had to support and follow his Patron in his political and military campaigns, and in case his means were insufficient to contribute freely according to his (the Client's powers) towards paying his Patron's debts, his or his sons' ransom if prisoners of war or his daughters' dowry.

The Clients belonged to the " Gens," family, of their Patrons and therefore could take their cognomen or surname, somewhat like the Scottish clans. Neither could be called upon to come forward as the accuser of the other, or to bear witness or vote against him. If the Client committed a crime against his Patron he was considered in the light of a parricide and dealt with accordingly. If a Patron was guilty of a crime against his Client, he was outlawed, and anyone could injure or kill him unpunished, and they were both equally foredoomed to penalties in the next world, which was then held in more account than now. The power and pride of the illustrious Roman families depended quite as much on the number and importance of their Clients as on their lineage, wealth and public services or offices.

This was, since there must always be leaders and followers, a useful and admirable system of give and take, a free arrangement by which one side gave a protection derived from an influence based on the best elements, independent position, culture and high tradition, and the other in return gave a support arising from numbers and business, resulting in a fair and sensible combination and co-operation of moral, material and mental factors, reciprocally beneficial and which practically as well as theoretically proved successful.

Closing the digression we resume. Besides those temples in which Minerva figured as a member of the Pagan Divine Trio with Jupiter and Juno, there were naturally also other temples and shrines dedicated exclusively to her worship. Of these all have disappeared almost even as to name, date and site, with the exception of three, so far as we know, viz.: Minerva Chalcidica, Minerva Medica and Minerva, the third being the only genuine Temple of the Goddess of which some ruins survive in Rome.

So far as regards the Templum Minervae Chalcidicae, we only know that it was constructed by the Triumvir Pompey who decorated it with some of his numerous war trophies, and reconstructed by the Emperor Domitian, on the site now occupied by the Church of Sta. Maria Sopra Minerva, which took this sobriquet from having been built over the ruins of the ancient temple, and that a statue of Minerva, now in the Vatican Museum, was discovered here. This statue was given the distinctive epithet of " Medica" or " Medicea," having been appropriated by the grand ducal family of the Medici of Florence, as that of " Farnese " was tacked on to the statue of Hercules found in the Antonine Baths, appropriated by the Farnese family.

Skirting the Viale Principessa Margherita is a ruin, decagonal externally and circular internally of about 165 feet in circumference, denominated erroneously the Temple of Minerva Medica. The origin of this misapplication of name seems to have been that, according to common report, among the statues of Aesculapius, Antinous, Adonis, Hercules, Pomona and the Farnese Fawn found here, there was also a statue of Minerva,

TEMPLE OF MINERVA, A.D. 94-97. VIA CROCE BIANCA. ROME.
Plate xviii.

though the reason of her selection as the titular Deity of this building, which was not, it appears, a temple, in preference to the others as above discovered here, has not been explained. The lower section of this structure was lined by marble with nine niches, seven of the occupant statues having been as aforesaid found *in situ*, and the upper part coated with stucco culminated in a vault which survived till 1828 nearly intact.

In the Middle Ages this building was called "Le Galluzze," or "Terme delle Galluzze," which has been interpreted by some as a corrupt contraction of Caius and Lucius and by others of Gallienus. The more probable hypothesis is that these ruins are the remains of a Nymphaeum of the Gardens of Gallienus, co-Emperor with Valerius, A.D. 253–260, and sole Emperor, A.D. 260–268, which covered the site of the former Horti Luciniani the property of the Lucinii, a prominent plebeian family of Etruscan extraction that first rose to distinction through L. Lucinius Calvus who obtained valuable privileges for his order. The Lucinii comprised conspicuous branch families, such as the Crassii and Lucullii, and personalities of note such as Verrus, Macrinus and Nerva. Up to the time of the construction of the railway this ruin standing amid vineyards was picturesque enough to attract the attention of tourists and serve as a subject for artists.

The ruins of the temple consecrated to Minerva, the divine miraculous offspring of Jupiter's brain and the personification of his wisdom, popularly known as the "Colonacce," are situated at the angle formed by the crossing of the present Vie Alessandrina and Croce Bianca, and consist of two half buried fluted Corinthian columns sustaining an entablature decorated with reliefs representing her in her dual capacity of patroness of the Muses or Fine Arts and of the Household Arts, such as spinning and sewing, and surmounted by the figure of Minerva also in relief. This temple was built by Domitian who professed great devotion to this deity, and rightly too, for wisdom comprises almost everything. This Templum Minervae formed part of the Forum of Nerva and this fragmentary ruin, although half submerged and badly damaged, testifies by its fine sculpture and its imposing and symmetrical architecture to what the entire edifice must have been in its palmy days.

Until the seventeenth century, that is, for about sixteen hundred years, seven superb columns, defying time, neglect and violence, were still standing intact, and who can say how much longer they would have continued so, had it not been for Pope Clement VIII, who volunteered as the active ally of the slower destructive agencies of decay and ignorance, and by one bold stroke knocked down these columns which with other marble fragments taken from this temple were afterwards employed for the well known Fountain of the Acqua Paola on the Janiculus. In a country like Italy so favoured by a wealth of marble and stone quarries of excellent quality, the preference which mediaeval and modern builders, Popes and Saints as some of them are called, for taking these materials precisely from the historic and superior monuments of their glorious forefathers, and thus destroying them, cannot be explained except by the innate dose of perversity with which humanity is afflicted.

Although it is more than probable that there were several temples and shrines dedicated to Neptune, the god whose sway extended over the greater portion of the terraqueous globe and whose importance augmented among the Romans as they developed more and more as a sea and colonizing power, he has nevertheless shared the fate of the other Deities, and there are no ruins of any temple consecrated to him with the exception of the remains of the Templum Neptuni in the present Piazza di Pietra, built by Agrippa 24 B.C. in commemoration of his naval triumphs.

The ruin now consists of a portion of a wall of the Cella incorporated in the present building and of eleven fluted Corinthian columns of Marmor Lunense, forty-one feet in height, the survivors of the original fifteen, seven of which flanked the length of the building and eight, four on each side, its breadth. On the shaft of the fourth of the said columns, to the left, is a diminutive figure of the Crucifixion, which may be taken as a token that this Temple, like so many others, was converted into a church in the Middle Ages. The decorations of the Temple consisted chiefly in reliefs illustrative of the conquered provinces and of symbolic trophies, some of which are preserved in the Capitoline and Neapolitan Museums and in the Odescalchi and Albani Palaces in Rome, but by far the greater number lost, or used for the following structures, viz.: the Arch of Claudius, that once spanned that part of the ancient Via Flaminia that is now the modern Corso, near the Palazzo Sciarra, for the restoration of the so-called Arch of Constantine, and later, for the adjacent mediaeval church of San Stefano del Trullo. This Templum Neptuni was burnt by a great fire in the reign of Titus and re-erected by Hadrian and Antoninus Pius. Pope Innocent XII, A.D. 1691–1700, converted it into a Custom-House and it subsequently became the Camera di Commercio.

Plate xix.

TEMPLE OF NEPTUNE, B.C. 24. PIAZZA DI PIETRA. ROME.

CHAPTER IX

TEMPLES, CHAPELS, SHRINES (*concluded*)

THERE are indeed very few subjects which are not regarded with entirely and often diametrically opposed views; this must be so and it is far better that it is so, because otherwise we would be condemned to utter monotony and stagnation. For instance, Music, embodied by Polytheism in Apollo, is regarded by some as an entrancing and refining sound and art, and musicians as interesting gifted persons, by others as a troublesome noise and its votaries as puerile, useless individuals. Hunting, personified by Diana, is for some an engrossing, invigorating pursuit, and for others a fatiguing and cruel sport. Militarism, or Mars, is held by some to be an element of order and discipline, war a field of glory and its professionals the representatives of courage; by others war is considered an immoral, bestial solution, the profession unproductive, and its members no braver than the average. Authority and Statesmanship, or Jupiter, by some viewed as a highly intellectual, elevated and indispensable calling, is by others considered a pernicious, intriguing business, and its professors mostly merely self-seekers. Physical beauty, or Venus, a rare and precious gift, productive of pleasure, soft emotions and satisfaction, or an ephemeral, animal snare, producing corruption and evil.

But perfect virility, the ideal of masculine strength, is liked by almost all and adored by many, for even those who are primarily intellectual admire this quality as expressed in their aphorism of " Mens sana in corpore sano." Therefore Hercules was an almost universal favourite and, though a demi-god, practically held brevet rank as the equal of any full-fledged deity of the first Order, except Jupiter, and in consequence had as great a number of temples, chapels, shrines and altars erected in his honour as any of the " Dei Majorem Gentium " or more, but nearly all have perished like those of the others. Among the few whose site has been identified is the Temple of Hercules Custos, the Custodian, which, as already mentioned, stood on one side of the Porta Capena, symbolic of the guardianship of the principal entrance of the Eternal City. The Temple of Hercules Musagetes, or Ludensis, the Muse or Sport Hercules, built 187 B.C. by the Censor Fabius Nobilior near the Circus Maximus in the demi-god's character of patron of athletic and other sports performed therein, was restored by Sylla and again reconstructed by L. Martius Philippus, step-father of Octavius, who surrounded it with a Porticus. Ovid and Martial both allude favourably to this temple.

The ancient city of Cora, between thirty and forty miles from Rome, possessed a temple erected by the Duumviri of Sylla's time and consecrated to Hercules, the ruins of which are the most striking of the antiquities of that town. The comparatively well-preserved remains on an elevated platform are those of a graceful and stately specimen of the Graeco-Roman Doric Order, probably one of the finest in existence, and consist of a pronaos of eight columns, four in front and two on each side, ending in two pilasters at the angles of the Temple wall, with the canonical entablature and the entrance door to the cella. The beauty and symmetry of this Temple impressed R. Sanzio, Palladio, and others so strongly that they devoted much time and care in several sittings to the study of this edifice, with the view of adopting it as a model for their instruction and imitation. As so frequently occurred this " Herculeum " was transformed later into a church which still contains a very fine antique altar carved with rams' heads and garlands of flowers and an equally handsome ancient vase, which was used later as a baptismal font. In 1899 a shrine dedicated to the demi-god was discovered near the Porta Portese of Rome, composed of a cave containing two small statues respectively of Hercules Victor and Hercules Cubans and seven diminutive busts of charioteers, now preserved in the National Museum of Rome.

Bacchus, Pluto, Proserpine, Ceres and Mercury had of course their edifices of worship, that have all equally vanished or nearly so. The present church of Sant' Urbano, not far from the vestiges of the Circumstadium Maxentii, was originally, it is stated, a Temple of Bacchus, identified by the name of a Bacchanalian priest inscribed on one of the columns and by a votive altar ornamented with a carved serpent, emblematic of the wisdom of the healing art he shared in a minor degree with Aesculapius. The tiger, the lynx, the ass and the goat were the favourite animals of Bacchus, and the latter his preferred sacrificial beast, possibly out of revenge, as the goat is the inveterate destroyer of the vine.

The worship of the other gods has waxed and waned, but Bacchus, in spite of the secular opposition from the Catoes of antiquity to the teetotallers and pussyfoots of our day, has traversed an interminable series of generations from Noah to us preserving his power, fascination and prestige over countless devotees, from Primates and Princes to the lowest strata, who have so practically proved their wholehearted devotion at such sacrifices to themselves and others in health, pocket, reputation, etc., to the jovial god, the curer often of the physically diseased, the consoler of the morally depressed, the bestower of a certain sort of courage nicknamed " Dutch," the mainstay of conviviality, etc. Indeed Bacchus can well afford to dispense with such purely material manifestations as temples and shrines, for his is a " spiritual " worship, and he is enshrined in the minds and hearts of his faithful and all-sacrificing followers.

The double Temple of Serapis and Isis formerly occupied the site of the present Via del Collegio Romano, and is said to have been a large and fine structure of Egyptian architecture and to have contained many objects of art, among which two surviving ones are noted—the recumbent figure of the Nile now in the Vatican and the Obelisk in the Villa Mattei—though the right to both is contested, the first by the Forum Vespasiani and the second by the Temple of Isis on the Capitoline Hill. Another temple to this goddess anciently stood on the juncture of the present Vie Macchiavelli and Labicana, near the Piscinae of Trajan's Baths, now known as the Sette Sale. In 1885 several fragments were unearthed here, among others the substantially intact statue of the Sacred Cow, Hathor. The first and second Christian centuries may be fixed approximately as the date of these and other buildings of Egyptian architecture in and about Rome,

TEMPLE OF HERCULES. CORA.

because before the Augustan era and after A.D. 200 this heterogeneous style was not much in vogue in the Eternal City and its environs.

The Mons Viminalis is the least known of the Seven Hills, its height originally, it is surmised, about 130 or 140 feet, is now lower, its area very problematically computed at 2½ square miles, because its limits cannot or have not been established precisely. There are two derivations offered for the name of this Hill, the one from "Vimen" or osiers, which grew in abundance thereon, and the other from "Vimen" or Caduceus of Mercury, who is said to have had a temple here, and there was also another to Sylvanus or Pan, two of the numerous vanished edifices of the Vicus Longus, the main thoroughfare that traversed the entire Mons Viminalis.

The Templum of Dea or Mater Matuta, by some supposed to be that of Hercules, commonly but erroneously known as the Temple of Vesta, in the ancient Forum Boarium, was undoubtedly of great antiquity, because we hear of a first restoration in 389 B.C. by M. Furius Camillus to commemorate the capture of Veii, which, like that of Troy, occurred after ten years' siege. The reason assigned for the selection or perhaps invention of this Matutinal Deity by Camillus, is that the surrender of the city took place in the morning. The small graceful temple we now see is, however, of a later period, built on the same spot and identical lines of the fabric of Camillus, of which only the podium survives. The present edifice, composed of white marble now thoroughly discoloured, measures about 156 feet in circumference, with a cella of twenty-six feet surrounded by nineteen fluted Corinthian columns out of the original twenty, of thirty-two feet in height, and its former marble cupola and decorated entablature is now substituted by a tiled roofing. The titular divinity was one of the numerous patronesses of childbirth, and some of the ritual ceremonies of her worship were rather peculiar. The feminine celebrants were not permitted to bring their own children here, but only those of their sisters, one female slave was alone admitted who was incontinently dismissed with a slap on the face, and it was forbidden for any woman once a widow, even if remarried, to place a garland on the head of the statue of the Goddess. This Templet was rededicated to Sta. Maria del Sole (St. Mary of the Sun) in obvious relation to its original titular "Matuta," as the rising of this planet heralds the beginning of the day.

The adjacent Temple of Fortune, to which is usually added the epithet "Virilis," was first erected by King Tullius Hostilus and rebuilt on the same shape and style during the closing years of the Republic by an anonymous constructor, mainly of tufo covered with stucco with the stylobate and projecting ornamental parts of travertine. The entablature was originally decorated in low relief with figures of children, oxen, candelabra and encarpus, which are scarcely discernible now. This Temple has twenty-two fluted Ionic columns twenty-five feet high, eighteen of which are Columnae Structiles, semi-attached columns, and the four of the portico entire detached columns. Though small and unpretending this Templet has two claims to interest: the one, that it is considered to be a canonical specimen of the Roman Pseudo-Peripteral, and the other, that it is one of the few genuinely ancient edifices now in Rome in a relatively good preservation; and if it were in the midst of harmonious surroundings instead of the mean buildings about, this Templet would make a most attractive picture. In A.D. 880 it was converted into a church and dedicated to Sta. Maria Egiziaca (St. Mary the Egyptian).

Its original titular Deity was credited with possessing a rare prerogative, that of blinding men's eyes to all the personal imperfections of the other sex; and though it is not specified that this power over the male vision extended to the mental and moral failings of women, or was limited merely to the physical, it would be, even in the latter case, an attribute exercising great influence in the intercourse of the sexes. Possibly this was the reason of the epithet " Virilis." In these conditions the fact that this particular Dea Fortuna was the object of sincere and especial adoration on the part of the matrons and maidens, particularly the latter, and that her rites were observed with exemplary zeal, need not of course surprise anyone. One ounce of luck is proverbially worth more, or rather is more profitable, than a ton of personal gifts; therefore to appear faultless is, so far as advantageous results go, to be faultless, and certainly this obscuring faculty, so pleasing to all around, the men no less than the women, was a decided piece of good luck, otherwise of Dea Fortuna.

At a short distance from the Porta Maggiore is the Porta Furba, and near the latter stands a covered mound commonly called Monte del Grano, said to be the burial-place of the Emperor Alexander Severus and his family, and though we do not hear of an Imperial Mausoleum being erected here, his sarcophagus, taken to the Capitoline Museum, and the famous Portland Vase were found on this spot. Near this mound are the ruins of the villa of Septimius Bassus, popularly known as the Sette Bassi, which included in its area the former " Aedes Fortuna Muliebris," a brick structure with pilasters and a mosaic pavement. A medal bearing a miniature reproduction of this Templet to Female Fortune proves that it was rebuilt by Faustina the younger, but the interest associated with it is chiefly historical, and though the event to which it owed its erection is known to readers of Roman history, it will bear repetition here as typical of the Romans of the time.

Gneus Martius, a scion of the patrician stock of the Martii, was distinguished for his ability and valour which were so conspicuously displayed in the capture of the Volscian city of Coriolo that gained for him the honorary agnomen of Coriolanus, by which he is best known to posterity. The Roman system of bestowing as a title the name of the place where the exploit had been performed, or of the achievement itself, or of a personal quality, was of a more elevated and useful character as a premium and an example than the mediæval and modern one of granting titles of nobility and knighthood unconnected in name with the service to the country, when indeed this is the only motive, which is not always the case, for the bestowal of honours.

This eminent man was never in favour with the plebs on account of his haughty bearing and of his uncompromising attitude with regard to the rights and privileges of the patriciate, and his open opposition to the gratuitous distribution of grain when there was no scarcity or other cogent reason to warrant the addition of so heavy a burthen on the State finances, brought his unpopularity with this class, or their demagogues, to a climax. On being summoned under pressure of popular clamour to justify his action on this occasion, he refused to appear, left Rome and was condemned in his absence. In response and retaliation for this sentence he allied himself with his former adversaries, the Volscians, and, being placed by them in command of their forces, his personality sufficed to change defeat into victory, for, after vanquishing the Romans sent against him, he led his men to the above spot near the city. It was remarked that though he ordered his army, as a military measure, to lay waste the country around Rome, the outlying estates of the patricians were respected. He had two reasons for this policy—first, that he did not intend to weaken that class which it had always been his principle to uphold, and secondly he wished to make it clear that he was not inimical to Rome but only to one class in Rome, that class of greater numbers but with the lesser brains and culture, who wanted to command when they were only fitted to obey.

While the citizens were a prey to consternation, especially the plebs whose ferocious courage evaporated very readily, as usual, at the enmity they had provoked, Valeria, a sister of the celebrated Publicola, while praying to Jupiter to avert the impending catastrophe, was suddenly struck by an idea that she took as an inspiration of the King of the Gods himself. This was to entreat Veturia, the mother of Gneus, Volumnia, his wife, and the matrons present performing their devotions with her, to go in a body to the camp of Coriolanus and implore him to spare Rome. This step, it was agreed, was to be kept secret because it was reasonably feared that the Senate would prohibit it, all the more as two embassies had been already despatched to Coriolanus, one of laymen, the other of clergymen, and both had been unsuccessful.

It was an unbending principle of the Conscript Fathers to refuse to treat with a foreign foe so long as he stood on Roman soil, but the above embassies to Martius did not constitute any infraction of this principle, firstly because he was not a foreigner, and therefore on the soil of his own country as well as theirs, and secondly because he was not warring against the whole Commonwealth but only against one of its classes.

In execution of her idea Valeria proceeded forthwith accompanied by the other ladies to Gneus' house, where they found his mother, wife and children, and revealed the project to them, pointing out that they might thus save their country and gain a greater glory than did the Sabine women by their memorable interposition between the Sabine and Roman armies. The mother and the wife of the conqueror consenting, they all went out to the besiegers' camp, where they were received with respect by the Volscian warriors and conducted to their chief, who on perceiving his mother and wife at the head of the procession ran forth to meet and embrace them. But Veturia motioned him back, requesting to know whether she was received as a mother or as a prisoner; she then asked him whether she was to consider herself and be looked upon by others as the unfortunate and accursed being who had borne and bred a son to destroy their own country, and whether he was bent on making it her duty to wish him unborn or dead, for in either case she would have lived a free and honoured matron in a free and honoured land. She added that for herself, kindly age combining with the shock his shame and her misery caused her, would quickly release her, but she urged him to think of his wife and children, of his relatives and friends, of his countrymen for whom and with whom he had governed and conquered, of the State he had improved and protected by his wisdom and patriotism, beseeching him not to sully his father's, his family's, and his own illustrious fame, and disgrace his class, a noble and patrician Order. Moreover, to bear in mind that he had now obtained a complete vindication and revenge by having proved to the Romans that he was as powerful as a friend as he was formidable as a foe, that with him they were strong and without him weak, and that to proceed further would be dooming their country to extinction in order to over-indulge in an already gratified vengeance on a mass of ignorant and misled plebeians.

When this great Roman matron had terminated her touching and elevated address, the wife and children of Gneus embraced him, and the other noble ladies knelt and implored his forbearance and mercy. At length he turned to his mother and said that she had conquered, that she had ruined her son but saved Rome, but from a penalty only as he had never intended to destroy but only to correct, and as he believed her chastisement would have been productive of excellent results eventually. But that out of affection for her and veneration for the names of his forefathers, because as regarded his wife and children it was their duty and he was sure their wish to follow him, he had decided to sacrifice everything else. But more than that, he intended the sacrifice to be complete and greater than his mother, wife and the others had asked for, that, therefore, he did not demand terms, guarantees or advantages for himself or his allies, which he was in a position to impose, and would not only withdraw his army forthwith unconditionally, but further engage that while he lived there would be no more hostilities on his part or that of the Volscians. That, with regard to himself, he was determined never to return to Rome, but to give up his property, prospects and family, and retire a voluntary exile to another land and people, those that had recognized and espoused his righteous cause. All this was fulfilled to the letter, and, after having returned his mother's, wife's and children's embrace, so dearly bought, he ordered his army to retire, while the cortége of ladies returned to Rome as the saviours of their country.

The initiative of Valeria, the action of Veturia and the co-operation of Volumnia, at such a cost to herself, on the one hand, and the full and unrestricted surrender of all his desires and interests in so generous a spirit by Coriolanus, on the other, furnish one of the many bright examples of Roman private and public virtue, of self-sacrificing and high-minded respect and love of country, lineage and family ties. The patrician and the conqueror sacrificed like the wife and the mother all they respectively held most precious for the sake of high principles.

The Senate, as usual doing the right thing at the right time and way, officially requested these matrons to choose for themselves the recompense they preferred without limitations, and they replied disinterestedly that they begged the Conscript Fathers to give them permission to erect at their own expense a temple in commemoration, in which they would be allowed to serve as priestesses. It is needless to add that their application was granted, the first High-priestess appointed being Valeria, and this was the origin of the " Aedes Fortuna Muliebris."

The Templet of Vesta at Tivoli, similar in general aspect and plan with the afore-noted Templum Dea Matuta, is usually but unfoundedly termed the Temple of the Sibyl, probably because the Tiburtine Sibyl Albunea was a conspicuous figure of Tivoli. The beautiful and striking situation of this small, graceful temple on a cliff overlooking the cascades, the woody, hilly region of infinite variety and the townlet around, are equalled harmoniously by the exquisite proportions and style of the ruin. Of the eighteen travertine columns which encircled the cella of opus incertus, ten are still standing; the frieze is tastefully ornamented with sculptured rams' heads alternating with festoons. Though it has been conjectured that this Templet was erected during the reign of

TEMPLE OF VESTA. TIVOLI.

Plate xxi.

Octavius, the exact date of its construction, as well as the name of its constructor, have not been ascertained.

Not far from this structure there stood another oblong religious edifice, likewise of travertine, with pilasters and a portico of four Ionic columns, supposed to have been dedicated to Tiburtus, founder, or rather refounder, of Tibur or Tivoli, named after him on account of a tomb found inside with the figure of a man, evidently of rank, in the habiliments of the times of Tiburtus, and with the allegorical effigy of the river Anio. According to Dyonisius of Harlicarnassus, who was a painstaking and accurate writer, Tivoli was originally founded by a colony of Siculi, by whom it was called Sikelion at a period prior to the birth of Rome. The second founders were Catulus I, a Theban Prince, descendant of Amphoras, King of Thebes, and his three sons, Tiburtus, Coras and Catulus. Coras has not left apparently any known trace of his presence, but the memory of Catulus is preserved in Monte Catulo, and that of Tiburtus in the name of the townlet Tibur.

Though Sibyl and Sibylline are terms frequently used by the cultured little or nothing is generally known concerning their historical or legendary origin, or the attributes and functions of their Collegium which so greatly influenced the destinies of the world. The word "Sibylla" is derived from the Greek verb "Sivyllo," to whisper, to prompt, to counsel. The Greek author Pausanius, of the second Christian century, describes the Sibyls as virgins born with the prophetic spirit. According, however, to M. Terrentius Varro, Virgil and others, they possessed, besides the divining faculties, also the Bacchanalian and Apollonian qualities. The number of these precursors of the mediæval witches and the modern clairvoyants was of course great, but the official Sibyls who counted as a power in the State were ten—namely, Cuma, Delphica, Eretria, Cumana, Persica, Lybica, Ellespontica, Erigia, Samica and Tiburtina. The Presidentess was the Cuma Sibyl either of Cuma in Campania or of Cuma in Ionia.

It is important to note that with the introduction of Christianity the belief in these prophetesses did not cease, for we hear of their predictions regarding the birth of the Messiah and of the triumph of the New Faith. The Tiburtine Sibyl foretold the advent of Christ, and this is the subject of a famous fresco by Baldassare Peruzzi, and another scene often represented in canvas, marble and metal, is that of the Sibyl who offered to King Tarquinius Priscus the Sibylline Books, first nine in number, and on his refusal, burning three of them, then six volumes, three of which were likewise rejected and burned, and then the remaining three Books were proffered and acquired at the same terms asked for the entire number. It appears that for a long time the identity of the above Sibyl was a disputed question, but, after some controversy, it was established to be that of the Cumana Sibyl, otherwise Amaltea, Demophila or Erophila, as she is indiscriminately referred to by either of these names. In the Church of Sta. Maria della Pace in Rome there is to be seen in excellent preservation the justly celebrated painting of four of the Sibyls by R. Sanzio.

The Sibylline Books contained the "Fata Urbis Romae," or the Destiny of the City of Rome, and as their sentences were applicable to every event that occurred, they were consulted systematically. These fateful Books were kept, as has been mentioned, in the Metropolitan Temple of Jovis Capitolinus, in charge of the College, originally composed of two members, called "Collegium Duumviri Sacris Faciendis," was successively increased to ten "Decemviri," with two presidents, and then to fifteen "Quindicemviri," with five presidents, all drawn from the Patrician Order, but by a subsequent reformation, or deformation, according to the views with which similar changes are regarded, divided equally between the three Orders of the State. They were all life members, exempted from military service, and usually chosen from those who had held high public offices. Under the Imperial régime, all powers being concentrated in one individual, the number of the Collegium fluctuated, and the Emperor was the *ex officio* Magister or President with a Pro-Magister or Vice-President to assist or replace him.

The functions of these officials consisted principally in the custody of the Sibylline Books, regarding the contents of which absolute secrecy was rigorously enforced, in copying them with their own hands whenever a new addition became necessary, in examining and judging relatively to the legitimacy and orthodoxy of any new work in connection, and in interpreting any sentence or sentences, when authorized to do so by the Senate. The Sibyls being of Greek origin the language adopted in the Books was Greek in hexameter, wherefore two linguistic interpreters or translators were always attached to the personnel of the Collegium. The earlier sentences were inscribed on "Libri Palmes," Palm-Books, and the later on "Libri Lentii," Linen-Books. It is noteworthy that neither these prophetesses nor the members of the Collegium had any connection with, or place in, the Hierarchy.

Regarding the "Aedes Magnae Matris Deorum," Great Mother of the Gods, otherwise Cybele, Consiva, or Ops, on the Palatine, nothing more has been gathered than that it was circular with a cupola, and contained the statue of the Goddess with the sharply-pointed conically-shaped stone called "Acus Matris Deorum" set on the shoulders, which is the peculiar headpiece of this divinity instead of the usual head, and that there was also, according to Tacitus, a painting inside depicting the Cybelline priests.

These clergymen had three distinctive apellations: "Corybantes" composed from the Greek "Kyripto" and "Veno," to move the head and to walk, "Carete" from "Kura," tonsure, and "Datuli," from "Thactila," fingers, because they were imagined to have been borne by means of the pressure of this Goddess' digits, when she was hiding on Mount Ida, in Crete. Among their rites was striking violently on bronze targets so as to produce a deafening noise that arose from the following curious origin:

One of the articles of faith was that Saturn, spouse of Cybele and sire of Jupiter, Neptune and Pluto, was not such an absorbingly tender father as to subordinate everything to the paternal character. In his divine capacity he foresaw that he would have trouble with his progeny, that they would on reaching adult age rebel against him and try to dethrone him, as he himself had done by his own father Uranus. To prevent this unfilial conduct on their part, with its accompanying undesirable results to himself, he thought it expedient to nip the evil in the bud by eating the infant Jupiter to begin with. Cybele, however, with all her attachment to her spouse and wish to maintain their power, demurred at this drastic treatment of their offspring, and accordingly gave Saturn stones to swallow instead of the toothsome baby, which it seems he did with all the satisfaction arising from a successful accomplishment of a wise act of policy and without apparently a sign of indigestion, a mighty gastronomical feat impossible to any but a superhuman, the only hitch being that the trick could not succeed if after the heavy meal, the cries of the infant were audible.

So long as the baby Jupiter was good, as nurses phrase it, otherwise quiet, all went well, but when he began to cry the danger of discovery returned, with its consequences. So whenever the divine infant commenced squalling the priests drowned his probably inharmonious voice by the louder cacophony produced by hammering violently on the bronze targets. Saturn, not hearing the customary yellings at intervals, concluded that no baby existed in his family, because no one not even it seems, a god, could imagine such an unheard-of miracle as a baby that never made any inharmonious noise. The result of this benevolent fraud of Cybele was not altogether bad even from Saturn's point of view, because though Jupiter did eventually rebel and assume supreme authority by force, Saturn retained great power and prestige even after that event.

The Sibylline Books, sometimes productive of tragical consequences, as in the instances mentioned in the Forum Boarium, had, generally speaking, an innocuous or beneficial influence. Their contents in reference to Cybele and Hannibal may be quoted as a case in point. One of their sentences was officially interpreted as a declaration that so long as the Acus (the symbolic form of this Goddess) was not transferred to Rome, the great Carthagenian would never be vanquished, and, moreover, only on condition that the miraculous relic was consigned to, conveyed and deposited in its place in the Eternal City by the worthiest and most virtuous man and by a woman of absolute chastity —that is, by the two stainless representatives of the two sexes, only the male's qualifications had to be positive and the female's negative.

The precious Acus was in Phrygia in the possession of King Attalus, an ally of Rome, who, having consented to deliver it up to the Romans, P. Cornelius Scipio, a cousin of the renowned Africanus, was unanimously recognized as the possessor of the above rare qualities and accordingly deputed, 204 B.C., as Envoy Extraordinary, to receive and bring the wonderful relic to Rome. He performed this mission to Attalus successfully and conducted his sacred cargo up the Tiber till the vessel stranded, where the Vestal Claudia was summoned to draw it up the river by a rope. This Vestal, it is added, was labouring under a suspicion of having violated her vows, it may be assumed in some other direction than that of chastity, and she was offered this opportunity of clearing herself, and the test proved successful, because she towed the vessel to its destination without a hitch. This episode has been illustrated in various productions, and among others there are two reliefs representing it respectively in the Vatican and the Capitoline Museums.

Hannibal, after his marvellous many years' campaign in a distant enemy country against the whole power of Rome, unsupported and frequently opposed and thwarted by his own countrymen, at length loosened his mighty grasp and relinquished his prey, only to depart to defend his compatriots at home, who were commercially, manufacturally and colonially capable but politically inept, morally without high ideals, and stupidly and shamefully ungrateful to him to their own detriment and ultimate destruction. The struggle was thus practically terminated, the great State had conquered the great man, the superior race without a genius to lead it had gained the mastery over the genius alone heading the inferior race. The miraculous prediction of the Sibylline Books was therefore fulfilled, and the Temple of Cybele, on the Palatine, consecrated 191 B.C. The discovery here of a headless sitting statue of the Goddess propped up against the wall helped to identify the site of this ancient structure, but except for this and a few fragments of columns also near the walled mound crowned with a clump of trees, there are no vestiges of it now.

In one of the valleys or hollows that abound in the undulating Campagna, called Valle della Caffarella, there is a small, quaint rectangular brick building approached by a flight of steps with hexagonal Corinthian pilasters in the niches of the walls externally and an interior of two stories of groined vaulting, which is by some authorities pronounced to be the Mausoleum Herodes and by others the Temple of the God Redens (God of Return). If we accept the second version, this structure was erected in grateful recognition of the titular Deity's signal service in dissuading Hannibal, who had reached this spot, from besieging or assaulting Rome, the God Redens having, in addition to his spiritual arguments, also sent a material providential hailstorm. Although it is a well-built, comely little fabric, and we hear studied by the Rebirth artists, it does not seem a befitting memorial for the enormous service rendered by a God, moreover, little indebted to the Romans who had never previously shown him any veneration or even recognition, and who was probably invented for the occasion.

Anyhow, the above miraculous interpretation of Hannibal's apparently inexplicable retirement in the full tide of success, did quite well for the consumption of the plebs, for whom it was intended, but could hardly recommend itself to any individual then or now of average sense and knowledge. In consequence other reasons were suggested for the "intelligentia" for this sudden departure of the formidable foe. For instance, that the Roman Authorities had decreed the sale of the land outside the city occupied by the invader, as if they had already recovered it, and that an army had been despatched from Rome to Spain, at this moment. But Hannibal, being a master of statecraft and strategy himself, could hardly have been deceived by these rather transparent devices, considering, too, that the first was a replica response to his own previous proclamation of the sale of various quarters of the Eternal City itself as if already captured, and as for the second, as he had defeated a very short time before, with great slaughter, the Roman armies sent against him, and as he also knew the man-resources of Rome, he could by a simple calculation be sure that the said expeditionary force to Spain was, if not quite a phantom army, at any rate a simulacrum, otherwise what is now colloquially and somewhat vulgarly termed "Bluff."

Hannibal, being a profound Statesman, had conceived much broader and greater plans than a mere military chief would have been capable of. He knew and estimated as a consummate general to an iota the capabilities of his motley army, the main strength of which lay in the cavalry, and this arm, excellently fitted when handled by him, preeminently a cavalry officer, to deal sudden, dazzling and even deadly and decisive blows on the battlefield, was ill adapted or equipped for a siege or even an assault on a fortified city. In consequence he used the instrument he possessed incomparably in defeating the Romans in the open field, and the Statesman had to accomplish the remaining and more important part of his programme. He calculated that the moral affect of his striking victories would be twofold: internally, that is in all Italy, the discontented elements, submissive to what they thought the invincible power of Rome, would rise against her once, or rather thrice vanquished, and for this he treated well and liberated all prisoners taken by him who were not Romans; externally, that is the foreign free States, Macedon in particular, would, he concluded, seize this unique opportunity of asserting themselves and securing their independence by coalescing with him to overthrow the dominant and growing power of Rome.

Therefore to capture the Seven-hilled City then with his army alone had never entered his calculations at the time, and his approach to Rome was rather in the nature of a demonstration to show how he had humbled her. If none of the peoples of Italy or of foreign States possessed his foresight and broadness of view and failed towards him and their own interests, either by opposing or by abstaining or by offering a belated and insufficient support, that does not diminish the greatness of his project, but only proves their inferiority—that is, that they were too small and backward even to understand his superiority or to grasp the situation.

Evidently fate had decided otherwise—that is to say, that the downfall of Rome was to come later and by her own hand, a national suicide, to be accomplished when she had fulfilled her mission, which was that the Roman spirit, and not the Phoenician or any other, was destined to exercise a paramount influence in the universe, and that fate had so decreed seems corroborated in this case by Hannibal's own words, "that he was alternately deprived of the 'power' and of the 'will' to deal the Eternal City her death blow." And much as we must admire this extraordinary man, the greatest of his great family and that Carthage ever produced, his disinterested patriotism, his unsurpassed statesmanship, his splendid generalship, his chivalry, his resourcefulness, his unconquerable spirit and magnetic influence over those he led or with whom he came in contact, it was best probably that he was ultimately unsuccessful—in other words, that the Phoenician spirit did not become predominant.

The decline followed by the fall of the Aristo-democratic institutions of the Roman Republic was accompanied by the decay of belief in Pagan Polytheism, as originally established, because the men who had usurped all the powers of the State also began to share with the Gods the honours of worship. Hence the first temple erected to a mortal in Rome was that of Octavius to Cesar, 42 B.C., and dedicated to the latter, 29 B.C., thus coinciding chronologically with the definite overthrow of the Republic.

The Aedes Divi Julii was built in the Roman Forum close to the Rostra Julia. It was of the Ionic Order but with a Corinthian Porticus facing the Forum Square, contained an altar and a portrait of Venus Anathyomene (Undressed Venus) painted by no less a personage than Apelles, and having in front an Honorary Column of Giallo Antico dedicated to Cesar, bearing the laconic epigraph of "Parenti Patriae," a phrase then as yet unprostituted, with the statue of the Dictator on the summit. Some faint idea of the Columna Caesaris might be conveyed by the half-effaced relief on one of Trajan's screens, but a somewhat better one is furnished by the miniature reproduction of the Templet and Column on the coins of Octavius and Trajan. The marble of these works, like those of the greater portion of the Temple of Castor and Pollux, were burned into lime by the Farnese Potentates.

The site of the Templum Divi Augusti adjoining the Bibliotheca Augusti, is now occupied by the ruins of the church of Sta. Maria Antiqua in the Roman Forum, and was commenced by Livia and Tiberius to be terminated by Caligula, the third Roman Emperor. Damaged by fire during the Neronian conflagration of A.D. 64, it was rebuilt by Domitian, who, whatever his faults, delinquencies and sins, was a notable and talented restorer and constructor. It was again recreated by Hadrian on the customary splendid style that distinguished his works.

The exact dimensions and divisions of these two joint edifices, temple and library, have not been ascertained despite the ruins, excepting the vestibule, measuring, it is said, 105 by 20 feet, but it is evident that these buildings were lofty and relatively extensive. There were two façades and two porticos, the one on the Via Etruscus consisting of eight columns and a colossal statue of Octavius, to which was afterwards added the galaxy of those of his deified successors, with the pronaos and cella, the present remains of which are the wrecked brick walls entered by the archway. The other façade and portico, lined with tabernae, fronted the Forum Square, and gave egress to the above Bibliotheca Publica, not to be confounded with the Bibliotheca Imperialis of Augustus on the Palatine. This public library consisted of the Peristylium, Atrium and Aula backed by the Triclinium and Alae of the apartment assigned to the "Curator Palatii."

The Atrium of the Bibliotheca was transformed later into the nave and aisles of the aforesaid Byzantine Church of Sta. Maria Antiqua, and the Triclinium and Alae into the Presbytery and side chapels. This disfiguring transmutation of the ancient library occurred probably during the sixth Christian century, and the frescoes, of the typical Byzantine style, which is equivalent to saying that they are by no means attractive or artistic, are attributed to the Greek monks who escaped and took refuge here from the persecutions of the Iconoclasts (from Icon, image, and Klastis, breaker) who in that epoch exhibited extraordinary activity in their fanatical and mischievous destructiveness.

The Templum Panthaeum, the temple "All Godly" or "Of all the Gods," because "Pan," all, and "Thaeum," Gods or Godly, signifies both, was constructed by Marcus Vipsansius Agrippa, 27 B.C., originally as a section of his Baths here; but shortly after he detached this hall and converted it into a temple, adding a pronaos with the intention of dedicating it to his deified father-in-law Octavius. But the latter, faithful to his systematic dissimulation of feigned moderation and modesty for the edification of the public, refused the honour as he consistently did all other distinctions provided they did not carry with them substantial advantages. This temple was therefore at the Emperor's initiative consecrated instead to the Gods and Goddesses of the Seven Planets, viz., Jupiter, Saturn, Diana, Mars, Mercury, Venus and Apollo, Jupiter being the titular.

In conformity with the statutory canons regulating Pagan worship, a temple could only be dedicated to a single titular Deity, and if vowed to two, as for instance Mars and Venus, Serapis and Isia, etc., then there were two joint structures, which though under one dome, had separate entrances and were in all other respects distinct buildings. There was also a third category termed "Delubrum," which while containing sacelli (shrines) for the worship of other divinities, were nonetheless dedicated to one titular, precisely as in the Roman Catholic churches, consecrated to the Saviour, the Virgin Mary, or to one Saint, that also possess minor side-chapels or shrines assigned to others. Consequently the Panthaeum, intended for the God Octavius, and failing him, the carnal living Divinity,

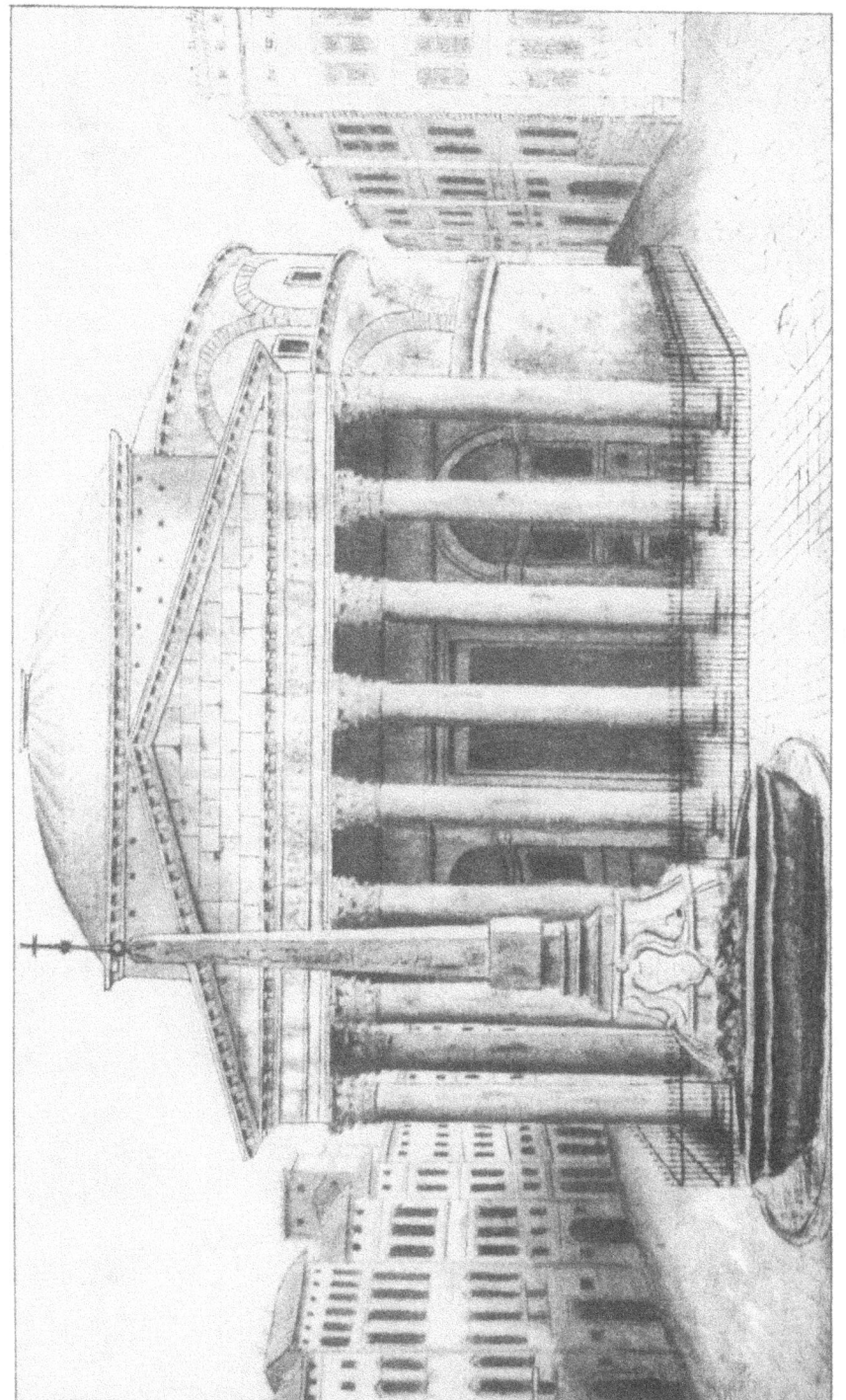

PANTHEON, B.C. 27. PIAZZA DELLA ROTONDA.

Plate xxii.

was dedicated to Jupiter the "All Godly," as the presiding God at the Ara Maxima or High Altar, with shrines for the other deities.

Unless therefore we accept the hypothesis that the then obsequious priesthood of the period had granted a dispensation for the omnipotent Ruler, who declined " to be called " but not " to be " Emperor, permitting the infraction of the canonical nomenclature of temples in this case, we may assume that the meaning of " Panthaeum " relatively to this Temple signifies " All Godly " and not " All the Gods," especially as only seven of them were specifically named, as we see above.

This edifice, measuring 396 feet in circumference, was not originally below or level with the street, but approached by steps, now covered by the risen soil and pavement, which obviously added to its imposing aspect. The pronaos, 100 by 44 feet, is adorned by sixteen monolith Corinthian columns with shafts of Elba granite and capitals of white marble, 45 feet high by 5 in diameter, of which eight form the front series and the other eight divided into four on each side in double rows, both sides having niches formerly containing the statues of Octavius and Agrippa. These columns and entablature, on account of their strictly canonical design and proportions, have been taken as the model of the Roman Corinthian Order. The tympan was decorated with reliefs and the vault formerly coated with bronze also in reliefs. There are three inscriptions on the frieze, the brief earliest one, recarved in 1898, refers to the erector as follows: " M. AGRIPPA. L. E. CONSUL. TERTIUM. FECIT"; the second records the restoration effected by Septimius and Caracallus and runs thus: " Panthaeum vetustate corruptus cum culta resituerunt" with the two Emperors' names, the third complacently eulogizes the plunder of the building by Pope Urbanus VIII, though in justice it must be recalled that, as an inadequate compensation, this Pontiff replaced three of the missing columns which may be identified by the family cognizance of the " Three Bees." Nearly a century previously to the Septimian restoration this building, having been much damaged by lightning, was restored by Hadrian.

The circular cella of equal diameter and height, 142 feet, was lighted from the summit by a single central aperture furnished with the movable disk of bronze, called the " Clypus." The dome consisted of a core of concrete covered externally with plates of chiselled, gilded bronze and internally by a casing of rare marbles, porphyry, serpentine and luna, inlaid with silver. The supporting fluted columns of Marmor Numidicum, excepting four of Phrygian marble, with shafts 29 feet in height, were intersected by niches containing statues of the Deities, the central one being, of course, Jupiter's, and above rose semi-circular arches sustained by Caryatides, the whole surmounted by the moulded bronze cornice running round the cella with bronze tubes at intervals reaching to the roofing. The walls were lined with costly marbles and chased silver like the dome, and the pavement was composed of granite and variegated marbles.

This temple, though not one of the largest, admittedly one of the finest of antiquity, has been reduced by spoliation and neglect to the structure we now behold with its scarred dingy columns, walls and pavement, and the ignoble roof, and yet even thus it stands as a specimen of the admirable work of a bygone generation. But besides its historical and aesthetic value the Panthaeum has the privilege of being the sole monumental edifice of Roma Vetus which preserves something of a resemblance to its original state, because, quite exceptionally, the bronze doors and cornice have been left *in situ* as well as the walls, vaulting and colonnades, internal and external, all standing still coherently together, although the building has been defaced, mutilated and reduced. In other words, most of the fundamental substance has remained, but much of the costly material, lustre and beauty has departed.

After the fall of Paganism this temple, like others, was abandoned till A.D. 391, when it was definitely closed. Over two centuries later the Emperor Phoca presented it as a donation to Pope St. Boniface IV, who consecrated the whilom many-godded Pagan Temple into the many-sainted Christian Church, dedicating it to Sta. Maria ad Martyres in A.D. 609, on which occasion twenty-eight wagon loads of martyrs' bones from the catacombs were transported here, and it was to this protective transmutation that this building owes mainly its comparative immunity from ruin. The Emperor Constans III, A.D. 641–668, however, relieved the Temple-Church of many of its silver and bronze decorations by taking them for his palace at Constantinople, but on his return journey from Rome the despoiler was in his turn despoiled and moreover killed in Sicily, and many of the spoils found their way back to the countries from which they had been taken six centuries earlier by Octavius and brought to Rome.

In A.D. 1087 the Panthaeum was temporarily fortified and used as a stronghold by the Anti-Pope Guibert in his struggle against Pope Victor III. The latter was one of the Pontiffs supported by the alliance of the celebrated Matilde, Marchioness of Tuscany, Modena and Ferrara who was one of the mainstays of the Guelph or Papal party against the Ghibelline or Imperial, and a woman of strong will and intellect. In consideration of her services Urban VIII had the remains of this staunch adherent of Papacy exhumed at the Convent of San Benedetto di Pontino, near Mantova, and transferred to St. Peter's Cathedral in Rome, where he had the monument erected to her memory. Popes Martino V, Eugenius IV and Gregory V made some attempts at extricating the building from the accumulated overlaying rubbish and at a partial restoration, and Gregory III is responsible for the leaden roof, if that be accounted as a restoration.

The above-mentioned Urbanus VIII (Maffio Barberini), A.D. 1623–1641, replaced, as has already been said, the missing columns of the pronaos, effected some other repairs and had the roofing disfigured by the addition of two hideous belfries, known in derision as Bernini's Ass' Ears, because that artist was employed to erect them, and they were fortunately removed in 1885. This Pope was one of the chief plunderers of the temple, taking away much that his precursors in pillage had left. The bronze tubes and the gilt-bronze coating of the vault of the pronaos, were used by him for the present Tabernacle of St. Peter's of the Four Fathers of the Church—Augustine, Ambrose, Athanasius and Chrysostom—and for making eighty, or as some affirm, one hundred, pieces of cannon placed in the Castel Sant' Angelo. Benedict XIV (Prospero Lambertini), A.D. 1740–1758, took likewise his share in the spoliation by stripping off much of the marble lining.

Pope Urban VIII, who is to this day a well-remembered and prominent figure among the Romans, was as remarkable for his creative energy as for his destructive activity and rapacity, but, as is generally the case, the distinctive vices remained more forcibly impressed than the distinctive virtues, and were embodied in Pasquino's epigram which mellowed into the well-known Roman proverb " Quod non facerunt Barbari id

Plate *xxiii.*

TEMPLE OF ANTONINUS AND FAUSTINA, A.D. 142. ROMAN FORUM.

facerunt Barberini," in allusion to his surname, to signify that this Pontiff and his family outdid the Barbarians themselves. But it is fair to acknowledge that if by his high-handed and grasping methods of government he enriched and elevated his family, he only followed in this the system then almost universally and openly adopted (though not perhaps always with the same consistency and thoroughness) by those in power, Spiritual and Temporal, and if he signalized himself as a wholesale and ubiquitous ravager of historical monuments, he was also, according to his lights, a creator and restorer for the Church's benefit and that of the public, as well as for his own fame and his family's aggrandisement. The evidences of his handiwork in these two opposite directions are to be met with in Rome, and it is not altogether his fault, but rather that of the times, that he could not unfortunately indemnify by any works of equal merit those he had helped to destroy.

The Panthaeum became, in the course of time, the burial-place of artists. The third chapel to the right contains three tombs, the one in the centre of Raffaele Sanzio, with those of Taddeo Zucchari and Annibale Caracci on either side. The celebrated artists Giovanni da Udine, Baldassare Peruzzi, Pierino del Vaga and others are likewise interred here. Close to the first-named three tombs was buried Maria, Cardinal Bibbiana's niece, whom Sanzio refused to marry out of love, it is said, of the Fornarina, though the latter, from what has been gathered, seems to have been a very commonplace woman, who only gained a reflected renown through his fame as a painter. With regard to the other candidate, Maria, little is known except that, being a Cardinal's niece, she was well dowered. Several Popes and Cardinals were remarkably prolific in nephews and nieces, and from the marked favour shown them by their uncles in power arose the term "Nepotism" to signify a family favouritism. Near the High Altar is a monument to Cardinal Gonsalvo, Minister of State to Pope Pius VII, the work of Thorwaldsen.

At Pentecost the Popes frequently officiated *in propria persona* formerly in this Church, when it was customary to shower down rose leaves on the congregation in symbolic representation of the Holy Spirit descending on them. This Temple-Church, on which of late years care has been bestowed, has since the unification of Italy been adopted as the Mausoleum of the reigning House of Savoy, and already three members—namely, the two first Sovereigns of Italy of this Dynasty—have been interred here under their sarcophagi, Victor Emanuel II of Sardinia and I of Italy, A.D. 1848–1878, and Humbert I of Italy, A.D. 1878–91, and in 1925 Queen Margherita, consort of Humbert I.

The Temple of Claudius on the Caelian Hill has been mentioned, and though we do not hear that Tiberius, Caligula or Nero had temples erected to them as gods, it is quite probable that they received or took this honour, with the exception, perhaps, of the saturnine Tiberius.

The Temple of Vespasian, at the foot of the Capitoline, between the Portico of the Twelve Gods and the Temple of Concord, was built by Domitian to his father, A.D. 94, on a raised platform in the form of a Corinthian, or, as some say, a composite Hexastyle with a quadrangular cella, and it was restored by the Emperors Antoninus and Severus as was recorded by the inscription on the entablature, " Divo Vespasiano Augusto Senatus Polusque Romanus: Imperatores Antoninus et Severus Pii Felices Augusti restituerunt " of which only the " unt " the last syllable is decipherable now. That this was a beautiful edifice is guaranteed by the proved ability of the creator and attested by the three handsome fractured original columns and entablature *in situ*, and by a fragment of the frieze preserved in the Capitoline Museum. Of the Temple of Trajan the only reliable record is, remarkably enough, limited so far as we know, to its name alone.

The Temple of Antoninus and Faustina in the Roman Forum, between the Chapel of Romulus and the Basilica Aemilia, was erected A.D. 141 by the Senate as the inscription reads to " DIVO ANTONINO ET DIVAE FAUSTINAE." The twenty-five steps that led up to the platform on which the Temple stands bordering the Via Sacra, were taken away in A.D. 1364 by Pope Urban V and adopted for repairing San Giovanni in Laterano, and the marble casing of the entire edifice was used in the Fabbrica di San Pietro in A.D. 1540. The main part including the cella was converted into the present Church of San Lorenzo in Miranda, A.D. 1602, and the actual genuine remains of the temple consist of a pronaos of ten Corinthian columns of cipollino, the favourite marble of the Antonines, 43 feet in height, sustaining a canonical entablature with a frieze ornamented with griffins and candelabra, and a portion of the walls denuded of their marble coating. This is one of the best preserved of the classic monuments of the Eternal City.

The adjacent Chapel of Romulus, " Aedes or Aedicula ad Divo Romuli," was constructed by the Emperor Maxentius A.D. 306–312, and dedicated to his son Romulus, like the other one of the Circustadium Maxentii, but it was rebuilt and altered into the present Church of the Saints Cosimo and Damiano overlooking the Forum. This church, similarly to so many others, was divided into two sections, an upper and a lower. The lower, now subterranean, otherwise the crypt, was originally the Cella of the Temple and was adopted by Pope Felix IV, A.D. 526–530, for the church. The upper was built much later by Urban VIII, who had the level of the soil raised artificially for the purpose. The façade of the ancient Aedicula had been adorned with Corinthian Cipollino columns, of which one is nearly intact, part of the shaft of another, both with their pedestals, and two more columnless pedestals with some fragments around, are all that survive of this chapel now. As Maxentius was one of the two last great Emperor-builders, and this Aedicula was erected by him in honour of his son, to whom he was evidently extremely attached, it was doubtless a work worthy of admiration, and it is to be regretted that we know so little about it.

TEMPLE OF VESPASIAN, A.D. 94. FOOT OF CAPITOLINE HILL.
Plate xxiv.

CHAPTER X
WALLS AND GATES

ROME, like the majority of ancient cities, was surrounded by walls, which in those times served as defensive fortifications much more effectively than they do at present. There were two distinct city boundaries recognised by the Romans. The material "Murus," or "Moenia," with its "Aggeres" or mound-ramparts and the spiritual "Pomoerium," a term derived from "Post-Moerium" (after or beyond the walls). This religious circle was consecrated by the Augurs and thus rendered holy ground, wherein they consulted the will of the Gods, and which it was prohibited to inhabit, cultivate or otherwise use. This constituted the legal circuit also, that is, only that portion of the town buildings which were within its limits were considered the "Sacra Urbs," Sacred City, and the permanent residents thereof, the "Civis," or citizen. The Pomoerium could only be extended or removed by one who had previously also extended the confines of the State, and then subject to the authorization of the Pontifex Maximus. Sylla, Cesar, Octavius, Claudius and Trajan all exercised this privilege with the approval, as above, of the religious authorities.

Whatever may be our opinion relatively to the value of this religious circle from a moral or spiritual point of view, there can be presumably only one as to its beneficial effects in respect to the health of the inhabitants. Public parks, especially in overcrowded cities, are rightly called the "city lungs," but these were substituted in antiquity by the Fora and the Nemus of the temples. The Pomoerium did, however, more than this, it was a broad belt of land round the inhabited area covered with groves of trees growing wild, free from every pollution, the whole being kept scrupulously clean, and thus functioning as a sanitary cordon of the city and therefore combining the advantages of town with the naturally more hygienic properties of the country.

The terms "Augur" and "Auruspicis" with their derivations, though frequently used, do not generally convey more than a hazy notion of their original meaning, if, indeed, many trouble themselves to attach any meaning whatsoever. Nonetheless it would be more sensible and ought to be more satisfactory to know the origin and significance of the words we employ, and in consequence a brief notice relatively may be acceptable. The title or epithet of Augur was originally bestowed on men credited with the power of divination by means of watching and interpreting the actions of birds, such as their flight and song, but later it was applied in a wider and more important sense. The Collegium Auguralis was composed, under Romulus, of three members, under Numa of five, under Tarquinius Priscus of nine, under Sylla of fifteen, and during the Empire the number was not fixed.

The Augral dignity has been described by Cicero, himself an Augur, as endowed with great privileges and consideration. Their principal duties consisted in the observation and explanation of supernatural occurrences, signs and omens, in the supervision of everything appertaining to ceremonial and ritual regulations and laws, and in the consecration of religious edifices, of the Pomoerium and of all places to be rendered sacred. It was their prerogative to suspend all public deliberations, elections or assemblies, until the inaugural rites had been previously performed, the omission of which rendered, *per se*, the discussions and decisions illegal and invalid. In the old medals the members of this Corporation are represented attired in a long and ample cloak over their robes which covered their heads and hung from the left shoulder to their knees, holding the "Litius," or curved stick, somewhat resembling a pastoral staff, only shorter, in the right hand, and the "Capis," a large drinking vessel of clay, beside them. This institution was abolished definitely by Theodosius, A.D. 379–395.

The Auruspices were likewise diviners, only their science consisted in interpreting the will of the Gods from the aspect of the intestines (Orta) of the animals sacrificed and from the thunder and lightning and other phenomena of nature. They were held as inferior to the Augurs, and never included in the hierarchy or constituted into a Collegium. Nevertheless it seems that this branch of divination, attributed to Tagetes as the founder, its professors like him being usually Etruscans, was held in considerable estimation by the Romans, as we hear that the Senate sometimes consulted them.

In the course of twenty-four centuries the walls of the Eternal City were built and rebuilt seven times, not counting, of course, partial repairs and extensions, and her chief mural constructors were namely as follows: 1st, King Romulus, 753–716 B.C.; 2nd, King Servius Tullius, 578–534 B.C.; 3rd, Emperor Aurelianus, A.D. 270–275; 4th, Emperor Honorius, A.D. 395–423; 5th, General Belisarius, A.D. 546–558; 6th, Pope Leo IV, A.D. 847–855; and 7th, Pope Urbanus VIII, A.D. 1623–1644. Two kings, Ancus Martius and Tarquinius Priscus, were also mural builders, but the first reared a wall to encircle the Janiculan Hill and connected with Rome by the Pons Sublicius, and the second did not live to finish more than a fourth of his work.

The wall of the first Roman Sovereign was, it is affirmed, low and about one and a half miles in circumference. On the west side of the Palatine some vestiges of this primitive wall, consisting of unequal blocks placed together in irregular courses, are still to be seen, but the original are mixed with additions of a much later date, presumably of the fourth pre-Christian century. These nucleus walls had three gates, some say four, but this is doubtful, the "Porta Rumanula," the "Porta Mugonia" and the "Porta Scalae." The first was the water-gate of the townlet, its name deriving from Rumus, the earlier appellation of the Tiber, which, according to polyglot etymologists, signifies "River," like Rhone and Rhine. The second took its name from the sound emitted by the lowing of cattle, driven in and out of this gate, and it is probably the identical one alluded to by Livy under the designation of "Veteram Porta Palatii." The third stood at the steps of Cacus at the Roma Quadrata facing the Aventine.

During the period that elapsed between the reigns of Romulus and Servius Tullius the rustic townlet had developed into a town and a capital. It is one of the modern fallacies that progress is much more rapid now than formerly, that twenty years, for instance, at present do the work of one hundred before, but going by historical tangible evidence it must be admitted that few, if any, at any period, surpassed the ancient Romans in rapidity of development. But besides this, the best proof of progress is not its rapidity but its reality, because to move quicker does not necessarily imply to move better, and obviously apparent and artificial improvement, however speedy, is no progress in the true sense, but sometimes even the reverse.

Judging superficially, it seems evident that we ought, on the whole, to be more advanced than those who have preceded us, because every generation has contributed its quota to the fabric of human knowledge. But this assumption, though apparently conclusive in theory, is not corroborated by fact, for man is too ephemeral, too feeble and too limited and incomplete a being to grasp so much contemporaneously, that is, to retain the past and attain the future, and hence his advance in one direction is accompanied by his retrogression in another. It is impossible for him to advance all along the line. To cite an example in point among many, if we, on the one hand, have invented, or reinvented, or resuscitated or diffused certain mechanical contrivances, it is undeniable, on the other, that our artistic and many of our constructive productions are inferior to those of the ancients, seeing that we are reduced to the rank of their humble imitators.

The majority, that is the ignorant and unreflecting, of every generation are the same in one respect, they each flatter themselves that they have surpassed the previous one, and each is successively quite right, but only from their respective one-sided standpoint, that is to say, in the one branch of knowledge peculiar to each generation, and also, only at the cost of losing ground in some other equally or more important direction, if not in the material, in the moral, spiritual or intellectual regions.

The giant strides that Rome made during her age of developing adolescence in real all round progress was reflected in her constructions, and the walls of Servius Tullius were not only vastly superior to those of Rome's founder, but such as have been declared by competent experts excellent for any period. Various fragmentary specimens still survive in confirmation of the above estimation of the Muri Servii. One of these may be seen at the foot of the Capitoline Hill. Another, consisting of peperino blocks opposite the main railway station of Rome, with its agger. This site was, as Horatius relates, one of the favourite promenades of the Imperial times. Other isolated sections of these walls are near the Castra Praetoria, in the Piazza Magnanopoli, incorporated in the Palazzo Antonelli and in the Trastevere quarter beside the rough old arch of San Lazzaro skirting the present road along the Tiber leading to the Porta San Paolo.

Above this arch is a "specus," or water channel, of the Anio Vetus, and in the vineyard behind is one of the earliest known specimens of concrete used in fabrication to be seen in the massive ruins of the "Emporium," or Public Magazines, founded by M. Aemilius Lepidus and L. Aemilius Paulus. But the best preserved remains of the Servian walls are those below the Aventine, bordering the Viale di San Paolo, formed of twenty-five courses of large blocks in the Etruscan style with two arched gateways, one of which is much damaged and the other substantially intact.

Annalists and archaeologists differ widely as to length and dimensions of the Muri Servii, though all more or less refer to them in terms of admiration, Virgil particularly so. The nearest approach to an accurate calculation seems to be that their height varied according to the undulations of the soil, from thirty to forty feet, their depth about twelve feet and their length from nine to ten miles. These walls were pierced by eight principal gates, namely beginning from the south: Capena, Radusculana, Trigemina, Salutaris, Collina, Viminalis, Esquilina and Caelemontana.

The exact site of the Porta Capena had long been a subject of dispute among the learned, when the excavations of 1857 conducted by Parker solved the problem by the discovery of the traces identified to be those of the ancient gate between the Caelian and Aventine Hills, at a short distance from the southern extremity of the Circus Maximus. Not far from the Porta Capena was the Porta Rudusculana and next came the Porta Trigemina. The site of this gate was marked by two erections left standing until comparatively recent times, an arch and a column, raised by public contribution to L. Minucius the Praefectus Annonae, who reduced the price of corn. This Porta Trigemina witnessed, among others, two historic exits; the one being that of Camillus who, in consequence of the enmity of the plebeian faction, left Rome, and in passing under this gate prayed the Deities to vindicate him by compelling the plebs to require and solicit his aid and protection. This in fact took place shortly afterwards, for his pardon was implored and his help invoked by the "Pullati," when he was recalled to defeat and expel the Gauls, to be loaded with honours and to earn the title of "Second Founder of Rome," as the man who, having saved her from annihilation, gave her second birth. The other exit alluded to was that of Marius who fled from this gate to Ostia to escape from his victorious antagonist Sylla.

About a mile of the Trigemina once stood the Porta Salutaris, or Sanqualis, on the site of the present Church of S. Silvestro, near the central Post Office. This Porta was the egress of the Imperial Fora to the Quirinal and Viminal Hills. To the northeast was the Porta Collina, situated at the angle of the Vie Sette Settembre and Goito. It was by this gate that the Goths entered Rome, A.D. 410. The Porta Viminalis came next close to the former Diocletian Baths, now National Museum, and then the Porta Esquilina, near the present Arcus Gallieni, or Arco di San Vito, and proceeding we reach the spot where the Porta Caelimontana opened.

As the original walls were extended other gates were naturally added. Among these are recorded the Portae Triumphalis, Carmentalis, Fontanalis and Flumentana. The Triumphalis, though of supreme historical importance as one of the triumphal gates of the City, is so little known that even the exact site is uncertain. The Porta Carmentalis stood close to or on the site of the Hospital of Sta. Galla, named after a very charitable lady.

This gate has an historical and legendary association attached to it, and took its name, together with the adjacent Aedicula dedicated to her, from Carmenta, who was a deity or semi-deity of Sabine extraction, gifted with three special qualifications. She was the reputed mother of no less a personage than Evander, a prophetess who according to Ovid predicted the future might and glory of Rome, and the patroness, or rather one of the patronesses, of women in childbirth, in her latter capacity an earlier Pagan counterpart of the Christian Saint Anna. It may be noted that the Latin word "Carmen," obviously the root of her name, signifies not only "song" and "chaunt," but also "spell." An unexplained peculiarity of her worship was the exclusion of leather in any

AURELIAN WALLS, A.D. 270-275. ROME.

Plate xxv.

shape within the limits of her temple. The Porta Carmentalis consisted of two twin gates or Jani, the one for ingress the other for egress. It was from this exit that all the members of the patrician family of the Fabii, 306 in number, with 4,000 of their clansmen, passed out, 477 B.C., to meet their death with the exception of one, Quintus, spared on account of his extreme youth, by an ambush prepared by the Veii, this family having alone sustained for a time the cost of the war against them. After this catastrophic holocaust of the patriotic Fabii this Janus Carmentalis was renamed "Porta Scellerata."

The Porta Fontanalis was built, it is said, where the palace of the Counts Antonelli now stands, and its substruction and arch testify to the fact that concrete was employed in Rome even at this early period. This is the Palazzo of the nephews of the celebrated Cardinal Giacomo Antonelli, A.D. 1806–1878, Prime Minister of Pope Pius IX, who was the last man who united in his person, like Richelieu, Mazarin, Alberoni and others, the double offices and dignities of Prince of the Church and Prime Minister of the State.

The Porta Flumentana was probably an original gate of the Servian wall running from the Capitol to the Tiber. It may claim some interest also on account of its locality, the Rione della Regola, in which was the family house of Rienzi, whose father, Lorenzo Gabrini, kept an inn here, helped by his wife, the Tribune's mother, who also worked as a laundress and water-carrier.

It appears that the celebrated Emperors of the Julian, Claudian, Flavian and Antonine dynasties, who proved themselves such mighty constructors in other directions, did not devote their ability and activity to wall building, and the reason is probably threefold. Firstly, the great growth of the city during their sway, to keep pace with which would have necessitated continual demolishing and rebuilding of walls. Secondly, Rome's unique position in their times as the undisputed Metropolis of a world composed mainly of subject or tributary peoples, without one independent State of sufficient importance to threaten her security and consequently her perfect immunity from the remotest possibility of a siege, which rendered walls as fortifications a work of supererogation. Thirdly, the fact that mural constructions are not of a nature to offer a field for the application and display of artistic talents, at least not in the same measure as other buildings. In consequence the Muri Servii, with some local extensions, remained substantially the city walls of Rome for over eight centuries and the next important mural builder was the Emperor Lucius Domitius Valerius Aurelianus, A.D. 270–275.

The Aurelian Walls were of much greater extent and entirely different construction to the Servian Walls. Their length has been variously computed at twelve, at twenty and at thirty miles, their height at twenty-five to fifty feet, their depth at from ten to twelve feet, and the number of their gates from thirteen to thirty-seven, comprising some of the Servian ones. In his circumvallation this Emperor included the Campus Martius, the Janiculus, Pincius and Vaticanus and such "extra murus" buildings as the Castra Praetoria and the Amphitheatrum Castrense. There are several remains of the Muri Aurelli, though all that are pointed out as such are not genuine vestiges of them, because these walls have been much built upon and altered, the wall-towers especially being mostly of later date.

The question whether the Servian or the Aurelian wall-type was the best for the city defences has not been answered decisively in favour of either, but as regards the attributes of durability and aspect there can be little hesitation in assigning the preference to the former.

There is a difference between the two in height, style and material, the earlier walls being composed of massive tufo or peperino blocks set together in courses of ledgers and stretchers, with aggeres at intervals, the later of brickwork with loopholes, turrets and bastions. The names of the gates of the Aurelian Walls, taken in sequence from the southeast, were the following: Metrovia, Latina, Appia, Ardeatina, Ostiensis, Portuensis, Aurelia, Flamminia, Pinciana, Salaria, Numentana, Chiusa, Tiburtina, Praenestina and Asinaria.

The Porta Appia, now Porta San Sebastiano, still flanked by the two towers of the Aurelian Walls on marble basements, spoils of the Appian Sepulchres, was wrecked during the Gothic invasion and rebuilt by Narsus, the successor of Belisarius. Under the arch is a Gothic inscription refering to the repulse here, A.D. 1327, of Robert King of Naples by the Romans led by Jacopo dei Ponziani. Most of the triumphal processions of the Imperial times passed through this historic gate. The last witnessed, arranged with all the pomp and forms of the ancient Roman ceremonial, was the procession headed by Marcus Antonius Colonna in A.D. 1571, after the naval victory of Lepanto won by the coalesced Christian States over the Turks, in which he figured as one of the allied commanders in charge of the Roman contingent, the Commander-in-Chief being Don Giovanni, an illegitimate son of Charles V, Emperor of Germany and King of Spain. The latter himself had passed through this gate in triumph forty-four years before, after the capture of Rome by his general, Duke Charles of Bourbon. At a short distance from the Porta Appia was the Porta Ardeatina, destroyed together with nine towers, by Sangallo, by order of Pope Paul III (Alessandro Farnese) A.D. 1534–1549, to make way for the erection of his bastions.

The Porta Appia and the adjacent Portae Latina and Metrovia were all not far from the spot where the more ancient Porta Capena once stood, from which they branched out fanlike. From the first two issued and still issue the omonymous roads, and close by the second gate is the little chapel of San Giovanni in Olio to commemorate the site where Saint John suffered or rather enjoyed martyrdom by being thrown into a cauldron of boiling oil. "Out of which," says the chronicler, "he emerged as from a refreshing bath," which was an easy and agreeable way of acquiring eternal glory by the pleasant process of an exhilarating bath, instead of the painful one of being scalded to death. The third gate, Porta Metrovia, now closed, was at the angle of the crossing of the Via della Navicella and the Via delle Ferrantelle, the latter being the lane beginning from the front of the Antonine Baths and leading to the Baptistry of St. John Lateran.

Westward of the Porta Appia was the Porta Ostiensis, opening on the road bearing the same name conducting to the town of Ostia. This gate is now replaced by the well known Porta San Paolo, and next in order came the Porta Portuensis, now substituted by the Porta Portese. By this gate the Vandals under Genseric entered Rome, and it was demolished by Urban VIII, who constructed on nearly the same spot, the Porta Portese, which in its turn was wrecked during the siege of Rome by the French in A.D. 1848 and rebuilt as it now is by Pius IX.

Outside this gate was the Campus Tarquinius, granted by the Senate as a free gift to C. Mutius in reward for his patriotic heroism. This episode may be briefly related, or repeated, as follows. Lars Porsenna, the Etruscan king was besieging Rome, and Mutius entered his tent with the intention of killing him, but mistaking the secretary for the enemy Sovereign, slew the former instead. On being arrested, Mutius boldly expressed his disappointment at the error whereby the persistent foe of Rome had been spared, but assured Porsenna that several Romans had pledged themselves to renew the attempt until it succeeded, and, to punish himself for his failure he held his right hand over the sacrificial fire and kept it burning till the king, marvelling at and honouring such daring and fortitude, allowed him to return to Rome free and unmolested. It was for this feat that C. Mutius received the additional agnomen of "Scaevola" (Scaevus signifying left or left-handed) and the donation, as above, of the Campus Tarquinius outside the Porta Portuensis. In one of the halls of the Capitol there is a painting illustrating this act of C. Mutius Scaevola. Later, this land became the "Horti Caesaris," a personal property of the Dictator, which he bequeathed by testament to the Roman people.

The ancient Romans, wiser and juster than we are, rewarded the intention and the example, irrespectively of the mere success, which is frequently the result of chance and not of merit, and there can be no doubt that deeds of heroism and self-sacrifice, in which Roman history abounds, recognised and rewarded by the State whatever the result might be, went far towards erecting and consolidating the mighty and durable fabric of Rome's world domination.

Proceeding in the same direction, we reach the place where the Porta Aurea, or Aurelia, once stood, which, like the Portuensis aforesaid, was similarly destroyed and replaced by the Porta San Pangrazio near its site, and likewise reconstructed by Pius IX after the siege of 1848. Close to the ancient Porta Aurea was the "Arx" or Fort of the Aurelian walls and from it issued the Via Aurelia crossing over to the Janiculan Hill.

During this siege a very singular defensive strategem was gravely proposed by the beleagured Roman Republicans. This was nothing less than to line the walls between the two gates, Portese and Pangrazio, with nuns, who certainly were numerous enough to man, or rather to woman, all the walls of the Sevenhilled City. It was sagely opined by some that this device would suffice to arrest the fire and assault of the French, as a double barrelled spiritual and moral bulwark, consisting of holiness and femininity. This was carrying out the formula of "Place aux Dames" with a vengeance, a similar practical application of which could hardly be as agreeable to ladies as a preference shewn, for instance, at an entertainment or a theatre in the matter of the best or front seats, etc.

But this laudable project was not put into execution, firstly because some very reasonable doubts occurred to certain of the members of the Council of defence as to the efficacy of unarmed nuns in the place of men and guns, and secondly on account of some hesitation on the part of the holy Sisters themselves, who were not, it appears, particularly anxious to be made targets of, either to gain the palm of martyrdom or the worldly renown accruing from warlike achievements. So both, laic and ecclesiastic, from the different standpoints of common sense and common timidity, were at one in rejecting this extraordinary plan, and agreed with exemplary unanimity that bombs, shells, bullets, swords and bayonets are distressingly impervious to the claims of immunity advanced by sanctity and sex. That, therefore, the artillery-men at a distance and the infantry at close quarters, despite veneration for the Church and her ministers and ministresses inculcated in all good Catholics, and gallantry to the female sex, rightly or wrongly attributed in particular to Frenchmen, would not be one wit more considerate in the circumstances than the unfeeling weapons they handled, and deliberately knock down walls and kill nuns with equal promptitude, impartiality and zeal.

The Porta Flaminia was erected by the same Flaminius who constructed his omonymous Via and Circus. This gate was subsequently renamed when saintly appellations came in vogue, "Porta San Valentino," from the neighbouring basilica and catacombs until the fifteenth century, when the name was again altered, as popular nomenclature became the fashion instead of ecclesiastical, to "Porta del Popolo," which it retains to the present day. Near this gate, that in pre-railway times was the main northern entrance to Rome, was discovered a pyramidical monument and reliefs of five horses that were taken from the tomb of the champion, Publius Gutta Calpernianus. The inner tower of the walls here, known as the "Trullo," was imagined to be haunted in preference by Nero's ghost.

Next comes the Porta Belissaria, now Porta Pinciana, from which Belisarius issued and routed Vitiges, A.D. 538, though it is not certain that this was one of the regular gates of Aurelianus, but possibly only a postern until it was rebuilt by the above Exarch whose name it took. Then follows the Porta Salaria, so called because the city received her principal supply of salt (Sale) by the Via Salaria on which it opened. After this gate is the Porta Numentana, walled up since 1564, close to the present Porta Pia. This ancient gate evidently took its name from Numentum (the modern Mentana where Garibaldi was repulsed by the French and Pontifical troops A.D. 1867) and derived from Numentanus Sylvius, the maternal grandfather of Romulus and Remus, the paternal being, it appears, Jupiter. This gate, which is asserted to be the Porta Collina of the Servian Walls, was entered by the Gauls 390 B.C., and it was near here that a decisive battle was fought 83 B.C., between the Romans under Sylla and Crassus, and the Samnites, and Lucanians under Pontius Telesius, terminating in the complete victory of the former, in which, it is related, that 50,000 men fell on each side.

We next reach the Porta Chiusa, the former site of the Castra Praetoria and the Vivarium, where the wild beasts for the arena were kept. Consecutively to this was the Porta Tiburtina, replaced later but not exactly on the same spot by the present Porta San Lorenzo. The reconstructed gate, from which issues the Via Tiburtina leading to Tivoli, was built by the Emperors Honorius and Arcadius, A.D. 402, against an aqueduct-arch of the Aquae Marcia and Julia as the inscription also records.

The Porta Praenestina, now called Porta Maggiore, originally likewise a main aqueduct-arch of the Aquae Claudia and Anio Novus, was first erected by Claudius, A.D. 52, restored by Vespasian A.D. 71, and by Titus A.D. 80, repaired and converted into a city-gate by Aurelianus, and finally renovated by Honorius A.D. 405. In the Middle Ages the Colonna incorporated it in one of their numerous strongholds. It is a fine and imposing ruin, and the two ancient roads, Via Praenestina and Via Labicana, still diverge from it. The Porta Praenestina was the outer-gate of the more ancient

PORTA TIBURTINAE, A.D. 402. ROME.

Plate xxvi.

Porta Esquilina of the Servian walls, with which it directly connected by the part of the Via Labicana inside the city.

The Porta Asinaria, named after the Gens Asinaria, a conspicuous family residing near, and now built up, was the gate by which Belisarius entered Rome, A.D. 536, King Totila in A.D. 546, and the Emperor Henry IV with his Anti-Pope Guibert in A.D. 1081. A few years later this gate was known by the name of "Porta Porusta," on account of the damages caused by Robert Guiscard, who came in support of the Pontiff Gregory VII. At a little distance from it Gregory XIII opened the present gate, called Porta San Giovanni. The next gate is the closed Porta Metrovia with which our circle of Aurelian gates began.

The Porta Septimia, or Settimiana, situated at the entrance of the present Via Lungarina, was built by Pope Alexander VI, it is stated on a former unrecorded building of the Emperor Septimius, from whom this gate took its name. It forms, with its Guelph turrets, a picturesque, typical work of the fifteenth century.

The mural additions of the Emperors Honorius and Arcadius, A.D. 395-423 were chiefly limited to the south-eastern quarter of the city, beginning, as some assert, from the Vivarium and terminating at the Porta Maggiore.

Belisarius, A.D. 505-565, whose name is the latinized transformation of the two Slav words, "Belic," White, and "Zar," Prince, rebuilt a great portion of the old walls and added to them, and has therefore as much right as the Emperors Honorius and Arcadius before him and the Popes Leo and Urbanus after him, to be numbered among Rome's mural constructors. The work of this celebrated general, Exarch of Italy of the Emperor of the East Justinian, consisting mainly of brickwork, was of a type resembling the Aurelian Walls, but somewhat higher and thicker. In his extensions and renovations Belisarius refrained from touching one small portion of the northern section, the part known as the "Muro Torto," or Twisted Wall, which has remained to this day in the same shattered, bulging condition it had in his time. It appears that the popular belief in the Church legend that Saint Peter had undertaken the responsibility for the integrity of this portion of the wall, and had actually appeared here, *in propria persona*, during the assault of Vitiges, is answerable for this public opposition to repairs in this section. And for the same reason succeeding mural builders abstained from laying sacrilegious if repairing hands on it. For it would be hardly reasonable to expect that the Roman populace would prefer any wall made by mortal hands, however perfect, in exchange for even a falling, broken fragment under the special protection of the Prince of the Apostles, who is also the Patron Saint of their City.

The Papal walls were mainly reconstructions of the Imperial ones, with occasional curves and additions of bastions and commemorative tablets affixed thereon. Leo IV, A.D. 847-855, seems to have been a man and a ruler of some merit, besides having the advantage of being a canonized Saint. During his pontificate the States of the Church were much troubled by the incursions of the Saracens, who successfully advanced to the suburbs of Rome. This warlike Pontiff, with the aid of the peoples of Naples, Gaeta and Amalfi, repulsed and drove them back. The sharp lesson taught by the invasion bore fruit, for San Leo proceeded without delay to provide more effectually for the protection of the city in view of possible future aggressions. He repaired and strengthened the old walls and erected a new fortified area around the Cathedral of St. Peter and its appurtenances and environs.

This fortified quarter extended from the ancient Pons Neronis to the Janiculus, and thus constituted a townlet of itself, named after this Pope " Urbs Leoninae," Italianized into Città Leonina, an appellation it retains to this day. And in proof that this quarter continued to be regarded as a distinct section of the Eternal City, it is affirmed that in the treaty of surrender of 1870, after the assault of the Italian army, there was a clause whereby the Città Leonina was excluded from the dominions of the King of Italy and remained and was recognised as a Papal domain. A serious disturbance, however, occurred in this quarter and as the Pontifical forces had been disbanded, the Italian troops were called in at the request of the Pope to restore and maintain order, and remained in occupation.

Considering that the Pope is the Supreme Head of the Roman Catholic Church of all countries professing this form of Christianity, and not of any one of them alone, it has long seemed wise and equitable, in conformity with his polynational Spiritual authority, that he should have some independent domain under his own exclusive jurisdiction. In consequence of the Treaty of A.D. 1929 between the Holy See and the Kingdom of Italy, the Pope now possesses and rules a small dominion of his own, with all the attributes of a State, large enough to render him independent but not large enough to weigh internationally as a temporal Power. A most satisfactory solution for all concerned.

The above mentioned enterprising Pope S. Leo IV also entirely rebuilt the town then called Centumcellae, which had been razed to the ground by the Saracen invaders. From this event arose its second name, for the inhabitants on their return to their original place of residence, reconstructed and rendered habitable again, called it in their dialect " Civita " (Città) " La Vecchia," contracted into its present appellation of Civitavecchia.

The famous Urban VIII, who it seems could not refrain from laying his either destructive or constructive, desecrating or consecrating hands on almost everything within his reach, repaired, refortified and in some parts replaced the ancient walls, wherever the exigencies of the population or his own views called for a change.

In a manuscript of an anonymous writer of the ninth century there is a description of the Roman walls, with their fourteen gates and three hundred and eighty towers and bastions, still standing in his time. These old walls, so dissimilar in origin, material and type, ruined, demolished, restored, patched and altered, are capacious enough in some parts to afford space within their thickness for dwelling places, as for instance in the section near the Tre Archi.

The main work of modern times in connection with these ancient and mediaeval walls has been to strengthen them and in making at intervals open gateways to facilitate communication. As fortifications they are not now of much use, but they might perhaps form a nucleus in some parts for new walls. Or, if these historic walls, the guards, mute witnesses and memorials of the former universal Metropolis, be considered solely as national monuments, the intelligent national sentiment will see to it that every measure is taken for their preservation.

ARCH OF THE MARTIAN AQUEDUCT (CALLED "ARCH OF DRUSUS"), B.C. 146.

Plate xxvii.

CHAPTER XI

AQUEDUCTS AND DRAINS

THE "Aquae-Ducti," or water-conduits, offer one of the most remarkable examples of the typical Roman constructions, as well as of their wise appreciation, thus early in their history, of the importance of an abundant and regular supply of this element of a good quality. With all the enormous facilities rendered in our times by steam and electricity the best waterworks of the most modernly equipped cities are not more reliable and efficient, and, if our uniform experience be worth anything, less durable than those enjoyed by the Romans even as far back as three centuries before the advent of Jesus Christ, and as regards their aspect aesthetically there can be no comparison between the former and the present. But as if to mark the contrast more forcibly by proximity, beside these superb structures of antiquity, imposing even in decay, one sometimes meets a mean little modern aqueduct, with its low arches, frailness and architectural ugliness. To the self-satisfied presumption of superiority in most directions, and particularly in works of this nature, so complacently arrogated by the majority of moderns, the above proof, one of many, of the capacity and thoroughness of the men of those times comes doubtless as a shock, all the more as it is a material fact.

The number of Roman aqueducts has been variously calculated. Sixtus Frontinus, Curator Viarum under the Emperors Nerva and Trajan, in his treatise " De Aquae Ductibus Urbis Romae " mentions nine, Procopius, a Greek historian of the fourth century, fourteen, and Victor, a later writer, twenty. This discrepancy is probably to be attributed to a different system of computation rather than to a numerical increase due to the course of time. For while some, such as the first-named author, reckoned as one unit each main aqueduct, whether consisting of a single channel or of two or three conveying waters from different sources, other writers counted each of the several channels, though incorporated in one main structure, as separate distinct aqueducts. We have instances of this in the Martian and Claudian aqueducts, the former carrying three conduits, the original and lowest for the Aqua Martia, the central for the Aqua Tepula and the highest for the Aqua Julia, and the latter similarly with two separate channels for the passage of the Aquae Claudia and Anio Novus. The total aggregate length of the various aqueducts has been calculated at about 360 miles, of which 60 were above and 300 under ground, and the quantity of water supplied to the city, was, according to Renatus Flavius Vegezius, a writer of the reign of Valentinian II, A.D. 375–392, estimated at 285,000,000 pounds per diem. This abundance of water presents a striking contrast to the scarcity prevailing in later times, when this element had occasionally even to be brought in carts or barges to Rome as in Venice.

The most ancient aqueduct recorded was that constructed 313 B.C. by the Censors Appius Claudius Caecus and C. Plautius Veluscius almost entirely subterranean, and covering a distance of twelve, or as some assert eight, miles from its source, not far from Praeneste, the modern Palestrina, to Rome. The water and the conduit were both called " Appia." The second in point of date, 225 B.C., was that of the Censor Marcus Curius Dentatus, thirty-five miles long from its source of the River Anio to the city, was named Anio Vetus to distinguish this aqueduct from another drawing water from the same parts built over three centuries later by the Emperor Claudius and therefore denominated Anio Novus. The third, constructed by the Censor and Praetor Quintus Martius Rex, 146 B.C, conveyed water from the Sabine mountains to Rome, a distance of about forty-five miles. It is from this Aqueductus Martius, restored in 1869, that the capital receives her principal water supply to our day.

The fourth was the Augustan Aqueduct, which brought over from Algidus, in the ancient Latium, the water required for the Naumachia of Octavius Augustus. The Emperor Trajan subsequently restored and made use of this aqueduct for bringing water from the lake of Bracciano to Rome, about thirty miles and it was renamed after him. The fifth, a fourteen mile aqueduct, was the work of the celebrated Marcus Vipsanius Agrippa (the Baron Haussman of Octavius), 19 B.C., and it was thoroughly renovated by Claudius A.D. 46, and by Hadrian A.D. 130. This water was called Aqua Virgo, according to some authorities on account of its purity, according to others from the legend that it was a girl who first indicated this spring to a body of thirsty soldiers. The Aqua Virgo, Italianized now into Acqua Vergine or Virgin Water, issues in Rome from the fountains of the Piazze di Trevi, di Spagna, Navona and Farnese, yielding, it is estimated, a total of 12,000,000 cubic feet of water, of a quality very highly prized in the city. The channel of the Aqua Julia, to which this name was given in honour of the Julii, was also constructed by the same M. V. Agrippa. The ruins of the tower-like reservoir of this water are situated in the Piazza Vittorio Emanuele, which occupies part of the ancient Forum Esquilinum. The memorial trophies of Caius Marius' victory over the Cimbri, now on the terrace of the Capitol, were originally placed here, where, in sight of these emblems of his triumph, so diversely does the wheel of fortune revolve, his opponent, P. Cornelius Rufinus Sylla, arriving by a forced march with his legions from Nola, and entering by the Porta Esquilina, encountered Marius here and compelled him to flee precipitately to Ostia.

To the right of the above reservoir, affixed to the wall formerly at the entrance of the Villa Palombara, may be seen a marble slab with an inscription referring to an occurrence which may merit a few words as one of the numerous instances exemplifying the aspirations and vagaries of an extra-natural character inherent in humanity in all times and countries.

In the year 1680 the Marquis Maximilian Palombara observed an unknown individual enter his villa and proceed to examine the ground attentively. The intruder, on being interrogated by the servants, replied that he knew that the proprietor was interested in the mysterious science of transmuting into gold other substances, presumably less valuable, which is, by the way, a common enough process on an infinity of different lines in which we see a vast number of people keenly engaged. The visitor added that he was searching for the necessary ingredients to accomplish this laudable and profitable purpose, which he desired to convince the Marquis, practically, was no impossible feat. The man apparently belonged, or pretended to belong, to the tribe of adventurers and illusionists by no means rare in the seventeenth century, of whom later the notorious Guiseppe Balsamo was a specimen, and gave his name as Francesco Bona. All this was duly reported to Palombara, evidently a devout believer in the " Philosopher's Stone," the " Elixir of Life," and all the rest of it, who at once welcomed the alchemist with open arms and assigned to him an apartment in his mansion consisting of two rooms, a bed-chamber and a laboratory.

The magician commenced his operations in the presence of his host by pulverising the herbs he had gathered, throwing them into a professional looking crucible containing a liquid as mysterious as himself and going through the usual manœuvres of his trade in a very creditable fashion. He then promised the Marquis that by next morning he would not only have completed his task but, furthermore, would initiate Palombara into its secrets, and it must be admitted that the man shewed some consideration for the feelings of his excited host by not inflicting on him a longer probation. In due course the seemingly interminable hours passed, but with the morning no wizard made his appearance, and the anxious Marquis, possibly apprehending some accident to his guest, and certainly unable to curb his impatience any longer, decided to break open the locked and barred doors occupied by the conjurer, but with no better result, for he had vanished "into space" or "thin air" according to the ritual phrase, after the manner of his kind, without a farewell, a rudeness condoned in these "superior beings." However, in return, doubtless, for the interested hospitality he had received, he left two objects behind him, the broken crucible on the floor, from which flowed a stream of gold, and a document purporting to be explanatory but which was the reverse, because, as the narrator naïvely says, " No one ever could decipher or understand the enigmatical and cabalistic characters traced on it." But the Marquis was a staunch devotee of the Magic Art, and, nowise discouraged, caused a memorial inscription referring to the gold manufacturer and his recipes to be carved on a marble tablet affixed to the walls of his villa, where, as aforesaid, it is still to be seen.

This story is somewhat incomplete, because we are not informed if any outlet was discovered by which the wonderful Bona escaped, nor if the stream of gold retained its precious properties on being handled, or turned into ashes, stone, charcoal or any other less valuable substance, as the productions of these magical beings have so often the disconcerting knack of doing as we know. But in any case, if this nobleman did not become any wiser or richer in consequence of the alchemist's visit, we do not hear, on the other hand, that he was any poorer thereby, and that nothing of his was abstracted may perhaps be regarded as the only surprising part of the whole affair. An explanation that might fit more or less, is that Bona was either a harmless monomaniac or an incompetent burglar, and that the Marquis was a man known to be under the influence of a hobby of the mystical variety.

There is, however, another version of this incident. The alchemist is always there, as the protagonist, only the patron or patient is no longer the Marquis Palombara but the celebrated Queen Christina of Sweden, A.D. 1626–1689, who abjured Protestant

Lutheranism for Roman Catholicism, and acquired or hired this villa, and that it was she, therefore, who had the tablet attached to the wall, to be deciphered by some one wiser than herself. It is added that the wizard, whether Bona or another, was not so disinterested as Palombara's, but that he made gold " for himself " in no magical manner out of her credulity, if not " for her," with much ease and abundance. From the classic standpoint this villa can claim an interest also as the place where the famous statues of the Discobulus and the Meleager were discovered.

With due excuses for this digression, we will return to our subject. The sixth and seventh aqueducts were constructed by Claudius Tiberius Drusus Nero, who has been about as consistently underrated as Constantine I has been overrated. This conduit, named after its creator, measured, according to some accounts, forty-three miles, and according to others eighty, in length from its source at Subiaco, and the other, called Anio Novus, from the homonymous river source, about fifty miles to Rome. Approximately a fourth of both was built over ground and the two were united into one double channelled aqueduct that entered the city by the main archway aforementioned converted subsequently into the gate now known as the Porta Maggiore.

These two aqueducts were probably the most important of the Eternal City from the structural, architectural and engineering standpoints. They were built of neat hewn blocks of stone of two kinds, travertine and selce, the sustaining arches, with their strong piers were lofty, occasionally reaching the height of 105 feet, and the route was traced deviously to avoid the great and abrupt inequalities of the soil and to moderate the gathering impetus of the water coming from so long a distance, which would have otherwise inevitably damaged the channels. The preliminary and accessory work, too, of transporting the material in vast quantities and from afar, levelling mounts and perforating rocks, was, especially in those times, no facile undertaking in itself. Frontinus, already quoted, a recognised authority in these matters, says in reference to the Claudian aqueduct, " Opus magnificentissime consumatum." Of course if man could continue to be now what he was in those ages and also have the aid of artificial agents, the ideal of power would be attained; but this is impossible, because in proportion as his personal work is not done by him but by other factors outside him, man must degenerate physically, and even mentally in some respects, and the progression, as already observed, in one direction is counterbalanced or overbalanced by the regression in another.

The eighth aqueduct was built by the Emperor L. Septimius Severus, A.D. 193–211. Its principal ruins are still to be seen near a locality called Torre Mezzavia, between Rome and Albano, and some of its fragmentary wrecks are on the Palatine, and it is mainly from these that some hazard a guess as to its proportions and structure. Certain writers assert that the water of this Aquaeductus Septimii was derived from the Alban lake.

The ninth, of which Caracallus has the credit of being the constructor, A.D. 211–218, began also from the Alban district and terminated at the extensive and luxurious Antonine Baths, more commonly known by the name of this monarch. Some writers allege that these two aqueducts were branches of the same aqueduct commenced by Septimius and completed and deviated by Caracallus. The tenth, the magnificent ruins of which are still existing between Rome and Praeneste, attributed to the Emperor

AQUEDUCT OF CLAUDIUS, A.D. 41–52.

Plate xxix.

Alexander Severus, A.D. 222–235, brought water, called Aqua Alexandrina, from the heights of Colonna and Praeneste to Rome. The branch-aqueducts of Nero, Titus, and some add, the above ones of Septimius and Caracallus, were annexations, deviations or prolongations of the Claudian to the Caelian, Palatine, Aventine and Esquiline Hills, mainly for the purpose of furnishing the water necessary for the palaces, baths and circuses of these emperors.

The "Cisternae," the "Piscinae," and the "Castelli," the first for rain-water, the second for spring-water and the third as the main reservoirs of the aqueducts, were all, likewise, perfectly constructed to serve their several purposes of collection, purification and preservation of water. Two utterly wrecked specimens of these works still to be seen in Rome are the aforenoted Julian Reservoir and the Sette Sale of Trajan's Baths.

During the Republic the superintendence and custody of the water works devolved on the Censors and Aediles and under the Empire the official in charge was the "Curator Viarum," or Road-Inspector, who had under his orders, besides a host of mechanics and labourers, an organized body of trained men employed in guarding and keeping the aqueducts and their accessories in a sanitary condition and good repair.

With all due respect for Pliny, who says that the Martian and Virgo waters were not much appreciated in his time, the Aquae Martia, Virgo and Claudia have, on the whole, enjoyed the best reputation, and the Anio Vetus and Alsietina the worst, the latter being only adopted for washing and irrigation.

The best known water conduits of the Middle Ages or rather of the transition period between them and the modern, all restorations or deviations of those already mentioned, were three in number. The ancient Virgo aqueduct repaired by Pope Nicholas V (Tommaso Parentucelli, A.D. 1447–1455) who conducted it to the present Fontana di Trevi (a name derived from Trivio or triple outlet). The Aqua Felice by Pope Sixtus V (Felice Perretti, A.D. 1585–1590), who gave it his baptismal name and who made use of the Martian and Claudian aqueducts to carry water from the highlands near Colonna to the Fontana delle Terme in Rome. Thirdly, that of the Pope Paul V (Camillo Borghese, A.D. 1605–1621) which was mainly the Augustan aqueduct renovated and prolonged up to the Janiculus to issue from the Fontana Paolina. This water, as has already been stated, has been pronounced unpotable.

The drainage system of ancient Rome was based and arranged with that combination of efficacy and durability that signalized all their public and private works. According to the most competent authorities probably the only drainage in existence that is comparable to that of the Eternal City over five centuries prior to the Christian era, is the present one of London, but the latter is more than 2,500 years younger, so that we cannot predict yet that it will wear so well and last so long as we know the former has done.

The Latin word "Cloaca," from the verb "Cloaco," to befoul, was used to describe a subterranean conduit to receive and discharge liquids and solids for the twofold purpose of drainage and purification. Of the ancient Cloacae of the Sevenhilled City we know two, in a way, surviving, and to these two it appears other tributary drain-pipes converged from various directions. The "Cloaca Maxima," or Greatest Drain, was begun by Tarquinius Pricus (the Elder) fifth King of Rome, 616–578 B.C. The spot where this drain commenced is marked by the stone altar, Ara Veneris Cloacinae, and crossing under the Roman Forum descended to the quarter denominated the Velabrum (from Vela, sail) that is, the space between the above Forum and the Boarium and passing under the latter, issued into the Tiber. Before the Tarquins drained this low, swampy region it was sometimes covered with water deep enough to float flat-bottomed boats or rafts, oared or sailed, and even, later, temporarily and rarely during inundations, water craft were employed. In its course the Maxima passed to the left of the Arch of Janus and here there is a spring, said to be that of Juturna, the waters of which, apparently more abundant then than now, were collected into a capacious basin and discharged into the Cloaca, thus producing a current throughout the rest of its course, which, after receiving the contents of the minor drain-pipes of the city, passed to the left of the Templet of the Dea Matuta to empty itself by its "Os," or mouth, into the river just under the Forum Boarium.

The height of the Maxima, the "Receptaculum Purgatorium Urbis," has been calculated at twelve feet, constructed of blocks of tufo fitted and fixed together without cement, but with layers and binders of travertine at intervals, except the mouth, which consists of concentric blocks of peperino. The renowned Strabo states that its capacity sufficed for the passage of a wagon laden with hay, and it is recorded that M. V. Agrippa, who had the tunnel cleaned and repaired, traversed its length in a boat. That conscientious historian, Titus Livius, informs us that the Tarquins had the best known workmen brought expressly from Traquinii (the modern Cornetto) and other parts of Etruria, then considered superior to Roman builders, and in fact the most expert in all Italy, for the construction of the Cloaca Maxima. Pliny is full of wonder and admiration for the "Opus omnium Maximum," as he terms it, which he declares so perfectly made, and which withstood with impunity the assaults of inundations, earthquakes and the wear of service for over 600 years in his time, while in ours it has exercised its functions for well over 2,400 years, that is, from about 570 B.C. to A.D. 1892, when it was blocked up. The Maxima possesses the threefold attraction of great antiquity, of grand construction and of being one of the three, and the most important, representative structure of Etruscan architecture surviving in a way in Rome.

On the same bank of the Tiber and not far from the mouth of the Maxima is that of the other main drain of ancient Rome, the "Cloaca Circensis," which traversed the valley between the Palatine and Caelian, receiving in its course the tributary drain-channels before discharging its contents into the river. The Circensis is of later, but as yet unrecorded date, and of an unidentified constructor, and though its dimensions were slightly smaller than those of the Maxima, it is held to have excelled the latter in respect to more finish in its workmanship. Otherwise, the two seem to have so closely resembled each other that to give a description of the Cloaca Circensis would be an almost superfluous repetition. This Cloaca served also as the drain of the Circus Maximus.

CHAPTER XII

CIRCUSES AND STADIUMS

THE only buildings for spectacular diversions and sports permitted in Rome during the Royal and Republican eras were the Circuses. Their origin is, according to some authorities, Etruscan and according to others Greek, but history does not favour the second hypothesis because the Greek Ippodrome (from " Ippos," horse, and " Thromos," road) the nearest corresponding structure and the ancestor of the modern race-course, differed essentially from the Roman Circus.

The most ancient, the largest and, during the Royal régime, the only building of this class, was the Circus Maximus. In the course of time other similar buildings were erected, but the " Maximus " continued to the end to merit and retain unchallenged its distinctive title of the " Greatest." Romulus had built a small rough nucleus of what became in after years the Circus Maximus, and he invited here his Sabine neighbours with the ostensible object of thus cultivating amicable relations between the two peoples, but with the real one of supplying by this step an important need of his infant city, namely: women. This numerical insufficiency at this stage of Rome's existence will not surprise anyone who knows that at the initiation of all colonial settlements in all epochs, naturally founded by the pioneers, discoverers and inventors of humanity, the male sex, the other one must necessarily be in a minority, when not altogether absent. After the newly constituted communities have survived their infancy the contrary usually happens by degrees, and the numerical superiority passes to women which is also, for obvious reasons, quite natural and inevitable.

With regard to the above wholesale match-making scheme of Romulus it is to be inferred that it was not crowned with, at any rate, the requisite success, for we know it had to be supplemented by the practically effective measure of the Rape, which took place either on this first invitation or some other subsequent occasion. Be this as it may, whether Romulus first tried persuasion and diplomacy and failed or partly so, and then decided on employing force, or did so at once, founders of colonies might take lessons from him in more ways than one, seeing that he gave premiums to and systematically patronized married men.

This giant sire of Circuses was built by King Tarquinius Priscus between the Palatine and Aventine Hills. It is said to have measured 2,260 feet in length by 675 in width, was furnished with three tiers of seats termed collectively " Cavea," bisected longitudinally by the wall-like platform called the "Spina" (from spine or backbone) and encircled internally by the " Euripus " (Canal) which separated the arena from the audience. The north extremity, the starting point, was quadrangular and the south one semi-circular, with its "Oppidum," or tower-like erection, on which was placed a box for the editor who directed the games, and beneath were the stalls for the horses and chariots. At each end of the Spina stood the "Metae" (goals) between which were the columns bearing the seven "Ovae," or egg-shaped balls, with as many "Delphinae" (Dolphins) corresponding in number with the courses marked by the dropping of a ball as each circle was completed by the racing chariots.

The public "Ludi," or games, being theoretically consecrated to the gods various temples, chapels and altars were raised about the circuses. Livy mentions a rather remarkable temple near the Circus Maximus, that is, remarkable in so far as regards the origin of the funds collected for its construction, which were provided from the fines imposed on Roman ladies convicted of adultery, but it must be remembered that he referred to the Imperial times, incomparably less moral than the preceding ones. Tacitus records temples dedicated to Bacchus, Prosperpine, Hercules and Flora, and Plutarch relates that a colossal statue was brought from Carthage and placed here. The two obelisks which adorned the Spina were erected thereon, the first by Octavius and the second by Constantine II or Constans.

During the republican times the expenses of these exhibitions were paid out of the private means of the Aediles, and it is said that Cesar had to sell his villa at Tivoli to defray the cost of the spectacles given during his Aedileship. But perhaps the most magnificent were the games given by the Emperor Carinus, A.D. 283, who had the circus transformed on this occasion into a primaeval forest with wild beasts, birds and reptiles. The last public Ludi took place here in A.D. 549 under the auspices of Totila King of the Ostrogoths. At the time of the first Triumvirate the Maximus is reported to have been capable of containing 150,000 persons, in the reign of Trajan 250,000 and in that of Valentinian III, A.D. 425-455, is said to have reached 360,000, which progressive numeral increase is accompanied by the records of the successive extensions, reconstructions and embellishments of the original edifice by Cesar, Octavius, Claudius, Trajan and Constantine. In the Imperial epoch, too, it was rendered more ornate and imposing by the addition of the Podium for the Sovereigns and the aristocracy.

The Circus Maximus, originally intended as a general centre for public sports of a nature calculated to develop amicable and useful emulation and to invigorate the race, became gradually more and more limited to chariot racing and the scene of the display of pomp and the spirit of faction, as the majority of the people ceased to participate in the healthy and inspiriting sports as actors to become spectators and partisans of the four orders of professional Aurigae or charioteers, distinguished severally by the colours red, blue, green and white in allusion to the four seasons. The chariots were of three kinds: the "Bigae," or two-horsed vehicles; the "Quadrigae," or four-horsed; and the "Sejugi," or six-horsed. Suetonius indeed mentions that Nero, participating personally in these chariot-races, made use also of the "Decemjugis," or ten-horsed car, but this was probably a unique, certainly a very rare example. The party feeling among the supporters of the different factions ran so high in these later times, especially at Constantinople, that the races degenerated into tumultuous meetings, rarely terminating without the accompaniment of free fights.

In 1900 a mosaic was discovered in the Castel Sant' Angelo representing figures of four charioteers in the colours of the four orders and an inscription referring to the effigy of Avillius Torus, a victorious auriga. These relics were affixed to the wall of the rooms of the National Museum of Rome, known by the name of " Museo Nationale delle Terme Diocletiane."

All those whose rule is mainly based on the unstable and ignorant favour of the multitude, by whatever appellation it may be disguised, had then as now, to satisfy the old cry of the populace of Rome of " Panem et Circenses," in other words to feed and amuse the multitude in order to be thus enabled to dominate and tyrannise, which would be impossible if those in power used it rather to develop the moral and mental qualities than solely the animal instincts of those placed under them. The Bourbons of Naples, much later, relied a good deal as instruments of government on their three " Fs," viz: Feste (fêtes or games), Farina (flour or bread) and Forca (gibbet). For though the third " F " was added by this Dynasty consistently with the Divine Right principle professed, it was, of course, only resorted to exceptionally as a final argument, and the regular system of government remained that of the old formula, " Panem et Circenses," that is: to keep the herd in order by pandering mainly, if not solely, to the grosser material wants and pleasures. But so long as the Roman Republic was the *de facto* constitution, being founded and working on entirely different ideals, it did not descend to these reprehensible methods of rule.

Though the Circus Maximus was much damaged by fire under Nero, it was entirely restored by Claudius and Trajan, and the deliberate and thorough destruction of this historic edifice, the most ancient and extensive of its class in Rome, that had withstood the assaults of time, service, neglect and disorders throughout the Royal, Republican, Imperial, Gothic and Greek governments, was left to be perpetrated under the Papal Rule by the Pontiffs Pauls III and V, and so completely that even its original limits can hardly be traced, though its name survives in the Via dei Cerchi, the broad road that now passes over its former site.

The Circus Agonalis, whose name is derived from the Greek word " Agon," struggle, was, it is said, originally founded by King Numa in honour of Janus, whose festivals were celebrated in January. It is doubtful whether this ancient Circus Numae was ever finished, but we hear that on its site the present Piazza Navona, or Agonale, since it has resumed its classic name, the above Circus Agonalis was built about eight centuries later by the Emperor Domitian, reported to have been large enough to contain 30,000 spectators. The obelisk on the Spina was transferred to the Circumstadium Maxentii and afterwards returned to its former place here in the Piazza Navona or Agonale.

The Circus Flaminius, in the Campus Martius, outside the Porta Flaminia that spanned the Via Flaminia, by the Censor Caius Flaminius. The precise date of the construction of this circus is uncertain, either 237 B.C. or 224 B.C., but that of the road is fixed at 220 B.C. No information has been gathered relatively to the dimensions and architecture of this edifice, and no vestiges of it remain. There was one feature peculiar to this circus, viz.: that it was built and used exclusively for the plebeians, the games being directed by a plebeian editor; a wise measure of the builder, himself of this Order, who afterwards encountered Hannibal at the battle of Trasimene, 217 B.C., in which action he was vanquished by the latter, and, moreover, lost his life.

Of the following circuses little is known beyond their names and sites. The Circus of Flora, between the Esquiline and Viminal, where the Floralia were celebrated on the 1st of May, the Circus of Sallustius, the Circus of Caligula and Nero, begun by the first and terminated by the second in the Vatican district, on the space now covered by the Basilica of Saint Peter. The Circus of Hadrian, behind his famous mausoleum, of which, strangely enough, no records have been attainable and no traces survive, and the Circus of Heliogabalus, on the site of the present Basilica of Sta. Croce in Gerusalemme.

The buried ruins that form, with the accumulated earth, the elevation in the Piazza Montecitorio, were once erroneously supposed to be those of the Circus of Taurus, but have since been ascertained to be those of the Imperial " Ustrinum," a construction adopted for the ceremonial cremation of the Emperors' corpses and their apotheosis.

The Circus of Maxentius, on the left of the Via Appia, close to the mausoleum of C. M. Crassia, was built by that Emperor near his villa with which it was connected, as stated, and measured 1,482 feet in length by 244 in width, and was calculated diversely to contain from 18,000 to 40,000 or 150,000 individuals, an even larger disparity than usual. Judging broadly from its dimensions as above, by its present few ruins and also by its ten tiers of seats instead of the customary three or four rows, the number of possible spectators, performers and attendants, might perhaps be fairly assumed to be between 50,000 and 60,000.

This edifice, which was partially unearthed and identified in A.D. 1825 by two inscriptions over its Porta Triumphalis referring to its builder, is interesting for three reasons: firstly because it is the sole one of which some vestiges of some of the features of a Roman Circus exist, secondly, because it is probably the only circus outside the city boundaries, and thirdly, because it is, so far as we know, the last building constructed of this class. The Spina, richly adorned with statues and obelisks, was placed in an oblique line in order, it is alleged, to equalise the chances of the racing-cars. Recent excavations have demonstrated that the Spina was a regular museum in its way; among the numerous statues of which relics have been found are those of Venus, Paris, Victory and Phoebus, and a curious earthenware vase wherein were kept the palm-branches for the victors. In another section of the building were statues of Hercules, Prosperpine and of an Amazon and columns of grey marble, belonging to the Temple of Neptune. The fragments of the Metae show that they were decorated with reliefs.

The two main entrances were surrounded with porticoes, the one facing the Via Appia included the round Aedicula or Sepulchrum, still standing, dedicated by Maxentius to his son Romulus, and the other gate was placed opposite the Via Pignatelli. There were, besides these, two lateral entrances, named respectively " Libitinensis " (from Libitina the Goddess of death) and " Sanavivaria," the first serving for the conveyance of the dead, the second for the wounded. On the towers were stationed the Tibicini, or flute-players (from Tibia, thighbone, also flute, flageolet, fife) whose office it was to regale the audience during the spectacle. The scattered, scant ruins, with their background studded with other ancient remains and the Sabine range, are exceedingly picturesque as well as otherwise interesting, though unaccountably they have not attracted the notice they deserve.

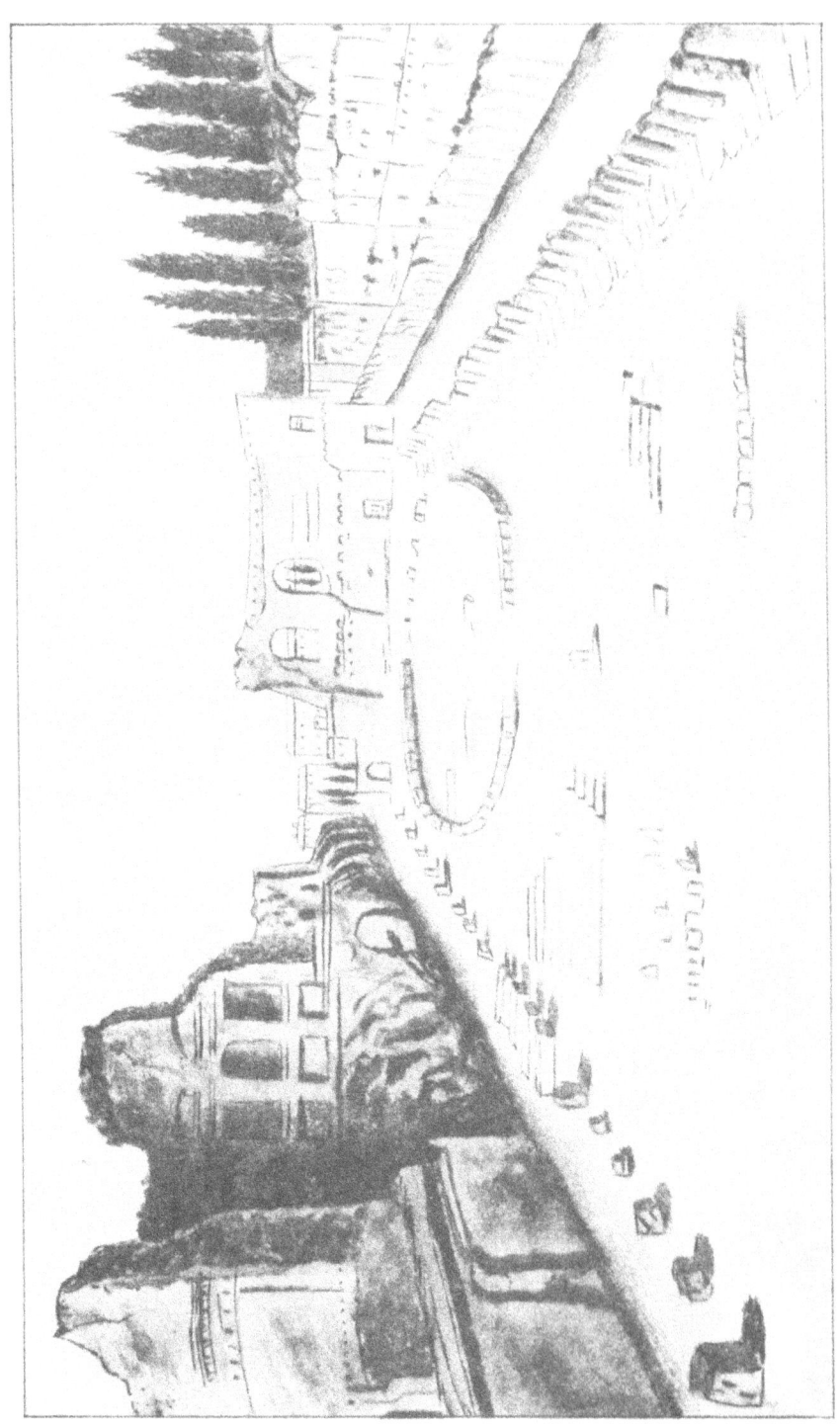

STADIUM OF DOMITIAN, A.D. 81–96. PALATINE.

Plate xxxi.

CIRCUSES AND STADIUMS

To the Emperor Maxentius is due the honour of being the last Sovereign or prominent man of Rome, except Diocletian, whose public constructions were designed and executed on the scale of grandeur and artistic skill of the ancient classic Roman works, or at least closely approaching them; and this is all the more remarkable becasue he lived in a period of decadence, and because his reign, A.D. 306–312, was brief and troubled, and moreover shared by other co-emperors. We have come across another of his buildings, the Basilica Maxentia, in the Roman Forum.

In character, mental powers and activity he showed himself superior to his rival and brother-in-law, Constantine I, called the Great, but he espoused a losing cause and history, or rather many of the writers of it, do not quite divest themselves always of the characters of *courtesans* and partisans, and hence see merit in what is merely success, due to luck or accident. But this biassed estimation is no reason for accepting error uninvestigated, frequently originating in partiality and solely consecrated by time and repetition, for we are all aware of the fact that " The race is not always to the swift or the battle to the strong." The conclusion is if we wish to appreciate history fairly and truly, we must take more pains to examine and weigh ourselves the facts, actions and worth of everyone on their own merits and independently of success or non-success, and uninfluenced by any glamour of power, name or artificial reputation. This necessitates more study and mental exertion, but it is well worth the extra trouble in order to have a right knowledge of history and to make a proper use of it.

The Circus and Stadium, so often confounded, were two branches of the same architectural stock, and therefore, while presenting a general resemblance, differed in some respects in form and purpose. The first was in shape an incomplete oval, being quadrangular at one extremity, bisected midway and lengthwise by the Spina and serving either exclusively or principally for chariot races. The second described a perfect unbisected oval oblong and was intended for foot-races and other athletic sports, wherefore it was sometimes termed " Palaestra," signifying a wrestling-arena. The fact that circuses were not uniformly used for chariot races only, may also account for the confusion between the two. The vast Circus Maximus, for instance, was, as has been said, a general centre for a variety of sports besides racing, and that of Maxentius combined the two, and hence is termed by some " Circustadium," although it has not been definitely ascertained whether his annexed stadium was an independent structure or incorporated in his circus. But it is evident that neither of the above were exclusively or chiefly stadiums, which, indeed, rarely constituted of themselves isolated buildings, but usually formed integral sections of other edifices, such as for examples the Stadiums or Palaestrae of the Antonine and Diocletian Baths.

The race-course of the Olympia, in Greece, the archetype, measured one stadium or 183 metres in length and this word, indicating a unit of measure, was adopted in the course of time to describe conventionally all edifices of this nature. So far as we know at present there is only one ruin in Rome of an independent, isolated stadium and that is the Stadium Domitii or Septimii on the Palatine.

This structure, known generically as " The Stadium," about 255 feet long by 150 wide, was built by Domitian, reconstructed by Septimius, transformed into a garden by Theodoric and excavated for the most part between 1881 and 1898. At the extremity facing the Monastery of St. Bonaventure there is an elevation conjectured to have served for the accommodation of the Senators, at the opposite end there is an open half-domed vault which was the main entrance originally; to the left of this are the vestiges of the Imperial box about midway between the two extremities. This Pulvinar is attributed by some writers to Hadrian, and consisted of three compartments, of which the almost effaced stucco decorations are apparently additions of a later period, when their preservation had become an unknown and lost art. Near the two extremities of the Stadium were fountains, and a marble Euripus ran round the entire building internally. A passage to the left led up from the arena to the galleries above the Imperial and Senatorial boxes, and a double row of piers and attached semi-columns traversed the arena longitudinally. The composition of these in material was unusual, the core being of bricks and the casing of two species of marble, white Lunense and red Pietrasanta for the shafts. These ranges of marble Columnae Structiles are attributed to Septimius, as likewise the recesses formerly occupied by statues. Some fine sculptural works were found, which were transported to the Palazzo Mattei and the Villa Albani, but the most important and best preserved are the statues of a Muse, found in 1868, and of Juno in 1878, kept in the Museo Nazionale of Rome.

We are informed that St. Sebastian underwent his martyrdom, or at least the first part of it in which he is almost invariable represented, in this Stadium. He was born in Narbonne in the third century and enlisted as a volunteer in the army of the Emperor Carinus, in order, it is stated, to assist Christians condemned to death, though it would seem that he could have served this purpose more appropriately if he had enrolled himself under the banner of the Church instead of that of Mars, as a priest and not as a soldier in the Pagan army. Anyhow, he was discovered and reported as a conspirator and inciter to insubordination, probably a true accusation, and a death sentence by serving as a target for archery practice was passed on him, and put into execution under the aforesaid Senatorial box, where he was tied to a tree-trunk and well riddled with arrows in the guise we so frequently see him depicted. However, he survived this drastic treatment and in due course recovered, and presented himself anew imprudently to the Emperor, who, not a little scandalized at this inopportune and almost impertinent resurrection and presentation, determined this time to be on the safe side, and seeing that the Saint had proved himself if not impervious at least immune from the effects of steel in the shape of arrow heads as missiles, resorted to wood at close quarters and had him beaten to death by rods. It is noteworthy that we do not see St. Sebastian represented in this his last and mortal martyrdom.

The "Naumachiae" may likewise be considered as appertaining to this category of buildings, and as their designation denotes ("Nafs," vessel and "Máhe," battle), were exclusively intended for Naval combats. They consisted of a vast and deep natural or artificial lake, encircled with the usual "Gradatio," or enlarging circle of seats, with its partitions for the spectators. There are reasons that explain why the Naumachiae did not equally become the theme of writers or engage the attention of archaeologues or otherwise ever attain the prominence of other edifices destined for spectacular exhibitions. Firstly, the Naumachiae were limited to one purpose not capable by its aqueous nature of as much variety as the land performances; secondly, they were mostly of a temporary character, as for example the naval combat given by Claudius, in which Tacitus tells us, 19,000 "Naumacharii" (ship combatants) were engaged; and thirdly, because the permanent circuses and amphitheatres were also occasionally used as Naumachiae and had water-conduits opening on them to inundate the arena when required for naval fighting.

The Naumachia of Octavius, near the Horti Caesaris, for which he built his aqueduct, must have been a permanent structure, and there was another mentioned on the Campus Vaticanus, which was, it is said, a work of Nero, but which may only have been another name for his circus there, already noted, also sometimes called his amphitheatre, or perhaps it may have been an annex of his said circus. The theoretically mimic naval battles waged in these Naumachiae were not much, if at all, less sanguinary than the gladiatorial land fights, or even real battles, in those times absolutely harmless mock combats would scarcely have suited the taste of the Romans under the Imperial rule.

CHAPTER XIII

AMPHITHEATRES

AS the severity of the principles and customs of the Royal and Republican periods began to relax, the thirst for amusement, fostered by those in power for their own ends, began to develop and spread, and in consequence edifices for spectacular diversions and sports increased in number, costliness of material, artistic display and variety of performances.

Nine amphitheatres are recorded in ancient Rome, most of them temporary buildings. Pliny describes an ephemeral construction of hybrid character which served as two separate semi-circular theatres for plays, each containing a distinct body of performers and audience, but which, revolving on an axis, closed and formed one amphitheatre for other spectacles. This is probably the structure indiscriminately denominated amphitheatre, theatre and circus, built by C. Scribonius Pariones for public exhibitions on the occasion of his father's obsequies, possibly 76 B.C., when he held the offices of Consul. If Pliny is to be trusted, who, moreover, in this instance confirms the testimony of others, this fabric showed a power of machinery not inferior to that of the present day, although doubtless worked on a different system.

Cesar, we are told, erected an amphitheatre, by some styled a circus, near his Forum Julium when he inaugurated the latter, and Octavius another larger one in 29 B.C. Caligula and Nero followed their example, the amphitheatre of the former being partly of stone and partly of wood, but, it seems, unfinished by him, and soon after demolished; that of the latter, possibly a reconstruction of the former, consisted entirely of wood with a velarium, or awning, painted blue with gilt stars in imitation of the firmament. These two structures are by some affirmed to be the circuses already noted, because the epithets of circus and amphitheatre were often promiscuously applied to the same structure. The Amphitheatre of Statilius Taurus, one of the generals of Octavius, in 16 B.C., when he was Praefectus Urbis, was situated on what became in mediaeval times an Orsini quarter, and the foundations and ground storey formed the under core of the present Monte Giordano, so called after one of the baptismal names of this feudal family. This amphitheatre is said to have been the first one entirely built of stone in Rome. It was destroyed in A.D. 64, presumably by the all-devouring fire of Nero's reign. Much later Trajan likewise began to construct an amphitheatre of stone and concrete, of which the exact site is uncertain and which was soon after also destroyed.

The Amphitheatrum Castrense, of which there are still some very scant vestiges, behind the present Monastery of the Cistercians, an annex of the Basilica of Sta. Croce

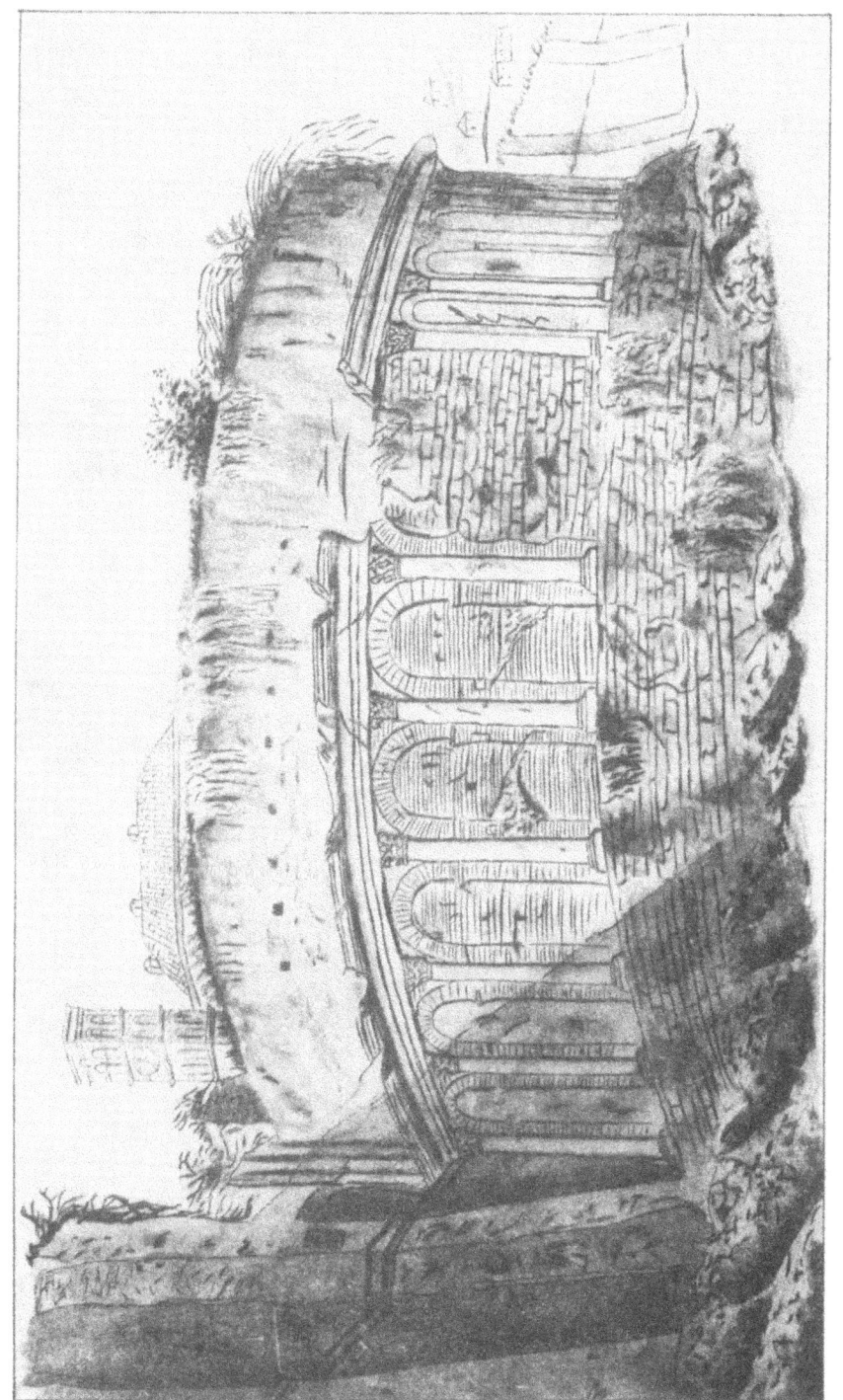

Plate xxxii. AMPHITHEATRE CASTRENSE, A.D. 14–37. SQUARE OF ST. JOHN LATERAN.

AMPHITHEATRES

in Gerusalemme, in the shape of a few arches supported by Corinthian pilasters attached to a wall. This building was probably composed mainly of brick, though marble and stone may have been adopted, as was customary, for the decorative parts. Its length has been estimated at about 175 feet and its width at 125, but otherwise nothing has been gathered. There are two versions regarding the date and proprietorship of the Castrense one, that it was built by Tiberius I, second Roman Emperor, A.D. 14–36, for the games called the Ludi Castrenses for the two cohorts of soldiers quartered in the neighbourhood, the other, that it was constructed about a century later, by, and belonged to, the Equites Singolares, one of the several Equestrian Orders. It shares with the Flavian Amphitheatre the distinction of being one of the only two surviving structures of this class whose remains have been discovered, identified and to some extent still exist.

All spectacular requirements were, however, amply supplied by the magnitude and magnificence of the above-mentioned Amphitheatrum Flavium, said to be the largest and certainly one of the most famous and imposing edifices of ancient, of mediaeval, or of modern times. This amphitheatre was begun by Vespasian, A.D. 72, and raised up to the third tier, and completed by Titus A.D. 80, who inaugurated it with spectacles that lasted consecutively for one hundred days in which sea-fights were represented realistically enough and five thousand wild beasts were slain, while the number of human beings that perished has not been computed. It is situated in the hollow between the Caelian and Esquiline Hills, on the space previously occupied by the artificial lake, an appurtenance of Nero's Golden Palace, which was built by him after the great fire of Rome with such lavish splendour and doomed to such rapid and total decay and almost extinction. Martial writes in reference to the site of this amphitheatre textually as follows:

" Hic ubi conspicui venerabilis Amphitheatri
    Erigitur moles stagna Neronis erant."

The actual construction of this mighty pile took less than four years because up till two years before Vespasian's death, in A.D. 79, the time was employed in the drainage of the above lake and other preliminary works. It was composed of a core of bricks and tufo covered externally by a coating of travertine and internally by a lining of marble, all held together by iron clamps, the numerous jagged holes now visible being caused by the extraction of these iron bars. There were, however, also other regularly cut orifices which served as the mouths of pipes for the emission of hygienically scented water sprayed to purify and perfume the atmosphere during the performances. It is affirmed that besides a multitude of other artisans and labourers, twelve thousand captive Jews were engaged in building this oval edifice which measured, according to the least inaccurate calculations, 157 feet in height, 620 feet in length, 525 in width and 1,780 in circumference, and the arena 279 by 174 feet

It consisted of four tiers, the first, second and third formed of arcades supported by semi-columns on their piers in the following gradations of Orders, Etruscan, Ionic and Corinthian, the fourth being a wall with apertures intersected by pilasters of the Composite Order sustaining the entablature that crowned the edifice. The arcades of the first or ground storey or tier served as entrances for the spectators, and were numbered to indicate the various sections, of these the numbers from XXIII to LIV are still traceable. Between the columns of the second and third tiers there were life-sized statues on pedestals, as may be seen on miniature reproductions of the amphitheatre on old coins. The stucco decorations were particularly fine and were chosen as models among other artists by Giovanni da Udine. There were four principal entrances, two of which were assigned for the exclusive use of the emperors and Imperial families. One of these has been identified by the numbers 38 and 39 still visible on the piers of the lower arch which had to be passed before reaching the great Imperial entrance. The other main entrances intended for the sacrificial processions that invariably preluded the spectacles and for the introduction of the wild beasts and the requisite mechanical appliances. There was also a cryptoporticus evidently destined as an escape-tunnel that issued facing the present church of San Gregorio Magno.

The foremost row of seats was called the "Podium" and reserved for the Sovereigns, Senators, highest officials, Ambassadors, Vestals and Pontifices. On an elevated dais in the centre was the "Seggestum," or canopied box, for the Imperial members, and, on this again the "Pulvinar" for the Sovereigns on thrones of carved ivory and gold. Certain philologues reverse the above noted relative positions of the Seggestum and Pulvinar, others, again, make no distinction between them, adopting the terms indiscriminately, but there does not seem to be any valid reason for accepting their dictum in this case. The seats of the Senators were thrones of finely sculptured marble, many taken from the theatres of Athens and Corinth, and these were in after years used as the Episcopical Cathedrae. Behind the Podium was the "Cavea," or more correctly "Equestria," consisting of twenty tiers of seats of marble, for the Equestrian Order, the second of the State, subdivided again into three grades of Equites or Cavaliers. The two Orders, Patrician and Equestrian, were seated on "Pulvili" or cushions. The Equestrian section was separated by the marble Praecinctio, or divisional wall from the "Popularia," destined for the ordinary citizens, the "Tiers État," the burgesses of Rome, consisting of series of stone seats. Divided from the latter by another similar wall was the top section composed of wooden benches allotted to the "Pullati" the populace or rabble.

These various sections of the entire "Gradatio" were separated horizontally by the "Praecinctiones," and vertically by the aforesaid stair-cases, the space between each being termed "Cuneus" from its wedgelike shape. The spectators who were most exposed because the nearest to the arena, were those of the highest dignity in the State, the occupiers of the Podium, but they were protected by the gratings of spiked iron bars and by the intervening open passage encircling the arena, constantly patrolled by guards. Some authorities opine that the arena was floored with wood, others that it was paved with stone and others that the ground was not covered but only levelled, but all concur that it was strewn with a layer of sand, whence its name of "Arena."

This amphitheatre, as others of its class, was open at the top, but the Velarium attached to lofty pine-masts fixed around the building and managed by sailors of the Imperial fleet, acted as a movable roofing quite sufficient as a protection against the sun and rain in such a fine climate and far preferable in other respects to a stable roof. Below were cages for the wild beasts sloping upwards to the level of the arena and the wards of

FLAVIAN AMPHITHEATRE (COLOSSEUM), A.D. 80. ROME.

Plate xxxiii.

the gladiators, and there was a regular service of lifts, and beneath all, a magnificent drainage system. The official appointed as general director of the entire personnel and machinery was styled Villicus Amphitheatri.

The number of spectators which this vast edifice was capable of containing has been variously estimated at 40,000, at 50,000 and at 87,000. A statistical discrepancy, even so great as this, might perhaps be admissible in the case in question when two-thirds of the building have disappeared and in dealing with a public place of amusement where the audience may easily be almost indefinitely multiplied by crowding. But the inaccuracies and contradictions continually to be met with in the measurement of the length, breadth, height and circumference of these material works which exist, are not equally excusable or explicable.

The nickname of "Colosseum" began to be applied to this amphitheatre in the eighth century. At that time culture had sunk to a low level, wherefore material objects were all in all, the words "Flavii," "Amphitheatre," "Architecture," conveyed little or no meaning to the ignorance of the men who were, however, none the less impressed by the colossal skeleton of the architectural giant looming visibly before their eyes, and hence gave it the generic appellation of "Colosseum," or "The Colossal." Some writers, while endorsing the above explanation of this epithet in principle, opine that it is due to the adjacent statue of Nero, the main objection to this conjecture being that the said statue had vanished some time previously to the period when the nickname came into use. In any case, it appears to have been a matter of size alone to which this edifice is indebted for the name by which it has been incorrectly but generally known ever since.

It is stated that the above statue of Nero, of which the scarred pedestal survives, was 110 feet high and represented this Emperor with the nimbus as Apollo. The "Nimbus, Aureole," or Halo, otherwise the circular gold, bronze, gilt or coloured disk, with or without rays, was placed round the heads of the statues and effigies of the deified emperors as an emblem of their godliness. It appears, however, that originally this projecting circlet or disk was adopted by the ancient Greeks as a protective cover for the heads and faces of their statues against the effects of rain, hail, dust, etc., and that the Romans, imagining it was a symbol of divinity, or considering it as an appropriate ornament for divine majesty, employed it as such for the effigies, images and statues of the deified Rulers. The Christians till the fourth century in their productions represented Supreme Divine Beings, or Saintly human beings, with a member of triangular or quadrangular shape about the head as a sign of Divinity or Saintship, but after that epoch, the identical Pagan Aureole was copied and adopted and its use has continued as we see, to this day. From the same eighth century also dates the prophetic distich of the Pilgrims:

"While stands the Colosseum, Rome shall stand.
When falls the Colosseum, Rome shall fall;
When Rome falls with it shall fall the world."

This prediction, which it must be confessed does not err on the side of modesty, despite the apparently devout belief with which the Venerable Bede, who died A.D. 725, alludes to it, seems uncommonly like a nursery rhyme to send tiresome youngsters to sleep.

The subsequent historical events associated with this structure have not all been transmitted to posterity, but the principal recorded are briefly as follows. The succeeding Emperors naturally gave great spectacles here upon which it is not incumbent to dwell in this work. Among others may be noted those of Hadrian and Commodus as offering some exceptional features; the former as he signalized his exhibitions by most realistic representations of a forest of living trees and shrubs on the arena, enlivened by wild beasts issuing from yawning clefts and caves, and the latter by his personal participation in the Ludi impersonifying Hercules, with the lion's hide and club, where he killed a number of gladiators and wild animals. The feats of Commodus in this character, although he was undoubtedly a powerful man, were not always so difficult of accomplishment as might appear at first sight, because his human adversaries spared him out of awe and fear, and the bestial ones were duly weakened beforehand artificially.

Among the Christian martyrs who met their death here may be cited Gaudentius, who, tradition relates, was the directing builder of the edifice, and the Saints Sempronius, Olympius, Theodulos, Exuperia, Ignatius, Prisca, Martina and others, all having their legends which it would take a volume to record. In A.D. 246 the Emperor Philip celebrated in the amphitheatre the thousandth anniversary of the foundation of Rome. In A.D. 403, on the occasion of the victory of Stilichus over Alaric at the battle of Pollantia a series of gladiatorial combats were given here in celebration of the event, during which a monk named Telemachus rushed into the arena and besought the spectators to renounce similar exhibitions. The immediate and personal effect of this intervention was that Telemachus was stoned to death by the outraged auditorium, the ultimate and general one, that from that day these savage spectacles were condemned and ceased, and the Emperor Honorius, A.D. 405, in consequence issued an edict formally abolishing gladiatorial combats as contrary to the spirit and principles of Christianity, though wild beast combats continued till the time of Theodoric the Great.

It is remarkable that so obvious a truth, or rather a truism, should not have occurred long before during the lapse of four centuries to Princes and Primates, and that it should have been reserved for an obscure monk to point out to the public the glaring inconsistency between their professions as Christians and their patronage of these inhuman sports, and who, in order to awaken their dulled perceptions and torpid consciences and feelings had to seal his appeal and protest with the sacrifice of his life. Nor has the failure of the Roman Catholic Church, so lavish in its beatifications and canonizations, to bestow an adequate mark of approval on this truly courageous and enlightened man, to whom humanity owes such a debt, ever been satisfactorily accounted for, unless, perhaps, by the axiom that very few, if any, alive or dead, get impartial appreciation and strict justice from their fellow men.

No useful purpose can be obtained by narrating the numerous religious legends connected with this famous building, but the one relating to Pope Gregory, First, Saint and Great, may be cited as a specimen. This Pontiff presented certain ambassadors with some soil from the arena to be conveyed by them as relic-gifts to their respective Sovereigns, which these personages evidently did not receive with befitting reverence, being diappointed, possibly, in their expectations of presents of a somewhat more substantial and worldly nature, whereupon Gregory proceeded to squeeze the sand, from which blood instantly oozed; a miraculous proof and reproof. In the lives of Saints we read of several almost identical miraculous episodes to the above of which there are also several versions.

The celebrated Robert Guiscard, A.D. 1015–1085, who was summoned to Rome by Pope Gregory VII to defend him against Henry IV of Germany, demolished the fortifications of this structure so as to render it unfit for further use as a bulwark of the Eternal City. Subsequently the Feudal Barons, notable the Frangipani, possessed themselves of the ancient amphitheatre and converted or reconverted it into an enormous fortress again. Two Popes, Innocents II and III, chose it as a place of refuge during their conflicts with their rivals the two Anti-Popes Anacletus II and Pascal. The Annibaldi, A.D. 1305–1312, who were masters of the Septizonium, the former Palace of Septimius, also annexed the Flavian Amphitheatre, and afterwards ceded it to the Emperor Henry VII, who returned it to the Senate and People of Rome.

During the fourteenth century, when the amphitheatre was in possession of the Municipality of Rome, it was sometimes used for bull-fights, and we hear that in A.D. 1332 many nobles participated in a fight of this nature, eighteen of whom were killed, relatively to these combats a heavy toll of life that may be attributed to the lack of skill of the mediaeval Romans as compared to the Spanish bull-fighters.

In A.D. 1381 the Senate made it over to the Canons of the Lateran, who transformed the building into a hospital and renamed it " Hospital Sancta Sanctorum," which explains the presence of the Arms of the Chapter, the Saviour's Head between two Candelabra, still traceable on some parts of the walls. It may not be generally known that St. John Lateran is the Metropolitan Church of the See of Rome of which the Pope is the ex officio bishop. On the platform of this basilica is written " Haec est Papalis Sedes et Pontificalis " and on the front is inscribed the Papal and Imperial Decree declaring this basilica to be the Mother and the Head of Churches. Moreover the Canons of the Lateran have the prerogative, in the absence of the Cardinals, of replacing the latter in the Sacred College in the most important of their functions, the election of the Supreme Head of the Church.

Necromancers subsequently plied their trade in this ancient amphitheatre, and B. Cellini narrates that on one occasion he caused the magician in possession to people the place with demons, one of his fantastic tales, unless, indeed, he meant human incarnated fiends, which would be no arduous task to find without magical powers, as there are always plenty of these at hand everywhere. The remonstrances of Angelo Paoli, a Carthusian monk, relatively to the impropriety of permitting a site hallowed by the blood of martyrs of the Christian Faith to be desecrated, induced Pope Innocent XI (Benedetto Odescalchi), A.D. 1676–89, to consecrate or reconsecrate the place, and it became henceforth again the resort of pilgrims. Seven churches and several shrines of which no vestiges remain, were erected in the arena, the former being dedicated respectively to San Salvatore, in Tellure, in Trase, de Insula, de Rota Colisci, San Giacomo, Sta. Agnese and one for the Saints Abdon and Sennen.

The beatified Leonardo di Porto San Maurizio preached his zealous sermons here, and founded the religious association styled " Amanti di Jesu e Maria." Benoit Labré, a Frenchman by nationality and a holy beggar by profession, used habitually to make these ruins his haunt, praying by day in the shrines and lying by night under the arcades. A little old house in the neighbouring Via dei Serpenti, where his relics are now kept and exhibited yearly on his anniversary, was his occasional dwelling place as the honoured but not paying guest, though this does not mean that the two characters are incompatible, for even in our money-making times we meet occasionally an individual who combines both. Labré died in Rome, A.D. 1783, was beatified by Pius IX and subsequently, it is reported, duly canonized. This huge pile of ruins became later the centre for the revolutionary meetings of 1848, and it was here that Gavazzi delivered his fiery orations, and from these ancient arcades issued again a crowd of Romans, no longer in the character of spectators of the grand and inhuman exhibitions, but as actors in the political drama then being played.

The first time this edifice needed and underwent thorough repairs was in the reign of Antoninus Pius, A.D. 138–160. In the single year of the reign of Macrinus, A.D. 217, it was nearly annihilated by a conflagration caused by lightning and restored successively by the Emperors Alexander Severus and Gordianus, and subsequently repaired by the Emperor Valentinian III, A.D. 425–455, after the severe damage occasioned by the earthquakes of A.D. 444, and again by Theodoric, A.D. 489–526. The secular Sovereigns, Roman Emperors and Gothic Kings, who frequently restored, replaced and guarded the monuments bequeathed by previous generations, gave an excellent example to the religious potentates, the Popes, which the latter failed to follow until comparatively recent times.

The earthquakes of the seventh, thirteenth and fourteenth centuries, notably those of A.D. 1231 and 1255, reduced this building to nearly, but not quite, its present dimensions, not quite, because it was reserved for the men of the fourteenth century and onwards to deliberately complete this wholesale ruination. From this period the ancient amphitheatre came to be regarded as a convenient quarry, near at hand, and abundantly provided with excellent material ready and hardened for immediate use. Besides other constructions the well known Farnese, Barberini and Venezia Palaces were built mainly of the stone abstracted from it. Under the Pontificate of Nicholas V, a certain Foglia was authorized to carry away 2,522 cart-loads of material from the amphitheatre, and Cardinal Farnese obtained permission from Pope Paul III, A.D. 1534–49, to remove as much stone and marble as he could within twelve hours, and the Cardinal, making the best use of the time limit accorded him, employed 4,000 workmen to do the work. Cardinal Riario constructed out of the travertine of the "Flavium" the Pontifical Cancelleria, an edifice which later, during the Papal constitutional government of 1846–47, was transformed into a Chamber of Deputies, wherein Count Rossi, the Pope's Minister of State, was assassinated. Clement XI likewise built of its material the principal landing stage of Rome on the Tiber, called "Ripetta Grande," much less frequented now than formerly. Sixtus V and Clement XI both attempted to utilize the arcades for practical purposes, the first as shops, the second as manufactories for saltpetre.

In the eighteenth century this secular plundering came at length to an end, and the long interrupted restoration and repairs, carried out formerly, were resumed. The Bull of Clement XI, aforesaid, by decreeing that all acts of pillage or injury would be henceforth considered as sacrilegious crimes, and be visited with the usual penalties, placed this historic pile under the Church protection, which shielded it, though rather late, from further wreckage. It was at this time that a chapel was erected within to Sta. Maria della Pietá e il Sangue dei Martiri (Saint Mary of Pity and the Blood of the Martyrs) but on the murder of the hermit in charge, A.D. 1742, Benedict XIV had the building closed for a time by bars and gates, and after reopened and reconsecrated not any more to the Virgin, but to the "Saviour and the Blood of the Martyrs," and a Via Crucis constructed terminating in a lofty iron cross left standing till 1872.

The last named Pope and eight of his successors namely: Clement XIII, Clement XIV, Pius VI, Pius VII, Leo XII, Pius VIII, Gregory XIV and Pius IX, all contributed, more or less, in saving this grand creation from total annihilation by sustaining vaults, buttresses, iron clamps, etc. It was unfortunate, in a sense, that the Government after entrusted Rosa with the direction of the excavations, who, however capable he was otherwise, committed the grave error, endorsed by the authorities, of extracting the parasite shrubs and creeping plants, that seem provided by nature to bind together and preserve ancient structures, an office they certainly perform, and by this measure the wear of time was anticipated by many years.

Although approximately only one-third of this famous edifice now exists, and in a very ruinous condition, it is still stupendously impressive and pre-eminently interesting as the tangible evidence of the historical, architectural and structural power and genius of the men who created it. An architect of the preceding century estimated the money value of the present much reduced remains at 1,500,000 scudi. Close by stands the crumbling mound usually called the "Meta Sudans," erected to quench the thirst of the combatants, and not, as some supposed, for the washing of their wounds, because the disabled gladiators were attended to, as already said, in the wards of the amphitheatre.

One of the most stringent articles of the unwritten but draconian code of tourists is to view this edifice by moonlight, but this choice of light is equally applicable to all, considering that it is a generally acknowledged fact that all works, all scenes of nature, as well as all persons, old or young, look to advantage, as a rule, if viewed by the softening light of "Selene" than when otherwise illuminated.

CHAPTER XIV
THEATRES

THE ancient Roman Theatres (this word derives from "Théama," spectacle, "Théatron," theatre) similarly to the amphitheatres (double theatres) may be divided into two categories, the earlier temporary or semi-temporary ones consisting of wood or partly of wood and partly of stone, which were often dismantled at the termination of a series of performances, and the later, permanent buildings of stone, bricks or marble. Of the former, in the natural course of things, no traces and scarcely any records survive, of the latter the remains of one only, the Theatre of Marcellus, are still standing.

The earliest we find mentioned authentically is that by Livy, on the Capitol, near the Temple of Apollo, about one hundred years before the fall of the Republic, belonging to the ephemeral class, which were tolerated, while the construction of permanent theatres was prohibited as long as this constitution was a fact and not merely a word. By a strange counter-coincidence, the two most celebrated Roman actors, Quintus Roscius in Comedy, and Claudius Aesopus in Tragedy, flourished at the times when there was no permanent, nor probably any temporary theatre, suitable for the display of their talents. The former died 62, B.C. and though the latter made his last public appearance at the inauguration of Pompey's Theatre, he had then terminated his professional career and had retired previously, and on this occasion broke down during the performance and was unable to proceed. Roscius was protected by Sylla; both were personal friends of Cicero as well as his clients professionally. The great orator styles Aesopus "Summus Artifex," Horatius and Valerius Maximus also eulogize the merits of these two eminent artists, the latter in referring to them uses the phrase "Ludicrae artis vires prestissimi."

The ephemeral "Theatre of Scaurus" was erected 60 B.C. by Marcus Aemilius, junior (son of the able and unscrupulous Marcus Aemilius Scaurus), on his return from his service as Questor under Pompey in the war against Mithridates. This theatre capable, according to Pliny, of containing 80,000 spectators, was built and furnished with great luxury and splendour, as is attested by its recorded 360 columns, 3,000 movable bronze statues, numerous paintings and the three sections of its stage composed respectively of marble, of glass and of painted tablets. Scaurus, at this time, occupied the office of Aedile, and is said to have nearly ruined himself financially by the enormous expenses he incurred in this undertaking, and the construction of a Palace on the Palatine, but, it is added, refunded himself by extortions in Sardinia, where he had been nominated Propraetor 55 B.C. It is satisfactory to know, however, that he was, in consequence accused of illicit appropriation, and that though he succeeded in obtaining his acquittal of the criminal charge, in consideration of his services to the State and of having spent most of his own patrimony, as well as his ill-got profits, mainly for public purposes (which, with the Romans covered a multitude of sins) he was not allowed for this " to feather his nest," and that he became in every sense, prospects, consideration and means, the poorer instead of the richer as the nett result of his delinquency. The Aemilii Scauri, a family which could boast also of men of unblemished reputations, were a branch of the illustrious stock of the Aemilii, their second name signifying swollen or large heels.

The magnificent " Theatre of Pompey " built by him 55 B.C. and the first permanent structure of this class, was calculated to provide accommodation for over 17,000 spectators. It was situated behind the present Palazzo Pio in the Via dei Giubbonari, and near the well known Campo dei Fiori, where once a week the usual sale of flowers, edibles and other articles is exchanged mainly for that of antiquities, mock and real, of all descriptions. Theatrical performances, with the exception perhaps of the pantomime, were not as much to the taste of the Romans as they were to the Greeks, the devoted lovers of the histrionic art. The former preferred witnessing the pomp and action of the grand and realistic spectacles of strength and courage. Pompey evaded the letter of the prohibitive law concerning the construction of permanent theatres by nominally dedicating his to the worship of " Venus Victrix," to whom he built a chapel within. This famous Roman, like others seeking power through popularity, had necessarily studied the psychology of the times and peoples, and had come to the conclusion that a formal recognition of a law, then practically obsolete, would suffice to preserve to him the favour of the conservative elements, while the erection of an imposing edifice for public spectacles would attract the others and dazzle all.

The two rivals, Gneus Pompeius Magnus and Caius Julius Caesar, in their race for power, initiated pandering to the people's appetites as a system, which, reacting on the critical transition stage the Roman world was then traversing, could have but one result and that was, the beginning of the end. The Patrician, Equestrian and Plebeian Orders, with their well-defined duties and corresponding rights, were practically swept away, and in their stead seethed a demoralized multitude, venal and frivolous, less brave and more ferocious, less dignified and more insolent, which inevitably paved the way, by the twin gates of licence and tyranny, to the disgraceful downfall that followed. Yet, like the candle flame which often blazes up more brightly before it begins to flicker and expire, so the might and glory of Rome never appeared greater or more resplendent than in this memorable epoch of her history, when already the germs of corruption had fastened fatally on her vitals, comprised in the closing years of the Republic and the opening ones of the Empire. And it is suggestive, but not reassuring, to note a certain resemblance in some respects between the present conditions of society in some of the leading States and those prevailing in Rome at the period referred to. For instance, the same ominous decay of public spirit, the tendency to shirk duty for its own sake, the craving for excitement, continual change and irresponsible life, in short, the development of humanity's feebler, grosser and duller qualities at the expense of her stronger, finer and more intellectual ones.

It would be in vain to seek now for any vestige of the superb theatre on its former site, but on the fragmentary ancient plan of Rome may be traced the outlines identified as those of this edifice by their form and proximity to the other constructions of Pompeius here, viz.: the Porticus, Halls and Ambulatories. It is to be noted, however, that the above outlines of this theatre do not represent the original building that had been repaired by Tiberius, but of a reconstruction of Claudius about one century later, but which, nevertheless, being authentic, will enable us to form some conception of the plan and style of the Roman Theatre of the times.

The stage was divided into four sections, namely: the "Pulpitum," where the actors performed; the "Proscenium," where they appeared and stayed; the "Scena," where the scenes, unlike our shifting ones, were fixed and immovable, and the "Postscenium," which served as the modern foyer. A lane separated the stage from the orchestra, and another the latter from the audience. The aristocratic Podium as customary came first, next the "Equestria" or sixteen rows of what we would now call reserved seats, for the Equites, and the remainder for the plebeians, the entire "Gradatio" being divided horizontally by partitions into the various sections and vertically by the staircases as mentioned in the Flavian Amphitheatre. No positive and detailed record of the decorations has been obtained, excepting the general one that the building was profusely and tastefully adorned within and without, and there can be little doubt that was the case, considering the power and purpose of the creator, who possessed ample pecuniary means and competent men at his disposal, and who, in furtherance of his aim, spared neither pains nor resources to impress and please.

Cesar, his rival in every direction, contemplated building a theatre calculated to outshine this one, but though he went so far as to design and begin that of Marcellus, death frustrated his complete realization of his project.

One of the halls which faced the magnificent Porticus Pompeii was called the "Curia Pompeia," and contained the statue of the Triumvir, its founder, which is conjectured to be the identical one now in the Palazzo Spada in the Session-Chamber of the present Council of State, a body corresponding somewhat to the British Privy Council. While the ancient Curia in the Roman Forum was being rebuilt, the Senate held its meetings in this Curia Pompeia, and it was here that Cesar was assassinated in 44 B.C., by what might seem a sort of retaliatory destiny, at the foot of his rival's statue, and the dark red stains visible on the marble are pointed out as the indelible marks left by the Dictator's blood. The colossal statue of Melpomene was also found here in A.D. 1775 or 1779, and transferred to the Vatican, but it was afterwards taken to France to be preserved in the Louvre, in Paris.

The "Theatre of Marcellus." Issuing from the small, busy and typical Piazza Montanara, much frequented by the peasantry, is an old, narrow street named Via Teatro Marcello, skirting which, on the site previously occupied, it is affirmed, by a Porticus and temporary theatre of Metellus, are now standing the ruins of the above Theatrum Marcelli, which was commenced, as aforesaid, by Cesar and terminated by Octavius, 13 B.C., who dedicated it to his nephew, son-in-law and heir apparent Marcellus, who, however, predeceased the erector. This edifice, built of travertine and marble, consisted of three tiers, the first and second certainly, the third possibly, formed of arcades resting on semi-columns attached to the walls of the Roman Doric, Ionic and Corinthian Orders in their usual gradation. Of these three series, the lowest is half embedded in the soil,

THEATRE OF MARCELLUS, A.D. 13. ROME.

Plate xxxiv.

and the exposed parts over the level, are in a dilapidated condition, the second also much damaged and broken, and the third, or highest, has entirely disappeared.

The interior was adorned with numerous works of art, principally of Greek creation, and has been calculated as capable of accommodating, with the usual diversity of computation, 3,000, 4,000 and 15,000 spectators. The third estimation is probably nearer the truth, if only because we know that the smaller neighbouring Theatre of Balbus contained, as recorded, about double of either of the first two numbers given. It is said that a double temple to Jupiter and Juno was annexed, constructed either by Metellus in 149 B.C. on this site, or by Octavius in order to evade the prohibitive law regarding theatres, which by this means became theoretically dedicated to the gods, otherwise a religious edifice. It is true that Octavius was in a position, at the time, to have overridden any law, but he was so scrupulous and politic an observer of forms that it is quite likely that he erected the said Jupiter-Juno Temple 13 B.C., if Metellus had not done so over a century and a quarter previously.

The Theatrum Marcelli was twice nearly burnt down, in A.D. 80, and in A.D. 203, on the first occasion restored by Domitian and on the second by Septimius. In the twelfth century this theatre was seized by the Pierleoni, who, according to custom, converted it into a feudal castle, retaining it till the fourteenth century. The family name of these Barons of Jewish extraction is still commemorated in the contiguous Via Pier-Leone. This Theatre-Fortress was afterwards alternately appropriated by the Orsini and the Savelli. From the architectural standpoint this ancient theatre has been considered by some as superior to the Flavian Amphitheatre and in support of this opinion it is known that the renowned Andrea Palladio, who is an authority in the canons and purity of classic architecture, and who came to Rome expressly to study the models of antiquity, selected its Doric and Ionic Columns in preference.

The inauguration of this theatre was heralded as customary by gladiatorial and wild beast combats, but subsequently, like the Theatrum Pompeii, it served for dramatic and musical performances. The ruins of this ancient edifice are now in a way inhabited by human beings, that is in a way not unlike the manner of birds in the orifices and crevices of the old walls, and the ground tier of arcades is used as shops by blacksmiths, retail coal sellers and the like, but degraded, blackened, wrecked and built upon as it is now, it is still a grand ruin, rising majestically among the squalid, pigmy, deformed, crowded dwellings around.

The "Theatre of Balbus." Until A.D. 1556 the Jews of Rome inhabited the quarter termed the Trastevere (Trans-Tiber) but in the above year Pope Paul IV (Giovanni Pietro Caraffa, A.D. 1555-1559) assigned to them that region of the city still known as the Ghetto (from the Hebrew " Ngedah " signifying a congregation) the generic name in Italian towns for the Jewish quarter. Here they were formerly separated from the other inhabitants of Rome, as was customary all over Italy and her dominions, and confined by boundaries and gates, opened and closed at fixed hours in the morning and evening by the authorities, between which no ingress or egress was permitted. During the revolutionary upheaval of 1848 the propulace, headed by Angelo Brunetti, better, known by his nickname of Ciceruacchio, whose bronze statue has been erected in Rome, near the Ponte Margherita, tore away the Ghetto gates, which were never afterwards replaced, any more than the restrictive regulations affecting the Israelitish community re-enacted, even after the restoration of Pius IX at the suppression of the short-lived Roman Republic, though the Jews continued to inhabit that quarter of the city till 1870.

In an old street of the Ghetto, now partly renovated, stands a church previously dedicated to San Salvatore in Cacaberi and subsequently to Sta. Maria del Pianto, its present appellation since the occurrence of a miracle of the Image of the Virgin on an adjoining wall, which shed tears on beholding a murder committed near it. Proceeding along this street also named Via del Pianto (Street of Weeping) from the Porticus Octaviae a little old square is reached called Piazza Giudea, and at the angle formed by the street and the square are some sculptured fragments which comprise, with the substructure of the theatre (converted into the underground church called San Paolo Hospitium et Schola) nearly all the existing remains of this ancient building on its former site. The Theatrum Balbus, capable of containing about 7,500 spectators, was constructed 12 B.C., by Cornelius Balbus, a general who had naturally seen active service, for it would have been difficult in those times and race to have singled out any prominent Roman, of whatever profession, who had not taken a turn in military command, and he decorated this theatre chiefly from the spoils he had secured in the African wars against a people called Caramantes, though the marble was taken from the Temple of Apollo. In the year 1556 two rough statues of Castor and Pollux, later placed on the summit of the flight of steps to the platform of the Capitol, were discovered here, and over three centuries after in 1888, some broken columns, conjectured to have belonged to this theatre, and also a cryptoporticus. Caius Velleius Paterculus, whose work might serve as a sequel to that of Livius, relates the following incident at the inauguration of the Balbus Theatre. An overflow of the Tiber had inundated this part of the city, and the spectators were in consequence obliged to come in boats, from which it may be inferred that the building was raised on a natural or artificial elevation. Researches relatively to its exterior and interior have not hitherto it seems yielded any precise information, so far, but it may be assumed that it resembled, on a smaller scale, rather the Theatre of Marcellus than that of Pompey.

CHAPTER XV
BRIDGES

THE bridges of ancient Rome, like her other constructions, nowise inferior in solidity and efficiency to their modern counterparts, often excelled them in material and aspect.

The " Pons Sublicius," the earliest known, was built by King Ancus Martius, and consisted of two distinct sections, the stable portion, the fragments of the foundation of which were still visible in low water up to 1877, when they were wantonly destroyed, and the movable part of beams " Sublicies," whence its name. The latter section, capable of being severed with comparative ease and rapidity, cut off, in case of necessity, the communication between the Trastevere on the one side of the river and city on the other.

It is related that the historical defence of the bridge begun by Horatius Coclitus with his two companions A. Larcius and T. Herminius, and continued by him alone, against the Etruscan army led by Lars Porsenna, lasted until the beams were cut or broken behind him, and thus all approach of the enemy over the bridge effectually stopped. His grateful countrymen presented him as a free gift with as much land as he could encircle with a plough in one day, and erected to him a statue, one of the first in Rome. The heroic defence of H. Coclitus and his two comrades, the equally heroic sacrifice of C. Mutius and the courageous escape of the hostage, Cloelia, with her companions, caused Porsenna to realize practically the unconquerable and magnanimous character of the Romans even more than their armies' achievements. It may be added that the Etruscan King proved himself a chivalrous as well as a formidable adversary, not only in the case of C. Mutius but also in that of Cloelia (to whom an equestrian statue was afterwards raised in the Via Sacra) for when she was returned to him by the Roman Senate, too proud and honourable to break its faith by retaining the fugitive hostages, he treated them with consideration and set them free unransomed and unconditionally.

It is probably not generally known that the origin of the name of an important class and profession in Rome is closely connected with this bridge. " Pontifex " is a composite Latin term derived from " Pontem," bridge, and " Facere," to make, to do, wherefore " Pontifices " signifies literally makers and keepers of bridges. Some philologues give a Greek etymological origin to " Facere," which, according to them, means " Sacrifices or Sacrificers," or sacrificing on the Pons or bridge, but whichever etymology be preferred, or both together, does not affect the case in question, because to keep the Pons Sublicius in order and to sacrifice upon it were among the duties of the earlier Roman priesthood, and it is noteworthy that in the Middle Ages a corporation of monks, a revival of the ancient Pontifices, was appointed to tend the bridges and to facilitate the passage of the pilgrims over the river.

King Numa Pompilius, the legislator, and also the prototype of the Popes " Rex " and " Pontifex Maximus," otherwise Secular and Spiritual Sovereign in one, was the institutor of the Collegium Pontificalis or Synod, a directive religious College composed of four members drawn exclusively from the Patrician Order. Under Servius Tullius, four more members were added, chosen from the Plebeian Order. In Cesar's times they were increased to fifteen, equally divided between the two Orders, and during the Imperial régime their number was no longer limited, but depended, like everything else, on the will of the monarch.

This Sacerdotal Body was endowed with extensive powers and functions; it was the Bench to judge and sentence all, clergymen and clergywomen, laymen and laywomen alike, accused of transgressions and crimes of a religious character, and it constituted the electoral corporation (of which the present College of Cardinals is an imitation) that elected the Pontifex Maximus or Supreme Head of the State religion. Besides, this Synod was the initiator, regulator and guardian of all canons, laws and dogmas, as well as of all rites and ceremonies. The Pontifex Maximus, on his part, was invested with the prerogatives of choosing, ordaining and consecrating all the members of the hierarchy, the several Orders of the Flamens or priests (who took this epithet from " Flammeum," flame, their conical flamelike head-piece) and the Vestals. The punishment of any one of these consecrated ministers or ministresses, if corporeal, could only be inflicted by his hand, if of confinement by his order, and, if capital, only after he had unconsecrated them himself and delivered them personally to the executioners. It was also one of the functions of the " Highest Pontiff " to record the events of every year in the chronological order of their occurrence which he inscribed on the " Album," or White Board, and exhibited to the public, but a copy of these " Annales Maximi " was also kept on a roll, and this explains how after the Gauls had destroyed or carried away all they could lay hands on including the " Album," Livy and Dionysius were able to quote so liberally in their works from the " Copy-Roll " of the " Annales Maximi " which had been rescued when the original Album had disappeared. Cicero reports that this registration was coeval with the foundation of Rome, " Ab initio rerum Romanorum," he says, but this date of the greatest Roman orator need not be understood literally, as we know that the office of Pontifex Maximus was instituted by Numa, and we may therefore assume that he intended thereby to indicate the time when Rome could be considered as a constituted State.

It was also one of the functions of the Supreme Pontiff to expound the very obscure meaning of the oracular utterances, omens and miracles, and to decide on the manner, day and hour of the expiatory or thanksgiving ceremonies, when in his opinion the case called for either. During the latter years of the Republic the last named duties were entrusted to the College of Augurs, but subject always to the ratification of the Pontifex Maximus. It may be noted that there were eight Sacred Colleges, viz.: 1st, the aforesaid Synodical Council to assist the Pontifex Maximus; 2nd, the Flamens Diales or Priests of Jupiter; 3rd, the Salii or Leapers of Mars; 4th, the Curiones or Chaplains for each Curia; 5th, the Vestales or Fire-Priestesses; 6th, the Augurales or Diviners;

AEMILIUS BRIDGE (Ponte Rotto), B.C. 180–142.

Plate xxxv.

7th, the Fetiales or Heralds; and 8th, the Celeres or Priests of the Equites or Knights. To these some authors add a ninth, the College of Corybantes or priests of Cybele.

The example of Numa was revived, after the lapse of centuries of the Republic, on the establishment of the Empire. The first emperor who voluntarily renounced this double sovereignty was Gratianus Augustus, A.D. 367–383, on the ground that for the same individual to hold the two most exalted earthly offices of such a different nature, was incompatible with the teachings of Christianity. After several centuries again this twofold sovereignty was assumed by the Popes (not the earlier ones, however) who borrowed even the Pagan title, Pontifex Maximus; only as their temporal dominion was much smaller than that of the Roman Emperors while their spiritual power was much greater, the Catholic rulers were first priests and then kings, the Pagan rulers were first emperors and then priests. In modern times, too, many Sovereigns such as the Emperors of Russia and Turkey were similarly the *de facto* and *de jure* Spiritual and Temporal Sovereigns.

The "Pons Aemilius" was begun 180 B.C. by the Censors, M. Aemilius Lepidus and M. Fulvius Nobilior, and completed after an interval of nearly forty years by the Censors P. Scipio Cornelius and L. Mummius. This bridge, close to and parallel with the Sublicius, spanned the Tiber from the Forum Boarium by the Porta Flumentana to the Trastevere. According to Buffalini, it had originally seven large arches, which remained standing till the inundation of A.D. 1598 carried away two, and of the surviving five, four were quite aimlessly and barbarously destroyed as late as A.D. 1887. This bridge of marble, when intact, must have been a thing of beauty, a combination of artistic design and execution and of engineering skill, as is attested by the single arch and the third of another of the solitary wreck existing now, which presents such a striking contrast from the massive foundations to the panelled parapets, to the inferior, unattractive modern bridge near. It was from the Pons Aemilius that the body of Heliogabalus, and later those of the martyred brothers, Semplicius and Faustinus, among several others, were thrown into the Tiber.

The contention of certain archaeologues that this bridge was constructed by the Emperor Marcus Aurelius Valerius Probus, A.D. 276–282, is effectually disposed of firstly by the style and plan of this work belonging to a period prior to the third Christian century, and secondly by its ancient generic appellation of "Pons Lapideus," applied to it because it was the only bridge entirely of stony substance then in Rome, while it is known that there were several of similar materials in the times of Probus, who, it seems, built another bridge in the vicinity, which may account for this error. Between the Pontes Sublicius and Aemilius were anciently two gigantic Lions' Heads to which a chain was fastened and drawn across the river to prevent hostile vessels from passing. In the modern masonry the Lions were reproduced in a way, but lacking the charm and dignity of their classic predecessors.

The "Pons Fabricius," another adjacent ancient bridge reached by the narrow old street called the Via Monte Savello, connected the ancient Forum Boarium with the Insula Tiberinae, or Tiberine Isle. It was built, to replace a former wooden bridge, of peperino coated with travertine, by the Curator Viarium L. Fabricius, 62 B.C., and consists of two arches with a small floodgate between them in the central pier. It took its first name of "Pons Fabricius" from the builder, its second of "Pons Judaeorum" from the Jewish community inhabiting the Trastevere before their removal to the opposite bank, and its third and present common denomination of "Ponte Quattro Capi," or Four Headed Bridge, from the bust of Janus on the parapet.

Though much smaller and incomparably inferior to the Aemilius in every respect, it is a well built, well proportioned construction, and as it had already had nearly twenty centuries of existence and is still quite serviceable, it may be regarded as a creditable testimony to the durability of Roman works, whenever they were not deliberately destroyed or almost as badly repaired. And if the Pons Aemilius has not attained an equal longevity this is not due to inferiority in work but to superiority in material and artistic worth, qualities which seem to have attracted the destructive propensities of *bona fide* destroyers, or of incompetent restorers, who often substitute disfiguration to demolition. The inscriptions on the bridge, still traceable, read as follows:—" L. FABRICIUS C. F. CUR, VIAR. FACIENDUM. CURAVIT. RIDEMQ. PROBAVIT" and "Q. LEPIDUS. M. F. M. LOLLIUS M. F. Cos, EX. S. C. PROBAVERUNT."

During the construction of the present river embankment there were found in the "Favissae" (pits) close to this bridge several votive offerings to Aesculapius consisting of arms, legs, trunks, hands, etc., moulded in terra cotta, just as votive offerings representing diseased parts or limbs of the human body are similarly appended in the Roman Catholic Churches to the Images of the Madonna and Saints which are credited severally with the faculty of curing certain illnesses of their devotees. The trunks discovered here were opened in front, leaving exposed the heart, lungs, bowels, etc., shewing a knowledge of anatomy and accuracy of reproduction of the internal component parts nowise inferior to those of the present day after the passage of twenty centuries.

The "Pons Cestius" was built 46 B.C. by the Praetor Lucius Cestius, a kinsman of the Caius Publius Cestius of the well known pyramidical mausoleum, to connect the Insula Tiberinae with the Trastevere on the other side. The Roman Senate, with its characteristic provident sagacity, made it a rule not to grant its final formal approval until forty years had elapsed from the completion of public works, during which period contractors were held responsible for the collapse or other deterioration resulting from incompetent construction. The restorations made by the Co-Emperors Valentinian and Valens, and by Gratianus with travertine taken from the Theatre of Marcellus, were marked by their Sacerdotal title of Pontifex Maximus as well as their Imperial one, a curious anomaly, because these monarchs (with the exception as aforesaid of Gratianus) and others, while professing Christianity, retained the title of Pontifex Maximus of the Primates of the Pagan Faith which they had abjured.

After the construction of the church dedicated to the Apostle St. Bartholomew, A.D. 1113, on the Tiber Isle, the Pons Cestius was re-named Ponte San Bartolomeo, a designation it bears to this day. This bridge was much mauled about and rebuilt in part by the Municipality in 1888, save the central arch, which somehow escaped their meddling and muddling.

The Insula Tiberinae or Insula Sacra (Sacred Isle) to which as aforesaid these two bridges converge from the opposite river banks, linking it thus with the mainland on either side, has a rather curious origin and philanthropic history. It is related that

FABRICIUS BRIDGE, B.C. 62.

Plate xxxvi.

after the fall and expulsion of the Tarquins their extensive cornfields, like their other possessions, were seized, and enormous quantities of corn were thrown into the river at this spot, in conformity with the more than bestial habit of all revolutionary mobs who destroy the resources and works of their countries in order to demonstrate their animal animosity to a system or an individual. The masses of cereals, owing to their agglomeration and their cohesive and elastic nature, stayed and swelled, thus forming a nucleus around which the river-bed soil and stones gathered, augmented by the flowing weeds, rubbish and other materials continually brought by the current and stopped by this obstacle, which, in consequence, gradually grew in size and height, and thus, in the course of time, formed an islet in the middle of the river, large and solid enough to be useful and to justify the placing of a protective border of neat hewn travertine blocks as a bulwark on its shores.

Three Templets, consecrated respectively to Aesculapius, Jupiter Lyaconius and Faunus, besides a chapel to Semo Sanco and other accessory buildings, were subsequently raised upon it, the principal of which was the first named, built 292 B.C., on the occasion of a plague visitation. It is affirmed that the chapels or shrines of Semo Sanco, being built on sites struck by lightning, were open at the top in order that this Sacred Fire could have free access, if it should return.

It is related that in obedience to certain oracular paragraphs of the Sibylline Books a special embassy was despatched to Epidaurus, a small town in Greece, that contained several temples dedicated to Aesculapius, charged with the mission of obtaining and bringing to Rome a statue of the medical Deity, which they succeeded in accomplishing. Legendary lore, so frequently interwoven with history, further adds that on their return journey up the Tiber a serpent, till then invisible during the voyage, glided out of the vessels and landed on the Tiberine Isle, and that this was interpreted by the faithful as a token that Aesculapius had chosen this spot for his residence, this reptile, the symbol of his widom and his constant companion, being taken as his Alter Ego on this occasion. In consequence this islet was duly honoured by the erection of his temple forthwith and also given the commemorative form of a stone ship, a part of which with Aesculapius' bust can still be seen at the south extremity under the convent, the mast being represented by an obelisk, now long since vanished. During the floods this vessel-shaped isle took formerly the illusive appearance of a floating galley, while in the ordinary conditions of the river it assumed that of a stranded one. In the gardens of the Villa d'Este, at Tivoli, there is a model of the Insula Tiberinae in its ancient vessel-form, and in the Villa Borghese, in Rome, there is an Aedicula with a statue to Aesculapius on the islet of the artificial lake there, of course a modern construction.

The treatment of patients submitted for cure to this Divinity of the Sacred Isle, a mixture of medicine and magic, was characteristic enough. They were first drugged and then placed in the peristyle of the Temple, where, in their dreams, produced by the threefold agencies of narcotics, excited imagination and disease, Aesculapius was supposed to visit them and by hints, directions and prescriptions, indicate to the sleepers the remedies required, which method, it is quite possible, may have sometimes proved as effective as any other. The High-Priest received the reports of the patients on their returning to consciousness, and forthwith attended to the administration of the recipes, and if the cure was successful, the patient or his friends presented the votive offerings and donations, which were suspended at the sanctuary of the health-giving Deity.

Naturally this treatment did not in all cases succeed, but the usual explanations were ready at hand to justify the failure without compromising the infallibility of the God. Aesculapius may have been wroth with them for some reason or other and deliberately misled them in order to punish them, or the sufferers had not duly comprehended or reported the hints and recipes, etc., all quite possible contingencies considering, on the one hand, that the patients could not be all or most of them sinless and faultless, and also that they were often delirious or partly so, while, on the other, the miraculous advice was frequently ambiguous and vague. If this system were adopted of making remuneration conditional on recovery of health it would suit the patients admirably, who would either thus regain their health or keep their money, only it would not be equally advantageous or often just to the physicians. Among the wily Chinese another custom is said to prevail or to have prevailed, the doctors were paid so long as their clients retained their health and ceased to be so as soon as the latter fell ill, when the physicians had to attend them gratis. So in direct opposition to what happens with us, medical men there lived by the health and not by the diseases of their clients, otherwise, it was thus made the pecuniary interest as well as the moral interest of the physician to keep his client well continuously, and it is possible that neither party were the worse either hygienically or financially for this custom.

The Isola Tiberina, with the exception of some few and comparatively brief intervals, has for over 2,000 years served as a refuge to suffering humanity. The most important interlude occurred during the latter years of the Empire, when this islet, with its buildings, exchanged the benevolent character of hospital for the punitive one of prison. The Emperor Claudius decreed that all sick slaves placed within its sacred limits should, in the event of their recovery, obtain at once their unconditional freedom, so that once within the river-bound Tiberina they were *ipso facto* released from their bondage, either by life or by death. On the site of the ancient Temple of Jupiter Lycaonius, from whom the isle is also denominated "Insula Lycaonia," was built in A.D. 1575 the Hospital of San Giovanni, also styled "Dei Benfratelli," because it was administered and served by the Brethren of the Order of "Fate bene fratelli" founded by San Giovanni di Dio. This hospital contains seventy beds for male patients only, whose number averaged during the year about 1,200. Thus, after the lapse of many centuries, this isle, with its buildings of church and convent, reverted to the original purpose and use of its foundation of the ancient Pagan times, a refuge for the sick.

On the site of the Aesculapian Temple the German Emperor Otho III, in A.D. 997, built a church he dedicated to his friend, St. Adalbert of Gnesen, which, however, he endowed, or intended to endow, with the body of the Apostle St. Bartholomew as its chief relic, which he had brought, or believed to have brought, from Beneventum, the doubt being caused by the Beneventans declaring afterwards that they did not give up the body of the Apostle, too precious to be surrendered, but kept it, delivering instead the body of San Paulinus of Nola. Pope Gelasius II, completing the reconstruction of this church initiated by Pope Pascal II, A.D. 1113, rededicated it to the Apostle St. Bartholomew.

The "Pons Janiculus" of Caracalla's times may be said to have practically disappeared, because the ancient foundations and piers we now see of the present Ponte Sisto are almost entirely those of the Pons Valentiniani built A.D. 366 by the Prefect Symmachus, and named after the Emperor Valentinian. This bridge collapsed owing to an overflow in the pontificate of Adrian I, A.D. 772–95, and henceforth was popularly known as the "Pons Fractus," or Fractured Bridge. Its third supplanter, the present Ponte Sisto, was constructed by Pope Sixtus IV in A.D. 1473, and was subsequently completely remodernised, which does not mean rendered beautiful. One of the innumerable Roman superstitions persistently clings *ab antico* to this bridge in all its changes, viz : That unless on crossing it one sees a priest, an old woman or a white horse, any of the three being equally efficacious, one cannot hope for good luck, which is hardly respectful enough to the two first who might justly claim, one would think, some sort of precedence over a quadruped, even in these levelling days.

The "Pons Agrippa." The spot, about 125 yards from the Pons Janiculus, of this bridge was identified by an inscription on a cippus found near, but no records or remains of this bridge have, so far as we know, been as yet discovered. With regard to the "Pons Vaticanus," otherwise "Neronis" and to the "Pons Aelius," See Chapter XXIII.

The "Pons Scaurus," which subsequently took the name of "Milvius," from the Milvii, a conspicuous family residing in the neighbourhood on the adjacent Monte Mario, and now known as the Ponte Molle, was constructed by the Censor Marcus Aemilius Scaurus. Chronologically, therefore, this bridge should have had the third place, coming after the Pontes Sublicius and Aemilius and before the prementioned succeeding ones, but the latter being city bridges and locally adjacent it was deemed advisable to adhere, in this case, to sequence of topographic vicinity rather than strictly to date of construction. Four of the original arches remain, but Pope Pius VII built the other parts in A.D. 1815, and it was about this time that it took its present name of Ponte Molle. The triumphal arch was, however, erected by the architect Valladier in A.D. 1805. The statues of the Saviour and St. John are by the sculptor Francesco Mocchi, whose most successful works are held to be the group of the Annunciata at the Duomo of Orvietto and the statue of Sta. Veronica in St. Peter's Cathedral in Rome, and he also made the well-known stucco figures in the church of St. Bernardo and the twin statues of Saints Peter and Paul that flanked the Porta del Popolo, both in the Eternal City. To narrate the various historical and legendary episodes of which this bridge has been the theatre would be to take too deep a plunge into the annals of the past for a work of this description, but two may be mentioned, the one on account of its historical value, and the other, ecclesiastical, in virtue of its typical character

The first is, that the epoch-making battle of Saxa Rubra, A.D. 312, whereby Christianism triumphed over Paganism, was fought here, in which the Emperor Maxentius, the Pagan champion, was drowned in the Tiber near, or under, this bridge.

The second is the following. The severed head of St. Andrew, Apostle and Martyr, well preserved either by miracle or by embalmment, was brought over from Patras, where it had been in danger of being sequestrated by the Turks, to Narni, from which town Pope Pius II (Aeneas Silvius Piccolomoni), A.D. 1458–1464, resolved to have it transferred in solemn procession to Rome. The Pontiff, assuming, apparently, that the trunkless heads of Saints are disposed to behave in about the same manner as whole live sinners, opined that on such occasion when St. Andrew's head had risked such peril and had come from a distance, it would be incumbent, or at least becoming, on the part of the heads of Saints Peter and Paul to go, or be carried, to meet and give a welcome to the travelling head of their brother Apostle on its arrival at the place of their habitual residence.

But excessive piety has its drawbacks, like everything else; the faithful devotees, in their generous zeal, had loaded the iron shrines or safes of the two Saints so heavily with their donations and votive offerings of massive silver and gold that they could not, it is asserted, be transported, which is nevertheless an odd confession of impotence in the descendants of those Romans who have moved and erected enormous masses and fabrics from considerable distances, as is proved by the colossal constructions of antiquity. In any case, the result was that the Pope had to forego his project and proceed, unaccompanied by the Holy Heads, but accompanied by a number of Cardinals and Court officials and followed by a crowd of people, to meet the procession bearing the incoming Apostolic Head over Pons Milvius.

The Pontiff, in this meeting, thereupon addressed an eloquent peroration to St. Andrew's Head, and had a hymn chanted invoking the alliance and intercession of the Saint against the Ottomans, towards whom the Pope reasonably concluded this Saint in particular could have little cause to be indulgently disposed. A halt of half a day was then ordered, during which the Head was temporarily placed in the Church of Sta. Maria del Popolo, wherefrom it was conveyed with due pomp and ceremony to the Basilica of St. Peter, where it was deposited.

The "Pons Narsus," otherwise Numentanus, which it is reported was built on another bridge of more ancient times. The name Numentanus has given work to philologues. Some maintain that it arises from Numentanus, or Numitor, the maternal grandfather of Romulus and Remus, others from Numentum, the name of the district, the modern Mentana, others from Numentanus Crescentius, its constructor or reconstructor, and others again from Numen, gods. The reason of the name of Narsus being applied to it is obvious. Narsus was first sent to Italy as the lieutenant of the more celebrated Belisarius, whom he succeeded as Exarch of the Emperor of the East Justinian for Italy, A.D. 552–556, and it was during this period that he built this bridge. As we view it now, with its picturesque shape and turreted walls, it could never be mistaken for an ancient bridge, any more than for a brand new one, the mediaeval constructions being in aspect quite as distinctly typical and superior to the modern, as the classic ancient style was in its turn distinct and superior to the mediaeval. It may be noted here as possibly not generally known, that the mediaeval Guelph and Ghibelline parties marked their antagonism even in their architecture, for instance, the bifurcated turrets are Guelph and the apex turrets are Ghibelline. It was over this bridge that the Italian troops marched on to the Eternal City in 1870, which, by its capture, sealed the unification of Italy under one Sovereign.

But even more interest can be claimed by the River Anio, which this bridge spans near the Basilica of Sta. Agnese, Fuori le Mura, and by the land around, than by the bridge itself. The legend of Rhea Sylvia connected with this site, who shipped her twin baby boys here in their cradle boat to become, when adults, the founders of the most renowned City and the greatest State known, has been mentioned. It was likewise here, on the neighbouring Mons Sacer, that the Roman plebeians twice retired in a body, until, in the first instance, the recalcitrant Patricians granted some of their demands, and in the second, until the iniquitous government of the Decemvirs had been abolished. The eloquence of Menenius Agrippa and his apt and ingenious apologue of the " Belly and the Members," went far to smooth all differences. The second secession of the Plebs under their leaders, Virginius and Icilius, was, however, of another character, being organized and carried out on the advice and co-operation of the Patrician Delegates, Horatius and Valerius, as in this case both Orders were equally determined to have done with the men and system of the Decemviral rule. About four centuries later, another scene was enacted within this site and river, this time associated with the defeat of the plebeian faction, when P. Ruffinus Sylla, the patrician leader of the triumphant aristocratic party, had the body of Caius Marius, the plebeian leader of the vanquished democratic party, thrown into the river Anio.

To all intents and purposes the two above exoduses of the Plebs were regular "strikes," only, like most things ancient, were more just, practical and thorough than the modern frequent attempts of this nature, whose origin, often sordid and puerile, and almost always entirely selfish and unpatriotic, is usually signalized by unreasonableness in the demands and feebleness in the execution. Our claim, therefore, that "strikes" are quite a modern invention sounds rather comical. But these demonstrations of ancient times were not called "Strikes," therefore they were not "Strikes," because with our superficiality, as already observed, the "word" is everything and the "fact" nothing. The title of "Mons Sacer," or Sacred Mount, applied to the above elevation, here arose, according to Dionysius of Halicarnassus, from an altar thereon erected to Jupiter. This historic hill has been levelled by the Municipality and the material used for building purposes.

The "Pons Lucanus," See Chapter XXV, and the "Pons Aquoria" are the two recorded and surviving ancient bridges, though in ruins, of Tivoli, so far as has been gathered. The latter, situated near the foot of Mount Catulus, dates probably from the second century of the Christian era. The builder is unknown, but it derives its name from a spring close by, whose waters have a golden hue, "Aqua-Oria," otherwise "Aqua-Aurea," Only one of its arches consists of stone, the others being of bricks, which at first sight might seem strange in the land of huge travertine quarries, but the brickwork is that of a later reconstruction, and we must remember that there was such a demand probably for travertine everywhere for great edifices that in its place of production it had become too scarce to be used for the more ordinary constructions. However this may be, this bridge is a solid, useful structure, without any claims to artistic value.

It may be noted that the ancient Romans proved by their bridge-building their knowledge and mastery of waterways in a degree sometimes lacking in the present day. To cite one case in point, the Pons Aelius, for instance, was constructed with the great arches for the bed and flow of the river in ordinary conditions, and the side arches, or floodgates, to give vent during an overflow.

CHAPTER XVI
ARCHES

AS Rome gradually assumed the position of Queen of Nations, she gathered round her and absorbed, besides the genius of her own race, all the talents and resources of the other tributary or subject nationalities. In similar circumstances it would have been strange if her architecture were not distinguished by arches and columns, these two main architectonic sections, many in number, superb in design and execution and costly in material, whether standing alone as complete isolated monuments, or as integral parts of other structures. The Arch of Titus and the Column of Trajan, household words among the cultured of every nation, continue to this day to hold their undisputed supremacy as the most perfect creations extant respectively, to which the civilized world of succeeding generations pays the sincerest of all appreciations and homages, that of taking them as the best models for imitation.

A number of these works have so utterly disappeared that the very site they occupied is uncertain or unknown, but of the more or less ruined specimens left, a summary account and the respective illustrations may serve to convey some remote idea of what they were originally.

The "Arch of Romulus," which stood in some spot as yet unidentified, was built, it is conjectured, mainly of tufo, as this was the usual material used at that period, without decorations and naturally of a primitive, crude, solid style.

The "Arch of Camillus," erected over three centuries later, was composed of blocks of superior stone, a distinct step in advance. The plan of Buffalini, places this arch where the present Via Pié di Marmo joins the Corso. During the long period that elapsed between the erection of these two arches and also between the second and the succeeding one, it is more than probable that others were built of which no positive records or traces remain.

The "Arch of Scipio Africanus," said to have been erected 190 B.C., was situated on the platform of the Capitoline Hill. This arch was decorated with two horses and some gilded statues, among which was the noted group of Aristides teaching a youth to play on the lyre.

The so-called "Arch of Drusus," standing just within the Porta San Sebastiano, built of blocks of travertine, the flanking columns of African marble being additions of a later date, was, in fact, a main archway of the Martian Aqueduct, those near or within the city being more elaborate, and it was subsequently used as such by Caracallus. During this period and later it was known by the name of "Arcus Stillae," from the dripping water of the conduits above. Pope St. Stephen held a Synod here, where he was

ARCH OF TITUS, A.D. 81.

Plate xxxvii.

incarcerated, A.D. 257, and issued his official documents with the formula "In carcere ad Arcum Stillae." This site was formerly spanned by three arches, erected respectively to Drusus, to Verus and to Trajanus, all vanished, which may explain but does not justify the choice of Drusus to give a name to this archway. This conjecture can, moreover, be effectually disposed of by the style and plan of this work belonging to a period of over a century prior to the times of Drusus. But even if it were a contemporary work it is next to impossible to admit that a rough arch of this antiquated type, though well built in its way, would be the appropriate monument erected in honour of a man of the exalted position and great popularity and reputation of Drusus, in times, too, when the members of the Imperial families were regarded as demi-gods, and when art, luxury and splendour had reached, in this Augustan Age, such a high degree of development.

The "Arch of Fabius" (Fornix Fabianus) built by the Consul and Censor Quintus Fabius Maximus, 109 B.C., near the Temple of Antoninus and Faustina, was, it is asserted, the first triumphal arch in the Roman Forum, which, crossing the breadth of the Via Sacra, marked the limits of the earlier Forum in this direction, as a memorial of his decisive victory over the Allobrogi, near the river Iser, 120 B.C., for which he received, as was customary, the honorary epithet or title of "Allobrogicus," in addition to his names. A few mouldering vestiges testify to the former existence and situation of this Fornix, which, it is affirmed, was of the severe simplicity of style characteristic of the earlier Republican times.

The "Arch of Dolabella and Silanus," raised A.D. 10 by the Consuls P. Cornelius Dolabella and Caius Julius Silanus, is likewise composed of travertine, small, simple and unadorned, but its proportions are perfect, and the hermitage over it and the convent near it combine to give a general picturesque effect to the whole scene. Both Nero and Domitian included this arch in the passage of their aqueducts to the Imperial palaces, and there are some crumbling remains of the former's water-conduit near this spot. The person to whom, or the occasion for which, if any, it was originally intended are unknown, the probability being that the above Consuls of the illustrious families of the Cornelii and Julii signalized their tenure of office by this as by other works of convenience and embellishment to the city. The street which terminates at this arch was the ancient "Clivus Scaurus," now called "Via SS. Giovanni e Paolo," opening on the little Piazza della Navicella (vulgarly "Barcaccia") that takes its name from the small marble boat (Navicella) which stands in the square, a thanksgiving offering of the centurions of the Legions in foreign parts, who were detached from their units, sent to Rome and stationed here, on a service somewhat similar to that of officers of the Intelligence Department.

The "Arch of Augustus," the foundations of which, discovered in A.D. 1888, were identified by the following paragraph of the Aeneid "Juxta Aedem Divi Julii," allusive to its junctaposition either to the Temple of Cesar or to his Basilica, both in the Roman Forum, both near and both referred to indiscriminately by the above designation. This arch, that spanned the Vicus Vestae and bounded the limits of the Forum on this side, was a triple vaulted structure with the inner piers larger than the outer ones. Nothing has been gathered relatively to its decorative or other details and it was finally destroyed in A.D. 1540-46.

The "Arch of Tiberius," near the Temple of Saturn, also in the Roman Forum, has been probably only partially unearthed. According to Tacitus it was erected A.D. 16, in commemoration of the recovery by Germanicus of the Roman standards taken by the Teutons from Varus, the defeated General of Octavius, on which occasion the heavy losses they inflicted on the Romans drew from the Emperor the well-known reproachful and dolorous exclamation of "Varus, give me back my legions." A portion of a half buried arch, a fragment of a huge column and pieces of a massive, finely sculptured frieze are the remains of what was undoubtedly a handsome and imposing monument.

The "Arch of Nero," stated to have been erected somewhere on the Capitol and quite vanished, is said to have been begun during the Armenian wars, in which, by the way, the Roman Emperor's army was vanquished. The only interesting item gathered concerning this Arcus Neronis seems to be that the well known and much travelled bronze horses, now on the façade of Saint Mark's Basilica in Venice, and previously in Byzantium, were placed on this arch originally, but they are certainly not specimens of the highest classic art.

The Arches of Claudius, Domitian and Aurelius formerly crossed that part of the ancient Via Flaminia now called the Corso. Of the first named two fragments of carved marble were preserved in the Capitoline Museum and the Borghese Gallery respectively, of the others nothing, so far as we know, has been as yet identified. The three Gordian Emperors had, it appears, two arches near the above locality and the third in some part of the Roman Forum, not yet specifically established.

The "Arch of Titus," commemorating the conquest of Jerusalem, was erected in A.D. 81 on the summit of the Via Sacra, in honour of this Emperor by the Senate and People of Rome and dedicated to him by his immediate successor and brother, Domitian. There are two inscriptions on this monument, the ancient original one facing the Roman Forum is brief and as follows:

"Senatus Populusque Romanus Divo Tito
Divi Vespasiani Filio Vespasiano Augusto."

The other, fronting the Flavian Amphitheatre, more prolix and of a much later date, records the restoration effected by Pope Pius VII, which was conducted in a niggardly and slovenly fashion, the missing portions of the damaged structure originally of marble being replaced by travertine. But we ought to be thankful for small mercies, and even inadequate and unsuitable repairs are better, in some cases, than none at all.

This was the first public monument of importance in which columns of the Composite Order were introduced exclusively in Roman architecture. The reliefs of the frieze represent a sacrificial procession, and those of the soffit of the arch illustrate, in the centre and summit the Emperor borne to heaven on an eagle, and, on one of the sides lower down, Titus again in a quadriga drawn by the Genius of Rome and crowned by Victory, and on the other, the triumphal cortége of the captive Jews, the Shew-Bread and the Seven-Branched Candlestick. In the Middle Ages this arch went by the name of "Septemlucenarium," evidently originating from the above famous Jewish candlestick. Later the Arcus Titi was appropriated by the Frangipani, lords of that part of

ARCH OF JANUS QUADRIFRONS.

Plate xxxviii.

Rome, furnished with a portcullis and battlements and incorporated in the fortress they built there. The complete demolition of the sustaining fortifications in A.D. 1823 necessitated the above mentioned restoration by Valladier, by order of Pius VII.

The drawing of Giuliano di San Gallo shows how much, even since his time, A.D. 1443–1517, the finely executed reliefs and columns have been vitally injured, but mutilated, wrecked and patched as we now behold this arch almost beyond resemblance to what it once was, it is still, owing to its graceful simplicity and exquisite symmetry, style and work, the most beautiful monument of its class, ancient or modern, surviving in Rome. It is remarkable that though this arch has naturally been chosen by posterity very frequently as a model, there is no absolute facsimile reproduction of it of monumental size and importance so far as we know, existing. These solitary Arches did not invariably open on streets and roads, nor were they always left on the spot where they had been first erected, but sometimes removed according to the requirements of the times, the one in question, for instance, changed places, it is affirmed, more than once.

The "Arch of Janus." The date of the construction of this Arcus Compitalis is very uncertain, and might be fixed at any time between the closing years of the first Christian century and those of the second, and by some writers at a still later period. But it is known that Domitian, A.D. 81–96, erected several magnificent Jani in various parts of the Eternal City, and as we do not hear of others doing likewise, at least on so extensive a scale, it might conjecturally be attributed to him. The Roman Fora were usually provided with these two vaulted Jani, of which this one is the solitary survivor, built generally at the crossway meeting of two streets and intended chiefly as a shelter from the inclemencies of the weather. Similarly, in modern times we also have sheds or other covered erections in our parks, piers, etc., but the difference in aspect, solidity and materials between the two is so vast that it is difficult to realize that they both were intended for the same purpose. The ancients, while effectually providing in their works for the useful and convenient, also produced the durable, grand and handsome in the same structure, while we unfortunately favour the mean, fragile and ugly. And, there can be little doubt that this continual view and contemplation, from birth upwards, of splendid art creations in every direction for the service and comfort of man, was bound to exert an elevating influence on the Romans of which we are deprived.

This quadrilateral arch is composed of blocks of Parian marble, now discoloured and defaced so as to resemble old grey stones, and consists of four arches with forty-eight external tenantless niches; statues, pedestals, cornice and other sculptural decorations having disappeared.

During the dark and dreary mediaeval epoch it was included as a section of a stronghold of the grasping feudal barons of the Frangipani family. In A.D. 1583 Pope Sixtus V contemplated demolishing this monument to use the material for a huge pedestal to the obelisk of the Lateran Square, but his factotum, Domenico Fontana, fortunately became aware in time that the Romans had not utterly lost, or rather perhaps had been partially reawakened to a natural pride in the ancient glories of their city, and thus out of a wholesome dread of the consequences of their indignation, the project was abandoned. In this case, as occasionally happens, it was not the shepherds who guided the flock in the right path, but vice versa.

The "Arch of Trajan," another artistic treasure lost to posterity, adorned the entrance to the Forum Trajani, of which it was one of the seven sections. This arch was erected by the Roman Senate and people and stood here until Constantine I, about two centuries later, laid his desecrating hand upon it, dismantled and plundered it, to make up the arch now known by his name, and its complete annihilation was the feat of Pope Clement VII, who being a Medici, ought to have known better. There is unluckily little data to depend upon relatively to this arch, but as Trajan was distinguished for his discernment and taste, was the possessor of almost unlimited power, which, moreover, he knew how to wield, a rare quality, and an ardent lover of the artistically beautiful, and there is his existing column in evidence of his success in this direction, we may safely assume that unless this arch were in harmony with the other structures of his famous Forum he would not have permitted its erection there.

This monarch, a wise statesman and an able general, has been styled "The Justest of Princes," and was held in such high esteem and repute by posterity as well as by contemporaries, that Pope St. Gregory, nearly five centuries after, only voiced the general opinion when he offered up private and public prayers that in so great and benevolent a man and ruler Paganism might be considered as an involuntary error and not as a heinous sin, and that he might exceptionally, Pagan though he was, receive the same heavenly reward conceded to the most deserving of Christians. This spontaneous and public recognition of his worth was all the more remarkable as coming from so eminent and pious a personage as St. Gregory, the Head and Guardian of Christianism, in those times, too, of intolerant zeal and fanaticism prevalent among the earlier Christians, the more immediate descendants of the victims of the Pagan persecutions.

The "Arch of Septimius" was raised by the Senate and people of Rome to him and his two sons, Caracallus and Geta, in A.D. 203 in the Roman Forum. Independently of the surmounting Quadriga in which the Emperor's statue stood crowned by the Genius of Victory and accompanied by those of his two sons, long since vanished, the height of this arch has been calculated at seventy-five feet and the width at eighty-two. In one of the piers there is still an internal staircase leading to the summit of the monument and formerly an external flight of steps from the arch led upwards to the platform of the adjacent temple of Concord. The reliefs illustrate the victories of the Emperor L. Septimius Severus over the Dacians, Arabians and Adeabeni (a people inhabiting a region of ancient Assyria, now part of Kurdistan). To particularize: Facing the Capitol, "the capture of Babylon and the tower of Belus, the crossing of the Euphrates and Tigris and the conquest of Ctesiphon and Seleucia." Facing the Roman Forum," the raising of the siege of Nisibis, the treaty with the Armenians and the siege of Atra." On the spandrels of the central main arch, which is flanked by two smaller ones, are the figures of Victory, of the Seasons and of the River-gods of the conquered countries, and on the pedestals of the fluted Corinthian columns that border the three arches the reliefs represent Barbarians.

This structure is entirely composed of marble except the foundation of travertine coated with marble. Caracallus, after his father's death and after he had slain Geta with his own hand, ordered the portion of the epigraph of this arch referring to the latter, viz.: " Fil. Getae. Nobiliss. Caesari " to be erased and " Optimis. Fortimisque. Principibus " substituted in its place.

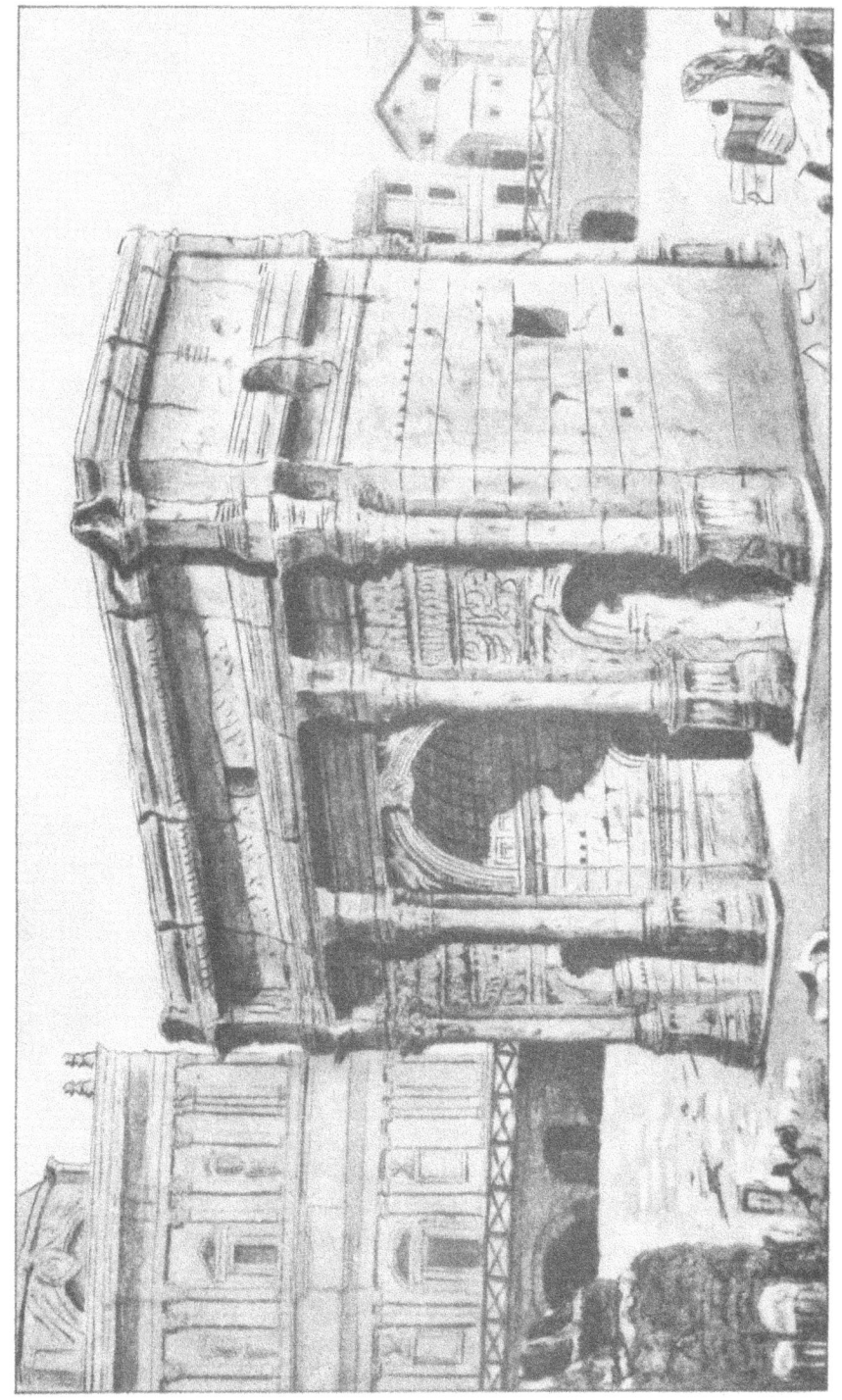

ARCH OF SEPTIMIUS, A.D. 203. ROMAN FORUM.

Plate xxxix.

ARCHES

It seems to have become the fashion (that poor deity that had no devotees among the sensible and virile ancients) for connoisseurs and non-connoisseurs to depreciate this monument, to omit to do so, would be they opine, equivalent to avowing themselves, what they mostly are, no judges of art. Their adverse, second-hand, stereotyped criticism generally condemns the execution of the details rather than the plan or proportions of the work. Unfortunately the fire of A.D. 282, which destroyed nearly the whole of the neighbouring Temple of Saturn and a great part of the Curia and Comitium, also effectually mutilated, discoloured and partially cancelled the reliefs and other decorative parts of this monument. In consequence, though an opinion may be advanced relatively to the form and style of the arch none can be fairly hazarded in respect to the sculptural work. To sum up the case: one may possibly judge of the general proportions and the number of figures (wherein perhaps lies the defect, that of overcrowding) which one can see, but not of the sculptural execution which one cannot now properly discern. Wherefore, with all due deference to the supposed infallibility of the majority, which has gradually become an article of faith nowadays, we have to admit that in this case, as in numberless others, this consensus of opinion is lacking in foundation and value, being neither reasonable, original, nor competent.

In the Middle Ages two turrets were superstructed on this arch, one of which served as a belfry, whence it was named " Turris de Braccio," but quite exceptionally, we do not hear of its having been converted into a fortress or part of one, as was the fate of most monuments of antiquity in feudal times. This arch was in a way restored by Pope Pius VII.

Another " Arch of Septimius," completely of marble, was erected, A.D. 204, in honour of this monarch, his consort, Donna Julia and his aforesaid two sons, by the " Argentarii," or silversmiths, who had their shops in that quarter of the Forum Boarium, wherefore it was termed " Arcus Argentariorum." The unusual shape of this monument, similar to what is called a " Pylon " (only not of trapezoidal form), its vaulting being quadrangular instead of semi-circular, and its minute dimensions, render it unique in its way. The reliefs represent a sacrifice performed by the Imperial family and allegorical figures and deities. The decorations of the cornice and piers bordered by pilasters of the Composite Order, though disapproved of by some critics, are nevertheless finely wrought. The particular paragraph of the inscription referring to Geta was erased and replaced by Caracallus on his assumption of the throne, precisely as has been noted in the other Septimian Arch. The Vicus Jugurthus which connected the Fora Romanum and Boarium made its ingress to the latter, it is said, through this arch, but this statement may be challenged on account of its inadequate size for the passage of traffic, and the probability is that the Aeditus of the Boarium was some other Gate-Arch close by, or the Arcus Janus aforementioned.

The " Arch of Gallienus," erected between A.D. 255-260 by Marcus Aurelius Victor to this Emperor and his consort Salomina with the dedicatory epigraph of " Clementissimo Principi cujus invicta virtus sola pietate superata est " gained for their author the unenviable reputation of a Court Sycophant. Considering that Gallienus was chiefly noted for his extravagant architectonic projects (he intended to raise among others a monument to himself 120 feet high on the Esquiline) which was the least of his evil propensities, for his self-indulgence and cruelty in general and his unfilial conduct to his aged father, Valerian, in particular, whom he deliberately left to die a prisoner in the hands of the Persians, and that Salomina was not noted for anything, the above monument and inscription were so out of place as to smack of the ironical.

This travertine arch occupies the site, it is affirmed, of the former Porta Esquilina and is now on the Via San Vito adjoining the church dedicated to this Saint, not far from the Basilica of Sta. Maria Maggiore, and hence is popularly called the " Arco di San Vito." Being literally swamped with modern buildings it is difficult to decide whether it was originally a single or a triple arch, but what might be the trace of another vaulting on the side of the church, besides the one surviving, seems to favour the latter hypothesis. However this may be, it is evident that the Arcus Gallienus could never in its best days have boasted of much intrinsic or artistic value, which is not to be wondered at considering the decadence of art at the period.

The " Arch of Diocletian " probably crossed the Via Lata, and in the crypt of the church of Sta. Maria in Lata some huge peperino blocks are preserved said to be the remains of this monument, which was erected by the Roman Senate between A.D. 284–305 and demolished by Pope Innocent VIII (Giovanni Battista Cibo) in A.D. 1484–1492.

The " Peperino," or Pepper-stone, has been given this name on account of its speckled pepper and salt hue which, blending into a dark grey, presents a fine aspect, though in some of its varieties brownish or reddish shades predominate owing to the presence of volcanic substances. Its component elements are chiefly granite and tufo and it is very durable, particularly as regards colour, on which wear or time appear to have no effect. This stone was and is adopted on a large scale for a variety of constructions, ranging from the immense substructures of the Tabularium on the Capitoline slope to monuments such as the fine sarcophagus of Cornelius Scipio Barbatus in the Vatican, and to edifices such as the handsome and vast palace of the Princes Brancaccio in the city.

It may be as well to mention that in the ancient Via Lata were also formerly the sectional porticoes, called " Septa Julia," begun by Cesar and completed by Agrippa. These constructions, which corresponded as regards purpose with our polling stations, were first made of wood and afterwards of marble, and derived their name from " Septem," enclosure, and " Julia," from their founder. These stations were erected here when the capacity of the Forum Romanum, the official electoral centre, became insufficient to contain the ever-increasing number of voters.

The so-called " Arch of Constantine " was erected on the Via Triumphalis now Via San Gregorio, in A.D. 312 in commemoration of the battle of Saxa Rubrae won by this Emperor as leader of the Christian and progressive party over the other Emperor, his brother-in-law, Maxentius, the champion of the Pagan and conservative, or perhaps it might be styled, the reactionary one. The inscription runs as follows:

" Imp. Caes. Fl. Constantino Maximo Pio Felici Augusto Senatus Populusque Romanus quod instinctu divinitatis mentis magnitudine cum exercitu suo tam de tyranno quam de omni ejus factione uno tempore justis rempublicam ultus est armis arcum triumphis insignem dicavit."

ARCH OF SEPTIMIUS (ARGENTARIORUM), A.D. 204.

Plate xl.

The fulsomeness of the adulatory epigraph, with its "Divine-minded Greatest Constantine, etc," is not surprising, nor can it, of course, be taken as an expression of the truth or even of the public feeling, because long before this epoch the Senate, which was responsible for it, had degenerated from being one of the best, if not the best, of deliberative, legislative and administrative assemblies any nation ever had the good fortune to possess, into a body of courtiers who were characterized by all the baseness but not much of the wit and grace of their professional successors, the courtiers of Charles II of England and of Louis XIV of France.

This "collected" arch is composed of different kinds of white marble, except the eight columns of Marmor Numidicum and seven of the eight statues of Dacian captives, which are of Phrygian marble. The eighth statue and the heads and hands of some of the others are comparatively recent substitutions. It appears that Constantine and those about him had little to do with this work, except plundering other monuments and piecing the spoils together into a species of huge puzzle, wherefore it was generally known in former times by the epithet of " Cornix Aesopi " or Aesop's crow.

Art, since the days of Vespasian and Trajan, had very sensibly deteriorated, and the opportunity offered by this monument of viewing, in proximity on the same structure, two specimens of two different periods, and of thus contrasting the finely-executed reliefs of Trajan's portion, by far the greater, with the misshapen, almost unmeaning, figures of Constantine's contribution, is exceptionally interesting and instructive. To the former monarch belong the aforesaid seven statues of the captives, the reliefs of the central vault representing in sequel: Prisoners supplicating this Emperor for mercy, conquered Dacians with their huts in the background, Praetorians fighting and Trajan in various positions; and the eight medallions illustrating hunting and sacrificial scenes as follows: Hunt and sacrifice of Apollo, Boar-hunt and sacrifice of Diana, Bear-hunt and sacrifice of Sylvanus, Lion-hunt and sacrifice of Hercules. These several sections were furnished by the gigantic frieze eighty feet long which decorated Trajan's Forum. The eight reliefs of the attica are of another sovereign, possibly Marcus Aurelius Antoninus, and the sides of the arch-piers are composed of marble taken from the vanished mausoleums of the Fabii and the Aruntii. Constantine's section consists of the smaller reliefs inserted below the above-mentioned medallions and were intended to illustrate his achievements with effigies of victory and prisoners of war.

This monument offers, on one hand, conclusive evidence of the vanity of this Emperor and of the flattery of his partisans, and on the other, of their inability to produce a work on artistic lines, which compelled them to have recourse to the device of fixing together heterogeneous materials and productions of their betters before them, that resulted in this queer conglomeration Arch, collected and joined but not created. Notwithstanding, however, its composition and its dilapidation, it is still a striking if not harmonious artistic monument, well worth studying in its details as some of the sculptural works are, as already remarked, fine specimens of a very brilliant period of art.

The pre-eminence accorded to Constantine in history is attributable not to the man but to the circumstances. At that time effete Paganism was irretrievably crumbling to its fall and Christianity was developing into the vigorous giant destined to give it its death blow. The epigrammatic French phrase, " Il se donna la peine de naître," if we add "et de choisir le moment de sa naissance," comprises about all or nearly all of the assets Constantine possessed. It was in the name of Louis XVI of France that serfdom and judicial torture were abolished and the representative system inaugurated; all great reforms, but the credit does not belong to him personally, any more or any less than the recognition and establishment of Christianity by the Imperial Edict of Milan, A.D. 313, were due to Constantine. Neither the one nor the other had the master intellect and character to be in advance of their times, to initiate and direct public acts of the highest importance, but were merely carried on by the force of events to register them. Moreover, if either of these two Sovereigns could be held to claim any sort of homage, it would be the French King who, as vacillating as the Roman Emperor, was at least gifted with a kindly nature and amiable disposition, qualities by which Constantine was not distinguished. Nevertheless, the Emperor is called and by some considered a great man, while the King at best a much pitied mortal, and this because the first happened, by chance, the times being ripe, to find himself the ostensible head of a mighty and beneficent change with a great future before it, whereas the second was destined to be the unlucky representative of an order and system that had run their course, were worn out and condemned to perish.

ARCH OF GALLIENUS (Arco di San Vito), A.D. 260. Esquiline.
Plate xli.

ARCH OF CONSTANTINE, A.D. 312.

Plate xlii.

CHAPTER XVII
COLUMNS

ALTHOUGH columns were, as we know, generally adopted in a series as an integral and important sustaining and decorative section of other structures, the custom of erecting them as complete isolated honorary or representative monuments was more prevalent with the Romans than with other peoples.

The " Columna Lactaria," or Milk-Column, raised in the ancient Forum Holitorium to serve as the rallying post for foundlings, who were placed at its pedestal by their unknown parents or kindred in token that they were themselves unable or unwilling to undertake the duty of rearing them, which, in consequence, devolved on the State, the parent of all in a far greater sense than is conceivable now to us. The form and style, materials and date of this vanished column, doubtless very ancient, have not been recorded, but in all probability, considering the remote epoch and particular purpose, it could scarcely have been an ornate, costly or artistic creation.

The " Columna Bellica," or Column of Bellona, the Goddess of War, was erected in that part of the extensive Campus Martius now occupied by the Piazza Paganica, and to this column was attached a great public function, for it was here that the " Fetealis", or Herald, had to stand when he was commanded by the Senate to proclaim a declaration of war. Two dates, very far apart, have been assigned for its erection. The one, about 430 B.C., near the Villa Publica, an edifice built in that year for taking the census, levying troops and for the reception of the Ambassadors of foreign States. The Consuls also, on their return from a campaign, had to wait in this villa, until the proclamation of the Senatorial Decree granting or refusing them a triumphal entrance into the city, the bestowal or refusal of rewards resting entirely with the Conscript Fathers, the head and mouthpiece of the Commonwealth.

The other date fixed for the erection of the Columna Bellica was that of the building of the adjacent Temple of Bellona, 296 B.C., in obedience to a vow by Appius Claudius Caecus for the decisive victory over the Etruscans. A difference of more than 130 years is hardly excusable, even in dealing with a subject like this, but the earlier of the two dates is the most probable one, if, indeed, not before that, since it is unlikely that the Romans, almost uninterruptedly at war from the foundation of their city, should have delayed so long as over three or four centuries, in order to erect a monument dedicated to such an important and frequent State function as the official declaration of hostilities.

The term " Fetealis, or Ferealis," is derived from " Feria," fête. The Collegium Fetealis, as first instituted by King Numa Pompilius, was a Corporation composed of twenty members whose functions comprised all acts and formalities connected with international questions, declarations of war and peace, conventions and treaties. In earlier times, when Rome was a small State and her restricted boundaries were contiguous with other Statelets like herself, in her transactions with her neighbours the formal opening of hostilities was announced by the Feteales proceeding to the enemies' frontiers, and, after pronouncing the ritual formula, flinging into their territory, according to some writers a lance and according to others a bloody sword. Probably the weapon was changed with the times, and the spear, the " Hastae Martis," the racial arm of the Sons of Mars, was first used, and substituted later by the " Gladium," the short, broad, strong, double-edged sword which became the typical Roman national offensive weapon subsequently.

With the extension of the Roman State, as its frontiers did not any longer always adjoin those of the other States, separated from her by distances, mountains, seas, this procedure had necessarily to be altered to meet the changed ethnographical and topographical conditions, and the Heralds, standing under the aforesaid Column accomplished their mission by throwing the emblematic weapon into a limited space assigned for the purpose of symbolically representing the enemies' territories and termed " Ager Hostilis," or Hostile Field. For peace conventions the " Caduceatores," or Peace-Heralds, were employed carrying an olive branch, and when it was a question of offering peace or war, the chief of the Feteales held in one hand the peace branch and in the other the war weapon. The " Praecones " were also a branch of the Collegium Fetealis, their particular office being to proclaim any edict or announcement in general, but especially in reference to internal affairs at the Curia, Comitium, Temples, Basilicas, Forums and in fact in all public places and assemblies. Briefly, the Fetealis was the international herald and the Praecones the home herald.

The " Lictors " were also a corporation of public functionaries first instituted, it appears, in Etruria, whose varied, and seemingly to us, incompatible duties are not very generally or definitely known. These officials partook of the character of ushers, of constables, of body-guards, of outrunners and of executioners' assistants.

Their functions were five, viz.: the " Submotio," consisting in keeping each tribe in its assigned place in public assemblies, in expelling the seditious and in maintaining order generally, the " Animadversio," that is, in announcing the arrival or in intimating the presence of the principal Magistrates to the assembled people, to enable everyone to render the due forms of recognition and respect as established, which were, to stand still if moving, to rise if seated, to dismount or descend if carried and to depose their weapons if armed, the " Praetio," that is, to precede the Magistrates on ceremonial occasions and if these were triumphal processions their " Fasces Lictorii," or rods of office, were wreathed with laurel, and finally in ordering the instruments of penalty for condemned persons and in binding their hands and feet previous to the execution of their sentences. Gallio derives their appellation from the verb " Ligare," to bind.

The insignia of office were the aforesaid Fasces Lictorii, or bundle of rods, bound round the helve of an axe in the centre which emerged from the top, and their attire the simple, manly and graceful costume of the Roman civis. The Chief Lictor was styled " Lictor Proximus," because he was always placed nearest the Magistrates to receive and transmit orders. The Kings and subsequently the Consuls had each twelve Lictors in attendance, the Dictators twenty-four and the cavalry Commander, the Praetors, the

COLUMN AND FORUM OF TRAJAN, A.D. 114.

Plate xlviii.

Proconsuls six, and the Vestals and Flamens Diales were also honoured by a similar escort, but the number assigned to each has not been exactly ascertained, any more than the total number of the whole Corps of Lictors; probably it fluctuated.

In connection we hear of Pontius Pilatus, Praefectus at Jerusalem, commanding the Lictor on service to send first for the scourges and then for the Cross for the execution of the two sentences pronounced on Jesus Christ, in the following words: " I, Lictor, expedi verges " and " I, Lictor expedi crucis."

The " Columna Duilia " was raised by the Senate, 260 B.C. in the Roman Forum, near the Basilica Aemilia, in honour of the Consul Caius Duilius, who had gained in that year the first decisive naval victory over the Carthaginians. It was of the Etruscan Order of Architecture, twelve and a half feet in height and consisted of parian marble with three pairs of bronze prows projecting at regular intervals on the shaft from the base to the capital, and surmounted by a statue representing triumphant Rome. At the foot of the stairs leading to the Palace of the Conservatori on the Capital there is a patched column which is said to be a recomposition of the Columna Duilia, by M. A. Buonarotti, who joined together the scattered fragments and replaced the missing ones to the best of his ability so as to form a whole somewhat resembling this ancient historic column. The Latin word " Rostrum " signifies Beak, a name given to the Beak-shaped prows of vessels of the times, and hence this Column was also called " Columna Rostrata," as for the same reason Pompey's house, similarly decorated, was likewise denominated also " Domus Rostrata."

The " Columna Caesaris " was erected close to the spot now occupied by the scant vestiges of the Rostra Julia and the Aedicula Divi Julii, in the Roman Forum. About all that has been gathered concerning this column is that it was composed of the costly marble now known by the name of Giallo Antico and that it bore the laconic but significant inscription, as yet unprostituted, of, " Parenti Patriae." It was thrown down by Dolabella, who, however, had to re-erect it owing to the insistent demands of the Romans, who had retained unimpaired their cult for Cesar.

The " Columnae Honorariae," or Honorary Columns. This collective denomination has been given to a row of eight brick pedestals, originally cased in marble, two of which a resurmounted by broken, capitalless columns, one of granite and the other of Pavonazetto found lying near, and placed on two of the above pedestals lining the Via Sacra of the Roman Forum opposite the Basilica Julia. Up to the present no reliable records seem to have been attained relatively to the erectors of these columns or of the personages or events in whose honour or memory they were raised.

The " Columna Trajani " of the Etruscan Order was erected in the omonymous Forum in honour of this Emperor in A.D. 114 by the Senate and people of Rome, and not to his memory as some misleading compilers of guide-books and other writers coolly assert, seeing that he died in A.D. 117. There is the usual divergence of calculation regarding the height and other particulars of this famed column. Some compute the total altitude at 147 feet, others at 128 feet, the second being, in all probability, the more correct estimation, because, according to the inscription, " Ad declarandum quantae altitudine mons et locus sit egestus," its height corresponds to the depth of the soil about 128 or 130 feet, levelled down between the Quirinal and Capitoline Hills for the construction of the Forum Trajani. Its diameter measures at the base eleven feet and at the summit ten feet, and the length of the shaft alone is either 87 or 100 feet, the latter being obviously nearer the truth.

The entire monument is said to consist of thirty-four monolith blocks of Luna marble and is decorated with 2,000, some affirm 2,500, figures in relief, two or two and a half feet in height, besides other accessories, illustrating scenes of the Dacian wars of this monarch, and by an encircling sinuous band, all increasing very gradually in size as they proceed upwards on the shaft, so as to produce the optical illusion, when viewed from below, that they are all of uniform dimensions. The summit was crowned by a statue of Trajan holding a globe. This statue has long since been removed, it is surmised by Constans Emperor of the East, A.D. 337–350, who signalised himself as one of the devastators of Roman monuments and as the seller to a Jewish dealer of the celebrated gigantic statue of Apollo. The globe fortunately escaped and was transferred to the Capitoline Museum. The post vacated by the abstraction of Trajan's statue was re-occupied after several centuries by the present bronze one of Saint Peter placed thereon by Pope Sixtus V in A.D. 1587.

At the foot of the monument was the sepulchral chamber wherein the ashes of the Emperor were deposited in a gold urn by his son-in-law and immediate successor, Hadrian. Inside the column there is also a staircase of 184 steps from which as well as from the external spiral lines, resembling those of a shell, it derived the nickname of " Columna Cochlis," which became after the generic appellation of all similarly formed columns.

The Columna Trajani has maintained its supremacy as the king and model of honorary columns for over eighteen centuries already, nor does there seem to be any prospect so far of its dethronement. But this is not surprising because in order to accomplish such works, which, as Marcellinus says, " The pen cannot describe and which man can only create and see once in the lapse of centuries," it would be necessary to resuscitate an Emperor Trajan and artists like Apollodorus, who also constructed all the superb edifices of the Forum Trajani and the magnificent bridge over the Danube in A.D. 104.

To mention two of the many monuments of this class copied from this Column of Trajan, there are in London the Duke of York's Column, which is said to be a plain imitation, but is rather no imitation save for the general shape, because as regards everything else the two are entirely dissimilar, and the other of plaster and cut in half, in the Victoria and Albert Museum, which is an excellent copy specimen.

The " Columna Antonini " was erected to the Emperor Antoninus Pius by his nephews and joint successors, Marcus Aurelius and Lucius Verus, and consisted of red granite with a sepulchral podium of white marble. This column was subsequently demolished and the granite used to repair the Obelisk of Psamtik I, King of Egypt, now in the Piazza Montecitorio, and the marble pedestal, among the reliefs of which is a prominent group of Antoninus and Faustina conducted to Heaven by a winged Genius, discovered in A.D. 1709 in the Via della Missione and transported to the Vatican. Pope Leo XIII (Conte Gioacchino Raffaele Luigi Vincenzo Pecci), A.D. 1878–1903, had a pillar and statue placed on this stylobate in the Giardino della Pigna.

The " Columna Aurelia," commonly known as the Colonna Antonina, very similar and little inferior to that of Trajan, is situated in the present Piazza Colonna,

COLUMN OF AURELIUS, A.D. 179.

Plate xliv

near the spot formerly occupied by the Porticus Vespasiani, and was erected, A.D. 176 or 179, by the Roman Senate and people to the crowned philosopher and philanthropist, Lucius Marcus Aurelius, one of the best rulers of any age or country. The height of this column, of the Etruscan Order likewise, has been calculated at 100 Roman feet, equivalent to ninety-six English feet, and is composed of twenty-eight blocks of marble. The reliefs, commemorating this Emperor's German and Sarmatian wars, are divided into twenty-three spirals winding round the shaft, and into two main sections, the upper referring to the German, the lower to the Sarmatian, wars, separated about midway by the figure of Victory leaning on a shield. Above there is a third spiral representing the miraculous downfall of rain in prompt response to the supplications of the Christian legionaries which providentially saved the Roman army.

In A.D. 1589 Pope Sixtus V had this column repaired, and placed on its abacus the bronze statue of Saint Paul, as he had done, as noted, with the Columna Trajana similarly with Saint Peter's statue. The Colonne Vendôme, in Paris, of Corsican granite, is said to be a replica, in a way, of this Columna Aurelia. It seems that the justice of fate ordained that of all the honorary columns of the Eternal City, these two, namely, the Columnae Trajani and Aurelii, of the two best Emperors, the two men who would have ennobled and graced any position in life, should retain to this day a relatively good state of preservation, as if, on the one hand, to perpetuate their memory tangibly to posterity, and, on the other, as masterpieces of art, in both respects surviving as models to be admired and imitated.

The "Columna Maxentia," a beautiful specimen of the Roman Corinthian Order, forty-seven feet high, belonged originally to the Basilica Maxentia, and was removed to its present site in the Piazza Sta. Maria Maggiore by Pope Paul V (Camillo Borghese, A.D. 1605-1621) in A.D. 1613, who also caused the two peacocks and four dolphins of bronze that ornamented the handsome old fountain in the Atrium of St. Peter, to be melted down to furnish metal, 10,000 lbs., for the statue of the Virgin Mary placed on the summit. This surviving column of the Maxentian Basilica has served as a model to posterity, and one of its offspring copies is supposed by some to be Viscount Nelson's Column in Trafalgar Square.

The "Columna Diocletiani" was, it is asserted, removed, rededicated and renamed "Columna Phoca," in A.D. 608, and is the last of the honorary columns of the Roman Forum. Though, according to apparently authentic authority, it was originally erected by Diocletian, it has not been ascertained to whom or on what occasion, and some free lances of antiquarian lore suggest that it appertained to an edifice anterior to the fourth Christian century. But it is duly reported that it was found and adopted by Smaragdus, a courtesan, as an honorary column for the Emperor Phoca, A.D. 602-610, after the dedicator had erased the original epigraph and substituted another very flattering one to his master.

These ancient columns teach a lesson by their successive phases born of evolution and time, that may be broadly divided into four stages. The first, when art was yet primitive and rudimentary but when public spirit had already attained an elevated standard, wherefore the columns were not raised and dedicated as a rule to individuals and did not possess any intrinsic or artistic value, being intended usually for purposes of public utility, such are the vanished Columnae Lactaria and Bellona. In the second stage art has progressed, and the columns are of more costly material and elaborate work, and erected preferentially to eminent personalities, but in relation to their services to the State, and of this category is the Columna Duilia, on the abacus of which not the statue of the Consul but that of Triumphal Rome was significantly placed. In the third period art had reached a very high, or rather the highest, degree of development, and the stupendous solitary columns are monuments in honour of great personages, as a manifestation of homage to their exalted station as well as an acknowledgment of their achievements in serving or rather ruling the State. Of these are the Columnae Trajani and Aurelii. The fourth stage marks a decidedly retrogressive and decadent stage. No purpose of public utility, no State services and no art appear now; men have become as indifferent to public welfare and honour and the services of eminent individuals, as they have become incompetent to produce artistic works, and nothing is represented by the columns of this period but a misappropriation and misapplication of the creations of earlier and better times, borne of degeneracy and servility incensing tyranny.

CHAPTER XVIII

OBELISKS

OBELISKS, like pyramids, are a typical foreign production which has nothing in common with Roman Art and ought not, therefore, strictly speaking, to be numbered among Roman works. But as obelisks have been for centuries in possession of the Romans and formed part of the ancient monuments of the Eternal City, any description of her antiquities not containing any reference to these erections as part of her monuments would be unanimously pronounced decidedly incomplete.

Art, as is known, is a copy, often a flattering one, of the most choice and remarkable, as well as the ordinary, in nature, to which imagination sometimes lends wings, launching further occasionally into fantastic creations, but it does not necessarily follow from this that Art cannot be an accurate reproducer of nature too, whenever a facsimile is sought for. With the exception of the Greek race, the Latin was gifted above all other ancient peoples with a temperament and mentality capable of conceiving and creating the beautiful, though if the Romans in their works excelled the Greeks in the attributes of virility, variety and majesty, the latter were superior in soft and serene loveliness. These racial characteristics of these peoples of a physique remarkable for grace of line, curve, contour and harmony and richness of colouring, were reflected in their attractive personal habiliments and ornaments, and in the style, symmetry and decorations of their private and public constructions.

The Egyptians, of a more uniform and sombre morale and cast of mind, and of a spare, dark physique moulded on more rigid lines, naturally reproduced these features with a corresponding monotony of outline, colouring and constructive material in their attire as in their works, as is exemplified by the characteristic stiffness and crudeness that pervades all down to the attitude, garments, hair and beard of the figures of their sculptural creations as well as of their architectonic constructions. Another of the main features of the Egyptian works is their dense massiveness and often their great dimensions, arising probably from their habitual contemplation of the vast and unvaried expanse of the country they inhabit. Though the surviving wrecks of the works of various ancient races such as the Indians, Assyrians, Persians, etc., prove that the Arts of Architecture and Sculpture were held in high repute among them, more so relatively and absolutely than these sublime Arts are honoured and valued with us now, the Egyptians, of all these peoples, have the first place, always excepting the Greeks and Romans, in the quantity and quality of the relics of this nature bequeathed by past civilizations to posterity.

The authentic specimens of the obelisks, entirely composed as a rule of red or grey indigenous granite, are the most ancient monuments of the Sevenhilled City, dating, it is understood, from their original erection in Egypt and not from their importation and installation in Rome. Regarded in the light of an earlier civilization and nationality they are certainly full of intense interest, but viewed from the true artistic standpoint they are far inferior in beauty and grace to the creations of the Greek and Roman schools. The copied obelisks of Rome, like the copied pyramids, are usually on a smaller scale, and reveal the Latin designer and workman out of their element in the reproduction of an alien and uncongenial work. Octavius was the first who brought over obelisks from Egypt to Rome, a transfer that could not well have occurred previously, because the definite absorbation of the former as a province of the newly-constituted Roman Empire dates from his rule.

The "Obelisk" of the Piazza del Popolo was the first seen in Rome. It is composed of the regulation Egyptian granite and measures, for the shaft alone about seventy-eight, and inclusive of the pedestal and cross above, 118 feet. According to Pliny it was erected in Egypt by King Psammetichus, contemporary of Pythagoras. Another version supposed to be corroborated by the hieroglyphics upon it mentioning the names of Meremptah I and Rameses III, fixes its approximate date at 1200–1100 B.C., and a third offers a still remoter period, attributing its existence to Seti and Rameses II or the Great. The outlined figures upon it are intended to represent a king doing homage to his predecessor.

This obelisk was brought to Rome by Octavius, 10 B.C., erected in the Circus Maximus and dedicated to his patron-deity Apollo in commemoration of and in gratitude for the naval victory of Actium and the subjugation of Egypt. It was placed in its present site in A.D. 1589 by Sixtus V, that enterprising, broad-minded and determined Pontiff who accomplished so much in his five years' reign. It may be noted that the statues of Apollo, like those of the other coeval Deities, were credited with the performance of all the miraculous glances and gestures with which we are familiar as being similarly attributed to the Images of the Virgin and Saints, on those occasions that their devotees choose to consider as momentous to their personal interests, or as omens of unusual events about to occur.

The "Obelisk of the Montecitorio" or "Obelisk of Psamtic I," was erected in Egypt, 864 B.C., in honour of this King. Pliny assigns its creation to Sesostris and Herodotus to Pheron, who raised, he relates, two obelisks of which this was one. Its height, including pedestal and globe, has been calculated at eighty-four feet, and its well preserved hieroglyphics bear the names of both the above kings in the genealogical catalogue with the accompanying eulogies, which is at variance with Pliny's statement that the inscription consisted solely of annals of Egyptian literature and science, wherefore it may be assumed that he refers to some other obelisk.

This obelisk was transferred by Octavius from Heliopolis (Helios, sun, and Polis, city) and placed in the Campus Martius near the present church of San Lorenzo, in Lucina, where it was found in fragments in A.D. 1797, or, as others affirm, in A.D. 1510. In any case Pope Pius VI (Giovanni Angelo Braschi, A.D. 1775–1799) had it reunited and repaired with the granite, as aforesaid, of the Columna Antonini, and erected in the

Piazza Montecitorio, on the site of the former Temple of Marcus Aurelius and opposite the present Chamber of Deputies where it still stands. This obelisk was adopted for a gnomon with a white marble sun-dial, and thence took the name of "Obeliscus Solaris." A phenomenally careless author writes that it began to be used in Rome for the above purpose in the year 60 B.C., but as it happens that Octavius, who imported this obelisk, was born 63 B.C., and was therefore a three-years-old child at the time assigned, the above writer anticipated the date of its adoption as a sundial in Rome by a good many years before even its arrival in this city.

The two obelisks, one of Smarus placed since A.D. 1587 by Sixtus V in the Piazza dell' Esquilino, and the other of Vaphrius since A.D. 1781 in the Piazza del Quirinale or Montecavallo, have many points in common. They were both, it is alleged, erected at about the same time, 1000 B.C., in their own country, both brought by Claudius to their new country, both destitute of hieroglyphics, both figured as twin ornaments before the façade of the Mausoleum of Augustus, and both are calculated as measuring forty-eight feet in height. A certain annalist nevertheless makes out the second, the Vaphrius Obelisk, to be ninety-eight feet, comprising pedestal and crowning piece. This computation can scarcely be accepted as accurate, because a difference of about thirty or fifty feet, even allowing for accessories above and below, would be too great between two obelisks equal enough to balance each other in front of such an artistic and important monument as the Imperial Augustan Mausoleum, in those times and people, too, of the classic Roman school, by whom the rules of symmetry were so rigorously observed.

The Obelisk of the Square of St. Peter, otherwise the Obelisk of Pheron or Nuncoreus, both sons of Sesostris, and both credited with being its creators. Herodotus relates that the former erected and consecrated this obelisk to the Sun-God of the Sun city (Heliopolis) on his recovery from loss of sight, but Pliny attributes it to Nuncoreus. The height of the shaft is eighty-three feet and of the entire monument, as it now stands, 132 feet. It has no hieroglyphics and owing to its well-finished work and good preservation, is probably the best specimen of its class in the Sevenhilled City. Caligula, A.D. 37-41, had this obelisk transported to his circus on the Vatican Hill, where the present Sacristy of St. Peter's Cathedral now is. It appears that Nero chose this circus in particular for his wholesale torture and slaughter of the Christians. It is affirmed, indeed, that St. Peter was himself crucified, A.D. 67, at the foot of the above obelisk of this circus, " Inter duas Metae," between two goals; wherefore it was popularly called later, " Aguglia di San Pietro," Needle of St. Peter, and the modern inscription at the base dedicates it to the Cross as follows: " Ecce Crux Domini-Fugite partes adverse-Vicit Leo de Tribu Juda." On the shaft the epigraph refers to the Emperors Octavius and Tiberius, " Divo. Caes. Divi. Julii. F. Augusto.—Ti. Caesari. Divi. Aug. F. Augusta Sacrum." In A.D. 1586 Sixtus V had this obelisk removed to its present place in the Piazza di San Pietro and its erection here was associated with an incident worth relating.

This Pontiff, after due consultation with the various architects, mathematicians and engineers, decided to entrust this difficult undertaking to his favourite, Domenico Fontana, who accepted, or had to accept, the responsibility of the charge, with the death penalty attached in case of failure. On the day appointed, 10th September, a vast multitude crowded the extensive square, on whom absolute silence was imposed under pain of death for the transgressor. The proceedings were inaugurated by the ceremony of exorcism of the obelisk as a Pagan Idol and its dedication to the Cross, followed by the celebration of High Mass in St. Peter's and the Pope's benediction of the 800 workmen employed, besides the 160 horses and forty-five cranes.

The obelisk, weighing 320 tons, was then moved on rollers to its present site, but if the plan and apparatus of Fontana were good they were not flawless. Their weak point proved to be that he had not allowed sufficiently for the strain on the cordage, and in consequence when the obelisk had been reared up, at a certain angle the ropes began to show by unmistakable signs and sounds that they were no longer to be depended upon to bring the many-tonned mass of granite to its proposed vertical position. To recede would be to confess failure not unaccompanied with risk, to proceed seemed equivalent to courting certain and immediate disaster, and to remain stationary partook of both these disagreeable alternatives. At this critical moment of tension and anxiety the situation was saved by the practical knowledge and fearless promptitude of a sailor, who, heedless of the Death Decree, called out amid the universal silence, " Aqua alle funi " (Water to the ropes), which, being done at once, produced the natural result that the ropes tightened and performed their office, and the obelisk, after fifty-two efforts, was raised entire and uninjured to its place, where it has remained up to the present for nearly three centuries and a half.

The delinquent was immediately arrested and brought before Sixtus, who, well aware of the salutary and general terror he inspired, was astonished that there could be found an individual audacious enough to disobey his orders in his very presence, and therefore proportionately curious to see him. The Pope, acting on his maxims, is reported to have said, " Before We attend to thanksgivings and rejoicings the claims of law and order must be satisfied." To the interrogations of the Sovereign Pontiff the sailor replied boldly and calmy enough, that " He had called out well knowing the penalty he had incurred, but that he considered the success of this great undertaking of much more importance than his life, which he was accustomed to risk daily for trifles," and Sixtus, elated with the success of his enterprise and admiring a promptitude and intrepidity so akin to his own, though he was hardly ever known to forgive, especially any disobedience, made an exception on this occasion, and, to the surprise of all, not only pardoned the man his delinquency, but moreover asked him to choose what recompense he would prefer for the service he had rendered.

According to an old writer the Pope spoke the following words, which it would be a pity to omit as they depict his character. " Owing to Our pardon the man convicted of crime has disappeared, precisely as the man of sin would through Our absolution, therefore We have before Us only the man whose meritorious action justly demands an adequate reward, this reward no one can choose to his liking so well as himself," and turning to the prisoner, added, " Choose therefore, my man of might, without hesitation, for if We are severe We are also just, and We know that you can not only act but also speak gallantly and well." The sailor at once replied with the same frankness that he would like to provide the palms used on Palm Sunday, adding that he could furnish much finer ones than those usually adopted and better fitted, therefore, for their high purpose, as His Holiness would admit if he saw them, and the Pope forthwith had a Bull duly drawn up in virtue of which the sailor and his descendants were appointed till Doomsday, sole purveyors of palms for all the churches, which besides being a moral privilege, much more highly appreciated in those times than in these, was also agreeably accompanied by a substantial pecuniary profit, far greater in that age of piety than can be easily realized in ours. Since then, it is asserted, a vessel loaded with palms, in which Liguria abounds, has been annually sent up the Tiber the week before Palm Sunday.

The sailor's name was Raimondo Brescia, from San Remo, in Liguria. The operations, it may be added, terminated with the cheers of thousands, the ringing of hundreds of bells and the roar of cannon from the Castel Sant' Angelo. Medals were struck also in commemoration of the event. As for Fontana he received a pecuniary recompense, between cash and material, of 135,000 Italian lire and the honorary ones of being created a Roman Noble and a Knight of the Golden Spur. The latter has always been a highly-prized distinction as being also accompanied by the rank and title of Count Palatine, and was divided into the Pontifical and Imperial Orders of the "Knights of the Golden Spur." The Imperial Order, instituted by Charles V, Emperor of Germany and King of Spain, A.D. 1500–1558, was conferred on the author's father in 1844, the Knightly title being personal and the title of Nobility hereditary for all the legitimate male descendants.

To resume, after our digression. In what is considered a standard work in this line, there is the following rather unintelligible paragraph relatively to the above obelisk: " In the centre of the Square of St. Peter stands the famous red granite Obelisk of the Vatican brought to Rome from Heliopolis by Caligula in a ship described by Pliny as being nearly as long as the left side of the Port of Ostia. It was used to adorn the Circus of Nero and is therefore of unrivalled interest, although it is only a Roman imitation of an Egyptian monument." The meaning of this passage seems to be, either that Caligula went or sent to Heliopolis, not to bring home an authentic monument but a Roman imitation of one, which somehow happened to be there instead of a genuine original Egyptian obelisk, or that this Emperor was capable of the equally eccentric and aimless proceeding of sending Roman artisans to Heliopolis to copy an original obelisk to be transferred afterwards to Rome, whereas he had at his disposal several authentic specimens to choose from in the Eternal City. Failing any other interpretation the above paragraph is illogical and inexplicable and had better have been omitted.

The " Obelisk of Rameses II, the Great," was likewise transported from Heliopolis to Rome, by whom and when is unrecorded. It was erected, it is said, by the Temple of Isis Capitolina on the Capitol, where it remained near the present church of Aracoeli till A.D. 1582, when the Senate made a present of this fragmentary obelisk, of which only the top is genuine, to Ciriaco Mattei, who took it to the Villa Mattei, or Celimontana, on the Caelian Hill, where it now stands. It is narrated that, on this occasion, when the obelisk was about to be placed on its position it suddenly fell, and, in doing so, cut off the hand of one of the workmen, the severed member being buried there under the monument.

Another obelisk of Rameses II, transferred from Egypt to Rome, it is affirmed, by Domitian, was adopted as an ornament of the Temple of Serapis, which was formerly situated near the present church of San Stefano del Cacco, where it was found in 1883. In 1888 it was incorporated in the monument erected opposite the central railway station of Rome in memory of the Italian soldiers killed at Dogali in the Abyssinian war of 1887.

The "Obelisk of Thothmes" has the triple distinction of being the highest and the oldest of all brought to Rome and also the latest imported from Egypt. The height of the shaft alone has been estimated at 105 or 115 feet, that of the entire monument at 151 or 155 feet and the weight at 440 tons. With regard to its antiquity there are several versions. One, perhaps the most reliable, is that it was erected, 1449 B.C., to the Kings Thothmes III and IV, another that King Tutmes raised it in front of the Temple of Ammon at Thebes, 1436–1427 B.C., a third, that it was erected by Radamantes, 1500–1460 B.C., to the Sun, and a fourth that it was the work of Mephres, 1700–1600 B.C., possibly because his name is inscribed on it.

The third distinctive, of being the last obelisk imported to Rome, is owing to the Emperor Constantine II having had it brought to the Eternal City in A.D. 357 from Alexandria, to which town it had been previously removed by Constantine I. On its arrival in Rome it was placed on the Spina of the ancient Circus Maximus, where it remained till A.D. 1587, when Sixtus V had it transferred to its present place in the Piazza San Giovanni, in Laterano, by Fontana, who having found it broken in three parts and the base damaged by fire, had to cut off a portion in order to reconstruct it as a complete monument with its own material, notwithstanding which curtailment it still exceeds all the others existing in Rome in altitude.

The "Obelisk of Sallust" is held by some archaeologues to be authentically Egyptian, and by others a Roman imitation, but nothing has transpired regarding either the Egyptian who first erected it in his own land, or of the Roman who brought it over, or, alternatively, of the Roman who copied it or had it copied. But whether an original work or an imitation (the latter being the more probable hypothesis) since the name of neither Egyptian nor Roman has been known in connection with the construction of this obelisk, while it is known to have belonged to Caius Crispus Sallustius, both by possession and erection in his renowned villa, his name seems to be, for the present, the rightful one to apply to this monument. Two trustworthy witnesses testify to its presence in the said villa or gardens of Sallust, namely Faunus, A.D. 1548, and Pirro Ligorio, A.D. 1552. In A.D. 1735 Clement XII (Lorenzo Corsini A.D. 1730–1740) had it removed to a small quadrangular space near St. John Lateran, and from thence it was again transferred by Pius VI, A.D. 1775–1799, to the front of the church of the Trinitá dei Monti, where it still stands.

The "Obelisk of Antinous" was a memorial monument originally raised by the Emperor Hadrian and his consort Sabina before the tomb of his favourite Antinous, who was drowned either by accident or by suicide in the Nile in A.D. 131.

Though the Egyptian monuments possess a sombre fascination, their great antiquity and the obscurity which, in spite of so many meritorious efforts still surrounds and clouds Egyptian history, render all attempts at giving a precise, well-authenticated and detailed account of them, never in any case an easy task, more than usually arduous, and certainly not a subject to be treated adequately, or even synoptically outlined, in a work of this description, especially as it does not profess to deal in any sense with the structural history of Egypt, but only to touch fleetingly on those works that were brought to Rome.

In works of fiction, even if they be historical Romances, the transposition and alteration of dates, events and personages, as well as imaginary creations to suit the plot, are, as aforesaid, a recognised mode of procedure, but in works of description, reference and information of all kinds, precisely the contrary is required. In the compilation and composition of the latter three courses, broadly speaking, appear to be open. First of all, a careful research and strict adherence to, and accurate statement of, facts, so far as has been gathered from authentic sources, recording at the same time the various versions in connection. Second, in default of these, to supply the void by reasonable conjectures based on known and confirmatory circumstantial evidence, but frankly acknowledged to be nothing more than conjectures. Third, failing even this, to keep silence, for it is far preferable to say nothing at all than to say something wrong, to be diffused by publication. All readers do not possess the time, faculty, knowledge or inclination to examine, analyse and verify the works they peruse; in short, all are not obliged to be critics or reviewers, but all are equally entitled to that consideration which is manifestly wanting when the authors, of the above class of works in particular, are guilty of incongruous and unfounded statements and gratuitous contradictions, sometimes to be met with in one and the same sentence, of which many examples might be cited.

Plate xiv.

OBELISK OF THOTMES. PIAZZA SAN GIOVANNI IN LATERANO.

CHAPTER XIX
PORTICOS AND FOUNTAINS

THE porticoes of ancient Rome, nowise inferior to her other constructions, may be divided, like their arches and columns, into two similar categories, those which were a section of their edifices and those which stood alone as independent structures. The Fora and most of the palaces, basilicas and baths were provided with porticos, and these are briefly dealt with or at least mentioned with the buildings of which they constitute a part, of the others, the independent porticos, the following may be noted.

The " Porticus Metelli " was erected, 149 B.C., by M. Caecilius Metellus, on the site afterwards occupied by that of Octavia, in commemoration of his victory over Andriscus of Macedon. Within this Porticus once stood two temples dedicated respectively to Jupiter and Juno, said to be the first built in Rome composed mainly of marble. It appears that one of these temples was of the Ionic Order and the other of the Corinthian, but that owing to some error the respective statues of the two titular Divinities changed places, that of Jupiter being placed in the Juno Temple and vice versa, and that, in the belief that this was the will of the deities themselves, the mistake was never afterwards rectified. In consequence the problem as to which the present remains appertain is still unsolved. Facing these temples, Metellus placed the famous bronze statues brought from Greece, the work of Lysippus, representing King Alexander the Great and twenty-four of his officers who were killed at the battle of Granicus, 334 B.C. This rivulet also gave the name to another important battle, which resulted in the victory of Lucullus over Mithridates, 75 B.C. The Metellus above mentioned was the direct or collateral ancestor of the Caecilia Metella Crassia of the well-known mausoleum of the Via Appia.

There were two porticos bearing the appellation of Porticus Libertatis. The one, near the Basilica Aemilia, possibly an annex, the other, on the Aventine, with a contiguous temple and library, constructed by Asinius Pollius during the latter days of the Republic. This Bibliotheca is recorded by Pliny as being the first public library established in the world. Confining ourselves to Europe alone, the Bibliotheca Apollinaris of Athens was certainly of greater antiquity, but it is doubtful if this was, strictly speaking, a public institution there, and certainly not such after its transfer by Sylla to Rome, because, among others, Strabo assures us that the dictator placed the contents of the Apollinaris in his own domicile for his private use and in consequence inaccessible to the general public.

PORTICO OF OCTAVIA.

Plate xlvi.

Of the "Porticus Philippi," built by Martius Philippus, stepfather of Octavius, northward and near the Theatrum Marcelli; of the "Porticus Liviae," near the Pantheon; of the "Porticus Vespasiani," over a century later, formerly in the present Piazza Colonna; and of the "Porticus Pompeii," except that the latter was a magnificent structure, there are few or no records so far as we know.

The "Porticus Octaviae," situated, as already mentioned, on and about the site of the Temples and Porticus of Metellus, was erected by Octavius in honour of his sister Octavia. From the Pianta Capitolina we gather that this portico was quadrangular, the entrance consisting of a double row of Corinthian columns, of which two of the outer range and three of the inner, though thoroughly wrecked, are still standing. Some authorities, however, dispute this, and maintain that the three latter columns belonged, as aforesaid, to one of the two above temples dedicated to Jupiter and Juno.

The total number of columns surrounding this structure have been calculated by some writers at 270 and by others at fewer, and the interior is said to have been adorned with paintings and sculptures of great masters. Pliny, in particular, refers eulogistically to a statue of Venus, by Phidias, which some archaeologues suppose to be the famed Venus of the Medici. There are, however, two reasons against this hypothesis; first that the purity and severe correctness of style characteristic of the above great sculptor, are not evident in our acquaintance, the well-known Medicean Venus, undoubtedly the production of a later though eminent artist, and second, that the Venere Medicea in question was discovered not in this portico but in the famous villa of Hadrian at Tivoli.

The following rather remarkable episode is connected with the construction of the Porticus Octaviae, though here again there are those who maintain that it relates to the said Jupiter-Juno Temples. It is narrated that two Greek artists, some specify them as Spartans, were charged with the execution of the columns, and that they were called respectively "Vátrahos," frog, and "Sávros," lizard. Both these sculptors were desirous of inscribing their names on their productions here, but that either through envy or policy they were forbidden to do so, and in consequence they hit upon the following ingenious device of proving their authorship and of perpetuating their memory, despite the prohibition of those in authority. On the capital of one of the columns Vátrahos carved a frog, and similarly Sávros on another a lizard, and although the animals were perfectly represented, the workers managed at the same time to conceal them so cunningly twined amid the complicated curves and lines of the ornate capitals, that they were effectually secured from detection from all observers, and even, it is affirmed, of artists, excepting, of course, those let into the secret, now no longer one. The above columns at present adorn the nave of the Basilica of San Lorenzo (Fuori le Mura), where Pope Pius IX is buried, and it must be confessed that the two reptiles can be discerned without much difficulty, now that we expect to find them there lurking among the foliage of the capitals.

On the occasion of the celebration by Vespasian and Titus of their triumph over the Jews in the Porticus Octaviae, among those present was Flavius Josephus, the Jewish historian, the author of the literary work of unique interest, the *Life of Jesus Christ*, from the standpoint of a layman and of an impartial and practically contemporary witness and writer. This structure suffered by fire under Titus and was renovated by him and again by Septimius and Caracallus as the inscription informs us. From the eighth to the eighteenth centuries this spot was used as a fish-market, and the church built here was, in consequence, distinguished by a sobriquet as well as a name, and hence called Sant' Angelo in Pescheria.

It was in this church that Rienzi, A.D. 1347, passed his vigil as Knight of the Spirito Santo, and from here he issued to proclaim the establishment of the "Buono Stato" (Good State), followed by its ratification on the Capitol, though we read in Bulwer's *Last of the Tribunes* that Rienzi's vigil took place in the Basilica of St. John Lateran. It may be that that gifted author only availed himself of the usual privileged license of all novelists with regard to transposition of places, dates, events, etc., but we need not for this exclude the possibility of both versions being correct in Rienzi's case as referring to two separate vigils.

Under the Pontifical rule, from A.D. 1584 to nearly 1870, the Jews were compelled to attend this church, once a year to listen to Christian sermons, in the pious hope of their conversion thereby, but this custom was abolished by Pius IX at the urgent and cogent representations of Duke Michelangelo Gaetano Sermoneta.

With regard to the "Porticus Paedagogium," See Chapter II.

The "Porticus Argonautorum," Portico of the Argonauts or Sailors of Argos, was erected by M. A. Agrippa in honour of his naval victories, but except that it was situated in the present Piazza di Pietra, near his Temple of Neptune and that this Porticus was built during his period of power, that is, approximately in the first years of the first Christian century, little reliable information has hitherto been attained.

The "Porticus Duodecim Deorum," containing statues of the Twelve Gods, at the foot of the Capitoline Hill and facing the Roman Forum, was constructed, A.D. 367, by the Praefectus Urbis Vettius Agorius Praetextatus, who chiefly distinguished himself as a potent and uncompromising supporter of declining Paganism. It was excavated in 1834, but of the original building nothing seems to have survived except some small shattered cells, because the low colonnade, we now see covering them, was erected in 1858 by Pius IX.

The "Porticus ad Nationes," near the Theatre of Pompey, was so called from the colossal representative statues of the nations subjugated by the Romans, a historical, interesting structure of which it is to be regretted we know next to nothing.

FOUNTAINS. Although we know that the Sevenhilled City was abundantly provided with water in the times we are treating of, and, it is stated, adorned with several small ornamental fountains, especially by Agrippa, it seems evident that the ancient Romans, unlike their successors the modern Italians, did not invest in or bestow much care on the construction of ornamental fountains, at least not on the scale of their other public and private works. The ancient structures of this category were obviously of a different style and plan to the orthodox, ornate monumental fountains we are accustomed to see at present in Rome, and might be rather described for the most part as tanks, sources, or grottoes, with sometimes a shrine, artificial basin or other small similar accessories.

There are two famed classical fountains, that of Juturna and that of Egeria, but the term must be understood as referring to natural springs rather than to structural fountains. The "Puteal," or Well-head, of Juturna, in the Forum Romanum, is the outlet of her spring rising near the Arch of Janus, and is of a small, unpretending work. As mythological lore informs us Jupiter, on the principle, doubtless, that a fair exchange is no robbery, conferred on the Nymph Juturna immortality in substitution for virginity, and her waters were consequently held as sacred and used exclusively for religious purposes. She was, it appears, of Royal lineage, being the sister of Turnus, King of the Rutuli, and according to the Aeneid, she assisted her brother in his conflict with Aeneas. It is related further that as a live carnal Nymph or Princess previous to her miraculous transformation (which might perhaps be called transubstantiation or transpiritation) she spoke at her habitual abode or headquarters at the Alban Lake, and it would be interesting to know the subject of her discourse and the terms in which it was delivered, and if it were limited to the ambiguous exclamations which comprise usually all the verbal efforts of these supernatural or semi-supernatural beings.

The site of the "Fountain of Egeria" had for a long period furnished one of the many bones of contention between archaeologues, but at length the question was decided by the excavations of 1857, which in fact solved two problems, that of the site of the ancient Porta Capena, which led to that of this fountain, known on good authority to have been near the historical gate, at the spot where the spring still sparkles on the grounds above of the Villa Cellimontana.

The erroneous locality ascribed previously to this discovery to the Spring of Egeria was the following. A winding path of the Via Pignatelli, a branch of the Via Appia, leads to a clump of trees, all that now remains of the more extensive Bosco Sacro or Sacred Wood, and is still dignified by that epithet, and it was here, where there was also a spring and a grotto still existing, that King Numa held his mysterious interviews with the Nymph Egeria. She was credited with three characters in connection with this Sovereign, viz.: his inspired supernatural guide, his friendly worldly counsellor and his lady-love or mistress, and it is quite possible that she combined all three, or that Numa, who was a sagacious man and psychologist, may have invented the first for popular consumption, the superhuman element adding to his prestige and at the same time covering the two other characters or exalting them. We have a somewhat similar case, minus the supernatural factor, many centuries later and in another land, in the romantic story of King Henry II of England and the Fair Rosamond. The above spring and grotto was constructed into a Nymphaeum anciently coated with marble, in which there are wrecked niches, now tenantless, with the exception of one containing a mutilated statue of the River-god Almones from which the water of the source flows past into an artificial channel. This Grotto-shrine of Almones was supposed, as aforesaid, to be the Shrine-fountain of Egeria, but has now been identified as the Nymphaeum, belonging to Herodes Atticus, an annex of his Villa Tropea.

There is a romantic tale attached to this man and his wife, Annea Regilla, which may be briefly narrated as follows. Atticus, evidently wealthy, but not of noble lineage, married Regilla, a proceeding which however agreeable to the two contracting parties, was vehemently opposed by her family, the Annei, who were connected with the aristocratic Julii, and who deeply resented this union as a mésalliance, for although the law prohibiting marriages between patricians and plebeians had been abolished by this time, the sentiment and custom long survived the formal legislative act, as it almost always happens, forming as strong a barrier usually as any law.

Regilla died shortly after her wedding and her brother, in pursuance of the family feud, accused the widower of being her murderer. Herodes was acquitted for lack of proofs and on account of the extreme grief he evinced in every imaginable way at the loss of his wife. Indeed, he went so far in his manifestations of sorrow and mourning as to rigorously banish from his villa all objects of a light colour, and to have them replaced by others of a sable hue, a measure that caused a waggish acquaintance of his to express his wonder at seeing beans of a white and not of the black mourning colour, as everything else, at the table of Herodes. Both husband and wife were successively buried near this villa in a sumptuous mausoleum. The Villa Tropea contained, besides habitation and tomb, also, according to Ligorio, a temple consecrated to the unusual Pagan Trinity of Plutus, Ceres and Prosperpine. The relics rescued from this villa, among which are two terminal columns in the Villa Borghese, are at present dispersed in the Capitoline Museum and Roman Palaces. It appears that there was a valuable quarry of pentelic marble on this estate which furnished Herodes with the superior material he required for these edifices.

A singular incident is connected with the wealth of this family which owed its origin to the luck of Julius Atticus, ancestor of the aforesaid Herodes. This man was appointed by the Emperor Nerva, A.D. 96–98, Praefectus, and found, on demolishing the citadel of Athens, immense treasures, which event he considered it his duty to report to the monarch, for the latter to decide with regard to their disposal. This successor of Domitian and predecessor of Trajan, who was a gentleman in the true sense and therefore disinterested, responded laconically to this announcement, " All the better for thee! " with one point of admiration. But Julius was not satisfied, thinking that Nerva had not realized the value of the find, and wrote again, " But, Cesar, it is no small amount that I have discovered, as, for instance, two or three millions of sesterces, but much more considerable." To this the Emperor again replied, " All the better for thee!! " emphasized by two points of admiration. Still the Praefectus, who was conscientious, imagined that he had not given his Sovereign an adequate idea of the value of the treasure in his first two reports and wrote a third time, " But, Cesar, I assure thee that what I have found is literally of enormous value." " All the better for thee!!! " answered the monarch, punctuated this time by three points of admiration. At this significant reiteration, the scruples of Julius were finally set at rest and he felt himself justified in keeping the riches he had discovered for himself, family and descendants, who erected splendid villas, palaces, temples, etc., in Athens, Rome, Naples and other parts.

It is added, however, that Atticus was destined to witness and deplore the decadence of his family in another and more important sense, for although he himself was an orator, poet and artist, and all the other members more or less distinguished for their mental powers, his grandson had so degenerated from the hereditary intelligence that his preceptors were obliged, in order to teach him his alphabet, to provide twenty-four slaves, each bearing on his chest a huge letter, to represent the alphabet.

To return to the semi-mortal, semi-royal Nymph Egeria. Between Albano and Genzno lies the townlet of Ariccia, near the fine forest, estate and huge palace of the Princes Chigi. The road at this point, crosses the valley below by a great viaduct, the massive and well-proportioned architecture of which offers a specimen of typical Roman work in this line, and which to be seen properly must be viewed from the beautiful valley beneath, the Val' Ariccia, where legend narrates that Egeria retired to mourn King Numa Pompilius. In this picturesque retreat she shed tears so copiously, says the chronicle, that she herself became in time mercifully dissolved into a spring, with its winding brook, which continued to murmur forth her lamentations to the woods and sylvan deities. In our times, however, her secular sorrow has apparently taken a tempestuous form, because the torrent now rushing from its source, nicknamed Fonte Gerulo, is impetuous and powerful enough to turn several mills, and thus it may be said that her grief serves mankind as usefully perhaps now in a material sense, as her counsels and influence over the second King of Rome did of yore in a mental and moral one.

The "Lacus Servilii" is said to have been situated where the Via Jugurthus left the Roman Forum near the Temple of Saturn, and to have derived its name from Servilius Alcalá, who on this spot slew the philanthropist S. Manlius. A fountain adorned by a hydra was constructed here by M. V. Agrippa, wherefore the lake, with its structural fountain, are denominated by some "Fons Servilius" and by others "Fons Agrippa."

Near the Flavian Amphitheatre is a crumbling conical mound known by the name of "Meta Sudans," or Sweating Goal. The original structure, dating approximately from the latter years of the Republic, was demolished by Nero when he reared his palace and gardens, and the present remains belong to a reconstruction by Domitian, as an accessory of the above amphitheatre. One of the halls of the Vatican Museum contains a marble tomb ornamented in relief. In general shape and outline this monument resembles a circus, while the reliefs represent a fountain-head between two lions, discharging water from the top, having the form of a Meta or Circus-Goal. This tomb is conjectured to have been the model of the above Meta Sudans Fountain, in its original condition, of which the waterless wreck we now see is all that survives. Other authorities opine that, on the contrary, the fountain was the model and the tomb the copy, a question that might be settled if the respective dates of each were established, granting always that the one is really the replica taken from the other, which is not beyond a doubt. But in any case this tomb, even if not connected with the Meta Sudans, may serve to give some idea of these fountain structures of the times in Rome.

Between the Comitium and the Septimian Arch in the Roman Forum there is a wrecked circular basin with a marble base which comprises all that exists of the handsome fountain erected by Maxentius probably A.D. 306 or thereabout and dedicated to Mars, Romulus and Remus.

The "Fons Orphei," Fountain of Orpheus, was a pond in the centre of which was a fountain-fabric composed of an artificial rock, surmounted by a group of statues of

Orpheus and the enchanted beasts around him in various attitudes, a design quaint and attractive enough to arouse the desire to know the creator thereof, which cannot be satisfied or at least has not been satisfied up to the present. This fountain was situated near the ancient Vicus Cyprius, probably the present Via degli Zingari, an old street that runs behind the Via Cavour. On this Vicus formerly stood a small house belonging to the identical Pedo Albinorum extolled by Ovidius, and which was tenanted subsequently by no less a personage than Pliny.

BASILICA AEMILIA, B.C. 179. ROMAN FORUM.

Plate xlvii.

CHAPTER XX
BASILICAS

THE term "Basilica" is derived from "Vasiliké," royal, the adjective of "Vasiléfs," king.

When public affairs ceased to be transacted, as was the earlier custom, in the open air, the more or less sumptuous edifices constructed for this purpose in Rome have been denominated basilicas, though the Roman words for them were "Regia," or "Aedes." Subsequently, that is after the commencement of the Christian era to our days, this epithet has been applied to the principal Christian churches.

There were naturally several structures of this class in the Eternal City and the following are those of which some ruins or records survive.

The "Basilica Portia," the earliest commemorated, was built, 184 B.C., in the Roman Forum by the Censor Marcus Portius Cato, the great and uncompromising upholder of morality and simplicity of life, to whose names were added the qualificatives of "Major" and "Priscus," to distinguish him from another eminent man, his homonymous grand-nephew. With regard to the plan and style of this basilica nothing, even traditionally or conjecturally, has been gathered, so far as we know, its very site being somewhat dubious, and of its history only its end seems to be recorded, which came about in a popular rising caused by indignation at the murder of the patrician, Clodius, by Milo, when the populace wrecked this building and seized also the wooden furniture of the adjacent Curia to use for the funeral pyre of Clodius.

The "Basilica Aemilia," situated between the Temple of Antoninus and Faustina and the Curia, was first built by the Censors M. Aemilius Lepidus and M. Fulvius Nobilior, 179 B.C., and greatly embellished by Aemilius Paulus the conqueror of Macedon, of the succeeding generation. In 54 B.C., L. Aemilius Paulus received, it is related, a subsidy of 1,500 talents from Cesar, then intent on improving the Forum, for the purpose of extending and beautifying this building. It is difficult to establish the corresponding value in modern current decimal coinage of this undoubtedly enormous sum. The word "talent" of Egyptian origin was adopted in that country to denote a unit of water weight, and afterwards used by other peoples to represent one of monetary value, which varied greatly in different epochs and nations, the equivalent for one talent being either 3,600, or 4,150, or 4,500, or 5,700, or 10,000 francs.

This superb edifice finally completed by Aemilius Lepidus, son of the above Paulus, in 34 B.C., while serving as the Central Exchange in Rome, was also regarded as a family appurtenance of the Gens Aemilii. This family, one of the most ancient, illustrious and influential of Rome, claimed their descent from Pythagoras and their surname from

"Emilion Lóhon," signifying "seductive word," otherwise to the persuasive eloquence attributed to Pythagoras' son, Mamercus, the founder of the family.

So far as has been ascertained the Basilica Aemilia measured 300 feet in length, and the Aula, or main-hall, 200 feet long by seventy-two wide. It was two storied, with a double colonnade, but it has not been established to which of the architectonic Orders it belonged, owing, perhaps, to the shockingly mutilated condition of the columns unearthed. The arcades and architrave belong to the Doric, and it has consequently been inferred that the rest was of this Order. This is not, however, an incontestable or even sound assumption, because though it is certain that the said hall, judging by the fragments, was adorned by Doric columns, it does not necessarily follow that both the stories, or the entire edifice, were of the same Order, but, quite the contrary, seeing that there is no example or record in Rome of any building of more than one story being constructed entirely of one architectural Order. The columns we now see here do not afford any clue because they were placed here after, and are of a later date and inferior work, and did not therefore belong to the basilica.

The gallery of the Aula was supported by unfluted columns of African marble, and the pavement consisted of slabs of white marble, on which the still adhering oxidized coins indicate that the smaller fry of the pecuniary profession, such as brokers, money-changers and the like, who congregated here, had for some cause or other to leave this building in great haste. From this main-hall diverged the ambulatories and the quadrangular "Tabernae" (a much and variously used term which in this case signifies the committee rooms and offices) built of blocks of tufa probably cased in marble, with a mosaic flooring of insertions called "Tesserae" of serpentine and porphyry, the whole adorned with richly sculptured cornices of which some fragments still exist, and surmounted by a series of statues. The "Aemilia" was damaged by fire, 14 B.C., and restored by another Aemilius, assisted financially by Octavius, and it was further repaired by Tiberius, A.D. 32. It is related by the celebrated historian and grammarian Caius, Tranquilius Suetonius, that the Praetorians rushed down from the Viminal through the Aemilia in pursuit of Galba, whom they overtook and slew near the Lake of Curtius, and that though some of his adherents sought the protection of the temple and shrines of Vesta and Juturna close by, they were not spared on that account. During the contest between Vespasian and Vitellius this edifice was subjected to much rough handling, but effectively restored by the former.

In A.D. 410 it was more than half destroyed by three enemies, viz.: earthquakes, fire and Alaric's hordes, but Theodoric, about A.D. 454–526, made some attempts at re-edification and repair. There is no doubt that this magnificent creation was both in detail and as a whole well worthy of the golden period of art to which it belonged. Publius Papinius Statius, an Epirote by extraction, a Neapolitan by birth and a Roman by choice, historian and poet, A.D. 40–96, in alluding to this basilica, terms it "Sublimis Regia Paulli." Cicero long before this had expressed his unbounded admiration and wonder for its design, superb decorations and precious material of which it was composed, and Plutarch, in his biography of Aemilius Paulus, reckons it as one of the most perfect and splendid of the Sevenhilled City. The "Aemilia" never really recovered from the effects of the above noted threefold catastrophes, and began henceforth to assume the

BASILICA JULIA, B.C. 46. ROMAN FORUM.

Plate xlviii.

character of a majestic wreck gradually wasting away, till about A.D. 1000 when it had almost completely disappeared, embedded under the rubbish and rising soil around, to be brought to light again in the nineteenth century, but only as part of a shattered, broken architectural skeleton.

The "Basilica Sempronia," relatively to which little has been gathered except that it was constructed in 169 B.C., in some as yet unidentified quarter of the Roman Forum. It is known, however, that the Gens Sempronia were a clan of great antiquity divided into two branches, patrician and plebeian, and that one of them was Consul as far back as 497 B.C., and that this basilica which bore their name was the work of this noted family, the eminence and prosperity of which began and ended synchronously with the duration of the Republic.

The "Basilica Julia," situated between the Temple of Castor and Pollux and that of Saturn, was a rectangular structure measuring about 330 feet in length and 160 in width. The precise date of its construction by Cesar is not quite certain but the approximate one is 52–50 B.C., about the time of his comprehensive renovation of the Roman Forum, and it was inaugurated though not quite finished in 46 B.C. Octavious extended this edifice, but even before he witnessed its completion it was destroyed by fire. Septimius, in A.D. 199, thoroughly overhauled and restored the building. This Emperor was a capable and ubiquitous builder and restorer, and a man of great energy, piercing intellect and iron will, before whom even his son Caracallus was awed into decent behaviour and only dared to manifest his evil propensities after his father's death. The "Julia" was subsequently repaired by Diocletian after the fire of A.D. 282, and finally by the Praefectus Gabbinus, Vettius Probianus, A.D. 416, as is recorded on a pedestal unearthed in the neighbouring Via Jugurthus.

This Basilica, built for the Law-Courts of the Capital, was composed of an Aula of 270 feet by fifty-four feet, encircled by double-aisled, double-storied Porticus or prolonged archway. The sessions of the Judges (simply called "Centumviri," or Hundredmen, three from each of the thirty-three Tribes, and comprising the President totalled one hundred) divided into four sections, took place in this hall, which was paved with costly Phrygian and African marbles, and open on three sides, the fourth being closed and occupied by the Tabernae. This pavement of the converging aisles consisted uniformly of white marble, and there are still traces on it of the incisions of the "Tabulae Lussoriae," or Dice-tablet, a game much favoured by the Romans. So much of the material has been abstracted, mainly for the construction of the Palazzo Torlonia in the Borgo, besides the secular ravages, that only one of the piers with a Roman Doric pilaster attached, is still standing erect, though grievously damaged, as a solitary sentinel facing the Via Sacra. The northern wall of the arcade of the basilica was incorporated in the Church of Sta. Maria, in Canepa, and is therefore in existence still, and, facing the present Via della Consolazione, are the walls of tufa and travertine, the core probably, which formerly was the section where the staircases leading to the upper story of this edifice were built.

If we may accept the more or less ideal reproductions by artists in recent times as fairly representative of what this basilica was originally, it appears to have consisted of a first or ground story reached by a flight of steps, of arches flanked by Roman Doric pilasters on the piers, and of an upper, likewise composed of arches, but with statues on pedestals within them, and bordered by Ionic pilasters. The interior of both stories consisted of vaults supported on pillars, and the roofing was surrounded with statues on pedestals.

This basilica, though handsome and stately, was less ornamental and of a simpler style altogether than the opposite one of the Aemilia, as became its judicial functions, more serious and weighty than the financial ones of the second. With the ancients of the classic times the idea and principle of the strictly appropriate prevailed much more than it does now, when we see a building serving as a miscellaneous shop, having not only the dimensions but also the style and architecture of a palace, and on the other hand the family residence of a great nobleman, which ought to be a palace, looking frequently not unlike a hugh, ungainly cottage externally, whereas in the ancient constructions there was no such unsuitable anomaly nor could there be any mistake, the temple, basilica, palace, etc., each possessing its specific harmonious character, representing to the least detail its purpose and status, similarly as the hut, shop, etc., had theirs.

Some writers assert that the Aemilian Basilica was intended to balance the Julian, but as the former was built before the latter, it would be more logical to conclude that the contrary might be the case. Possibly the parallel drawn was nothing more than the result of a vagary of some careless archaeologue, more bent on inventing a well-sounding phrase, whether applicable or not, than on accurate research and attention to dates.

The scant remains of this basilica were first exhumed in 1835–1847 during the excavations of Canina, and as we see it now in 1871 and 1883. It is recorded that the Sovereigns not unfrequently presided at the sittings of the Centumviri, and it is reported that Domitian and Trajan had sometimes on such occasions annulled sentences which they considered not strictly equitable through partiality or through error of judgment.

The "Basilica Flavia." The State-Hall of the Imperial Palace on the Palatine, begun by Vespasian and Titus and terminated by their successor Domitian, opened on the left to the Lararium, and on the right to the above Basilica or High-Court of Justice. It is said to have been semi-circular and divided internally into a nave with lateral aisles bordered by a range of columns with bronze ornaments. A transenna or balustrade separated the accusers and the accused from the Judges on the Apse, in the recess of which stood the throne on a dais, having above a gallery reached by a flight of steps. The entire building was of marble, except the walls which were cased with it, and its plan internally was subsequently adopted as the model of the larger Christian churches, styled basilicas. Octavius and Nero judged and sentenced in their palaces, Claudius, reverting to the system prevalent in earlier times, used to administer justice in the open air, and the Flavian Emperors in their above basilica, adjoining but independent of, their palace.

It may be as well to recall the composition of these Tribunals as regards their personnel. Under the Empire the members were Imperial Delegates of Consular rank appointed to judge all cases on appeal, one Judge being nominated for each province in virtue of a Decree of Octavius. The great criminal and state cases were heard by the Emperor in person presiding over a Council of twenty members, of which two were the Consuls of the year, and the other eighteen divided between Senators chosen by lot

BASILICA FLAVIA, A.D. 70–75. PALATINE.

from the whole body of Conscript Fathers, and by selected representatives of the various Magistracies of Rome.

This distinguished Bench, except for one defect, could not have been composed of better elements, enlightened, trustworthy, experienced, the very élite of the social, official, political and scientific Roman world. The defect alluded to, was, or rather might be, the President, who was at the same time the absolute Ruler of the greatest Empire known, and who might happen to be a Caligula or a Commodus as easily as a Trajan or a Marcus Aurelius. In the Roman and Venetian Republics this grave possible disadvantage, that might neutralize every other advantage, could never have existed, because the selection of the president no less than the other members, did not depend on chance or luck, but on careful and justified choice, and moreover his power was not in this capacity or any other unlimited.

The importance of incorruptible and competent Judges cannot be over-estimated, no care should be spared in the selection and no sacrifice be grudged in the remuneration of men on whose decision depend the liberty, honour, means and existence of their fellow creatures. These basic principles are recognized in theory by all, but they are not so uniformly and thoroughly realized and practised, as would be desirable. Cesar's famous phrase that " Cesar's wife must not even be suspected " ought to be applicable to Judges above all others, and with even more reason, because their unsullied reputation and high competence, as Judges, affects the whole of the community in all directions. The Israelites of old, themselves the chosen people, were governed by Judges, and Kings were accorded to them as a castigation. The administration of Justice has invariably and universally been held as the highest prerogative of all Rulers, from the greatest Monarch to the petty mediaeval Baron, who exercised high, middle and low justice on his dependents and vassals. There cannot be conceived any entity in the human or Superhuman world higher than the Judge, and in proof of this, one of the chief functions attributed to the Almighty relatively to us, is " To judge the Quick and the Dead," and we call Him the " Just Judge " and the " Merciful Judge." All this seems and should be self evident, nevertheless it is undeniable that most people look upon judges as on a par with other public functionaries, which is certainly not the case.

The " Basilica Ulpia " took its name from its creator the Emperor Trajanus Ulpius Crinitus, and was one of the seven sections of his Forum, the length of the basilica corresponded to the width of the entire Forum, that is, either 670 or 1,000 feet, and its breadth has been calculated at 165 or 220 feet. The descriptions of this basilica are as incomplete as they are conflicting, but the following seems to be based on the least dubious sources. According to this account the edifice consisted of three naves, the central one being the Court of Justice and was surrounded by columns of pavonazetto (peacock marble) marble, while the others were bordered by columns of black oriental marble with capitals and bases of white Parian marble, the entire building being lined with Luna marble, paved with Giallo Antico and roofed with a dome of gilded bronze. It may in any case be taken for granted that it was worthy of and in harmony with the superb Forum of which it formed part. It is recorded that it was in this basilica that Constantine I in A.D. 313 in the presence of the Senators, Magnates and Generals of the Empire formally abjured Paganism in favour of Christianism.

The "Basilica Sessoriana" is remarkable chiefly as the Law-Court instituted exclusively for the hearing of cases concerning slaves as petitioners, plaintiffs and defendants, to whom it was prohibited to appear in these characters in other Tribunals. This building stood in the area occupied later by the Horti Variani and the Circus of Heliogabalus and afterwards by the abode of Saint Helena, and was named from its origin the "Palatium Sessorianum," now covered by the Basilica of Santa Croce in Gerusalemme and the Cistercian Monastery with its garden. It would be interesting to know something of the plan, details and date of this basilica, so peculiar in its functions, but it does not seem likely that this desire will be gratified.

The "Basilica Maxentia." On entering the Roman Forum by the Arch of Titus, the first great mass of ruins we meet on the right are those of this edifice, erected by the Emperor Marcus Aurelius Valerius Maxentius, to serve as a High Court of Justice and designed to contain several Tribunals. It was built of a core of bricks with a marble casing and is stated to have measured 335 feet in length by 140 in width. The principal entrance originally faced the Flavian Amphitheatre, the one looking on the Forum being of a later date, and the former led to the main nave or hall, the domed arcades still existing being those of the aisles. The panelling of the soffits of these ruined vaults was of marble with gold rosettes, the design of which, still traceable, has been chosen by generations of artists as one of the best models extant of works of this nature. In front there were eight fine Corinthian columns, forming the Porticus, of exquisite proportions and workmanship as is testified by the only one now surviving, removed by Pope Paul V and placed in the Piazza of Sta. Maria Maggiore. The broken shafts of porphyry columns scattered about here with other fragments, did not belong originally, it is asserted, to this basilica, but were taken from the Temple of Venus later. In the western wall there was a spiral staircase conducting to the gallery closed in 1904.

Maxentius was a consistent admirer and staunch upholder of the earlier and more glorious epoch of Roman history, and this magnificent edifice, of which we know so little, was acknowledged to have borne the impress of the ancient Roman grandeur and finish in style, and to compare not unfavourably with the renowned creations of antiquity. With this Basilica Roman classic architecture, long lingering in decay, may be said, after this brief ray, to have closed its existence. Two vast nearly coeval constructions of Diocletian, namely his palace at Spalato and his baths in Rome, might also be included. This proves what one man can accomplish, if gifted with ability and individuality, even though as in the case of Maxentius, possessing only a share of power, encompassed by disturbances and obstructed by the full tide of degeneracy. This Sovereign sought even in his own family, by naming his son Romulus, to perpetuate the memory of the past and to relink it with the then present. Constantine, his brother-in-law and adversary, cannot be said to have any claim to this edifice, called by many Basilica of Constantine, unless we were to admit as such his illicit appropriation of it after the death of its constructor.

Apparently some people are beginning to realize the error of calling this building otherwise than by its proper name of "Basilica Maxentia," which is gradually becoming more diffused. Possibly also the name of Constantine may likewise, in the course of time, come to be eliminated from another monument, the well-known arch of Via San

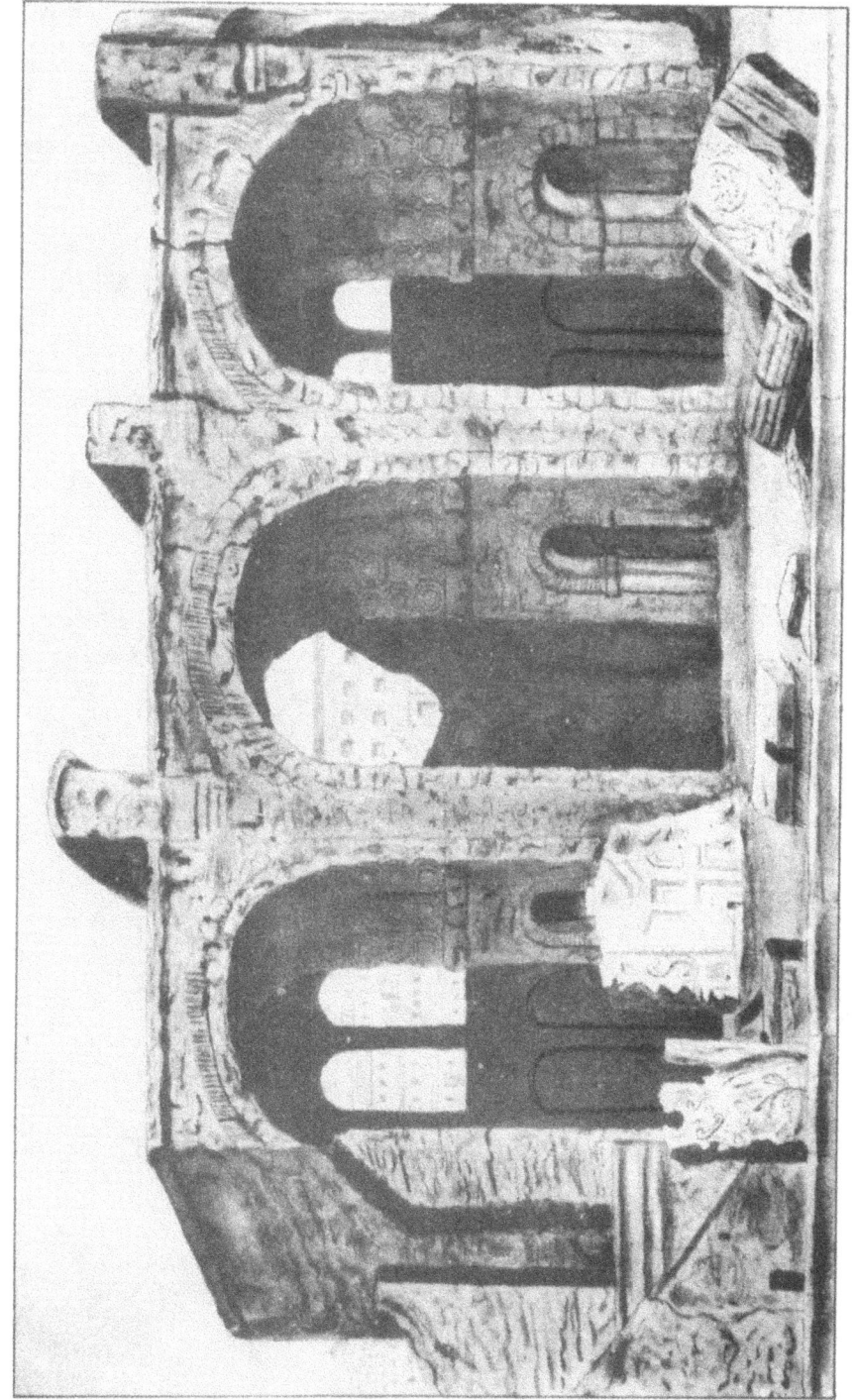

BASILICA MAXENTIA, A.D. 312. ROMAN FORUM.

Plate l.

Gregorio, to which it has hitherto been applied. In this case the choice of another more correct epithet would present some difficulty, because this arch cannot be said as already mentioned to appertain to any one in particular. Nevertheless perhaps the name of " Arcus Saxae Rubrae " might be suggested as it was intended to commemorate that battle, which might therefore be considered at any rate a somewhat more appropriate designation than that of " Arcus Constantini."

CHAPTER XXI

BATHS

THERE are perhaps few terms more misapplied than that of "Thermae" to describe ancient or modern bathing establishments. If the use of the ancient Roman parent tongue be considered preferable for the nomenclature of ancient Roman works, and there is something to be urged in favour of this view, there is the Latin word "Balneae," baths, which covers the entire subject, while the Greek "thermós," whence "Thermae," signifies only "hot." We know that the Roman establishments of this nature were not limited to hot water baths, but comprised tepid, cold, vapour and shower baths, besides music halls, libraries, gymnasiums, etc., wherefore the collective term is obviously the more appropriate. Nor is the argument or excuse that time has consecrated the employment of a misnomer logically valid, because if a term be inappropriate, time cannot render it correct, or turn wrong into right. And, it if be deemed advisable to adopt an ancient generic word for bathing establishments, ancient or modern, then the term, "hydro," derived from "ythor," water, might be less open to objection, seeing that these are Water Establishments.

We have our modern languages, to mention the four principal ones, English, German, French and Italian, emancipated from the parent tongues and constituted, as we flatter ourselves, in all essentials completely. If this be so, they ought to suffice severally to furnish words for eveything necessary, and there ought not, consequently, to be any need to borrow and travesty those belonging to others. The frequent introduction of Greek and Latin words to denote even objects of modern invention and use, many of which were not even in existence at the time when the above were living languages, may be attributed rather to a pedantic affectation of classical scholarship, and as regards the preference for words of another modern language reciprocally indulged in, when we have equivalent terms in our own and should know them, this is often an ostentation of knowledge of foreign languages.

Despite our "All Modern Appliances," the phrase so glibly squirted out at everyone and intended to produce satisfaction if not enthusiasm at the supposed wonderful progress attained in everything, which would indeed be most satisfactory if it were only founded on facts, our bathing establishments can ill compare with those of the Romans about two centuries before the birth of Christ. Inconsistently with the professions of most people nowadays of large-hearted liberalism and philanthropy but consistently with the prevalent snobbish, venal tyranny of our money grabbing times, we inexorably deprive all those who are indigent, not always through their own fault (as others are wealthy not invariably by their own merit but sometimes all the contrary) of the improvement and enjoyment derived from similar hygienic resorts.

Let us briefly compare the ancient and modern institutions of bathing establishments. Firstly, the Roman Balneae were more numerous and extensive in proportion to the population, secondly, besides being excellently planned, arranged and furnished with all requirements of comfort and even luxury, were also, an important difference and advantage, amply provided with the means for instruction, exercise, diversion, other than bathing, which are lacking in the modern public baths, thirdly, they were more durable and incomparably handsomer artistically and richer in material, and fourthly open indiscriminately to all. Thus the indigent in Rome could always enjoy a bath with its accessories at the nominal cost of a copper coin of infinitesmal value, less than a farthing, serving rather as a tally than as an entrance fee. In other words, they were not penalized for the crime of impecuniosity. And what a bath! Fit for a Sybarite in an edifice fit for an Emperor ! and it must be borne in mind that what has been said of Rome applies equally to all the cities which this marvellous people subjugated or colonized in Italy and the rest of the world. Nor must we overlook the fact that even these insufficient and inferior modern public baths have only been established recently, and that we have taken about twenty-two centuries to approach, but not to equal, the ancient Romans in this respect.

The " Baths of Decius," so called, it is said, from the Decii Albini, occupied formerly the land now known as the Vigna Torlonia opposite the old church of Sta. Prisca. There is nothing authentically known of their plan, size, architecture and structure and the exceedingly scant vestiges left, reveal nothing much either. Who were these Decii Albini? The Decii were an ancient plebeian family illustrated by the services, and, above all, by the deaths of two of its members, father and son, Decius Publius and Decius Publius Mas, who devoted themselves to the Manes, otherwise to voluntary death, in obedience to an oracular prediction in order to secure victory on two different occasions, in the fourth pre-Christian century. The third known Decius was the Emperor Decius Trajanus Gneus Massius, A.D. 249-251. The Albini, on the other hand, were a family of later date, who also gave two members to history, Albinus Posthumus, literateur and Consul as colleague of Lucullus, and Albinus Claudius, a general under M. Aurelius. The only recorded case in which we find the two names united in one individual is that of Decius Claudius Cejonius Albinus, first the co-Emperor and after the defeated and slain rival of L. Septimius Severus. But as his complexion was extremely fair and as the Latin word " Albinus " signifies white, this may have been an agnomen or nickname and not a cognomen or nomen, a surname or name. While, therefore, it cannot be affirmed positively that no such family as the Decii-Albini ever existed, it can certainly be stated that there are no absolute proofs that they did exist as one single " Gens " (clan or family). But all this does not help us to establish even the approximate date of the construction of these baths, which might possibly be any time between 450 B.C. and A.D. 190

It is noteworthy that the assumption of a double-barrelled surname as a distinction (for the second name is not usually tacked on unless it is a better or richer one) whatever the levelling theories of present times, betrays the almost universal existence of a strong sentiment within us which is diametrically opposed to equality. This is the inherent desire to spring from a high, or at least, a good lineage, rather than from a low or an indifferent one, and for this family and caste superiority to be recognised and distinguished by a designation. In the countries where the titles and status of hereditary nobility, derived originally from offices and then from feudal tenures, such as " Dux," leader, " Comes," companion, etc., are non-existent and not even personal knighthoods, as a sort of substitute, the peoples, and especially the plutocrats, have resorted to two ways to gain this coveted superiority, the one by adopting the double-barrelled surname, and the other by allying themselves by the daughters' marriages with some man bearing a title, and for this reflected titular aristocracy they make great pecuniary sacrifices. So we may logically assume that all the stale, drivelling talk about "democracy" and "equality" is only cant and humbug.

With the ancient Romans a different system prevailed relatively to social distinctions. There were no titles of nobility as we have inherited them from the Middle Ages, but there were the hereditary Patrician "Gens" with their well-defined rights, privileges and duties, and whenever any individual had deserved well of his country, the name or place of his achievement or the quality wherewith he distinguished himself were added to his name and surname, instead of the mediaeval " Baron, Marquis, " etc. Thus the name of Coriolanus " was bestowed on Gneus Martius as a reward for his capture of Cori, that of " Capitolinus " on Marcus Manlius for saving the Capitol, that of " Publicola " on Valerius for valuable services to the people or public of Rome, that of " Cunctator " on Fabius Maximus on account of his masterly waiting strategy, so successful in his conflict with Hannibal. There was the custom, besides, of adding an agnomen arising from a personal feature, also reckoned as an honorary epithet or title, because attached to distinguished persons, as for example, " Caecus," " Barbatus," " Scevola." Closing this digression we return to our immediate subject.

The " Baths of Aemilius Paulus " were situated on the isthmus uniting the Quirinal to the Capitol, afterwards cut down, as already mentioned, by Trajan for his Forum. It is to be regretted that there are no records that we know of regarding the style, plan, decorations and material of these baths, which have naturally entirely disappeared, in the first place because we are thus deprived of having a specimen, however ruinous, of the earlier Roman Baths, and secondly, because the Aemilii were capable and artistic builders, as we can perceive by the scant wrecks of their constructions of the Basilica Aemilia and Pons Aemilius aforenoted. The approximate date of these Balneae Aemilii is 180–160 B.C.

The "Baths of Agrippa" were built by M. V. Agrippa on the area now occupied by the Panthaeum and extended far behind and around this edifice, which from being originally one of the bathing halls of the Agrippa Baths was converted into a temple. The Virgo Aqueduct was constructed originally mainly to convey the requisite water supply of these baths. Some of the remains, exhumed in 1881, consist of portions of two other bathing-halls, with a large recess on the present Via Palombella, of a broken fluted column, a fragment of a fine frieze and reliefs representing dolphins and shells, and perhaps also the so-called Arco della Ciambella. But it is certain that these baths must have been of considerable dimensions as well as handsomely built, seeing that one

ANTONINE BATHS, A.D. 210-218.

Plate li.

of their halls alone was large enough and beautiful enough, though doubtless altered, to serve as an imposing temple, the Pantheon.

The "Baths of Tiberius" were an annex of his palace on the Palatine and that is about all that has been learned relatively to them.

The "Baths of Agrippina," on the Viminal Hill, were remarkable, so far as we know, principally for their purpose, being erected by this Empress for the use of women exclusively, as she objected, with a modesty somewhat alien to her character and reputation, to mixed bathing of the sexes. As there is no better explanation for this inconsistency, it may be that as she was the antithesis of modesty and decency herself, she might have been proportionately eager of exercising these virtues "vicariously," no very rare occurrence in our curious human nature.

The "Baths of Nero" stood on the site of the present church of San Luigi dei Francesi and the neighbouring buildings. M. Valerius Martialus, born in Spain and an epigrammatic poet, A.D. 43–104, alludes to these baths in a passage not complimentary either to the builder or the building. The two above baths of mother and son were constructed about the same period, approximately between A.D. 50 and A.D. 67, but there are no positive records or vestiges of them surviving so far at least as we are aware.

The "Flavian Baths," commonly but erroneously known as the Baths of Titus, were built by the three Emperors of this Dynasty on the declivity of the Esquiline facing their Amphitheatre. This establishment covered, it is said, an area of 1,150 by 850 feet and comprised a portion of the space previously occupied by Nero's enormous Aureae Domus. In two of the chambers, at present visible, there are alcoves for couches, and in a third, a cavity for a fountain with a trench around it, and there are also traces of a cryptoporticus, but the chief interest lies in the beautiful arabesques, much and irreparably injured now, which Raffaele Sanzio and Giovanni da Undine copied for the Vatican Loggia.

The "Baths of Trajan," extending from this spot to the churches of San Pietro in Vincoli and San Martino dei Monti, were of much greater dimensions than the above, which they adjoined, and with which they have sometimes been confounded. The excavations, first in A.D. 1774 and afterwards by the French in A.D. 1811, brought to light the substruction of a semi-circular exedra, placed in the centre of a rear wall, which is the portion of the building hitherto identified, but on the more elevated site above, in the enclosed property of the Princes Brancaccio, are still to be seen the "Piscinae," or reservoirs, now called the Sette Sale, from which, it is conjectured, the baths were supplied with water.

The "Antonine Baths," commonly known as the Baths of Caracalla, designed by Septimius Severus, begun by Caracalla, A.D. 212–217, continued by Heliogabalus A.D. 218–222, and terminated by Alexander Severus A.D. 222–235, were situated at the foot of the Aventine Hill, facing that part of the Via Appia, now renamed Via San Sebastiano, partly on the land previously occupied by the Horti Asinarii, the Gardens of Asinius Paulus mentioned by Frontinus. With the single exception of the Flavian Amphitheatre, these ruins are the most extensive of one building now existing in the Sevenhilled City. The area covered by the entire enclosure measured externally, as computed, 1,180 by 1,180 feet, and the rectangular bathing establishment proper inside

760 feet in length by 380 in width. These numbers are given, it is to be understood in this case as in all others, under protest of non-responsibility, regarding their accuracy for the reasons already mentioned before.

Ammianus Marcellinus, a Latin historian of Greek extraction, A.D. 330-390, voiced the popular impression, which, being such, was somewhat exaggerated, produced by their size, by the comprehensive phrase, " That the Roman Baths resembled provinces." The Balneae Antonianae were said to have contained 1,600 separate marble bathrooms, but could, of course, accommodate a greater number of bathers than 1,600 contemporaneously besides in the vapour and shower-bath compartments, &c., while the multitude of those dispersed before and after their ablutions in other non-bathing compartments, such as in the stadium as participators or spectators, in the gymnasium training or exercising, about the gardens strolling or sitting, in the libraries reading, in the concert and lecture halls performing, lecturing or listening, in the reception and refreshment saloons conversing and eating, in the exhibition and play-houses acting or looking on, was naturally very great.

Yet despite this vast concourse of frequenters of all kinds and conditions, no friction or delays occurred in the service, conducted smoothly by a perfectly appointed and directed, well-organised and numerous staff of attendants, freedmen and slaves, who circulated invisibly by the " Cryptae," or concealed corridors, that permeated the entire building. The head-porter or Janitor was called " Ostiarius," and the head wardrobe-keeper " Capsarius." The bathrooms were divided into two classes, each chamber being provided with a " Piscina," or basin, and an " Odeum," or tub, chairs and benches, those of the first class having, in addition, a dressing and massage room annexed.

The entire establishment was built over a substructure in which was the huge " Hypocaustus," the furnace, which by means of brick and lead pipes introduced steam into the " Laconium," or vapour-baths, and also served to warm the atmosphere, the temperature being regulated by valves, or for the hot or tepid water for the Caldarium or Tepidarium. The mouths of these tubes were, as customary in the greater edifices, of massive chiselled silver.

Passing through the " Propylaia," entrance portico, of the external enclosure, the first of the three principal halls was reached which occupied the centre, and bisected the entire breadth of the Balneae proper. This hall, termed " Frigidarium," or cold-water section, with its swimming pond, communicated directly with the second hall called " Tepidarium," or tepid-water section, both oblong and rectangular. On leaving the second hall and proceeding by a broad passage the third great hall, the " Caldarium," or hot-water section, was entered. On the right and left of the Tepidarium was the " Paleastrae," or " Arenae," with semi-circular alcoves and surrounded with columns of African granite encrusted with the valuable marble called Giallo Antico and paved with mosaic, some fragments of which are still adhering to the ground, but the well-preserved mosaic representing pugilists now in the Lateran Palace of Rome, though belonging to these baths, was not, it is affirmed, the pavement of the Palestrae, but of one of the bathing-halls. One of these two Arenae was designed for the exercise and diversion of men, and presided over by a statue of Hercules, the famous Farnese Hercules, and the other similarly for women, by that of Flora. These two statues, and, some also add, the Callypygian Venus, were discovered, A.D. 1534, here among other numerous art treasures, and carried off by Pope Paul III, together with large quantities of marble to decorate his Farnese Palace. Subsequently however, these statues were transferred to the Museum of Naples.

The Propylaia were composed of huge pillars of granite, which sustained the roof, and it is narrated that on their removal the roofing collapsed with such a tremendous crash that it was heard in the city like a close thunderbolt and a distant earthquake shock. Of all the numerous and various columns of the Balneae Antonianae only one is now known to be intact and identified, the one that supports the statue of Justice in the Piazza of Sta. Trinitá at Florence. The columns supporting internally the ceiling of the bath-halls were surmounted by bronze Telamones or Atlantes (the male figures corresponding to the female Caryatides). One of the ceilings, that of the Frigidarium, though some authorities maintain that they were all similar, was considered an architectural miracle, because it consisted of flat stone slabs held together by crossing metal bars, called "Soles," from their resemblance to the straps of sandals, wherefore this Hall is termed "Cella Solaria."

The three main bathing sections, namely the Frigidarium, Tepidarium and Caldarium, were surrounded symmetrically by smaller compartments, the principal of which were the "Apotheterium," or disrobing-room, the "Sudatorium," or sweating-chamber, the "Unctuarium," or anointing and perfuming saloon. Beside the swimming basin was an octagonal chamber, still in relative preservation so far as regards its outlines, supposed to have been destined for the use of the Imperial family, and opposite the Caldarium, on the other side, some traces are still visible of the contiguous Stadium. The lofty walls of the various apartments consisted of a core of brickwork cased by a thick coating of African granite, the latter again encrusted with the costly "Verde Antico" marble of Numidia, and decorated with beautiful mosaics and arabesques. The water supply of these baths was conveyed from an aqueduct from Mons Algidus.

There is a reconstruction of the Balneae Antonianae, as they are conjectured to have been originally, by a French artist named Abel Louet, and also an official plan of them affixed to the walls. But though no description by pen, pencil, brush or chisel can be expected to revive accurately the splendour of this vast edifice, still every account of it, however defective or incomplete, will be useful and interesting as helping to convey to our mind's eye some general idea of the Roman Baths, being typical of a class of monumental structures that had come to assume at that period the character of a national institution of manifold advantages to the public, which could be enjoyed by the powerful aristocratic and opulent patrician as well as by the poor "Pullatus," though, as was sensible and becoming, the different classes performed their ablutions separately.

The "Baths of Diolcetian," a portion of which has been reconstructed and transformed into the National Museum opposite the central railway station of the capital, were begun by the emperors Diocletian and Maximinus in A.D. 303 and terminated by Constantius Hlorus and Maximinianus, A.D. 305. Their dimensions were nearly double those of the Antonine Baths, but the scattered, scant remains of the Balneae Diocletiani, built upon and swamped by other constructions, are naturally less instructive and interesting than the isolated, concentrated ruins of the Balneae Antonianae.

In plan these two establishments were similar in most essential points; the entrance of the Diocletian Baths also led, it is asserted, to the Frigidarium opposite the Caldarium, with the Tepidarium between, also flanked by the Palestrae, and having around them the accessory chambers, viz: the Apotheterium, Sudatorium and Unctuarium. With regard to the materials and decorations of the Diocletian Baths nothing very positive or detailed is known. These baths, it is stated, could contain 3,200 bathers contemporaneously, besides, of course, a far greater number of non-bathers dispersed in the other sections of the establishment.

One of the above-mentioned bathing halls stood at the angle of the Viminal Hill, on the site of the Negroni gardens, near the Villa Strozzi, and was converted partly into a girls' school and partly into a granary later, and another of the halls into the well-known church of San Bernardo.

Cardinal Cesare Baronio, A.D. 1538–1607, who spent most of his life compiling and writing the annals of the Church, whence his title of "Father of the Ecclesiastical Annals," affirms that 40,000 Christians were employed in the construction of these baths, and the crosses found carved on the bricks are held to be an indication of their presence. The Gothic invasion of the fifth century coming after other vicissitudes, seems to have administered the *coup de grâce* to this short-lived fabric, for after that period it rapidly crumbled into a wreck. The sole surviving genuine complete relics at present in Rome, appear to be the eight columns of Egyptian granite, forty-five feet high, supporting the vaulting of Sta. Maria degli Angeli, conjectured to have been originally a hall of the Diocletiani, mainly built of " Pozzolana," or Roman cement, which, given the antiquity of these walls, proves the durability of this amalgamated substance of those times.

The origin of this church is due to a somewhat singular occurrence, worth perhaps relating as an instance of the vagaries to which mankind is subject, especially in the regions of the unknown. And it is also noteworthy as an exception in the Roman Catholic Church, which is decidedly sterile in sects, unlike the Protestants, which is so prolific in them.

In A.D. 1540 a Sicilian priest named Antonio del Duca conceived, or possibly thought himself inspired by, the idea of introducing a novel and distinct branch of worship in the Church, that of the Archangels. To promote the establishment of this new cult he brought over to Rome copies of the effigies of the Seven Archangels which were in the church of Sant' Angelo, in Palermo, namely: Michael, Gabriel, Raphael, Uriel, Santhiel, Gendiel and Borachiel. These, after obtaining due authorization, he proceeded to affix on the aforesaid columns, then standing in their original site, of the ancient Pagan Baths. It appears that the Reverend del Duca's idea fructified to a certain extent, for we find that some years later Pope Julius III (Giovanni Maria Ciocchi del Monte, A.D. 1550–1555) officially consecrated the spot and dedicated it to Sta. Maria degli Angeli, and though his successor Paul IV declared, " Ex Catedra," that Angel worship had never been sanctioned in the Church, except under the three first names mentioned in the Holy Scriptures, and even then not in the form advocated by the sectarian priest, and though, furthermore, this Pontiff ordered the removal of the pictures, he nevertheless implicitly accepted and permitted the qualified adoration of the Archangels and Angels collectively, because he instructed M. A. Buonarotti to convert this ancient Pagan bath-hall into a Christian church, with the identical dedication of his predecessor of Sta. Maria degli Angeli, a name it retains to this day, as it also remains substantially the structure of Buonarotti. Padre Antonio ought perhaps to have been satisfied with the measure of success his single-handed efforts had attained, although it was far from complete. There is, however, one obscure point in the whole proceeding that renders this advantage more apparent than real. So far as has been gathered del Duca's aim was to introduce a separate status and distinct form of worship, not for the Angels, but for the highest order of the Angelic Hierarchy only, the Seven Archangels, and this he did not accomplish, for though the latter were, it may be inferred, implicitly included, as belonging to the Angelic Body, they were not even mentioned as we see in the dedication.

The "Baths of St. Helena." Nothing much has been authentically known of this Bathing Establishment, except that it was built on the Esquiline Hill, where some fragments and an inscription were found that served to identify it. These relics were taken to the Vatican.

The "Baths of Constantine," built A.D. 335, on the Quirinal, on the space now covered by the Palazzo Rospigliosi and the Colonna Gardens. By looking down from the terrace to these gardens below may be seen a pit, some fragmentary vestiges and part of a flight of steps, that are supposed to have led up to these baths from the hollow beneath. The Porticus of this establishment with four statues stood till A.D. 1740, and two of the statues, representing respectively Constantine I and Constantine II, were placed after on the terrace of the Capitol, and eloquently betray the degeneracy of art at that period. In the Colonna gardens there is or was also a huge monolith Corinthian frieze, said to weigh twenty-seven tons and to be the largest single block of marble now in Rome. There are two versions regarding its proprietorship, the one that it belonged to the above Balneae, and the other, that it formed part of the vanished Temple of Apollo, constructed by the Emperor Lucius, Valerius, Domitianus, Aurelianus, A.D. 270–275, the noted mural builder and the conqueror of Palmyra.

CHAPTER XXII

MAUSOLEUMS AND TOMBS

THE sepulchres of the ancient Romans formed a very important class of their monuments, that could compare not unfavourably in architecture and often in actual dimensions with their palaces, basilicas and temples.

To satisfy and manifest by handsome and durable constructions the cult for the departed, originating in the noble and refining feelings of respect and affection for the pre-deceased by those successively left behind, a temporarily surviving part of them, to represent and mourn them, the ancient Romans, to their honour be it said, spared neither time, labour, care or money, utilizing the resources of talent and genius, to provide as adequate, or as sumptuous, abodes for their dead as the edifices destined for the living. This trait, so utterly free from all that is sordid or venal, a connecting and consoling link binding generations together, constitutes one of the most marked distinctions between men and brutes, and, to subdivide again, between class and class and individually between man and man. Among the most civilized peoples, that is, in the moral sense, the only true one, the best, the most gifted, with a deeper and more intellectual nature and higher conception of existence, are, generally speaking, the most devoted to the memory of their deceased.

The paucity of sepulchral monuments in Rome herself is due to the law strictly enforced during the Republic, prohibiting interments within the city boundaries. On exceedingly rare occasions exceptions were made in favour of a few among those who had rendered signal services to the State, as a public mark of gratitude and great posthumous reward, and though under the Imperial régime this, like everything else, depended on the will or humour of one individual over-riding all laws, custom is so difficult to eradicate, especially in strong races, that this privilege continued to be unfrequently bestowed. To the Vestals, as has been mentioned, the urban burial was accorded, but unaccompanied by sumptuous obsequies and tombs, in obedience to the other prohibitive law concerning grand funerals in general, and, as the monastic canons of this Order in particular forbade alike rich apparel for the Vestals when living, and imposing funerals when dead, the fact that no traces of authentic Vestal tombs have been discovered, is not surprising.

The "Tomb of Bibulus." At the Via Marforio, near the end of the present Corso, there is a travertine tomb, now hidden from view by buildings, bearing the following inscription:

TOMB OR CENOTAPH OF EURYSACES.

Plate lii.

"C.POBLICIO.L.F.BIBVLO.AED.PL.HONORIS.
VIRTVTISQVE.CAVSSA.SENATUS.
CONSVLTO.POPVLIQVE.IVSSV.LOCVS.
MONVMENTO.QVO.IPSE.POSTERIQVE.
EIVS.INFERRENTUR.PVBLICE.DATVS.EST.

The meaning of which is "That it was erected by the people with the permission of the Senate to the plebeian Aedile Caius Poblicius Bibulus as a family sepulchre on account of his worth and honours." The architecture of this tomb is Etrusco-Roman; it is a massive, simple rectangle in shape, having pilasters of the Roman Doric Order and the frieze decorated uncanonically with the encarpus instead of the triglyph. This monument is noteworthy for two reasons, firstly, as being one of the few relics of this architectural style and of the republican times, and secondly, for the exceptional privilege granted to a man not appertaining to the highest class. But the Romans of the republican era were neither sycophants nor snobs, and intrinsic, ungilded merit was given its right place and recompense among them. It may be mentioned, in connection, that Petrarch relates that he wrote one of his sonnets leaning on this tomb.

The "Tomb of Eurysaces." From the present Porta Maggiore diverge two ancient roads, the Via Labicana, now renamed Via Casalina, which, passing by Valmontone, connected Rome with Naples, and the Via Praenestina, which leads to Praeneste, the modern Palestrina, once the mediaeval stronghold of the Colonna. Between these two bifurcating roads, outside and contiguous to the Porta Maggiore, stands a remarkable rectangular monument on thick supporting pillars, half embedded in the soil, dating approximately from the closing years of the Republic, and unearthed or at least extricated from the overlaying rubbish, during the pontificate of Gregory XVI, A.D. 1830–1845. It was erected by Marcus Virgilius Eurysaces, baker by trade, and evidently of some importance in his line as he held the post of contractor or public purveyor of bread and also that of Curator Viarum, or Inspector of roads. The following epigraph on the monument records the erector's name, trade and public office as contractor.

EST HOC MONIMENTUM MARCEI VERGILEI EURYSACIS
PISTORIS REDEMPTORIS APPARET.

The reliefs, of no mean though not of the highest order, may be divided into two categories: those representing grinding, kneading and other processes of the craft, with the utensils used, such as kneading bowls and grain measures, and those depicting the baker in his office of public purveyor. Besides these there were, on the adjacent wall, two other reliefs representing Eurysaces and his wife and a sarcophagus with an inscription recording her merits, which were foolishly detached and taken to the National Museum, together with a row of arched windows formerly here. The inscription was as follows:

"FUIT ATISTIA UXOR MIHEI-FEMINA OPTVMA VEIXSIT
QUOIVS CORPORIS RELIQUIAE QUOD SUPERANT SUNT IN
HOC PANARIO."

A peculiar feature of this monument is its clear-cut, regular, circular orifices. We are indebted to the solidity and simplicity of the structure and to the protecting dense secular coating of earth, stones and rubbish for its relatively good state of preservation.

The sources at our disposal concerning this man, owing to the lapse of time, conjointly with the fact that he was no very celebrated personage, are necessarily very scant, nevertheless we may conclude that he was rather a notable character in his way.

There is a tradition regarding Eurysaces still extant among the populace of Rome, according to which " Il Fornajo di Porta Maggiore " was not merely an industrious, ingenious and wealthy man, but also more than half a wizard, of the white variety, and that in consequence he possessed such a marvellous power of producing bread of unique quality with miraculous rapidity, and of attracting customers, that all others of his trade were unable to compete with him, " were not in the running " as the slangily disposed phrase it. Moreover, that he was assisted by mysterious beings, at night, who vanished in the day (which last was neither supernatural nor unlikely, seeing that night workers usually disappear to sleep in the day) that peculiar sounds were heard in the bakery, that an uncanny atmosphere enveloped the establishment in general, and so forth. Thus, as is not uncommon, the result of superior skill, activity and luck, combined, in this case, it seems, with a prudent secrecy and reticence, was attributed to supernatural agencies and practices. It is only surprising that the unreasoning wonder and envy of the herd stopped short of labelling and libelling Eurysaces as a downright, black, infernal sorcerer, so prone is the majority of mankind to explain all abnormal success in whatever direction, in all countries and ages, as deriving from some evil source, whether it be Black Magic, cheating or other delinquency, an explanation which serves as a soothing balm to their self love wounded by a sense of inferiority in success. Eurysaces also escaped, then, the charge of infernal witchcraft, because the belief in sorcery of this nature never prevailed in these classic times, but was one of the obsessions and scourges of the superstitious and benighted men of the middles Ages.

The Sepulchrum Eurysaces itself seems to confirm, too, the opinion that he was above the average of his fellow craftsmen, or others of his class, as it is the sole structure of its kind existing within or adjoining the city of that numerous and useful corporation of artisans, the manufacturers of the " Staff of Life." It has been urged that neither has any sepulchre of the Vestals been yet discovered, though we know that they had the privilege of city interment, but the parallel is not a fortunate one, firstly because the number of the bread-makers was infinitely more numerous than that of the fire-feeders, and secondly, because the latters' tombs were, as aforesaid, of the simplest and plainest character, merely a grave-slab, and therefore easily obliterated.

The " Mausoleum of Caius P. Cestius." The ancient Porta Ostiensis was the gate from which the Via Ostiensis issued leading to Ostia, formerly the principal sea-port of Rome. The present excavated remains of this town, founded, it is said, by King Ancus Martius, 641–617 B.C., and after greatly extended, improved and embellished, especially by the Emperors Tiberius, Claudius and Trajanus, reveal an almost complete simulacrum in ruins of the prosperous sea-port of that period.

After the Eternal City came under Pontifical rule the reconstructed gate, in compliance with the system of nomenclature adopted, exchanged its classic appellation for the

MAUSOLEUM OF CAIUS. CESTIUS. POPLICIUS.

Plate liii.

ecclesiastical one of Porta San Paolo. This Saintly name was bestowed on the gate because St. Paul passed out of it on his way to be executed, which death sentence was, in his case, to be carried out by decapitation, owing to his rank and his quality of Roman citizen, and not by crucifixion, one of the supreme penalties allotted to plebeians, foreigners and slaves. According to religious legend and belief the severed head of the Saint rebounded three times, and from the successive spots touched by it, three springs of water miraculously issued and issue. The place of the execution is now covered by the church belonging to the monastery erected there, a very interesting spot well worth a visit for itself and its associations, not counting creature comforts in the shape of the excellent liquor of Eucalyptus manufactured by the monks, with which few real connoisseurs could find fault. Before reaching this monastery is the Basilica of San Paolo (Extra Murus) built over the place, it is affirmed, where St. Paul was buried, a monumental edifice of Byzantine architecture with its internal frieze decorated all round with medallions containing the portraits of all the Roman Pontiffs from St. Peter to our times.

It may be mentioned, in connection, that four of the seven principal basilicas of Rome were placed under honorary Royal patronage. The Seven in commemoration of the Seven Hills are those of San Pietro, San Paolo, Sta. Maria Maggiore, San Giovanni in Laterano, Sta. Agnese, San Sebastiano and Sta. Croce in Gerusalemme. The Basilica of St. Peter was under the patronage of the Emperor of the Holy Roman Empire, a title first borne by the Emperor of the Franks, then assumed by the Emperor of Germany, and lastly by the Emperor of Austria; the Basilica of St. Paul under that of the Sovereign of Great Britain, "The Defender of the Faith," the British kings being also *ex officio* honorary Canons of this basilica; the Basilica of St. John Lateran, under the "Most Christian King of France, the Eldest Son of the Church"; and the Basilica of Sta. Maria Maggiore, under the "Catholic King of Spain."

Of these four, two have long since lost their patrons, St. Paul's owing to the Sovereign's conversion to the Protestant Church, St. John Lateran in consequence of the change in the political constitution of France from a Monarchy to a Republic, the hereditary Sovereign, "The Lord's Anointed," being eligible where a four-year elected president would be ineligible. Nor have these two Royal patrons been replaced by two others religiously and politically orthodox patrons, at least so far as we know. To these absentees may be added a third, the Apostolic Emperor-King of Austria-Hungary, and assuming that this Empire be not restored to its *statu quo ante*, this vacancy in the patronage of St. Peter's Cathedral will be permanent, unless some other Catholic Sovereign be substituted, an arrangement that presents some difficulties in actual conditions, and all the more if they develop further in the direction they have taken.

Outside, and very close to the Porta San Paolo is the above-mentioned famous Mausoleum Cestii, unique now in Rome on account of its pyramidical form. The Romans, in imitation of the Egyptians, sometimes adopted for their sepulchres this alien architectonic shape and style, but the one in question is the only example remaining standing, so well did foreign barbarian invaders and native barbarous inhabitants carry out their work of destruction. To cite one example of the disappeared sepulchral monuments of this type, we may recall the pyramid, once on the site now occupied by Sta. Maria Transpontina (a church built A.D. 1566), that was erected in honour of Scipio Africanus, and which was first stripped of its marble coating by Pope Dono, A.D. 676–678, and after levelled by him to the ground. This disappeared monument, a miniature facsimile of which is to be seen on the bronze doors of the Cathedral of St. Peter in Rome, was, ignorantly enough, supposed once to be the tomb of Romulus, the victorious twin, as the existing one we are dealing with of Cestius, was assigned to Remus, the vanquished twin; but the origin of this double erroneous belief is unknown and probably not worth knowing.

Like many other Roman tombs and edifices of this period, this mausoleum consisted of a core of bricks with an outer covering of massive slabs of marble, mostly from the inexhaustible quarries of Carrara, with its base of travertine blocks. Its exact dimensions and the date of the death of Cestius are alike uncertain. The height has been severally calculated at 116, 125 and 140 feet, the diameter of its quadrangular base at 95 and 110 feet, and the year of the decease of Cestius either at 30 B.C. or at 12 B.C. The first discrepancies, almost incredible in a matter of measurement unless attributable to rise or fall of the soil as to height at the various times they were taken, are those of the officially responsible and of the estimations of independent archaelogues. The second, the difference in dates, is attributed by some to the posture and partial erasure of the Roman numerals on the monument, the heavy, strong strokes being nearly upright, instead of slanting, and the light ones somewhat indistinct, so that XXX might be mistaken for XII, and vice versa.

There is, however, in the records referring to the mausoleum, an almost irrefutable fact in favour of the earlier date. From these it is gathered that the deceased had appointed the celebrated M. V. Agrippa to be his executor, and that the latter, in this capacity, had the above pyramid constructed in the space of 330 days, to which two or three months more may be added for the decision, design and preliminary work, in all about thirteen or fourteen months. Agrippa died during the year 12 B.C.—that is to say, he could not dispose of more than six or eight months, perhaps, of the said year, and not of the entire year; in consequence we have to recognise by a simple calculation that it is difficult to reconcile the date of 12 B.C. with the time specified as above for the erection of the monument. This seems a probable if not absolutely conclusive argument favouring apparently the earlier date for the decease of Cestius, that is to say, 30 B.C.

The inscriptions on the sides of the monument are as follows: " C. Cestius.L.F. Pob.Epulo. Pr.Tr.VII.vir.Epulonum," which may be translated in full: "Caius, Cestius Poplicius, son of Lucius of the Poplilia Tribe, Praetor, Tribune and Member of the College of the Septemviri Epulones," that is the priests whose especial office it was to direct all arrangements relatively to the feasts of the gods. The inscription on the other side records that the monument was completed, as aforesaid, in 330 days, under the direction of L. Pontius Mela, a relative and heir of the deceased, assisted by a " liberto " or freedman, named Pothus.

The term " Epulones " survives to this day in the Italian language as synonymous of gourmand or gourmet, or rather a combination of the two. It was correctly assumed the Deities, for whom these dainty and abundant victuals were ostensibly prepared, did not consume them, but that these clergymen did so in their stead, and if the Superhumans systematically abstained from using, themselves, these exquisite viands and liquors, and human substitutes had to be selected, it does not seem unreasonable that these priests, their especial devoted servants, should have been chosen, as next best, to perform the eating and drinking functions. It is related of Vespasian, as doubtless happened to other Emperors, that he envied the Epulones their luxurious, godly fare and wished he were one of them, it is to be presumed only for this particular privilege, and that in other respects he preferred his own position, that of Emperor. It is said, moreover, that this desire was expressed only by this Sovereign when he felt fit and blessed with a fine appetite, for when he was unwell and lost it, he was wont to say humorously, "that he felt he was serving his apprenticeship in preparation to becoming a god," that is, to die and eat nothing.

The sepulchral chamber of the Mausoleum Cestii decorated with arabesques, a portion of which are still uneffaced, is 19 feet long by 13 wide and 16 high, its dimensions, as usual in pyramids, small in proportion to the size of the entire monument, and this may account for the exceptional accuracy in the measurement. It was the custom among many ancient peoples, notably the Egyptians and Etruscans, to ornament their tomb-chambers with paintings, etc., often of value, but intended solely for the dead therein, and not to be viewed, once finished, by the living, wherefore as soon as the ornamental work was completed and the deceased deposited there, the chamber was entirely blocked up by being bricked over, and after this the rest of the monument terminated. In the case in question there had not been apparently any departure from this rule, as no sort of entrance or aperture originally existed of this chamber previous to the present one opened by Pope Alexander VII (Fabio Chigi A.D. 1655–1667) who also had the whole structure extricated from the overlaying rubbish and repaired.

Caius Cestius Poblicius (probably the identical Cestius mentioned by Cicero in his oration, "Pro Flacco," as a rich speculator who having no offspring had set aside a great sum of money for his obsequies and monument) certainly a wealthy and apparently vainglorious man, desired expressly by his testament to have his body swathed in rich stuffs and his funeral to be on a magnificent scale. As has been already mentioned he appointed Agrippa as his executor, but the latter evidently opined that it was preferable to give the testator a more durable memorial than the transient pomp of a day, so not following out Caius' instructions in the letter but rather in the spirit, he applied the law prohibiting sumptuous funerals, and diverted instead the large amount provided, for the construction of this pyramid, with the colossal statues near it, in memory and honour of the deceased. Of these statues only one of the pedestals and a gigantic foot, unearthed near the monument, survive now in the Capitoline Museum.

If it had ever been a matter of doubt that the Egyptian pyramids were bona fide tombs, this Roman one built in imitation and except for the materials and dimensions, so perfect a facsimile, would furnish one more proof that these conical, colossal massive structures were sepulchral monuments. This mausoleum, like the Tomb of Eurysaces, though strictly speaking not precisely within the city circuit, because the first was though adjacent to the Porta Ostiensis and the second to the Porta Maggiore, both outside, still both may be considered as belonging to the City seeing that they are not on the borders of the country roads at some distance from its walls, as is the case with the regular "extra murus" sepulchres.

The "Mausoleum of Augustus." Considering the epoch and the importance of this structure, it is remarkable that so few and unsatisfactory records regarding it have been transmitted to posterity. It was erected by Octavius, 28 B.C., on the Campus Martius, close to the Tiber bank, between the Porta Flaminia and the more famous sepulchral monument of Hadrian, to serve as the Imperial Mausoleum.

So far as has been gathered, it appears to have been a huge circular edifice of white marble consisting, some say, of two, others of three tiers and resting on a quadrangular travertine base. These tiers successively decreased in circumference and height as they proceeded upwards, the outstanding spaces around each being planted with cypresses and laurels, and the entire building culminating in a lofty marble tower crowned by the statue of Octavius. Each tier contained the mortuary chambers in which were placed the "Olae," or cinerary urns, with the ashes of the departed members, appertaining, with one exception, either by consanguinity or affinity to the Imperial family, and also those of a number of their attendants, freedmen and slaves, in separate sections.

The remains of the founder of the Imperial régime in Rome and the creator of this mausoleum were interred in the central sepulchral chamber situated in a straight line perpendicularly and exactly under his statue on the summit of the crowning tower, and from this central hall the other chambers diverged. The entrance to the edifice was flanked by two genuine Egyptian obelisks, and the whole was surrounded by a fine park. If the hypothesis that the Emperor Claudius brought over these two obelisks be correct, it is obvious that they were placed here over thirty years after the monument was built. Strabo expresses his admiration of this edifice, and describes it as "a White Marble Mound in the midst of trees."

The following is the list and dates of those deposited here, indicating their connection with the founder: Marcellus, nephew, 23 B.C., Agrippa, son-in-law, 12 B.C.; Octavia, sister, 11 B.C.; Drusus, step-son, 9 B.C.; Caius Julius Octavius, the constructor, A.D. 14; Germanicus, step-grandson, A.D. 19; Drusus, step-grandson, A.D. 23; Livia, wife, A.D. 29; Agrippina, widow of Germanicus, A.D. 33; Tiberius A.D. 37; Nero and Drusus, step-great-grandsons, whose ashes were at first excluded and then brought here by their brother Caius, nicknamed "Caligula," A.D. 39; the Emperor Caligula himself, A.D. 41; Antonia, widow of Drusus, between A.D. 37 and 41; the Emperor Claudius, son of Drusus, step-great-grandson, A.D. 54; his son Britannicus, A.D. 55, and finally the Emperor Nerva Coccejus, no relative, A.D. 98.

The present discovered remains of this historic and magnificent mausoleum seem to be reduced so far to a section of a wall best to be seen from the courtyard of the Palazzo Valdambrini, in the Via Ripetta, *in situ*, of the two obelisks, if these may be strictly speaking included, the one on the Quirinal the other on the Esquiline, of the Urn of Aggripina, taken to the Capitol, of a grand alabaster vase, inscribed with the names of Nero and Drusus, the above-mentioned sons of Drusus, found in A.D. 1777 in the Piazza San Carlo, six other urns taken to the Vatican, a slab with fractured lettering bearing the name of Nerva or Nero, and later a block of marble with the following inscriptions: "Marcellus C. F. Gener Augusti Caesaris" and "Octavia C. C. Soror Augusti Caesaris." The continuous excavatory operations will no doubt bring to light, as time goes by, in this monument as in others more and more interesting relics. This edifice in the early Christian times was crowned by a shrine and statue to Sant' Angelo de Augusta, it was ravaged by the Goths under Alaric, and in the twelfth century converted into a fortress by the Colonna. The last cremation that took place in the whilom Imperial Mausoleum was of the body of Cola di Rienzi, which by order of the Colonna and the other coalesced Barons was burnt by a fire of thistles, the herb of asses, as a final sarcasm on the man, a plebeian, who dared to attempt and, for a brief space, succeeded in ruling them.

The interior was subsequently laid out as a garden, and later, up to the middle of the nineteenth century, was turned into a bull-baiting arena. After it had ceased to be used for these exhibitions it became an informal unofficial hospital for aged, lonely, indigent women, founded by the praiseworthy exertions of a laundress, known by the name of Sora Rosa, who began by taking in and attending one female centenarian. Later the open air plays of the Teatro Correa were acted here also. This theatre or concert-hall was called so, it is said, from the neighbouring Palazzo Correa, in which the first English Church service was performed in Rome.

The "Mausoleum of the Flavii." This was originally an annex of their Palace on the Quirinal Hill, for Vespasian and Titus, adhering to the ancient custom of interring the deceased members of the family within or adjoining the habitation of their surviving relatives, directed that they should be buried here. We know nothing regarding the construction of this mausoleum, as no ruins exist and no records have been gathered so far, or if it was altered or extended by Domitian, but we are informed that he had the place, possibly the Atrium of the palace, consecrated as a temple, and that he himself and his niece, Titus' daughter, were also interred here.

It may not be amiss to mention in connection that the word "mausoleum" is derived from Mausolus, King of Caria, who died 353 B.C.. His sister and wife Artemisia, inconsolable for his loss, and desirous of perpetuating his memory, had a tomb erected composed of white marble and alabaster, in which architecture and sculpture vied in perfection of design and execution, the handiwork of Scopas in co-operation with his rivals, Timotheus, Briasis, Leocaris and Petios. She succeeded so well in her twofold intention of raising to him a most splendid monumental sepulchre, and of transmitting his memory to future generations, that after the lapse of over twenty-one and three-fourth centuries, he still lives in memory, in the term adopted to signify a grandiose sepulchral structure. The elder Pliny is credited with having furnished one, or the best, description of this famous mausoleum, which he styles "One of the Seven Wonders of the World." After surviving many vicissitudes it was destroyed A.D. 1453 by the Knights of Rhodes in order to construct with the materials a bulwark against the Ottomans. In 1846 the Sultan Abdul Midjid made a donation of some valuable reliefs belonging to the monument to Great Britain, or rather to Queen Victoria, and in 1856 excavations were undertaken that brought to light precious fragments of friezes, statues and other decorations, which relics were conveyed to the British Museum.

With regard to King Mausolus, who reigned twenty-four years and extended his kingdom by conquest, it may be added that it seems indisputable that his much-loved remains were cremated, but that the ashes, or at least part of them, were not deposited in the superb mausoleum, because it is historically recorded that Artemisia drank his ashes mixed in liquid, so that his body would not be separated from hers, living or lifeless, and would thus continue their material union even after death.

CHAPTER XXIII

MAUSOLEUMS AND TOMBS (*continued*)

THE "Mausoleum of Hadrian." The ancient Pons Aelius, the present Ponte Sant' Angelo, was built by the Emperor Hadrianus Publius Aelius to be used exclusively as an approach to his mausoleum, because at the time of its construction there was another public bridge, the Pons Vaticanus close by, begun by Caligula and finished by Nero, the submerged remains of which are still visible when the Tiber is at low water. Except for the parapet and the statues the Ponte Sant' Angelo is essentially the Pons Aelius, as although some repairs were effected in 1892–94 on some of the arches, none were replaced, and the three middle ones, with the foundation and piers up to the parapet, practically untouched. The statues of the Saints Peter and Paul, the first by Lorenzetto and the second by Paolo Romano, at the entrance of the bridge, were erected A.D. 1530 by order of Clement VII, in substitution of the two chapels formerly there, and the statues of the Angels, from designs of Bernini, A.D. 1688, by order of Innocent XI, A.D. 1676–89, whose idea it was to represent thereby a heavenly array welcoming the pilgrims who traversed the bridge on their way to Saint Peter's Shrine in his basilica.

Facing, therefore, the Ponte Sant' Angelo stand the remains of the far-famed edifice begun and nearly completed by Hadrian A.D. 124–138, and terminated by Antoninus Pius A.D. 139, destined as the mausoleum of the Sovereigns and their families, and nearly confronting the other aforementioned imposing one of Octavius, which it admittedly outshone. The last Emperor interred in the Augustan Mausoleum was, as has been noted, Nerva Coccejus, and his successor, Trajan, was buried under his column in his Forum, and the first person whose ashes were deposited in Hadrian's Mausoleum was Aelius Verus, his first adopted son, who predeceased him. Seven Emperors were subsequently buried here, namely, Hadrianus, the constructor, A.D. 138; Antoninus Pius, A.D. 161; Marcus Aurelius, A.D. 180; Commodus, A.D. 192; Pertinax, A.D. 193; Septimius Severus, A.D. 211; and Caracallus, A.D. 217. Some authorities maintain that all the monarchs, from Hadrian to Caracallus, were likewise buried in this mausoleum, viz, Lucius Verus, Didius, Albinus and Niger, besides other members of the Imperial families, which is not probable, except in the case of L. Verus, and also other relatives of the reigning monarchs.

This sepulchral monument was composed of three stories, besides the substructure. The first and lowest section was quadrangular, measuring, it is said, 344 feet in diameter. It was adorned with pilasters of the Etruscan Rectus Order, with the spaces between engraved with the epitaphs of the dead on bordered tablets, and with equestrian statues of bronze at the angles. The second storey was a circular structure of about, it is affirmed,

Plate liv. MAUSOLEUM OF HADRIAN, A.D. 136-39. CASTEL SANT' ANGELO.

240 feet, surrounded with fluted columns of the Ionic Order, with intervening statues on pedestals. The third superstructed section, also round, and of smaller size, was encircled with columns of the Corinthian Order, alternating similarly with statues. The projecting spaces between the successive tiers had roofings of bronze plated with gold, the highest having its frieze surrounded by bronze pine-cones or, as some aver, by bronze peacocks, the whole culminating in a cupola of pyramidical shape of the same metal, crowned by a pine-cone of proportionately greater size. This pine-cone was transferred to the Vatican by Pope Symmachus, A.D. 498, where it is still to be seen in the Giardino della Pigna, named after it (Pigna, pine), between the bronze peacocks also taken, it is alleged, from this mausoleum.

The total height of this monument has been computed at 165–170 feet, and with the exception of the substructure and the inner lining of the lowest section, which were of massive travertine blocks, it was entirely composed of the costly and beautiful marble of Paros. Procopius, in describing this mausoleum in his work on Monumental Edifices, enthusiastically refers to the perfection of the marble casing of the lowest storey and the walls of the upper, consisting of huge squares of Parian marble, fixed accurately together without cement. The building was further surrounded by an outer circle of, according to some writers, forty-eight, and according to others eighty-eight, monolith columns of the Corinthian Order, some of which, it is related, were used later for St. Paul's basilica, afterwards burnt down and rebuilt.

But by no description, nor even probably by any stretch of the imagination, can we conjure up to our mental vision the graceful and stately pile rising, column above column, statue above statue, resplendent with the finest marble, bronze and gold most artistically wrought; nor recognise any resemblance to it in the present scarred, inharmonious, almost grotesque mass of masonry. The explanation of the surpassing magnificence and symmetry of this monument is to be found in the fact that it was designed and mainly constructed under the direction of Hadrian, who united a rare artistic nature, knowledge and taste, to a passion for architecture, tenacity of purpose, organizing ability, and almost unlimited power, which he, moreover, knew how to make the most of in a period when art was still at its prime, and when humanity was animated by very different ideals and spirit in this direction, as in others, to those prevalent in our times.

There are some archaeologues who opine, they confess conjecturally, that on the summit of the dome stood the statue of Hadrian in a quadriga, and not the pine-cone as aforesaid, an hypothesis probably arising alone from the idea that the statue of the creator would appropriately crown his creation for his own use. But it would be difficult to reconcile this assumption with the pyramidical form of the dome, on whose apex there would not have been enough space for the quadriga or even for a necessarily colossal statue, and besides this the pine-cone is not only recorded but the identical one is declared to be in existence, as aforesaid, in the Vatican. There were, it is true, the statues of Octavius on the tower surmounting his mausoleum, and of Trajan on his column under which his ashes were placed, but these are specifically and authentically mentioned, while the statue of Hadrian is not similarly recorded as crowning his mausoleum. In addition both the statues cited were respectively placed, the one on the platform of a tower, the other on the huge abacus of a gigantic column, both of which offered ample space for similar colossal erections. Moreover, it was not the usual custom of the ancient Romans to place statues of the deceased on the summit of sepulchral structures, but rather to represent them on the façade in low, middle, or high relief.

The subsequent history of the Mausoleum Hadriani is almost the history of mediaeval Rome. It did not escape the fate of nearly all ancient edifices of any importance, and in A.D. 423 it was converted into a fortress by the Emperor Honorius; and Theodoric the Great, A.D. 454–526, added to its warlike functions those of a state-prison, whence it took one of its after-names of "Carcer Theodorici." It is not irrelevant to note here that even late in the Middle Ages, although utterly changed and fallen from its high estate, this monument was very different and far superior to what we now see. The drawing of Sangallo, A.D. 1462, and the description of Martianus, A.D. 1582, furnish us with sufficient evidence that, though shorn of all its splendours, it had become a massive, well-built, typical mediaeval fortress, very dissimilar from the shapeless, patched bulk now decaying before us.

In its transformed character it naturally sustained many sieges, that of the Goths under Vitiges, A.D. 537, in particular, which considerably advanced the work of destruction, because the Greek garrison hurled down the statues as missiles on the besiegers. Totila captured the fortress in A.D. 548 after a protracted resistance by Belisarius, the Greek Exarch or Viceroy, and it was retaken by Narsus, the successor of the latter, in A.D. 552.

In A.D. 590 an event occurred here that gave its present name to the Mausoleum-fortress. Pope Saint Gregory, was conducting a procession to intercede for the cessation of the plague which was then depopulating Rome, when on approaching the Pons Aelius he declared that he beheld the Archangel Michael hovering over the castle and sheathing his sword, while a chorus of angels chanted the anthem, since adopted by the Church in the Vesper service, "Regina Coeli laetare-quia quem meruisti portare-resurrexit, sicut, dixit, Alleluja," in token that the scourge was over. This apparition and chant were visible and audible, it is added, to the Pontiff alone of all the multitude present on the occasion. In commemoration of the miraculous event Pope Boniface IV, A.D. 608–615, erected a chapel on the summit of the castle which he dedicated to "Sanctus Angelus inter Nubes." This structure was replaced after by a marble angel by Montelupo, still existing though dethroned and superseded, in its turn, by the present bronze statue elevated on the summit representing the Archangel in the act of sheathing his sword, the work of Verschaffelt, A.D. 1752, by order of Pope Benedict XIV.

From A.D. 933 this mausoleum-castle was used by the party in power for the purpose of intimidating the citizens of Rome, so that its possession became the object of contention between the Popes and Anti-Popes, as well as the lay rivals for power, whereby it was necessarily subjected to many vicissitudes and much rough handling. In the earlier years of the eleventh century we find it occupied by Marozia, a later edition of Messalina, who brought her three husbands and her other favourites here to tyrannise in security over the Seven-Hilled City.

From A.D. 974 to 1054 it was held off and on, but mostly on, by a very powerful noble family of the period called Crescentii, who have left behind them two, possibly three, material proofs of their passage: the Bridge Numentanus (doubtful), a street named after them, "Via Crescentii," and the ruins of a picturesque old house, originally larger, in the ancient Forum Boarium, now Piazza Bocca della Verità, which is the oldest existing specimen of this description now in the Eternal City. The inscription on this fabric informs us that "This lofty house was erected by Nicholas, son of Crescentius, foremost and descended from the foremost, not from motives of ambition, but to revive the ancient glory of Rome." Its proprietorship has been, curiously enough, quite unfoundedly ascribed to two very different personages, namely, Pontius Pilate and Cola di Rienzi. The reason of its supposed connection with the former has not been ascertained or guessed; probably it arose from one of those popular myths, inexplicable and perhaps not worth explaining. But the latter error may have arisen from the baptismal name inscribed as above, "Cola," being the diminutive of Nicholas, and also because the mediaeval Tribune was born in its neighbourhood. The first hypothesis is not only disposed of by the above epigraph, but also by the architecture and style of this house dating about half a score of centuries after the times of the Procurator Pontius Pilatus; and the second, by the low social status of Rienzi who could not possibly have inhabited a house of this description either as a proprietor or as a tenant, so long as he was only the son of a tavern-keeper and a washerwoman, and during his public career as Pontifical Notary, Tribune and Senator, he lived in abodes becoming his official rank, such as the Capitoline Palace.

The Crescentii had politically one main principle and aim, the abolition of the temporal power of the Pope, thus reverting to the original exclusively Spiritual Sovereignty of the Roman Pontiffs of several centuries before, and, at the same time, anticipating by more centuries still, the modern abolition of the Papal temporal authority. This political principle this family pursued hereditarily, and in consequence several Popes were incarcerated by the Crescentii in this castle and State prison, that at this time received another appellation and was called from its masters "Turris Crescentii," by which name it is referred to in the documents of the period.

In A.D. 1313 it was yielded to the Orsini, the most potent family of the Guelph party in the Roman State, who kept possession of it for several years, and it was from here that the Tribune, Rienzi, is said to have fled with his wife, Nïna Raselli, disguised as a friar, in A.D. 1347, on his fall from his first brief spell of authority. In A.D. 1373 the building was almost entirely destroyed, the marble coating still left being torn away by the revolted Romans, who had come to look upon it, not without reason, as the French, over four centuries later, regarded the Bastille.

From Pope Boniface IX (1389-1404) to Pius IX (1846-70) this fortress was held almost uninterruptedly by the reigning Pontiffs. In A.D. 1411 Pope John XXIII, constructed the walled turreted passage, called the "Passetto," or "Scapata," connecting the Castel Sant' Angelo with the Vatican Palace. Pope Alexander VI, A.D. 1492-1503, finished this corridor with the exception of the roofing, which was laid on by Pope Urban VIII, A.D. 1623-1644. This covered corridor, evidently built as an escape-tunnel, consisted of two stories, the upper a sort of loggia, the under, walled and lighted by loopholes, the keys of the two closed extremities, palace and castle, being kept in the personal custody of the Popes.

The "Passetto," whose ruins are still to be seen, served its purpose no doubt on many occasions, but the most notable evasions recorded are those of Pope Alexander VI who fled by this passage in A.D. 1494 when the French army, under Charles VIII, entered Rome, and of Pope Clement VII, who twice within one year, A.D. 1527, escaped by this two-storied tunnel, first, from Moncada, the Spanish Viceroy of Naples, and second, from the troops of Duke Charles of Bourbon.

The list of all the noted persons imprisoned, some of whom were executed here, would be long, tedious and difficult to compile, but the following may be cited as instances of some interest. Pope John, A.D. 931–936, son of the aforementioned delectable Marozia (who was herself also incarcerated herein) by his brother Alberic, who by forcing him to sign and seal from his State prison in this Castle whatever Edicts or Bulls he required, governed in the said Pope's stead. By the Crescentii, Popes Benedict VII and John XIV, imprisoned and executed, or assassinated here, and also Pope Gregory V, A.D. 998, confined, but liberated by the Emperor Otho III, who had Numentanus Crescentius executed in retaliation. Pope Gregory VII, A.D. 1084, incarcerated. Giovanni Colonna imprisoned, A.D. 1484, by Pope Sixtus IV on account of his antipapal tendencies and activities.* The able, unscrupulous and celebrated Cesar Borgia, son, or according to clerical writers, favourite nephew of Pope Alexander VI, was confined in this Castel Sant' Angelo by Pope Pius III (Francesco Piccolomini A.D. 1503) during his brief reign of twenty-six days, as a measure of security of the State, menaced by the ambitious and turbulent intrigues of this son or nephew of his immediate predecessor on the Pontifical Throne. The two brothers Caraffa, Duke and Cardinal, nephews of Pope Paul IV, were imprisoned here likewise by the succeeding Pope Pius IV (Giovanni de Medici A.D. 1559–1565) and subsequently both executed, only the manner of their death was different in conformity with the respective position of each, the Duke, as became his quality of noble, decapitated, and the Cardinal as beseemed his sacerdotal character, strangled.* *

During the pontificates of Clement VII, A.D. 1523–1534, and of Paul III, A.D. 1534–1549, the famous Benvenuto Cellini was twice imprisoned here, respectively on the charges of robbery and murder. While a prisoner he tried to escape, and broke his leg in the abortive attempt. It was from these walls, during the assault of Rome by the Imperial army under the Duke of Bourbon, that Cellini fired his celebrated shot and saw, as he asserts in his autobiography, the above leader of the besiegers apparently fall by it, one of his many amusing, sensational anecdotes that few seem to believe.

The well-known Beatrice Cenci was imprisoned here, A.D. 1599, on the accusation of parricide on the person of her father, Count Francesco Cenci, for which crime she was decapitated with her step-mother and brother Jacomo. It was in her cell in this castle that the condemned Beatrice composed her testament and selected her place of burial

---

* This historic family were, as is known, hereditary and consistent adherents of the Ghibelline or Imperial party, and as such opponents of the Guelph or Papal, and this is the real reason that this conspicuous race only gave one of its members to the Throne of St. Peter, namely : Martin V (Otho Colonna A.D. 1417-1431), while their peers of the other feudal families such as the Savelli, Orsini, Conti, etc., furnished their full quota of Sovereign Pontiffs.

* * The three usual forms in which the death sentence in mediaeval times was carried out were hanging for the commonality, beheading for the nobility and strangling for the clergy, but of course there was also death by fire, drowning, the wheel, etc., in certain cases. It is interesting to note that while the spilling of blood judicially of a member of the clergy was prohibited on the ground that it was that of a consecrated person, this was equally the case in custom and practice for the "Third Estate," the commonality, the gibbet, though an ignoble death, killing also bloodlessly. In respect to the nobles, whose heads were called upon to direct the State in peace and in war, and whose lineage or blood was held to be of higher value, the offending member was cut off from the trunk and the superior fluid was poured out in atonement.

in the Church of San Pietro in Montorio (St. Peter of the Golden Mount) so called from the scintillating yellow sand of the Janiculus, of which this is one of the elevations. The above church where she lies, which is visible from the Castle of Sant' Angelo, was built by Ferdinand and Isabel, joint Sovereigns of Spain. Cardinal Coscia, Minister of State, was incarcerated here, on the ostensible charge of embezzlement of public funds, but probably this was the pretext to cover other secret causes that rendered his confinement desirable by the man or men in authority during the pontificate of Clement XII (Lorenzo Corsini, A.D. 1730–1740).

The famous or rather notorious Count Alexander Cagliostro (Giuseppe Balsamo) condemned A.D. 1791 to perpetual imprisonment, not as a sorcerer but as a Free-mason. This condemnation on such a charge seems at first sight a rather remarkable proceeding, because one would naturally conclude that an accusation of sorcery in the eyes of the Church, then a capital crime and a mortal sin, would have been preferred to a charge of being a member of the Association of Free-masons.

But in explanation it must be borne in mind that in the eighteenth century the belief in witchcraft was in decay and nigh unto extinction for the general public, while the Free-masons were still a vital factor considered to be antagonistic to the Roman Catholic Church. To accuse Cagliostro as a professor of the Black Art would have provoked a sceptical smile of indifference, but to accuse him as a Free-mason, otherwise as an enemy of religion and order, was a stroke of policy. And to this day it is the rooted conviction of staunch Catholics that the Free-masons are a sinister Association conspiring to destroy religious faith, order and morality. It may be added that this astute adventurer did not remain in prison very long.

Last, but not least, may be recorded the case of Louis Napoleon Buonaparte, afterwards Emperor of the French, A.D. 1852–70, who was confined here in A.D. 1830–31 on the charge of armed rebellion against the legitimate authority of the Sovereign Pontiff Gregory XVI.

During the presence of the French auxiliary forces in Rome in 1848–70 this castle was garrisoned by them, and their tricoloured flag was hoisted here, except on the recurrence of great festivals when it was superseded by the Pontifical bicoloured banner.

Passing from this brief account of some of the principal events connected with this Imperial mausoleum in its transformed character of fortress and prison, we will make a cursory survey of the chief features and divisions of its interior. The excavations of A.D. 1823 laid open the sepulchral vault, in the centre of the substructure. By a narrow passage, on the left of which is a small museum with the busts of Hadrian and Antoninus, fragments of the frieze once encircling the upper section of the building, other relics and a model of the entire monument, we enter a square chamber with a huge recess that formerly held the colossal statue of Hadrian, the head of which has only been rescued and placed in the Vatican Museum. From this we proceed by a spiral staircase to the Tomb-chamber, which contained the enormous porphyry sarcophagus of the founder placed in the centre, with four niches for urns around. Innocent II (Giulio Papareschi A.D. 1130–42) had this sarcophagus transported to the Basilica of San Giovanni in Laterano to be used for his own tomb. It was almost entirely destroyed by fire in A.D. 1160, the cover only escaping the flames, but this massive and colossal lid sufficed alone for the sepulchre of Otho II in the atrium of St. Peter's, at least it is so affirmed, though there is a discrepancy in dates that is suspicious, but in any case the lid survived in the capacity of tomb for someone for about seven centuries, till it was transformed into the present baptismal font of the said basilica.

Ascending now a broader flight of steps we come out on the raised courtyard or terrace, styled the Cortile d'Onore, where the aforementioned marble statue of the Archangel, the predecessor of the present bronze one on the summit, and some marble balls in heaps formerly employed as missiles, are to be seen. Of the few sculptural units saved from the wholesale wreckage, the most valuable are the "Barberini Faun," now in Munich, the Dancing Faun in Florence, and the aforesaid head of Hadrian in the Vatican. From this terrace are entered the private and State apartments of the Popes, tolerably well preserved, decorated with carving, frescoes and stucco works, representing historical and mythological subjects and scenes, and with the immense typical finely sculptured marble mantelpieces of the times.

The "Sala del Consiglio" (Council Hall) and the Borgian and Farnese compartments are perhaps the most remarkable on account of the paintings and of the high class decorations. In the Armoury-hall there are also various specimens of antique fire-arms, such as culverins, petronels, blunderbusses, etc., and of the "arm blanche," such as pikes, halberts, axes. The pieces of heavy artillery on the platform of the summit of the building were moulded out of the bronze tubes taken by Urban VIII from the Panthaeum as aforenoted. In the Treasury-chamber are preserved quaint, old, massive metal-bound wooden chests with curious, formidable-looking locks, which served as safes of the Pontiffs Julius II, Paul II and Sixtus V.

Proceeding round we come to a complete mediaeval pharmacy, served by a real, live apothecary apparelled in the fifteenth century costume of his calling, so as to carry out the allusion harmoniously with his surroundings, with the difference, however, that in the dress of the apothecaries of the two periods, mediaeval and modern, there is a far greater contrast, than in the pharmacies of the two epochs, which were not much dissimilar. In the passages and corridors below are pointed out the bordering prison-cells, especially, of course, those wherein well known individuals were confined, and also the "Trabocchetti," otherwise the oubliettes and traps, the characteristic features of mediaeval fortresses. Below are the extensive vaults used formerly for the storage of food and ammunitions, the most important of which were the granaries and oil-cellars with their huge jars, the latter liquid being utilized then not only as an article of food but also, as is known, as a weapon of defence by being poured boiling on the assailants.

Of the entire monument only the substruction and the travertine inner lining of the first circular superstructure are the original authentic remains of Hadrian's magnificent mausoleum. Pope Paul III (Farnese) added the upper turreted section, Pope Nicholas V (Tommaso Parentucelli A.D. 1447–55) the four towers named after the Four Evangelists, Julian II and Alexander VI contributed greatly to its internal fittings and decorations. In concluding this summary account it may be observed that one is liable to be easily misled, no uncommon occurrence in similar circumstances, with regard to the dimensions of this structure, which are far greater than a casual view of its exterior would seem to indicate, and it may also be added, perhaps superfluously, that there can be obtained from the platform a particularly fine panoramic view of the Eternal City and its environs.

There can be little doubt that despite the prohibitive law regarding inter-urban sepulchres, and the wise chariness of the Senate in granting the privilege to anyone, even exceptionally, there were other tombs within Rome which have totally vanished, but those dealt with cursorily in these two chapters may be taken respectively as representative of the various types of the ancient Roman sepulchral constructions.

CHAPTER XXIV

MAUSOLEUMS AND TOMBS (*continued*)

Of the Via Appia

THE Via Appia, the " Regina Viarum " (Queen of Roads) as styled by Statius, was constructed by Appius Claudius Caecus, 312 B.C., the builder of the first recorded aqueduct. The Appii, like the Valerii, the Anicii and others were the patrician families of ancient aristocracy, mostly of Sabine extraction, a race that held in relation to the Romans and Etruscans a place somewhat analogous to that of the Normans with respect to the Britons and Saxons. This road, paved throughout, commenced originally at the vanished Porta Capena, and subsequently, in 272 B.C., further outwards, at the Porta Appia, now baptized Porta San Sebastiano, from whence, traversing the Pontine marshes, hills, valleys, rivers and streams, to terminate at Brindisium, was the main artery of communication connecting the Eternal City with the east and south of the then known world. This thoroughfare overshadows all others, even to our day, so completely that whenever an average Roman of the labouring classes is asked the name of any road outside Rome, be it the Flaminia, Cassia, Ostiensis or any other, ancient or modern, he answers in nine cases out of ten, that it is called " Via Appia," which for him is synonymous to a country road.

It would be superfluous to dilate on the excellence of its construction, because it is universally recognized that the Romans were absolutely first class road-makers, not to mention the fact that it has already stood the wear of nearly twenty-two centuries and a half, and is still perfectly serviceable. Two roads issue from the Porta San Giovanni, formerly Porta Asinaria, the Via Tusculana leading to Tusculum and the Via Appia Nuova conducting to Albano; the adjective " Nuova," or new, being added to distinguish it from its homonymous elder, which last, for the same reason, is often termed " Via Appia Vecchia," or old. These two Viae Appiae run in almost parallel lines for about eleven miles from Rome until they merge into one at a locality called " Le Frattocchie."

Like all the other principal ancient Roman roads, only in a greater degree, the Via Appia is bordered on both sides by a series of sepulchres, the remains of which at this juncture are the objects, which of all others that most forcibly arrest the attention in the whole extensive view, and which, impressing popular imagination and superstition, gained for this part the nickname of " Strada del Diavolo " that will recall the well known one of " The Devil's Dyke," in England.

In place, however, of an avenue of magnificent sepulchral monuments, besides other superb edifices of mostly renowned personalities, we have now some scattered ruins of, with few exceptions, unknown or unfamed dead. Though all have been more or less stripped of their marble casings and decorations and reduced to wrecks, there is a diversity of treatments meted out to different categories, for while some tombs of minor importance though dilapidated, still exist in a way, the most valuable historically, artistically and materially, have been almost entirely or entirely destroyed. Of the monuments erected over the graves of the great historic families of the Aemilii, Claudii, Furii, Fabii, Acilii, etc., or of those of the patricians of later creation, such as the Pompeii, Flavii, Crassii, etc., or over the remains of eminent men, such as Cato, Cicero, Hortensius, etc., or of the celebrated plebeian leaders, like Brutus, Gracchi, Marius, etc., no vestiges survive, with perhaps some rare and dubious exceptions, like, for example, the so-called tomb of Pompeius Magnus, a rugged cone near Albano being pointed as his sepulchre but without satisfactory proof. And this lamentable loss to us is not so much the result of the passive wear of time but of the active work of man in the wrong direction, whose inordinate destructive propensities appear to have been always especially excited in proportion to the greater artistic and intrinsic value of the works. Raffaele Sanzio, among others, writing on this subject deploring the wanton annihilation of these masterpieces in and about Rome in a letter to Pope Leo X, A.D. 1513–1521, from whose artistic nature Sanzio knew he would meet sympathy, says textually "That almost the entire city has been built with the lime made from the precious marbles that were once the glory of Rome."

The wholesale devastation, therefore, reduces the description of the ruins of the Roman sepulchres to very restricted and unsatisfactory limits sometimes consisting of merely a name, often an unknown and doubtful one. These vestiges of the ruined tombs of the Via Appia will be taken, not chronologically but topographically, because it is calculated that in this way their retention in the mind of the readers will be facilitated. It may be mentioned here, that it was customary in antiquity to provide tombs, whatever their style and size, with a tablet termed "Titulus Sepulchralis," on which was an inscription stating the dimensions of the façade, the depth of the monument and the name of the proprietor; a custom that has proved useful as a means of identification.

Between the Portae Capena and Appia, otherwise before reaching the latter, now Porta San Sebastiano, to the left in a locality called Villa Sassi, there are the remains of the Sepulchre of the Scipios, a branch of the illustrious family of the Cornelii, discovered in A.D. 1780, and consisting of an artificial cave in the tufo rock and divided internally into narrow passages between peperino tomb-slabs, over graves. Its original arched entrance and pediment faced the Via Latina, and what was formerly the back of the cave has been opened for the present ingress on the Via San Sebastiano. The epigraphs to be seen here now are copies of the authentic ones at present in the Vatican, the other relics, with the exception of the famous sarcophagus, have been dispersed and the entire sepulchral structure so much altered and damaged in the Imperial times, when many freedmen's bodies were interred herein and later by the unsatisfactorily conducted excavations of 1875, that few traces of its original state survive. The names found on the grave-stones unearthed are the following: Lucius Scipio Barbatus, and his son the conqueror of Corsica, Aula, the wife of Gneus Scipio Hispallus, son of Africanus, Lucius, son of Scipio Asiaticus, Scipio Hispallus and his son Lucius.

The burial place of Africanus, the greatest of the Scipios, is still a disputed question, three sites claiming that honour, namely: 1st, the above Hypogaeum Scipionis; 2nd, the disappeared pyramid in Rome; and 3rd, a spot close to Lake Liternum, where he retired and died. Livy favours the third hypothesis, and states that he saw the well known epitaph " Ingrata Patria nec ossa quindem mea habis," whence this little lake is to this day known by the name of " Lago di Patria." Africanus, like Coriolanus, Camillus and other great patriotic patricians, was treated with scant gratitude and sense by the plebs, as is not unfrequently the case in all nations and epochs, and this explains his desire not to be buried in the place of his birth. But instability, ingratitude and lack of judgment have always been and will unavoidably always be, the unalterable characteristics of the mob, for envy and ignorance are great demoralizers and blinders, wherefore those nations only are wise who do not entrust their destinies to such hands.

To cite one modern instance among many in proof that this class is always essentially and incorrigibly the same in all times and peoples, we may recall that the Duke of Wellington, on whose public services it would be superfluous to dilate, had iron bars placed in the windows of his mansion in London as a measure of defence against the assaults of the populace of his country, which he had done so much to save and glorify.

It may be noted that the conservative family of the Scipios adhered to interment, then like now, the older custom, in preference to cremation, the newer one, and therefore Lord Byron in his beautiful poem of Childe Harold, referring to the "ashes" of the Scipios being no longer here, is not precisely correct as to fact, but who could think of carping at or even considering such trifling verbal inaccuracies, moreover permissible by poetical licence, in his entrancing works, to my mind unequalled by any other poetical author within the last two hundred years.

One precious relic of the Sepulchrum Scipionis has been, as above noted, fortunately rescued, the well known and justly famed Sarcophagus of Lucius Scipio Cornelius Barbatus, buried here, who was Consul, 328 B.C., with C. F. Plautius, Dictator of the Comitii, 306 B.C., and Pontifex Maximus, 305 B.C., grandfather of the illustrious brothers Africanus and Asiaticus. This is one of the rare cases of non-contested identity in the monuments of antiquity, because besides being found in this Hypogaeum Scipionis, the names, merits and dignities of the occupant are engraved on the side of the sarcophagus, which was transported to the Vatican by Pope Pius VI, and placed in a recess of the " Atrio Quadrato " of the Museum, that contains also the celebrated " Torso " of Apollonius, to which M. Buonarotti declared he owed much of his success in representing the human form.

The sarcophagus in question is composed entirely of peperino, and belongs to the Roman Doric Order with the canonically dentellated cornice and frieze with rosettes on the metopes between the triglyphs. Its perfect proportions, virile and graceful style and exquisite workmanship justly entitle it to the place it holds as the world-famed model of its type. It is on the walls of this recess that the genuine epitaphs of the deceased Scipios, taken as already mentioned from their sepulchres, were affixed. The laurel-crowned bust, discovered with the sarcophagus and placed here on the top of the latter is conjectured to be that of the Calabrian Poet Ennius, the favoured protégé and friend of this family and buried in their above Hypogaeum.

MAUSOLEUM OF CAECILIA METELLA CRASSIA.

Plate iv.

MAUSOLEUMS AND TOMBS

The space after the Sepulchrum Scipionis is occupied by a veritable Necropolis of mausoleums, sarcophagi and columbariae in ruins, among which are recorded those of the Anicii, Massilii and Furii. The Columbariae, very numerous around Rome, were so designated from the Latin word "Columba," or pigeon, because the "Loculi," or cavities, of the interior were thought to resemble pigeon-holes. These structures were generally entered by the summit and provided with two staircases, one internal the other external for the purpose, and were either built by several families of the middle classes in association for their common use, or by more highly placed persons for their dependants, or, finally, by speculators for sale. In almost all the Columbariae there are still to be found some "Hermae" (Busts) and "Olae Cinerariae" (Cinerary Urns), but when one of them has been visited, it is not very necessary to inspect others of this category, because of their relative uniformity and lack of interest in other respects.

Passing from the Porta San Sebastiano and crossing the brook Almo or Marana, the first being the ancient name, the second the modern popular one, for a short distance, the almost obliterated vestiges of two tombs are reached nearly opposite each other, the one being assigned to Geta, son of the Emperor Septimius Severus, the other to a certain Priscilla, wife of Abascantius, a freedman of Domitian. The first-named tomb was, we hear, of pyramidical form, some assert, that it was a pyramid composed of seven tiers or steps, but both are in an extremely wrecked condition, and moreover, it is doubtful if they are, in fact, the sepulchres of the persons mentioned. As regards the Imperial Prince and Co-Emperor Geta it is not recorded that his ashes were deposited in the Hadrian Mausoleum, as the others of his family were, while it is averred that he was buried outside the Porta Appia, which may account for this wreck having been assigned to him as his tomb.

At a short distance further stands the church dedicated to St. Sebastian, one of the Seven Basilicas of Rome, from which after ascending a slight incline we reach the few scattered ruins of the Circumstadium Maxentii, in the background to the left of the Via Appia, and in the front bordering the road, the well known mausoleum of Caecilia Metella Crassia, a large, conspicuous, circular structure on the edge of a lava quarry formed by the solidified streams of lava of the volcanic eruption which stopped here, probably the pre-Roman one, that was one of the causes of the exodus from Albalonga. It is from this point that, less obstructed by side walls, modern buildings and estates, the view expands over the undulating plain of the Campagna, dotted with ruins of aqueducts, villas, tombs, etc., and the more interesting part of the Via Appia commences.

The diameter of this mausoleum has been estimated, as usual variously, at sixty-five, seventy and eighty feet, its original height being an unknown quantity owing partly to the demolition of its summit, said to have been conical, and substituted by the present turrets. The podium or base of this monument is composed of rough hewn blocks of lava and selce (the latter a coarse species of basalt) originally covered with marble, the superstructure of travertine slabs, but whether these were also cased in marble or not is uncertain. The fragments still adhering to the base, the encircling frieze and the tablet of pentelic marble facing the road are now the only parts of this material still existing *in situ*, of the building. On the tablet is the following brief inscription: "Caeciliae Q. Cretici F. Metellae, Crassi."

The interior contained the indispensable sepulchral chamber, first opened in the pontificate of Paul III, A.D. 1534–49, when her white marble sarcophagus found here was transported to the Farnese Palace, afterwards inherited by the Bourbon Dynasty of Naples, and later the seat of the French Embassy at Rome. It is stated that her gold cinerary urn was also discovered herein, but if so it has long since been lost or transmuted into coins or other articles of commercial value. Whether this sepulchral vault and other portions of this monument were originally ornamented or not must remain as yet an undecided question, but no certain traces of any such decorative work now survive, excepting externally the aforesaid frieze and the carved Gallic trophies, emblematic of the high post held by Cecilia's husband Publius, the constructor of the mausoleum, as Cesar's delegate in Gaul. He was the son of Marcus Lucinianus Crassus, the colleague of Pompey and Cesar in the first Triumvirate, and the lady interred here therefore, belonged by birth and by marriage to two of the most conspicuous and powerful families of the patriciate, though not of the most ancient nobility. The husband, in erecting this fine and imposing monument to her memory, made the world richer by a rare, touching and lasting example of conjugal love and regard. The date assigned for the erection of this mausoleum is 68 B.C. If so, as Publius Crassus was killed, 53 B.C., in the Parthian war with his father Marcus, the leader of the Roman expeditionary forces, this mausoleum was built previously to her death.

In A.D. 1299 the Gaetani completed its fortifications as a feudal castle, and extended it by a rectangular addition, the frieze, too, of the mausoleum has been attributed to them, because the Bulls' heads carved on it and from which this structure has been popularly nicknamed "Capo di Bove," or "Head of Bull," figure on the Coat of Arms of this family. They also built a mansion and a church dedicated to St. Nicholas near, of which there are some vestiges, and a village peopled by their dependants and vassals grew around, but of which there are naturally no traces now.

The Frangipani, an older race of nobles, had possessed this monument previously and it was they, it is affirmed, who first converted it into a fortress. It may be interesting to some to know that, according to tradition, the name by which this powerful mediaeval family became conspicuous originated from the charitable act of its founder, who, somewhat like St. Martin with his cloak, shared his loaf with a beggar, hence "Frangi" break, and "Pane," bread, after which they rapidly rose to power, and their opulence was proverbial in the Middle Ages. This race is now extinct, like the feudal families of the Conti, Savelli, Pierleoni and others, but besides, of course, the testimony of history, their memory has been revived recently in a material manner by the renaming of a street in the vicinity of the Flavian Amphitheatre, now called the Via Frangipani.

Subsequently this mausoleum castle fell alternately into the hands of the Orsini, Colonna and Savelli, till Pope Sixtus V took possession of it, and, in pursuance of his policy of curbing the power of the Barons and exterminating the robber-bands that infested the Campagna, effectually rendered it unfit for further use as a stronghold by thoroughly demolishing its fortifications. Sixtus V, Leo. I, Gregory I, Gregory VIII, Boniface VIII, Julius II, and Leo XIII (for obvious reasons excepting Saint Peter) may be numbered as among the greatest of Roman Pontiffs.

The marble casing of the base of this monument was carried away by Pope Clement

TOMB OF M. A. SENECA, A.D. 65. VIA APPIA.

XII and used for the well-known Fountain of Trevi, in Rome. It is one of the superstitions of modern tourists that if they neglect on the last day of their sojourn here, to throw a coin into the basin of this fountain, they will never again visit the Sevenhilled City, though they are careful that the offering wherewith they propose to bribe destiny cheaply should be nothing above copper coins, which ultimately end in the hands of little urchins, who thus substitute themselves, so far as taking the coins goes, for the agents of fate.

The interior of this mausoleum and its mediaeval extensions are now occupied in part with sculptural fragments, the cracked, scorched and broken relics of ruined or vanished buildings found in the environs, thus constituting a small, informal Museum.

Proceeding onwards from the Mausoleum Crassiae we reach a large rectangular brick ruin, the remains of the sepulchre of a certain Caius Duranius, and the Tomb of Marcus Sevilius Quartus, restored by Canova in 1818. The Servilii were originally patricians, but later one branch of them became plebeians. Two Consuls are recorded of this family, with an interval of over three hundred years, P. Servilius Priscus, 496 B.C., and Q. Servilius Selanus, 165 B.C.

A little further on are the remains of the tomb of Lucius Anneus Seneca, built of long bricks after the fashion of the period, with the summit in the form of an apex having "Mascheroni," or carved masks, at the angles, surmounting a broad frieze, the whole monument having been apparently coated with marble. The reliefs on the frieze and façade were intended to illustrate, according to some authorities, the life of Crœsus, but others differ from this version, contending that the figures in question are meant to represent the closing scenes of the life of Seneca, who put himself to death in his villa near here in A.D. 64 by order of Nero.

The condemnation to commit suicide as a death penalty was peculiar to the Imperial times of Rome, and, so far as we know, did not prevail there or elsewhere before or after that period, in an official form. It is about as inhuman as all capital penalties are, and which ought not to exist in any code for any crime, seeing that there are other and more effective methods for the prevention of crime and protection against it, in place of a cold-blooded, irreparable legal murder. The only difference between this form of violent, cruel death, always a brutal reprisal, and the other of enforced suicide, is that the latter presupposes a far greater degree of courage and determination in the individual sentenced thus.

The Senecas were of Spanish extraction, their birthplace being Cordova. Marcus Anneus Seneca, the father, born 60 B.C., migrated to Rome during the reign of Augustus and died there A.D. 32. He was a professor of rhetoric, and his school became one of the most renowned of the Eternal City, and besides his extensive learning he was also celebrated for his formidable and caustic wit and pen and his prodigious memory. Lucius Seneca, the son, born A.D. 3, was likewise a man of profound erudition, intellect and culture, held various high offices and amassed, it is alleged, in the space of four years, 300,000,000 sesterzii (about L.232,000). He was appointed by the Empress Agrippina to be preceptor to her son Nero, but unsuccessful in his attempts to eradicate and control the evil propensities of his pupil, he confined himself after a time mainly to saving appearances, in accordance with the maxim of St. Paul, of whom he was a devoted admirer. "If not chaste, then be cautious." This saying has often been adversely criticised as indirectly favouring hypocrisy, but the real lesson intended seems to be, that, first and above all, virtue ought to be practised, and only in cases when this is impossible, then the shadow, the appearance, ought at least to be maintained for the sake of avoiding the scandal and example of shameless, brazen-faced vice. Tacitus styles L. A. Seneca the defender of virtue as well as the practiser thereof, and attributes to him and to Burrhus the credit of having striven to prevent, and of having succeeded in a measure in moderating the excesses of their Imperial mistress and master, and it is certain that Nero changed incomparably for the worse in proportion as the influence of these two men declined.

In his celebrated letter to the Senate Seneca qualified the assassination of Agrippina as "A blow from Heaven to liberate the Commonwealth." This epistle has been characterized by some as that of a time-server condoning Nero's matricide, and by others, as that of an honest patriot, who though abhorring the unnatural felony, fully realized the providential relief to his countrymen resulting from the disappearance of so pernicious a person as Agrippina. His genius, learning and enviable position attracted, as they almost invariably do, numerous enemies, and he, foreseeing the storm about to burst upon him, endeavoured, but in vain, to protect himself by abandoning public life, voluntarily seeking retirement and repeatedly imploring Nero to accept the restitution of the wealth, with which the latter, unasked, had insisted on loading him in former times.

The plot of Piso gave Nero the desired opportunity to rid himself of a man whose admonitions and rebukes he resented, and whose very existence even at a distance and in retirement, constituted a standing and striking reproach to him; and though there was no evidence or likelihood of Seneca's participation in the conspiracy, this weighed but as a trifle once his death had been decided upon; sentence therefore was quickly passed and the time, mode and place of its execution as promptly chosen.

His villa, where he had retired owing to failing health, was surrounded by a cohort of praetorians, and their Tribune Grassus Sylvanus entered and consigned the death warrant to the condemned man. Seneca without any apparent emotion turned to his sorrowing friends and tried to comfort them by reminding them of the lessons of philosophy, pointing out that this was an opportunity of testing their value. His wife, Pompeia Paulina, he embraced, bidding her moderate her grief by the thought that he had lived an honourable life. She, however, in reply insisted on sharing with him the time and manner of his death, and he yielded to her earnest entreaties, on condition that she would withdraw to her chamber in order to spare both the pain of reciprocally witnessing each other's sufferings, and this injunction she obeyed.

As has been said the choice of the manner of death as well as the necessary orders for its infliction were permitted in these cases to the doomed suicides. Seneca selected a death by acute anaemia, and the veins of the arms of both husband and wife were according to his instructions severed contemporaneously though in different apartments, only, owing to a somewhat premature senile decay, meagre diet and asthma, Seneca's agony was prolonged and extreme. The blood refused to flow, and he had the veins of his legs also opened in vain, he then, by the advice of his friend and physician, Statius Annacus, swallowed hemlock equally without effect, a warm bath was next resorted to unsuccessfully, with the water of which, before entering, he sprinkled his attendants, saying it was a libation to Jupiter, the Liberator from all earthly ills, and ultimately he had to be placed in a closed vapour-bath where he at last succumbed to asphyxia. So true it is that where there is a less vigorous degree of vitality, there is also, in some cases, a superior power of resistance to certain forms of dissolution, which though apparently paradoxical, is nevertheless natural and explicable enough.

It is indisputable that Seneca was a man of high mental qualities and varied and profound knowledge, that he bore himself creditably in his public character, and that in his private capacity he proved himself a dutiful son, an excellent husband, a good relative and a staunch friend. With regard to the increase of his riches, this accumulation was not won by fraud or violence but the result of the voluntary lavish remuneration of the Imperial family, notably of Nero, and, moreover, Seneca more than once earnestly besought the donors to receive their money back. If he was not practically successful in the education of Nero, it may be remembered in extenuation that it would have been very difficult, if indeed possible, to have found anyone in those conditions who could have radically reformed that Emperor.

But whatever our estimation of the life and character of this celebrated man, there can presumably be only one opinion with regard to the manner with which he met his death, worthy of being compared to that of Socrates, which it closely resembled in many respects, furnishing an example of fortitude and unselfishness, not the result of the bestial unconsciousness and indifference of the savage, but of a consideration for others and a high-souled superiority to corporeal dissolution, even though violent, unjust, painful, and inflicted as a punishment. Nor can his wife's spontaneous decision to die in the same way and time with him be considered as less admirable in its spirit, for though excessive and unnecessary, and therefore not to be held up as a rule worthy of identical imitation, we cannot refuse our appreciation and homage to the devoted and elevated sentiments and principles, the admirable moral source, from which this decision of self-immolation sprung.

Continuing our way we come to a part of the Via Appia that is more thickly flanked with ruinous tombs, that may be broadly divided into three categories, viz., those which are nameless, those which are assigned to unfamed individuals, and those that are attributed to persons who have left some traces in history of their passage on earth.

Of the anonymous ones, especially as their architecture and present condition do not call for any particular attention, no mention need be made, though it is quite possible that if their owners and denizens could be identified some of them at least might excite a certain amount of interest. Among the second and third categories may be noted the sepulchres of P. Etticus, of C. Lucinius and of F. P. Philippianus. The last named, owing to its architectonic Order, commonly known as the "Sepolcro Dorico," is built of broad slabs of greyish stone called "Pietra Albana," or more specifically "Sperone," an amalgamation of lava and tufo of the Alban territories. This rectangular structure retains a relative degree of preservation, even to its decorations, which, being Doric, are simple, rectilinear and massive, but its conservation is also due to its durable material as well as its solid construction. The inscription informs us that this sepulchre was erected in memory of a certain tax-gatherer and his wife, recording his office and conjugal merits as follows: "Tito-Claudio-Secundo-Philippianus-Coactari-Flavia-Irene-Uxor-Indulgentissimo."

Not far from this is the "Tomb of Hilarius Fuscus," popularly known as the "Sepolcro del Frontispizio e dei Festoni" (Sepulchre of the Façade and the Festoons), on account of the garlands on the façades of the two front structures backed by a lofty, rugged columnar brick fabric, and it seems to have been handsome and of somewhat singular style and form. Three Fuscus of some note are mentioned in history, namely, Aurelius, rector in the reign of Octavius, the teacher of Ovidius, Fabianus and other celebrated men, and reckoned himself as an able writer, particularly in works of analysis. Aristus, grammarian and friend of Horace who dedicated an ode to him, and thirdly, Cornelius, partisan of Vespasian in the struggle with Vitellius, nominated Procurator of Pannonia by Galba, Praetor by Vespasian, Captain of the Imperial Guard by Domitian, and subsequently Commander of the forces sent against the Dacians, by whom he was defeated. But of the Hilarius of the above tomb no record has been forthcoming as yet.

The next monument we meet, that of the Secundini, a family or an association, is rather of the Columbarium class, only of somewhat superior architecture to the majority of these structures. Then follow the tombs of Quintus Apuleius, of A. Pamphilius, and of several unidentified persons or personages, among which is pointed out one attributed to the famous Gracchi, a wrecked mound, but this without sufficient authority.

Further on stands a monument alleged to have been constructed during the last century of the Pagan era, the much debated "Tomb of the Rabirii." Its good proportions and workmanship and comparative preservation entitle this ruin to be recommended as worthy of inspection. The summit is triangular and rests on a frieze sculptured with designs of twining flowers, while on the façade below there are three busts in relief in a framed tablet. The angles of the structure are supported by pilasters without capitals, and the podium is simple and large.

The Italians call this monument indiscriminately "Tomba dei Tre Rabirii," "Tomba di Uscia Prima Sacerdotessa d'Iside e dei Due Rabirii," and "Tomba di Uscia Prima Sacerdotessa d'Iside," while some foreign antiquarians name it "The Tomb of Rabinius," and these four epithets represent four theories regarding it.

Of the busts on the tablet, the central one is apparently feminine and the two lateral ones masculine, and though the inscription is partially erased the names of G. Rabirius and of Uscia, High Priestess of Isis, are legible.

1st. The monument is conjectured to have been erected to the three Rabirii, in number corresponding to the three men of the family recorded in history, and, if so, it is supposed that the name of this clergywoman was inscribed as that of the erectress to the memory of the three notable members of her family, who will be duly mentioned below.

2nd. That it was erected to Uscia and two male Rabirii, and in this case she replaced one of the men as one of the distinguished trio.

3rd. That it was raised to her only, though accompanied by her acolytes. The objection to this hypothesis being that in her character of High Priestess her official attendants should naturally be female, and the two flanking effigies are evidently those of males.

4th. The conjecture that this is the tomb of Rabinius may possibly be due to an error in substituting the letter "n" for "r."

TOMB OF HILARIUS FUSCUS. VIA APPIA.

Plate lviii.

The three members of the family who made their mark in Roman history are the following: Caius Curius, a Senator of conservative principles whom Julius Cesar, with his policy of breaking the power of that party of whom Rabirius was an influential member, caused Libienus to accuse the obnoxious Senator of having plotted the death of the Tribune Apuleius Saturnius, and a committee was formed to judge him—C. C. Rabirius had, however, powerful defenders, Cicero and Hortensius, as his advocates in the case, and the Praetor C. Metellus Celerus who, foreseeing that the sentence would be unfavourable to his friend owing to the partisan composition of the judges, ordered the flag on the Janiculus to be hauled down, which was the legal signal for the dissolution of the committees; Caius Posthumus, nephew and adopted son of the above, who, while holding the office of public treasurer, was accused by the same family and party foe, Libienus, of extortion in connivance with Gabinus, the Proconsul of Syria, in damage of the Egyptians, but by this time Cesar was no longer a demagogue, having rapidly veered round as he acquired power to conservatism (no uncommon occurrence and indeed a most natural and almost inevitable one) wherefore Caius Posthumus was not only easily acquitted of the unbacked charge, but was moreover promoted by the Dictator to a more important post in Africa as the head of the administration for the supplies of the armies there; Rabirius, the epic poet and litterateur, who flourished in the reigns of Octavius and Tiberius, mentioned by the historian Caius Valerius Paterculus, and also in highly laudatory terms by Seneca and M. Fabius Quintilius. Among the "Papirii" discovered and rescued there is a fragment attributed to this Rabirius which was published in A.D. 1804, 1809 and 1830.

A slight curve of the Via Appia is now approached, to the right of which there are two rugged circular mounds on which there are or were till recently five cones erected in commemoration of five men buried beneath, that are conjectured to be the tombs of the five slain of the two historic triplets, the Horatii and the Curiatii. These sepulchres of a primitive style could never have possessed any architectural or sculptural merit, they are too ancient for that, as at the period of their construction, the reign of Tullius Hostilius, 670–639 B.C., the fine arts had scarcely attained their embryo stage with the Romans, though already in their prime or their decline among other peoples, as for instance the Greeks, of whom it has been said that after the Romans had vanquished them in war, the vanquished had retaliated in their turn by conquering their conquerors in art, which to a certain extent is true.

Every reader of Roman history knows that the Romans and the Albans, being on the eve of a general engagement, mutually agreed to avoid it by choosing three men from each side to fight instead of the entire armies, binding themselves to abide by the issue of the combat and its consequences.

The three brothers Horatii were selected by the former and similarly the three Curiatii by the latter, and it was by a singular coincidence that in both armies there happened to be to champion their respective States three brothers serving contemporaneously, and still more remarkable that they were of about equal skill and valour, and above all that they were triplets, though some contest the veracity of the last point of similitude. The triple duel resulted, as known, in the victory of the Horatii, of whom one, though wounded, survived.

The story goes on further to relate that the surviving Horatius on his way to Rome met his sister who, instead of congratulating him on his and their country's victory, burst into tears and lamentations for the death of one of the Curiatii to whom she had been affianced, and her brother, intoxicated with triumph and transported with fury at conduct he considered unpatriotic, the greater crime, and unsisterly, the lesser one, thereupon slew her on the spot. Arnold narrates this incident as follows: " Horatius went home at the head of the army bearing his triple spoils. But as they were drawing near to the Capenian Gate, his sister came out to meet him. Now she had been betrothed to one of the Curiatii, and his cloak which she had wrought with her own hands was borne on the shoulders of her brother, and she knew it, and wept for him she loved. At the sight of her tears Horatius was so wroth that he drew his sword and stabbed his sister to the heart, and said, ' So perish the Roman maiden who shall weep for her country's foes.' "

She was buried on the spot near where the Porta Capena once stood, and Horatius was first condemned to death, but in consideration of his father's prayers not to be deprived of all his children, and, above all, on account of his brothers' deaths and his own victory in his country's cause, he practically received full pardon, his sentence being commuted to passing as a sign of repentence and penance under a yoke named "Tigillum Sororum," or Sister's Beam, which existed maintained at the public expense and custody for many centuries, as a token and example of the tragedy. The rigour with which impartial justice, without cruelty, was usually administered in the earlier times in Rome renders it probable that the father's supplications would have proved ineffectual to save his surviving son's life, had it not been that in this case the criminal was a patriotic individual to whom his country was deeply indebted for having secured her triumph, while the victim had shewn herself unpatriotic, and, as such, had forfeited her full claim to protection and vindication.

In a Hall of the Capitoline Museum there is a fresco illustrating the scene of the above conflict, with the leaders and parents of the six combatants at the extremities, and, in the centre, the fight verging to its close, two of the Horatii and two of the Curiatii lying dead, and the third Horatius dealing the death stroke to the falling third Curiatius.

It was this spirit of the sacrifice of the individual to the State (and her admirable constitution), though on this occasion pushed to excess, that held the secret of the supremacy of ancient Rome, of her invariable ultimate success over all adversaries apparently superior, that is, in numbers, science and wealth. The diminutive and indigent Spartan kingdom, with its 30,000 Spartans proper, owed its position as the dominant State of ancient Greece chiefly to these identical principles and substantially similar governing system, whereby all were reared from childhood in one Faith and Law,—that they belonged first to their country and after to themselves and families. The wonderful aristocratic Republic of Venice is another case in point. She attained and maintained her greatness and prosperity by the same exalted spirit of public duty and wise government. And if we duly consider that Venice was a single sea-bound city, and not a large one either, that competed in peace and war on equal terms with the great Powers of the times, such as France and Spain, with the overwhelming potency of Papacy and with the then mighty Ottoman Empire, the results she achieved may indeed seem little short of marvellous, though only natural and deserved. The practical advantages of these principles and institutions is that they are better calculated than others for the retention of everything ancient worth preserving, and the addition of everything new worth acquiring, and, as poor, blundering humanity cannot be expected to attain perfection in any direction, the best available, otherwise the least imperfect, is the utmost it can hope for. For in view of the one-sided notions often entertained, it cannot be too strongly emphasized that though we are undoubtedly dissimilar in some points to our forefathers, it by no means follows that we are superior in all respects. To maintain, therefore, as many do, that everything "new" must of necessity be "best," not for its own merits but only because it is "modern," is as illogical, narrow and shallow as to hold that everything "old" must be "best" merely because it is "ancient."

As is well known in the mediaeval times, characteristically the champion age, single combats were frequently resorted to, not only to decide religious and legal questions, but also in substitution of the conflicts of armies. The latest occasion perhaps on record in which an appeal to single combat on these lines was attempted was related to the author by a companion in arms of General Giuseppe Garibaldi, and as probably a unique resuscitation of an obsolete, ancient and mediaeval custom, as well as for the rather uncommon features of the case, it may be considered worthy of mention.

In the year 1860 Garibaldi captured Palermo, left almost undefended, the bulk of the garrison under General the Marquis Del Bosco having sallied forth with the object of intercepting and checking the advancing army of Garibaldi before it neared the city. The invader, however, managed to outwit and outmarch his Royalist adversary who, finding Palermo taken on his return from his fruitless expedition, sent a challenge to Garibaldi to decide by a duel between them the fate of the capital of Sicily and of the campaign, and thus avoid the effusion of blood in a fratricidal conflict.

Garibaldi was well aware of three things: First and foremost that his elementary duty forbade him to hazard in a personal encounter the fate of the Cause of which he was the soul; second, that though he had plenty of practice in the battlefield, he had not had scientific training in fencing, nor was he accounted a crack shot, whereas the Neapolitan Marquis-General was known to be one of the best swordsmen and shots of the kingdom; and third, that while the far-reaching disastrous results of the probable defeat of himself in the proposed encounter were obvious, the corresponding advantages of an improbable victory by him were by no means so manifest. To accept, therefore, would be in fact tantamount to a betrayal of the army, the expedition and the Cause; and Garibaldi, level-headed and independent as well as brave, felt that he could afford, after having given innumerable proofs of his cool intrepidity and daring courage in the field and elsewhere, to do what was certainly wise, conscientious and profitable instead of what was ill-advised, unconscientious and probably calamitous.

In consequence he and his advisors hit upon the following expedient to avoid the duel, without tarnishing the Commander's reputation, even in the eyes of the superficial and thoughtless, the great majority. The answer returned by Garibaldi was "That he would gratefully have accepted at once the General Marquis Del Bosco's honourable proposal, had he been himself like his adversary, a professional officer in command of a regular army, but he reminded his adversary that his own position was quite different as an elected Chief of an irregular volunteer force, and, as such, bound to consult his constituents, that is, his men, before taking any step affecting the Cause, and to submit to their collective decision. That therefore he had referred the matter to them, and their unanimous response had been an absolute negative, on the ground that one of the express and specified conditions in virtue of which he held his mandate distinctly prohibited him from engaging personally in any quarrel or fight while the force he represented and led was in campaign, and that, in consequence he had no option but to decline, reluctantly, the honour of crossing swords or exchanging shots with the Commander of the hostile army in a solitary duel but he added, nothing would delight him more than to meet him in the field of battle in a hand-to-hand fight."

Garibaldi had indeed laid the matter before his officers and men, but they of course refused to permit him, their one indispensable man then, to play into the hands of the enemy by exposing his life, without anything like equal chances, to deadly peril at the hands of the ambitious and vindictive Marchese Del Bosco, who, had he succeeded in thus inflicting a mortal blow on the Unionist Cause by killing Garibaldi, or even a serious one by disabling the latter for a time, with its incalculable moral effects, would not only have more than compensated for his recent strategic failure, but would have been justified in aspiring and obtaining any reward within the power of the King of the Two Sicilies to bestow.

The Neapolitan Government with its standing army of one hundred thousand men and its strong fleet, while ostensibly feigning to despise the " Filibustieri," the official term of contempt applied to Garibaldi and his one thousand followers (the famous "Mille") was perfectly well aware that this small, untrained body of men represented a great and popular current and aspiration, a cause constructive as well as destructive (a rare combination), which permeated all Italy, and which, moreover, was looked upon with favour, morally and unofficially, and even materially supported by other European States. Thus with all its immensely superior forces in discipline and numbers by land and sea, the Royal Neapolitan Government knew that the " Filibusters " were a very dangerous, probably an unconquerable adverse factor, so true it is that material forces are no match in the long run for the moral ones.

To return from our digression. Leaving the Horatian and Curiatian tombs we come to a cone-like sepulchre on a narrow base, assigned by some authors to the Gens Metelli, who gave several eminent men to the State, then to the Tomb of Pompeius Atticus, friend of Cicero, to that of Caecilius Sergius Demetrius, a wine merchant of the Velabrum, and to the Sepulchre of the Gens Aurelii, a celebrated family that furnished Rome with Praetors, Consuls and Emperors among who were Antoninus Pius and Marcus Aurelius.

Further on, near the Villa of the Quintilii, we find the mausoleum of Messala Valerius, a structure originally built of bricks by Corvus Marcus Valerius about 304 B.C., and long after in the first Christian century altered, enlarged and embellished by Cotta Valerius Maximus to serve as the memorial monument of the above-mentioned Messala Valerius Corvinus, his father, buried here. It is commonly and equally known by the names of " Casale Rotondo " and of " Tomba di Cotta," the first apparently on account of its round form and the second from the word " Cotta " on the epigraph. But although

MAUSOLEUM OF MESSALA M. VELERIUS. VIA APPIA.

Plate lviii.

this man reconstructed and constituted this building into a sepulchral monument, this work was done for another, his father, whose name ought therefore to be in preference applied to it. We are informed that it consisted mainly of bricks, the tomb proper being coated with marble, parts of which were carved, of which some fragments are still adhering.

M. Messala Valerius Corvinus, born 70 B.C., was a Conservative in political bias, and yet, or rather, because, he was so, belonged to the Republican party, that is to say, he was opposed to the autocratic faction of the Triumvirs. After the battle of Philippi, where he helped to rout the wing commanded by Octavius and very nearly took the latter prisoner, Messala led his corps in good order to Taso, from whence he concluded a treaty of alliance with Marcus Antonius, to whom he remained faithful until the latter subjected himself to the degrading and disastrous influence of Cleopatra. Octavius, appreciating his worth, received him amicably and appointed him Commander of the forces destined to combat Sextus Pompeius, and the Senate created him Consul in the vacancy caused by the death of his former chief, the Triumvir Antonius. At the battle of Actium Messala commanded the centre of the Augustan Fleet and contributed in no small degree to the victory, and he was subsequently appointed Prefect of Asia Minor, Proconsul of Aquitania, Prefect of Rome and member of the College of Augurs.

But besides being a distinguished statesman and military and naval leader Messala was also a poet, grammarian, historian, orator and a great and competent patron of science and art. Indeed, his literary merits surpassed his political and military talents. Plutarch and Suetonius both draw largely from his historical memoirs in the composition of their works. His style of eloquence was such as was to be expected in the transition stage that marked this period, when the traces and names of an expiring order and liberty survived though its spirit and substance were alike fast disappearing. He was an intimate friend of Horatius and the patron of Ovidius.

The massive construction of the Mausoleum Messala, its dimensions greater than those of the Mausoleum Crassiae, its favourable situation, all recommended it as an ideal stronghold, at the time that most ancient edifices even less adapted for this purpose, were converted into feudal castles, or incorporated as sections of them. The Orsini did not overlook its advantages in this respect, and in the fifteenth century, stealing a march on their hereditary rival Barons, seized this immense sepulchral monument and transformed it into a formidable fortress, and well were they repaid for their foresight and promptitude, as it served them to some purpose in the perennial internecine warfare. It subsequently fell into the hands of the Savelli. The rough treatment it sustained in its bellicose transformation is no doubt answerable for the state of extreme dilapidation to which it is reduced, because its solidity and style seemed calculated to guarantee to some extent its relative preservation from mediaeval devastators, who for the sake of sport as often perhaps as that of plunder, there is no accounting for tastes, habitually destroyed frailer and more ornate works. But in any case, we are in the dark so far, in respect to the details of the architecture of this monument in its original condition.

After this mausoleum the ruined sepulchres are more sparsely scattered. Among these have been identified the tombs of D. Philomusus with its eccentric relief of two mice nibbling, in allusion to the surname of the interred owner (Philo—Friend, Mus—Mouse), of P. Quintus, a military Tribune, of Marcus Julius, steward of the Emperor

Claudius I, of C. Flaccianus and a mound of unknown proprietorship surmounted by a tower, the latter probably Saracenic, popularly called "Torre di Selce." Then come the sepulchres of Titia Eucharis and of Atticus Evodus, a margaritarius (pearl-merchant or jeweller) of the Via Sacra, with its eulogistic inscription of "Hospes resiste aspice ubi continentur ossa hominis boni misericordis amantis pauperis." The last tomb identified is that of Quartus Verranus, and then the conjectured one of the Emperor Gallienus, who had a villa here, chiefly interesting now because of the famous statue of the "Discobulus" (disk-thrower) found among the ruins, though some authorities affirm that it was discovered in the Villa Palombara, possibly taken there from here, and eventually conveyed to the Vatican Museum. After this the Appia traverses a stream called Ponticello and then ascends to Albano, passing several possibly important but as yet unknown tombs, among which may be noted a high structure said to have been once cased in marble and decorated with monolith columns of three Orders and attributed to Pompeius Magnus as aforesaid and also a rugged mound surmised to be the tomb of Ascanius.

From this point onwards up to Brindisi the road continues to be bordered by ruined tombs, but which are less numerous and less explored.

CHAPTER XXV

MAUSOLEUMS AND TOMBS (*concluded*)

of the

Viae Cassia, Tiburtina, Latina and Labicana

THE direct road from Ponte Molle is the ancient Via Cassia which was one of the three northern arterial roads leading to the Cisalpine territory after traversing Etruria, the modern Tuscany. Cicero in referring to it says textually: " Etruriam discriminat Cassia." The other two are the Viae Aemilia and Flaminia. It seems almost superfluous to add that there are several sepulchral and other ruins besides those mentioned in this chapter bordering the above roads, as for example to cite a conspicuous instance, the conjectured Tomb of Sylla, but of these as yet either exceedingly vague information has been gathered or none at all.

The Via Cassia connecting the Capital with Veii and Bracciano is generally the route preferred by excursionists to visit these interesting spots, for the reason that it is one of the pleasantest drives in the environs, with its changing and varied panoramic views of the plain, backed by the rugged Sabine mounts and studded with townlets, hamlets, glades and groves, all embellished by the brilliant sunshine, clear atmosphere, blue sky and soft air prevailing usually during eight months of the year in Italy.

Not far from the Ponte Molle is situated the land anciently denominated " Saxa Rubra," or Red-stone Grotto, and though the rising soil has almost entirely covered the former strata with new layers, masses of volcanic rock of a reddish hue, whence the site derived its name of " Rubra," red, still occasionally emerge here and there to mark the spot that gave a name to the decisive battle fought here between Paganism and Christianism.

About three miles from Rome, to the left of the road, stands a sepulchral monument, of some interest on account of its style and of its disputed, or rather, erroneously reputed ownership. It must originally have been a rather handsome structure, coated with squares of marble, well proportioned and artistically wrought. It is popularly known by the name of " Tomba di Nerone," Tomb of Nero, but while no records confirmatory of this hypothetical proprietorship, born probably of some casual rumour or tale, arising who knows how or why (as so frequently happens in similar cases), have been gathered, we have direct written contrary evidence on the tablet of the façade assigning it to others, and besides this, the testimony of Suetonius, as will be seen further on, that Nero was not buried here. In spite of evidence, however, it still goes by the name of Nero's Tomb among the populace, and even among those who ought to know better, wherefore we may assume that in this case, as in so many others, " Vox Populi " is not synonymous with " Vox Dei," despite the frequent use made of this unmeaning saying. The epitaph clearly states that the tomb in question is that of Publius Vibius Marianus and of his wife, Reginia Maxima, erected by their daughter, Vibia Mariana Maxima, in the second Christian century, and records that he was Praefectus or Governor of Sardinia, and according to the text, a sweet father and she a dear mother. And this is all the information obtained of this couple and their daughter.

The Vibii, the paternal stock, were a plebeian family which though dating from the second Punic war and continuing to exist long after the establishment of the Empire, did not produce any man of mark. There were, it is true, two Emperors bearing that name, viz: Caius Vibius Tribonius and Vibius Voluscius, A.D. 251–52, but they can hardly be held as exceptions, because they were " distinguished " only by their official rank and not by personal eminence, and, moreover, they possessed that rank for a very brief space indeed, and during its tenure did not reach the level of mediocrity.

With regard, however, to the lineage of Reginia Maxima the case is different. The superlative " Maximus," or Greatest, was originally bestowed on Quintus Fabius Rutilianus, and became henceforth the second surname of the Fabii. Quintus was the sole survivor of the 306 members of this illustrious family from the massacre of Cremera. His long life of nearly one century of practically uninterrupted success as a Statesman and General, render him a unique personality of his times. He was " Magister Equitum " or Commander-in-Chief of the Cavalry, 322 B.C., five times Consul, twice Dictator, and " Princeps Senatus," or President of the Senate. But besides this, Quintus gave an example of Roman public virtue, even then not common and most rare now. When his son, Quintus Fabius Gargitus, who was far from being the peer of his father, and had been, moreover, defeated previously, was elected Consul, therefore one of the leaders of the army for the year, he acted with rare tact, self-denial and patriotism, for not questioning the advisability of his countrymen's choice, he resolved to prove it wise by his self-effacing co-operation as the subordinate of his own son. Having thus secured his country's victory by his unseen and unofficial but invaluable guidance, he took an unobserved place among the crowd of subaltern officers in the triumphal procession in Rome, seeking no other reward than that of his conscience; it is true that that was the best of all.

Among the eminent men of the Gens Fabii may be noted Quintus Fabius Verracosus, grandson of the above, nicknamed " Cunctator," from the Latin verb " Cunctare," to procrastinate, the celebrated antagonist of Hannibal, and to this day the expression of " Fabian tactics or strategy," signifies to play a waiting and harassing game in war. He was, likewise, four times Consul, thrice Dictator and President of the Senate, and he, too, nearly completed his tenth decade of life.

The present Princes Massimi, a noble mediaeval family, whose typical and picturesque Palazzo Massimi, in Rome, is still inhabited by them, claim descent from the Fabii Maximi, the followers of Remus, having dropped the first surname and Italianized the second, by the canonical substitution of the " x " by the " ss " and the termination of " us " into " o," Maximus-Massimo.

With regard to the other factitious candidate of this tomb, namely the Emperor Nero, it seems certain that he was buried A.D. 68, at the foot of the Collis Hortorum, Hill

TOMB OF P. V. MARIANUS AND OF R. MAXIMA. VIA CASSIA.

Plate lix.

of Gardens or Orchards, the present Pincio. Suetonius writes on this head what has been translated as follows: "When Nero was dead, his nurse, Eclogue, with Alexandra and Acté, his favourite concubine, having wrapped his remains in rich stuffs embroidered with gold, deposited them in the Domitian Monument in the Campus Martius which is to be seen under the Hill of Gardens." The tomb was of porphyry having an altar of Luna marble surrounded by a balustrade of Thasos marble. No remains of the costly Neronian Sarcophagus are now known to exist; if exhumed they have doubtless been dispersed or destroyed, as was customary during the period that divides the classic from the modern times. In fact, it is rather amazing that in those conditions any vestiges or traces still exist to attest materially the passage on earth of those cultured and artistic pre-mediaeval generations; from which we may conclude that these iconoclasts, or rather monumentoclasts and documentoclasts, of the dreary Middle Ages, incompetent even in their brutish, facile task, did not accomplish their work of destruction thoroughly. The partial rescue of classic monuments in Italy is also owing to the protection of some Gothic Rulers, notably Theodoric, and, as aforesaid, to the conversion of some of the larger ones into castles and churches.

There is a Christian legend connected with the disappeared sarcophagus and burial place of Nero worth mentioning. It is narrated that out of this grave a walnut tree grew with unnatural rapidity to an enormous size and became the habitual resort of crows, so numerous, so big, so black and so uncanny altogether as to render them an intolerable nuisance to all the neighbourhood. This uncomfortable state of affairs was brought to an end by the opportune dream or vision of Pope Pascal II, A.D. 1099–1118, in the following manner. The Blessed Virgin appeared to him in his sleep and informed him that the troublesome birds were not bona fide crows at all, but transformed demons, commanding him at the same time to have the said unique tree cut down and burnt, and the ashes thereof, according to the ritual phrase, dispersed to the four winds of heaven. The official version differs, however, with regard to the process of the disposal of the said ashes, inasmuch as it is recorded in an inscription of the church erected on this site, that the ashes of the tree, with those of Nero, were thrown into the Tiber.

The Pontiff otherwise seems to have scrupulously fulfilled the miraculously delivered instructions, and furthermore on his own initiative built a sanctuary on the spot where the infernal tree had grown up, presumably as a *pro tem.* bulwark, like a wise commander fortifies the ground he has wrested from the enemy against counter-attacks until a permanent stronghold could be raised. So in this case the small temporary shrine was replaced more imposingly and powerfully by the great Church later. In memory of the vision the church was dedicated to the Virgin Mary, and because the money for the construction was chiefly collected from the common people, the edifice was distinguished by the additional " Del Popolo," of the people that is, " Santa Maria del Popolo," a name it retains to this day, as, similarly, the square in which it stands is called " Piazza del Popolo." It may be added that this church is a fine edifice, and that the interior is well worth inspection and repays the trouble of more than one visit.

The legend does not proceed to relate the subsequent fate of the ejected fiendish crows or bird-incarnated devils in consequence of the summary and drastic suppression of their elected domicile, the walnut tree, but it may be fairly inferred that if they were really birds, as appearances vouched (only unluckily appearances are deceptive) they forthwith found some other suitable refuge, and, if evil spirits, returned to the habitat usually assigned to them as their headquarters, the lower or infernal regions, duly sobered and perturbed, it is to be hoped, after the signal defeat of their raid or escapade. At any rate, it seems that since the extinction of the abnormal tree and the dispersion of its ashes and those of the equally abnormal monarch, buried underneath, the extraordinary birds vanished entirely, to the greater glory of the church and the tranquillity of the inhabitants of the vicinity.

With regard to His Majesty Nero Claudius Cesar it is incontestable that he is one of the best known, and if fame consists in diffusion, the most famous of the Roman Emperors. One Nero in this respect overshadows a score of Aureliuses and Trajans, as, similarly, one Pope, His Holiness Alexander VI, a score of Leos and Gregories. Even those who are but little acquainted with the history of the Roman Emperors and Pontiffs, are generally familiar with the names of these two. It is eminently disagreeable to have to admit this fact, as regrettable as it is true, which proves that human nature, as a rule, is fascinated by evil deeds and evil doers, much more than by good actions and persons, and that this unfortunate instinct can only be remedied, though not always or altogether, by a wise culture.

The "Mausoleum of the Plautii." Leaving Rome by the Porta San Lorenzo which replaces the ancient Porta Tiburtina, and proceeding along the outgoing Via Tiburtina for about twelve miles, we reach the Dioryx or Canal cut by the Cardinal d'Este, brother of Pope Paul III, in A.D. 1540, to carry the bluish, opaque waters from their lakes of the Solfatara, commonly known as the "Colonelle," an outlet of the Apennines, to the river Anio. These waters, the "Aquae Albulae," were renowned *ab antico* for their curative qualities, and hence their subsequent appellation of "Santissime," and were patronized in consequence by many celebrities of antiquity, among others by Octavius and Zenobia.

About two miles further on, the Anio, nicknamed Teverone, is spanned by the Ponte Lucano, forming with the tower-like Mausoleum Plautiorum and the surroundings a most picturesque scene, that has provided a subject for many artists, of whose productions perhaps the best is a painting by Poussin. This bridge derives its name from, and probably owes its construction to, M. Plautius Lucanus, and although altered, decayed and damaged, especially during Totila's times, still retains its foundations of genuine Roman work in proof of its ancient Roman origin. The branch road, Via Constantina, passes over this bridge before rejoining the main Via Tiburtina.

The beautiful Mausoleum of the Plautii, standing on the left of the above Pons Lucanus, was built of travertine squares; whether originally covered with marble or not is still a disputed question, like that of C. M. Crassia, which it resembles in form but from which it differs by its smaller dimensions, absence of the external frieze and its Corinthian columns in front, the broken remains of which are still *in situ*. This sepulchral monument is especially remarkable for its exquisite proportions, by many competent authorities reckoned as superior to the aforesaid one of Crassia, to which it is often compared, though the latter is more generally known owing to its proximity to Rome. There are three versions regarding the date of the erection of the Mausoleum Plautiorum: the

MAUSOLEUM OF THE PLAUTII. TIVOLI.

Plate lx.

first, precise, fixes it at the first year of the first Christian century; the second, approximate, during the reign of Tiberius, A.D. 14–37; and the third, in that of Vespasian A.D. 69–79. It was built, it is stated, by M. Plautius Sylvanus, and used by him and his descendants as the family mausoleum, and if he be the identical Sylvanus mentioned below, for there were more than one named Sylvanus, the third approximate date might be the correct one. Of the various epitaphs recording the Plautii buried herein there are two decipherable on the façade—one referring to M. Plautius Sylvanus, recording his dignities of Consul and General, his wife, Larzia, and his son, M. Plautius Urgulianus, and the other of T. Sylvanus Elianus.

The Plautii during the earlier times appertained to the plebeian Order, but, rising rapidly in importance, became incorporated in the patriciate, in which they held a distinguished and influential place, numbering some eminent men among their members: C. Plautius, twice Consul, in 358 and 328 B.C., as colleague of Cornelius Scipio Barbatus; C. Plautius Voluscius, the Censor and Coadjutor of Appius Claudius Caecus in the construction of the Appian Aqueduct, 312 B.C.; M. Plautius Sylvanus, the possible builder of the mausoleum, Consul and General appointed by the Emperor Claudius in command of the army sent to subjugate Britain—this after four years of strenuous fighting, he succeeded in accomplishing, so far as regards the southern portion of the island, and for which he was awarded an ovation on his return to Rome (according to Suetonius, however, Aulus Plautius, in the reign of Claudius reconquered or resubjugated the Britons, led by the brothers Tagudamus and Caractacus, slaying the first and sending the second captive to Rome); the Plautius Lateranus, a powerful magnate, put to death by order of Nero, A.D. 64, on the charge of complicity in the conspiracy of Piso (for which Seneca was also condemned), which was evidently freely utilized as an exceedingly convenient machine for making a clear sweep of all those who for any reason or for no reason gave umbrage, or were merely antipathetic, to Nero Aenobarbus (Red-bearded) at the time.

According to one account of this obscure plot, if indeed it ever existed and was not an effective invention to suppress undesirables, the task of holding down the Emperor while the other conspirators despatched him, was entrusted to this Plautius because of his great physical strength, and it is also recorded that no word inculpatory, compromising, resentful, complaining or supplicatory escaped him during his trial, presumably a mock one, or at the announcement of his death doom, for which manly self-control he is much lauded by contemporary and postemporary writers. It is from this patrician that the Basilica and Square of St. John derive their distinction of " Laterano or Lateranensis." To the above Plautii may be added Tiberius Plautius Sylvanus, Juri-Consultus and Praefectus Urbis Romae, in the reign of Vespasian. The decisions and sentences of the Juriconsults, possessed the authority of laws, and their doctrines, compiled later by the Emperor Justinian, A.D. 527–66, termed " Pandette," formed the basis of subsequent civilized legislation.

In the Middle Ages, usually a rather vague and elastic term, the Mausoleum Plautiorum was converted into an embattled and turreted tower, and in this guise served as a bulwark for Tivoli. Pope Pius II, A.D. 1458–64, is credited or discredited, according to opposing views, as the author of this transformation, and if not the first or only one, he was certainly the chief agent in turning this beautiful sepulchral monument into a typical mediaeval castle, but, as so frequently happens relatively to names, its original appellation continued to cling to it, despite changes, and it was popularly known during these centuries as the " Plautiana." The very fact that these mausoleums and tombs of the classic generations were capable of being transmuted into the fortresses of the succeeding ones, testifies to their magnitude and solidity and to the striking difference in the vastness of conception and of existence between the men of the former and the latter periods.

In the vicinity of this monument there is a locality called " Barca," mainly a quarry of the " Lapis Tiburtina " (Tiburtine or Travertine stone) which furnished and furnishes such abundant and excellent material alike in ancient and modern times. The principal elements of its composition are the lime deposits of the mountain streams of the environs, which in this part of the peninsula are particularly rich in this substance brought down by the water impetus in great quantities. The travertine is soft and white when quarried, and while its pristine ductibility offers great facilities to the sculptor, its faculty of becoming absolutely hard and firm on exposure, and its extreme durability, justify the preference accorded to it both for structural and ornamental purposes. This stone is not to be confounded with the so-called limestone or freestone of England and France, with which it has nothing in common in respect to properties and capacities, for though the travertine and the limestone or freestone somewhat resemble each other in appearance when first cut, to the casual observer, the latter are far more brittle and friable than the former, and dissimilar in grain and texture.

The mausoleums of the Valerii and the Pancratii. The ancient Porta Latina, one of the few that has retained its original classic name, was one of the southern gates of the Eternal City. Inside and close to this Porta Latina is a small octagonal chapel of the Bramante style, called San Giovanni in Olio, built A.D. 1509 on this spot, where in the reign of Domitian Saint John gained the palm of martyrdom. From this gate issued the ancient Via Latina which, traversing the valley " Del Sacco," connected Rome with Capua. Some portions of its stone pavement of polygonal slabs of lava have been laid bare. As is known lava is the liquid burning matter discharged by volcanoes which, gradually cooling, solidifies into a useful stone that, owing to its mineral elements mainly, is hard and durable and excellent for pavements and walls, and much employed in this manner in southern Italy and Sicily. The active volcanoes from which this lava was ejected have in many cases been long since extinct, and the eruptions of some of them date from such remote antiquity as to be almost prehistoric. Their craters have been metamorphosed into lakes in several instances, such as those of Albano and Nemi, and their whilom flowing, burning streams into lava quarries.

Similarly to all the principal roads radiating from the Seven-hilled City, the Via Latina was bordered with sepulchral monuments. About three miles from the above homonymous gate a locality is reached of the Via Latina where the agglomeration of ruinous tombs is so considerable as to constitute a veritable cemetery, now commonly called " La Tombe Latine," and here also are the remains of the Basilica of San Stefano, the protomartyr, built by Demetria Anicia during the pontificate of Leo I, or Great, A.D. 440–461, and discovered A.D. 1858. Among the other wrecks here, attention is arrested particularly by two rather conspicuous monuments, standing nearly opposite each other. One is the Mausoleum Valerii and the other the Mausoleum Pangratii.

MAUSOLEUMS AND TOMBS

The Valerii were members of the ancient, probably Sabine, aristocracy, descended from Valescus, whose landed estates extended from this spot to the townlet of Marino, later for a long period the hereditary fief and fortress of the Orsini. The Valerii gave several illustrious men to Rome, among whom may be mentioned Voluscius, Consul in the first year of the Republic, 510 B.C., and therefore one of the first personages on whom this exalted dignity was conferred. Some authorities, however, write that the two first Consuls elected that year were Lucius Junius Brutus and Lucius Tarquinius Collatinus. It is not impossible, nevertheless, that one of the latter might have been replaced by Voluscius, or vice versa, which would reconcile the two versions. In any case, Voluscius was one of the foremost leaders in the political upheaval which resulted in the overthrow of Tarquinius Superbus and the abolition of the Royal régime, and who might be styled the "Beau Ideal" of a reformer in a liberal direction, without being in any sense a demagogue or place-hunter. So conspicuous was this quality and attitude in him that it earned for him the agnomen of "Publicola," then a synonym of "Friend of the people," and he was so beloved and venerated that at his decease the Roman matrons spontaneously went into mourning for him for ten months.

Marcus, his brother, also Consul and his coadjutor in several signal services to the Commonwealth, and Manlius, another brother, Dictator and victor over the Separatist Sabines. To this Manlius was awarded a unique honour never subsequently bestowed, it appears, to any other—that of having for life a distinct post assigned to him alone, whether he was in or out of office, in all public assemblies and ceremonies. F. Voluscius, son of the first named, twice Consul and conqueror of the Veii and Samnites. Lucius Consul, who, faithful to the traditional family principles, co-operated in liberating Rome from the tyranny of the Dicemvirs, and the vanquisher of the Equii and Volsci. Caius Marcus Valerius Corvus, born 370 B.C., first military Tribune under the celebrated Furius Camillus in the defensive Gallic campaign, then successively six times Consul and twice Dictator. He defeated the Samnites in the sanguinary and decisive battle of Cuma, which Neibour qualifies as one of the most memorable in the world's history, where the Romans, besides other spoil, took forty thousand shields and seven standards from the enemy; and he also vanquished the Sedicians, Ausoni and Etruscans. Octavius, after over three centuries, had a statue erected to this Valerius Corvus, in company with those of other celebrated Romans in the atrium of his palace. And, finally, Valerius Maximus, who united the two illustrious stocks in his person, viz, paternally the Valerii, and maternally the Maximi, Consul, historian and epic poet, who left many valuable works, some of which have been rescued.

The Valerii, it need scarcely be added, represented, like the Furii, Aemilii, Cornelii, and others, the best ideal of the Roman patricians, and their surname was in consequence so respected and renowned that it was assumed in addition, or in substitution, or as an honorary title, by various personages and Sovereigns, among the latter of whom may be cited the Emperors Probus, Diocletian, Maximus, Constantius Hlorus, Maxentius, Maximinianus and Constantinus.

The Mausoleum Valerii in question consists internally of an atrium, of which two pilasters standing here have been recently restored, of the Sacellum, or family chapel, also repaired, and of a sepulchral chamber decorated with exquisite reliefs in stucco representing sea monsters, nymphs and genii. These stucco ornaments are practically uninjured by the lapse of centuries, the fineness of the work being equalled by its durability. Nor is this to be attributed to the protection afforded by a covered condition, because there are examples of other stucco works exposed to the damage and attrition of time and weather, likewise resisting their deteriorating effects. It is alleged that the ancients invented a preparation of now unknown elements for the external protection of marble works termed " Circumlythius," but this does not explain the extraordinary conservation of the productions in stucco, presumably a more friable substance than stone or marble, or in fresco painting. This secret has not been handed down to posterity, nor has anything similar been rediscovered by the inventive faculties of artists or others in our times, despite our assumption that our era is the one for all round invention.

The intervening Middle Ages must be held responsible for the loss of the secret of preservation. Art, like literature, was numbed or wiped out, and if we are the richer for the survival of some of the literary works of antiquity, we must not forget nor fail to recognise, that we owe this mainly to the secular and monastic clergy, especially the latter, who, whatever the shortcomings attributed to them in other respects, certainly deserve our gratitude for having, amidst the deluge of barbarism of these dark times, almost alone kept alive, though languidly, the light of literature and rescued and protected, whenever religious fanaticism did not interfere, the precious productions of the classic ages.

The Mausoleum Pangratii was a construction of this family or association, there being no certainty as to which of the two they were, all that has been gathered relatively being that in the first Christian century a family of the Equestrian Order bore this name, while in the third and fourth centuries we find it applied to a noted burial society. The monument contains a chamber decorated with landscapes, and four stucco reliefs representing four different subjects, viz, 1st, The Judgment of Paris; 2nd, Alcestes; 3rd, Priam and Achilles; 4th, Hercules playing on the lyre, with Bacchus and Minerva as his auditors. This last scene is remarkable and probably unique, in the sense that it depicts the demi-god of virility in an unusual attitude and occupation. This chamber is also adorned with some fine illustrations of the Trojan War. This mausoleum, too grand for the use of the builders considering their station, is assumed to have been erected as an advertisement for their business.

The system of advertising is not, as some think, a modern commercial invention, but a device of very ancient origin. In the times of good King Solomon, in Tyre, Babylon, Carthage, etc., it was generally adopted. The only thing modern about it is the way in which it is done now, very inferior to the ancient method. In order to achieve a greater sale now we rely on disfiguring walls, etc., with glaring ugly pictures and prints, or in desecrating newspapers and books by filling them with boastful promises. They, as sellers, preferred to rely on presenting the real production itself to the purchasers, believing that true value, by being thus practically estimated, would hold its own, without the pseudo aid of empty self-praising phrases and slogans. Many think that our present curious advertising methods, counting on the shallowness and credulity of the public, pay well; others are of opinion that considering, on the one hand, the enormous cost in labour, time and material required, and, on the other, the relatively small number of those who read or look at these advertisements, and the fewer still who are impressed or decoyed by these rather childish appeals, the outlay in this direction is a loss to the sellers, unless the cost is deducted from the value of the article thus advertised, and in that case it is a loss to the buyers. Nevertheless it goes on, owing to custom, of which few indeed are independent enough to break the trammels, even when they disapprove and believe that a thing is useless or injurious.

Besides archaeology there is another inducement to visit this classic spot, the view from the Tombe Latine being particularly fine and impressive whether directed backward to Rome or forward to the long series of broken ruins of every description scattered so picturesquely and strikingly over the desolate but intensely interesting Campagna.

The Mausoleum of Saint Helena. Issuing from the Porta Maggiore, and following the ancient Via Labicana for about two miles, we reach the remains, bare, cracked walls, of an angular tower, popularly known as the Torre Pignatara. If this structure ever formerly possessed any architectural or sculptural beauties they are conspicuously absent now even to a trace. Nevertheless, it is interesting for two reasons: firstly, as being the sepulchre of the above personage, and secondly, because her superb porphyry sarcophagus was found here. This sarcophagus is now in the Vatican in a hall denominated "Della Croce Greca" (Of the Greek Cross), placed opposite another one similar in shape and scarcely less beautiful. The one on the right is the sarcophagus of Helena, the other on the left that of Constantia, both Saints and Royal Princesses, and standing in the relation of grandmother and granddaughter to each other, the former being the mother and the latter the daughter of Constantine I, called the Great.

The first-mentioned sarcophagus rests on four white marble couchant lions, and is adorned with middle reliefs illustrating battle scenes, presumably those of the above Emperor, and surmounted by small busts of Helena and Constantine. The restoration of this monument, remarkably well executed, cost, it is said, about 20,000 lire. Anastasius IV, in the single year of his pontificate, A.D. 1153, had this sarcophagus removed from its place on the Via Labicana to the Basilica of San Giovanni in Laterano for the purpose of using it for his own tomb, and it was from there transferred to its present place by Pius II, A.D. 1458.

The second sarcophagus, supported by four couchant marble wolves, is decorated by mezzo-reliefs representing vintage scenes, in allusion, presumably in its present character, to the Vineyard of the Lord. But this may have been originally a Pagan sarcophagus, and then the reliefs would be in reference to Bacchus, and adopted afterwards for the Christian saint, as not infrequently happened. Vintage scenes, however, do not essentially differ whatever the Faith, so these sculptures would do as well as a decoration for the Christian's as for the Pagan's sarcophagus without any other change than that of a name. This monument was taken from the Mausoleum of Constantia, over which was subsequently built the present church of Sta. Costanza, dedicated to her and close to the greater one of Sta. Agnese, on the road issuing from Porta Pia. From the Mausoleum Constantia the sarcophagus was transported by Pope Paul II (Paolo Barbo A.D. 1464–71) to the Piazza of San Marco, in Rome, and from there brought to the Vatican.

In the above Basilica of Sant' Agnese, Fuori le Mura, during the annual service performed on the 21st of January a curious ceremony is observed. Two white lambs decked with ribbons are presented and blessed by the officiating clergyman, high in the hierarchy, being either the titular Cardinal or Abbot. These two lambs are carefully chosen and reared for the purpose, and after being sheared, their fleeces are used exclusively for the weaving of the vestments of the Pontiff.

To narrate in detail the life of Saint Helena (the Holy title is preferred as she lost the right to the sovereign one of Empress since she became a divorced consort) would be too long for a work of this description, but some of its principal events may be touched upon here. She was of British extraction, and three towns dispute the distinction of being her place of birth, namely: Winchester, York and Colchester, the last of which has two points in favour of its pretention, though neither in the nature of proofs, firstly, because Helen is said to have been the daughter of Coel, King of Coel-chester or Colchester, and secondly, because the City Arms bear three crowns with a Cross in allusion to this claim.

The three Crowns of the Arms of Colchester (like the three Crowns of Cologne) symbolise the Three Holy Kings or Magi, whose remains, according to legend, were also discovered by St. Helena and taken by her to Constantinople with the True Cross and from thence removed to Cologne. With regard to the True Cross there is the version also that it was divided into four parts and sent respectively to the four parts of the world, north, south, east and west.

She was the first wife of Constantius Flavius Valerius Hlorus, first " Cesar," or associate, and heir to the reigning Emperor Maximinianus, and after " Augustus " or Emperor himself, Constantius, who was nicknamed " Hlorus " (hlorós signifying pale in Greek) on account of his pallor, had brought Britain again into subjection to Rome, about A.D. 297, whose yoke she had partially shaken off during ten years' rebellion, and it was probably in this period that this matrimonial alliance was consummated. He has been much lauded by both Pagan and Christian writers for his sagacity, humanity and justice, and he was the founder of the City of Costanza. After the birth of their son, Constantine, they were for some unknown reason, divorced. Helena remained in Britain and Constantius married again, returned to Britain after ruling Gaul and Spain, vanquished the Picts and died in York A.D. 306.

On Constantine's assumption of the Throne he invited his mother to Rome and Constantinople, where she renounced Paganism with him, embraced Christianity, and, as her biographer writes, " Favoured the progress of humanity, built churches and succoured the poor."

When Saint Helena reached her eightieth year she made a pilgrimage to the Holy Land, where, on visiting the site of Christ's sepulchre, she found an Aedicula erected by Hadrian to Venus. This edifice she ordered to be demolished and had excavations undertaken forthwith that brought to light three wooden crosses, assumed to be those on which the Saviour and the two thieves, Dimas and Gestas, suffered their sentence. It is alleged that in order to discover which of the three was the Sacred Cross the corpse of a woman, deceased some time previously, was alternately placed on each, that when laid on the two first, no change was observed, but that the contact with the third produced reanimation, we are not told whether ephemeral or permanent, but in either case the result was held to be sufficient, and the third Cross was thereupon pronounced to be the identical instrument of the crucifixion of Jesus Christ. It is further added that the wood was subdivided for distribution to the faithful into innumerable fragments, amounting together to treble the quantity of the timber originally composing the Cross, and that, notwithstanding this, it remained entire and unimpaired.

It would be curious to speculate how many crosses would now be required if crucifixion continued to be the legal and customary penalty inflicted on thieves in our times, on all the professors of the many branches of this lucrative business. There are, broadly, two classes of robbers, the violent robber, burglar, motor-bandit, window-smasher, bag-snatcher, etc., who are the drab and uninteresting successors in towns of the picturesque highwaymen and brigands of former days of the open country, who are still, it appears, lingering in Corsica, and the mild robber, the swindler, kleptomaniac, confidence trickster, blackmailer, etc., who may be termed euphemistically the apostles of " civil disobedience " to the law. But however much they differ in name and action, the principle is the same in all, to take what belongs to others, either by force or by fraud.

Saint Helena conveyed the Sacred Cross with her to Rome, where it was placed in a hall in her palace, transformed into a church named in commemoration of this event "Santa Croce in Gerusalemme," and which gradually developed into the present basilica, covering the area and supplanting the former Royal abode. This church was consecrated, according to some authorities, by Pope Sylvester, A.D. 314–335, and, according to others, by Pope Symmachus, A.D. 498–514; the first date is the more probable as being that of a contemporary Pontiff. The church was repaired by Pope Gregory II, A.D. 715–731, the monastery added by Pope Benedict VII, A.D. 975–993, in the first year, it is said, of his pontificate, and the entire edifice reconstructed by Pope Lucius II, A.D. 1144–45. Pope Benedict XIV, in A.D. 1740, had the basilica overhauled and remodernized, but not improved, far from it, but whether this unsuitable renovation was the Pontiff's or the artists' conception, or the latters' execution, has not been ascertained.

The words of fire " In Hoc Signo Vinces," with the Cross, said to have been seen by Constantine in the legend of his vision, were adopted as the motto and sign of his new Faith on the Labarium, or official, symbolic standard of the Roman Christian Empire. The monogram, we see so often, is formed of the two first Greek letters of the Redeemer's name, " X " and " P " Xristós or Christ, the initial letter being also of itself a Cross Decussate, the type known as St. Andrew's.

The ignorance of the mass of the people of the early Christian times rendered them quite incapable of grasping the spiritual character of Christianity without the aid of material, everyday objects to impress their senses. Hence the necessity for the introduction of effigies of animals, lambs, doves and fishes, representing, respectively, the denizens of the three elements, land, air and water, to typify figuratively two of the Holy Trinity and the Salvation of Souls. With Paganism, too, animals were adopted in connection with the Deities but with a different intention and system. They appeared either as emblematic accessories with the latters' statues or effigies, as for instance, the Serpent, the symbol of wisdom, with Aesculapius, the Eagle, that of Sovereignty, with Jupiter, etc., or when figuring as a disguise in which it pleased these Divinities to indulge for a while, but not to represent the gods and goddesses themselves.

The Lamb, in its religious formula of " Agnus Dei," was chosen as the symbol of Jesus Christ on account of its disposition and of its sacrificial end by the Jews, though the Pagans and others killed other beasts, bulls, hogs, etc., for the religious sacrifices. The lamb's two prominent characteristics are mildness and timidity; in respect to the first, mildness, it might be held to typify the Redeemer's gentleness, but as regards the second, timidity, and this creature's dullness, feebleness and selfishness, there can be no analogy with the exalted intellectual powers, unbounded courage, heroic self-abnegation and all embracing love, justice and mercy of the Saviour in His carnal existence.

The reason of the preference of the Dove as the representative of the Holy Ghost is presumably its softness and love. It was adopted perhaps more appropriately by Paganism as the emblematic pet of Venus, because these birds are noted for the tenderness of their sexual love, they live for it, as did Venus, only the bird's love is of a constant, faithful nature, whereas that of the goddess can hardly be qualified as such.

There are two explanations given for the selection of fish as symbolical of Salvation. The one is, that the Apostles were, at least in the majority, fishermen by trade, and hence from "Fishers of Fish" they became metaphorically "Fishers of Men." But this explanation is not strictly logical, for though they were "hunters" in both characters, the aim of each was diametrically opposed to the other, in the first, as fishermen, being "hunters" to destroy, in the second, as Apostles, being "hunters" to save. The profession and efforts of fishermen obviously aim, not at the salvation but at the destruction of the only existence these aquatic creatures are orthodoxically held to possess, their material life, while the principles and actions of the propagators of the New Testament were intended, on the contrary, for the salvation, above all, of the best part of human beings, their souls. Therefore, also, the implements of fishermen, the line, hook, bait, harpoon, etc., serving to lure and catch fish for the purpose of "killing" them cannot even figuratively be said to represent the means and instruments employed by the Teachers of the Holy Gospel, to catch souls in order to save them.

The source of the other explanation is probably etymological, and attributable to the fact that the five Greek letters that compose the word fish, "Icthis," are also the initials of the names, origin and mission of the Founder of Christianity, thus: JESUS CHRIST GOD'S SON, SAVIOUR.

But if it were previously absolutely necessary to identify, manifest and support the Christian Religion, so essentially spiritual, by the use of material symbols of this nature in those dark times, is this system equally so now? If so, we must admit that our over nineteen centuries of Christianity, our diffused literature, our varied and extensive legislation, have not done very much to improve and elevate us in the true and high sense, or, alternately, that we are incapable of any such improvement.

In view of the fact that everything relating to human concerns in the terrestrial, ephemeral existence, ends with the grave, these chapters treating of sepulchres seem to be a harmonious termination to this work, and thus, with the conclusion of the fourth of them on this subject, we will also bring it to a close.

THE END

www.ingramcontent.com/pod-product-compliance
Lightning Source LLC
Chambersburg PA
CBHW080330170426
43194CB00014B/2512